Complexity and Organizational Reality

Approaches to leadership and management are still dominated by prescriptions – usually claimed to be scientific – for top executives to choose the future direction of their organization. The global financial recession and the collapse of investment capitalism (surely not planned by anyone) make it quite clear that top executives are simply not able to choose future directions. Despite this, current management literature mostly continues to avoid the obvious – management's inability to predict or control what will happen in the future. The key question now must be how we are to think about management if we take the uncertainty of organizational life seriously.

Ralph Stacey has turned to the sciences of uncertainty and complexity to develop an understanding of leadership and management as the ordinary politics of daily organizational life. In presenting organizations as complex responsive processes, Stacey's new book helps us to see organizational reality for what it actually is – human beings engaged in many, many local conversational interactions and power relations in which they negotiate their ideologically–based choices. Organizational continuity and change emerge unpredictably, rather than as a result of any global plan. This is a radically different picture from the one painted by most of the management literature, which explains organizational continuity and change as the realization of the global plans and choices of a few powerful executives within an organization.

Providing a new foundation for understanding complexity and management, this important book is required reading for managers and leaders wanting to understand the reality of complexity in organizations, including those engaged in postgraduate studies in leadership, organizational behaviour and change management.

Ralph D. Stacey is Professor of Management and Director of the Doctor of Management Programme at the Business School of the University of Hertfordshire, UK.

Complexity and Organizational Reality

Uncertainty and the need to rethink management after the collapse of investment capitalism

2nd edition

Ralph D. Stacey

Routledge
Taylor & Francis Group

LONDON AND NEW YORK

First published 2010
by Routledge
2 Park Square, Milton Park, Abingdon, Oxon OX14 4RN

Simultaneously published in the USA and Canada
by Routledge
270 Madison Ave, New York, NY 10016

*Routledge is an imprint of the Taylor & Francis Group,
an informa business*

© 2010 Ralph D. Stacey

Typeset in Times New Roman by Keyword Group Ltd.
Printed and bound in Great Britain by TJ International, Padstow, Cornwall

British Library Cataloguing in Publication Data
A catalogue record for this book is available from the British Library

Library of Congress Cataloguing in Publication Data
Stacey, Ralph D.
Complexity and organizational reality: uncertainty and the need to rethink
management after the collapse of investment capitalism/Ralph D. Stacey.
p. cm.
Includes bibliographical references and index.
1. Organizational behavior. 2. Organizational change. 3. Management.
I. Title.
HD58.7.S732 2009
302.3′5 – dc22   2009023693

ISBN 10: 0-415-55646-5 (hbk)
ISBN 10: 0-415-55647-3 (pbk)
ISBN 10: 0-203-86365-8 (ebk)

ISBN 13: 978-0-415-55646-0 (hbk)
ISBN 13: 978-0-415-55647-7 (pbk)
ISBN 13: 978-0-203-86365-7 (ebk)

Contents

Preface

This book was first suggested by Routledge editor, Terry Clague, who felt that it was time for a new edition of a book I wrote called *Complex Responsive Processes in Organizations*: *Learning and knowledge creation*, published by Routledge in 2001. This followed a volume I co-authored with my colleagues Doug Griffin and Patricia Shaw called *Complexity and Management*: *Fad or radical challenge to systems thinking?* which Routledge published in 2000. The 2001 book was followed by chapters I wrote in some of the volumes published in the series *Complexity as the Experience of Organizing* which I co-edited with Doug Griffin and Patricia Shaw. At first I was a little reluctant to do another edition but as Terry and I talked about the possible new edition we began to think that it could incorporate key elements from all of the books I have mentioned. However, as we talked further and as I began to work on the book it quickly became evident that although some of the older material was being used, much new material was being added and what has finally emerged is far more a new book than a new edition of any of the volumes mentioned above. The main reason for the emergence of a new book rather than a new edition was my growing amazement at our continuing to talk about organizational leadership, management, consulting, research and education in the terms of system designs and strategic choices based on the assumption that top executives in corporations and government institutions choose outcomes. I found this amazing because, at the time of writing in May 2009, we are experiencing a period in which it is clear that no one is choosing outcomes and that no one is rationally designing whole systems that deliver chosen outcomes. Why do we continue to talk, explain and prescribe on an intellectual basis which completely contradicts our experience?

I think the answer to this question has something to do with the power of a dominant management discourse. Although the recent economic developments of credit crunch and recession make it very difficult to avoid questioning whether senior executives in organizations actually can do what the dominant management prescriptions call for, the vast majority of textbooks, business school programs and research projects around the world, most professional management and leadership development programs in organizations, most management consultancies and people in organizations, including executives, all continue to talk about how organizations *should* be governed and all make the same taken-for-granted assumptions. There is a dominant discourse in which it is assumed, without much questioning, that small groups of powerful executives are able to *choose* the 'direction' their organization will move in, realize a 'vision' for it, create the conditions in which its members will be innovative and entrepreneurial, and select the 'structures' which will ensure success and keep managers in control. No matter what happens and how it contradicts the dominant management discourse, managers continue to talk in its terms. In this book I want to explore how we might think about management if we conclude, contrary to management and organizational orthodoxy, that no one is choosing what is happening. Despite the obvious need, a great many people simply refuse to accept the possibility that we might be able to think differently, perhaps because to contemplate that no one 'up there' is in control is too anxiety producing for most of us and, also, perhaps because of a fear that the justification for huge executive rewards would disappear if we acknowledged the contradiction. Exploring the contradiction would lead us to the view that what is happening is somehow being co-created by all of us, although some play much more influential roles than others, and no one, no matter how powerful, can be choosing what is now happening around the globe nor have they ever been able to.

Alternative ways of thinking should avoid omnipotent fantasies about what leaders and managers can do and instead reflect carefully on what we all together actually do in organizations in the ordinary, daily course of doing our work as we live creatively in uncertainty. In other words, we need to move from fantasizing about what organization should be like and seriously explore the reality of organizational life and the way we might think about what we already do. After all, the world economy may be going through a tough time at present but most of it continues to function in a more or less 'good enough' way. Executives are clearly not choosing what happens to their organizations but they are doing something and often that something is creative and innovative, although sometimes it is repetitive and destructive and perhaps usually it is both at the same time. For these reasons we need to explore what is now happening around us, what roles executives and others might be playing in this, and how we might think more usefully about the reality of organizational life in the aftermath of collapsed investment capitalism.

The dominant discourse rests on the claim that there is an organization and management science and that it is appropriately based on the sciences of certainty. Despite the massive increase in numbers of professionally educated managers and the millions of pieces of research there is, however, no adequate scientific evidence base for the dominant prescriptions for managing and leading organizations. The key requirement of the sciences of certainty, an evidence base for the prescriptions, is lacking. This suggests that the basis of the dominant discourse in the sciences of certainty is problematic. If we are to turn to science then we should move from thinking in the engineering terms of the sciences of certainty to ways of thinking indicated by the sciences of uncertainty, the sciences of complexity. However, this should be done in a way that avoids the error of directly applying the natural sciences to human action and seek only analogies in the sciences of uncertainty which must be interpreted in terms of sociology and psychology. This book develops an alternative way of thinking that draws on analogies from the sciences of uncertainty, the complexity sciences, to propose a theory of organization as complex responsive processes of relating in which leaders and managers participate, along with all other organizational members.

The principal implication of a shift in ways of thinking is the re-focusing of attention. The dominant perspective quite naturally leads to a focus on decision makers and the problem situations they are required to deal with where the problem could be to do with correcting what has gone wrong or responding to new opportunities in innovative ways. The question immediately posed is that of how to make the *right* decisions and this is frequently taken to mean identifying and following *rational*, analytical techniques using the right decision-making tools to make decisions which *optimize* outcomes.

However, the perspective of complex responsive processes shifts attention to the organizational games we are all preoccupied with, in which we are perpetually constructing 'the organization' as patterns that emerge in our ordinary local interaction while at the same time the pattern of organization is perpetually expressed in our local interactions. Local interaction becomes central to our understanding of organizations, leadership and management. That local interaction takes the form of ongoing, ordinary conversation between members of organizations and between them and members of other organizations. It is in these ordinary conversations that patterns of power relations emerge not just in the local interactions themselves but across populations and these patterns of power relations take the form of figurations of inclusion and exclusion which confer identity on people. Furthermore the power relations of local interaction are reflections of ideologies and these ideologies are the basis, largely unconscious, of our choices, only a small fraction of which are made in the technically rational ways suggested in the dominant discourse. Together we are perpetually iterating and potentially transforming patterns of interaction across populations in our ordinary, everyday conversations, power figuration and ideologically based choices, all of which can be summarized as the ordinary politics of everyday life in which supposedly technically rational procedures may be used as rhetorical ploys or social defenses against anxiety.

From a complex responsive processes perspective, the practice of effective leadership and management is that of participating skillfully in interaction with others in reflective and imaginative ways, aware of the potentially destructive processes one may be caught up in. It is in this practice that one is recognized as leader, as one who has the capacity to assist the group to continue acting ethically, creatively and courageously into the unknown. The effective leader is a skilled participant in the ongoing ordinary politics of daily life. It is the role of the leader-manager to widen and deepen communication in organizations. In this way a leader may be exerting a powerful influence on what others think and do and so on what happens but all of this can only be done through the quality of the leader's participation in the conversation.

The central thesis of this book is that to deal with current crises we need far more than fiscal measures and new regulatory regimes to control investment banks and other financial institutions. I believe we need a radical re-think of our explanations of what leaders, senior executives, managers and the rest of us are all actually doing every day in our ordinary organizational lives. We need to be able to understand how people in organizations, in their many roles, produced the collapses and crises of the past few years while at the same time sustaining their organizations in a way good enough for the great majority of us to carry on, even continuing to develop and innovate. Instead of churning out prescriptions for how managers should act to be in control and undertake steps to achieve success, all reflections of the sciences of certainty imported into management thinking more than a century ago, we need to take seriously our inability to predict what is happening and the inability of any small group of people, no matter how powerful, to be in control of what happens while at the same they exert a significant impact on what happens. We may not be able to choose outcomes but we are together creating those outcomes which so often surprise us and we can know much more than we do now about how we are doing this. So what is it that we are doing when we create unexpected and unintended outcomes? I think we are continually engaged in local interaction with each other, which takes the form of what we might call complex responsive processes of relating. It is the purpose of this book to draw on the sciences of uncertainty to explore a way of thinking about organizations as complex responsive processes of relating in the belief that it provides explanations closer to organizational reality than currently dominant modes of discourse do.

What is radical about the way of thinking I am proposing is that it turns the dominant discourse on its head. From the dominant perspective, organizational continuity and change is the realization of the choices of powerful people. From a complex responsive processes perspective organizational continuity and change emerge in many, many local interactions as patterns across population which no one planned or intended. Outcomes emerge in the interplay of everyone's plans and intentions and no one can control the interplay.

I am extremely grateful to my long term colleagues and friends Doug Griffin and Patricia Shaw – I can hardly claim that what appears in this book is my thinking because what I think about organizational matters has emerged in our discussions over some fifteen years now. I am also grateful to the students who passed through on our research program, playing a key role in developing the thinking expressed in this book. I have learned a great deal from them and working with them has sustained my interest in organizations. I am very grateful to the community called the University of Hertfordshire. I have been there for nearly 25 years now and have always felt supported and encouraged by all in my work. I want to say thank you to Terry Clague for his role in getting this book going. And of course, above all, I am grateful to my family.

1 Contradiction

Experiencing the reality of uncertainty
but still believing that executives
choose an organization's 'direction'

Recent economic events of credit crunch and recession must surely be making it very difficult for all but the most willfully blind to avoid questioning whether senior executives in organizations really can do what the dominant management prescriptions call for. The vast majority of textbooks, business school programs and research projects around the world, most professional management and leadership development programs in organizations, management consultancies and people in organizations, including executives, all talk about how organizations *should* be governed, all making the same taken-for-granted assumptions. There is a dominant discourse in which it is assumed, without much questioning, that small groups of powerful executives are able to *choose* the 'direction' their organization will move in, realize a 'vision' for it, create the conditions in which its members will be innovative and entrepreneurial, and select the 'structures' and 'conditions' which will enable them to be in control and so ensure success. The problem is that to be at all effective, these activities rely to a significant extent upon the ability of powerful executives to know enough about what has been, is now and will be happening around them. Executives are supposed to know what is going on, because they are supposed to be avoiding emotion and personal politicking so that they can make roughly rational decisions on the basis of the 'facts'. If they cannot do this, then, on the basis of dominant thinking, they must simply be pursuing only their own interests and gambling with society's resources. However, recent and current economic developments are making it more than usually clear that executives of large corporations and their management consultants, as well as politicians and their advisors, are far from sure of what has been happening and they simply do not know what is now happening, let alone what will happen in the future as a consequence of the actions they are taking. However, surely there has to be more to what they are all doing than gambling. Despite not being able to know what the outcomes of actions will be as required by the prescriptions of the dominant discourse for choosing the 'big picture' over 'the long term', executives and others doing their jobs in organizations are, nevertheless, sustaining some kind of stability and change, producing growth and decline while generating all manner of technological innovations. If none of them knows enough to choose outcomes as prescribed, then how are they doing all this? It becomes a question of importance to ask what it is that they, and the rest of us, are all actually doing which the dominant discourse is making us rationally blind to.

Despite what is so obvious, a great many people simply refuse to seriously consider the consequence of not knowing what is happening, which is that there is a major contradiction between the organizational reality of uncertainty and the beliefs that we have about the capacity of executives to know what is going on and be in control. Perhaps to contemplate that no one 'up there' is in control is too anxiety-producing for most of us and, also, perhaps the justification for the fact that huge executive rewards would disappear if we acknowledged the contradiction. However, we surely have now to conclude, contrary to management and organizational orthodoxy, that no one is choosing what is happening. This applies to the executives of banks and other companies around the world, the executives running regulatory bodies, the government ministers and officials responsible for economic policies, the trade unions, consumers and taxpayers. What is happening is somehow being cocreated by all of us, although some play much more influential roles than others. But no one, no matter how powerful, can be choosing what is now happening around the Globe. If anyone is choosing what is happening at the present time then they must be virtually omnipotent and either psychotic or evil.

So what are we doing with this contradiction? I think that executives and politicians simply continue to ignore it and propose fiscal and monetary policies, bailouts and regulatory reforms, while the public and the media look for someone to blame and scapegoat bankers and politicians. I think that the situation which we are now in calls for a deeper response, namely, that of seriously reflecting upon the contradiction between our belief in control and our experience of uncertainty because, if we do, we may find, in addition to taking the kind of measures just outlined, that we will need to accept that currently dominant ways of thinking about organizations and their management are serving us very badly indeed and that what is called for is the *development of alternative ways of thinking*. The alternatives should avoid what seem to me to be omnipotent fantasies about what leaders and managers can and should do and instead reflect carefully on what we all together are actually doing in organizations in the ordinary, daily course of doing our work. In other words, we need to move from fantasizing about what organizations should be like and seriously explore the reality of organizational life in our experience and the way we might think about what we already do. After all, the world economy may be going through a tough time at present but most of it continues to function in a more or less 'good enough' way. Executives are clearly not choosing what happens to their organizations, but they are doing something and often that something is creative and innovative, while, of course, at other times, it is distressingly repetitive and destructive and it all could be, and usually is, both creative and destructive at the same time. For these reasons, we need to explore what is now happening around us, what role executives and others might be playing in this, and how we might think more usefully about the reality of organizational life in the aftermath of the collapse of investment capitalism. In other words, given that we do not know with any certainty what is happening, we can certainly know about what we are doing to enable us to live in uncertainty.

This chapter will first cover a rather brief review of some key economic events over the past few years in order to highlight the experience of organizational reality and raise questions about how we are thinking. The underlying justification for currently dominant ways of thinking and talking about organizations is that of rationality, ultimately that of science. One would therefore expect management prescriptions to be subjected to some 'scientific' examination of the evidence on whether they work or not. This chapter will review the evidence and conclude that the dominant discourse is not supported by reliable evidence. The chapter will end by considering what this lack of evidence might mean and how we might approach the task of developing ways of thinking which are closer to organizational reality.

Uncertainty and the actions of organizational executives over the past few years

Reflection on a brief account of key events over the past few years can provide some idea of the organizational reality within which executives of organizations find that they have to make decisions and take action. As with all stories, a beginning is somewhat arbitrary but I am going to start with newspaper reports nearly three years ago in mid 2006. At that time, some concern was being expressed about the state of global financial markets.[1] Housing demand was high in many countries, stock prices were rising rapidly on most markets, raw material prices were increasing rapidly and inflation generally was rising faster than expected. Fears were expressed that very high oil prices would soon create a crisis, imposing limits on economic growth. Commentators were saying that the Federal Reserve would continue raising interest rates, bringing the era of cheap money to an end. What a different set of concerns to those that came to pre-occupy us only a few months later. However, at the time, some commentators did recognize that it was almost impossible to predict whether cracks would appear in the global financial system or not. Some expressed some concern about the role of hedge funds which had more than $1.25 trillion in assets, largely in the form of derivatives and exotic securities. The number of hedge funds had been growing rapidly and no one knew how big the danger of hedge funds experiencing difficulties was. Trouble for the hedge funds could quickly spread to the whole global finance system. This rapid growth and the innovation in financial products made it difficult for the Federal Reserve to intervene. Others said that there would be no bust and that everything would soon settle down. The point is that at this time, less than three years ago, no one knew that there would be a global credit crunch and recession. Indeed, at the time, there was nothing particularly important about the newspaper article I have selected – it is only with hindsight that it becomes interesting, just as it is only with hindsight that we can know anything about what was then happening. The organizational reality of uncertainty means more than an inability to reliably predict the future; it also means that it is not at all clear what is currently going on and even what happened some time ago is open to many interpretations. However, we all continue to function in our organizations in these conditions of not knowing and while uncertainty means that we are not able to know in advance what the outcome of our actions will be, we can, nevertheless, know more about what we are doing in a world of uncertainty. We do cope with it, usually rather successfully, without being able to choose 'the big picture'.

Going back to August 2006, as it continued to increase interest rates,[2] the Federal Reserve announced that there was a 40 percent chance of the USA economy slipping into recession over the following twelve months and *The New York Times* suggested that the recession might already be occurring.[3] However, at the same time, others claimed that there would be a pause but not a recession, because the economy was still recovering from the 2001 recession and companies were still reporting positive earnings surprises.[4] Moody's gave a triple A credit rating to banks in Iceland on the grounds that they had been making high-quality investments and were unlikely to face a crisis, although, of course, two years later, they were to collapse in a dramatic fashion.[5] In February 2007, Alan Greenspan, former Federal Reserve chairman, said that a recession was a possibility by the end of the year[6] but not all agreed and later in the year, his warnings were dismissed on the grounds of his poor forecasting record, as were those of other gloomy economists.[7] However, after two years of rising interest rates, the US housing market experienced falling housing prices while numbers of homeowners defaulting on their mortgages rose. Some 20 percent of mortgages were subprime loans to borrowers with poor or no credit histories, colloquially known as Ninja (no income, no jobs or assets) loans. These loans were 'repackaged' into a great array of often sophisticated and difficult to understand financial securities and derivatives and then sold on by the mortgage companies to other financial institutions. It became possible to make huge profits from repackaging and passing on the risk to others in the belief that this was a high profit but very low risk activity. Incentives were provided for executives to sell as many products as possible, bonuses often being tied to targets set for numbers of deals without concern for quality. However, while one section of a financial institution might be passing on the risk to others, another part of the same institution might well be buying repackaged financial products from other financial institutions. So if any setback was experienced it would rapidly affect all institutions holding any of the high risk assets. With hindsight, it is possible to see how the problem could spread throughout the global financial system. This is another fundamentally important organizational reality, namely, interdependence.[8] Human beings are fundamentally dependent on each other and in the modern world, the web of interdependence stretches across the Globe. This fundamental reality must surely form the basis of how we think about life in organizations, but it features little in the dominant discourse, which focuses on the autonomy of individual organizations. In the dominant discourse, it is thus easy to miss seeing the possibility of knock on effects.

What later became the well known problem of subprime loans now began to feature in the press which expressed different opinions on what it might all mean. In March 2007, some were optimistically claiming that subprime problems would spread pain but probably not cause a recession.[9] However, by April 2007, subprime specialist New Century Financial went bankrupt. In July, the investment bank Bear Stearns informed its investors that they would get nothing from two of its hedge funds because of the collapse of the subprime market and the refusal of other banks to help bail them out. In Europe, by August, BNP Paribas also announced that investors could not take funds out of two of its hedge funds, but it offered to buy its clients' investments in subprime funds. The European Central Bank pumped over 200 billion Euros into banking markets and the US Federal Reserve cut interest rates to help restore liquidity. By now, everyone was talking about the 'credit crunch'. In September 2007, Northern Rock in the UK sought emergency financial support from the Bank of England and the next day there was a run on the bank with depositors withdrawing £1 billion. Northern Rock executives had pursued a strategy of relying on the interbank lending market for very short-term loans which it lent on as long-term mortgages to house buyers – these loans often exceeded the value of the house and the payment capacity of the borrowers. The spreading subprime crisis meant that nervous banks were refusing to lend to each other – the interbank market had dried up and Northern Rock was left without funding as well as increasing difficulty in mortgage repayments. Although buyers were sought for the bank, no satisfactory buyer emerged and by February 2008, Northern Rock became the first British bank to be nationalized. Even as late as August 2007, no one was seriously suggesting that a large British bank would be nationalized within the following six months. Once more, there is the organizational reality of uncertainty, unpredictability and high levels of interdependence. Furthermore, another organizational reality becomes clear. Northern Rock executives were pursuing an intentional strategy of funding its loans to high risk house buyers through the interbank loan market and this even seemed to work for a time, but eventually the intentions of the Northern Rock executives played into the intentions and strategies of executives at other banks according to which they all stopped lending on the interbank market. This is the organizational reality of the interplay of intentions and strategies.[10] Each group of executives can, of course, choose a strategy but what actually happens is determined by how these intentions play into the intentions and strategies of others as a move by one calls out responding moves by others. The patterns we call outcomes, for example, 'credit crunch', emerge in this interplay of responsive intentions to yield patterns that no one chose or wanted. The organizational reality is that no one, including powerful government figures, can control or plan the responsive interplay of intentions which is why the population-wide patterns that emerge are unpredictable, why we are continually surprised and find ourselves having to deal with unexpected events. Also, we can, perhaps, begin to see that organizational reality may well be paradoxically intended and unintended at the same time.

Going back to October 2007, banks in Europe and North America continued to announce bad news. The Swiss bank UBS declared large losses due to the collapse in the value of assets based on subprime mortgages. This was followed by large write offs by Citigroup and the revelation that investment bank Merrill Lynch was massively exposed to bad debt. Mortgages all but dried up in the UK and house prices began falling. The Royal Bank of Scotland bought parts of the Dutch ABN Amro Bank. Then on December 6, President Bush announced plans to help homeowners facing foreclosure by freezing subprime rates, followed by unprecedented action by the Federal Reserve to coordinate offers of billions of dollars of loans to banks by five central banks around the world. The Bank of England cut interest rates further and a few days later the European Central Bank made billions available to tide the banks over Christmas. The trouble was spreading to insurance companies, some of whose credit ratings were being cut.

The New Year arrived and while the World Bank predicted a slowing in global economic growth, White House advisors claimed that a recession was unlikely.[11] Indeed, some investment bankers were encouraged by China's acquisition of a hugely expensive stake in BHP to look forward to the return of the days of megadeals.[12] But Scottish Equitable in the UK delayed payments to investors and bond insurer MBIA in the USA announced large losses. In January 2008, it emerged that Société Générale had been close to being destroyed by a rather junior 31-year-old rogue trader, Jérôme Kerviel. It seems that he found his job boring, was irked at the lack of responsibility given to him and felt unrecognized. His skill with computer trading allowed him to take positions in the derivatives market which he then concealed with bogus offsetting entries. He rapidly earned over a billion Euros and then realized he had to conceal his profit because revealing it would bring down the wrath of his bosses. So he tried to lose it and only made more. As he realized that the auditors were closing in on him he became increasingly reckless and took positions of more than 50 billion Euros, which exceeded the bank's capital. Once this was discovered, secret efforts were made to reverse the positions but before this could be completed the news leaked out and the bank made a loss of 5 billion Euros.[13] Such was the popularity of banks that this rogue became a national hero rather than a villain. Here we see another organizational reality. Whatever the rules, people in organizations are not simply rule-following 'human resources'. They sometimes seek adventure and bear grudges which lead them into all kinds of destructive and sometimes also creative actions. The reality is that people in organizations are highly skilled in the arts of resistance.[14]

Then in March 2008, the Federal Reserve, with the approval of President Bush, made funds available to JP Morgan bank to buy the failing Bear Stearns for $240 million compared with its value a year before of $18 billion, while the White House continued to claim that the fundamentals of the economy were still strong. However, in March, the Fed cut interest rates again and made further funds available to the banks. Some commentators now said that recession was unavoidable.[15] The chairman of the Fed told congress that there might be a recession.[16] News emerged that Credit Suisse had to write off $2.85 billion due to intentional misconduct by a handful of traders who had been suspended or sacked. Through April, central banks continued to cut interest rates and pump funds into the banking system in an effort to get lending going again while house prices in the UK and the USA fell further. The funds pumped in by the central banks did not get through to borrowers, because the banks were using the money not as the government intended, for making loans, but to improve their balance sheets in order to stay out of the clutches of the state. Towards the end of April, the Royal Bank of Scotland wrote down a substantial amount on its investments, a major reason being the falling value of its ABN Amro acquisition, and announced a plan to raise £12 billion from its shareholders. The Bank of America announced large falls in profits and write offs in the billions. Bank of America, however, adopted an aggressive strategy of continuing to acquire a troubled mortgage lender and a Midwest bank. Swiss bank UBS also announced a rights issue in May and in June, Barclays bank sold a 7.7 percent share to Qatar Investment Authority in a move to avoid having to take freedom–curbing assistance from the government. In May, US Treasury Secretary said that the worst of the credit crunch might have passed.[17] Then, in June, investment bank Goldman Sachs declared a second quarter profit of $2 billion while one of its competitors, Lehman Brothers, declared its first quarterly loss. In July, the US financial authorities stepped in to assist Fannie Mae and Freddie Mac, insurers of home loans and crucial to the stability of the housing market. In August 2008, the Royal Bank of Scotland announced a loss of £691 million and wrote off £6 billion because of the credit crunch. Before this, the Royal Bank of Scotland had been considered by financial regulators to be a model of proper corporate governance.[18] It did everything by the book and ticked all the right boxes. It provided an exhaustive analysis of its corporate governance performance with nonexecutive directors meant to restrain the executives, although by early 2009, the Financial Services Agency was investigating the allegation that the CEO, Sir Fred Goodwin, had bullied the nonexecutives into compliance. Some commentators are now calling for more actively involved shareholders to correct such problems but others point out that it was active shareholders who had pressed the short-term profits culture on executives so compelling them to take bigger and bigger risks. Here is another organizational reality: people 'game the system' and they cheat, often for what they think is the good of the corporation, as well as genuinely acting ethically and seeking the good of the whole corporation and society. Systems of quality control and evidence of compliance are often simply covers for what is actually going on which might be bullying and greed.

Events took another dramatic turn when, in September, Lehman Brothers collapsed, while investment bank Morgan Stanley was in talks to be taken over by Wachovia. With the exception of Goldman Sachs, the once mighty Wall Street investment banks had disappeared as separate independent entities. President Bush then asked Democrats to support a $700 billion bailout for the US financial sector in a similar move to Prime Minister Brown in the UK, who had put together a package of £50 billion to part nationalize banks in trouble. October saw similar action taken across the world to shore up the banking system. Also in October, President Bush announced a $250 billion plan for the government to buy shares in leading banks. The President denied that this was to supplant the market – it was intended to support the market. In the same month, the UK government announced a £37 billion package to shore up Royal Bank of Scotland and the soon to be merged HBOS and Lloyds in a bid to save HBOS. In return, the state would own 60 percent of RBS and 40 percent of Lloyds/HBOS. The latter merger turned out to be a disaster so that not long afterwards, the state shareholding went up to 75 percent. Here is another important organizational reality: ideology plays a central part in the decisions made and actions taken in organizations. Belief in improvement and progress as a 'good thing', belief in markets as optimal ways of organizing human action, belief in the need to minimize regulations so as to avoid interfering in efficient markets, belief in government as an important intervener to compensate for market failure, belief in the primacy of shareholders and the importance of maximizing profit, belief that science is the only route to true knowledge; these are all ideologies which profoundly affect what executives in organizations do.

By December 2008, it was announced officially that the US economy was in recession and that it had started in 2007. The same was true for the countries of Europe, indeed of most countries throughout the world. And so the story continues into 2009 and as I write this chapter in May, with interest rates about as low as they can go and further huge budget stimuli planned for the economy, no one knows whether all the interest rate cuts, massive bailouts and huge budget stimuli are going to lift us out of recession. Some think these measures will end the recession and are now concerned that it might all be a massive overkill soon supplanting recession with unsustainable boom and high inflation. In the meantime, politicians, media and public have turned on executives in financial institutions who continue to pay themselves huge financial rewards despite their failure. The executives in AIG have received death threats and the home of Sir Fred Goodwin, by then Britain's favorite hate figure, was vandalized. We see yet another organizational reality: the idealization of the 'great' leader lasts while times are good and then rapidly turns to denigration and even persecution when they do not live up to expectations. What is also clear is the organizational reality of executives' personal agendas, emotion, greed and neurosis. The speculation now, in May 2009, is whether the 'green shoots' of recovery can be discerned, which country will recover first and whether the bear stock market phase has ended or not. Surveying all the recent developments, some commentators herald the end of investment capitalism while others draw attention to the recovery of Goldman Sachs which, as the only independent investment bank left, now faces much reduced competition.[19] Perhaps they still are masters of the universe! Or will the worldwide pressure for tighter regulatory control and the political backlash against large payments to executives lead to a rather different form of capitalism? Whatever changes, and surely some things will, the need to rethink management, after the events of the last few years, remains.

The story of the last few years, taken as a whole, reveals further important aspects of organizational reality. First, there is the striking organizational reality of little local interactions escalating across a population to produce major patterns that none intended or wanted. Falling house prices trigger mortgage foreclosures, which reveal subprime market risks, which cause collapse of banks in Iceland and elsewhere, as profits fall in banks across the world. Second, consider how the story taken from newspaper articles is told. It is told in the same manner as case studies in management textbooks are told and that is almost entirely in abstract terms. It is the story of what the Bank of England and the Federal Reserve did, of the actions Citigroup and Royal Bank of Scotland took, the derivative products hedge funds designed and the collapse of the subprime market. The story is primarily told in terms of impersonal forces and the actions of institutions. But, of course, institutions cannot decide nor do anything. It is the people who are their members who decide and act. People largely appear in the story as rogues and hate figures that are messing things up with the implication that if only they would all do what they are supposed to then there would be no problems. The organizational reality, however, is that organizational 'wholes' are our own imaginative constructs with no physical existence. The organizational reality is people and the communicative interaction between them through which they accomplish all the good and the bad that they accomplish.

I have been telling the story of crunches, collapses and recessions but at the same time, in and around these gloomy happenings, other more promising stories are being constructed. For example, smaller supermarket chains in the UK, Morrisons and ASDA, operating at the cheaper end of the market, have been growing market share and by March 2009, were reporting higher profits.[20] One of the larger supermarkets, Tesco, was responding to its own falling market share by taking advantage of the public anger against bankers by opening bank branches in its stores and operating as an Internet bank.[21] The entrepreneur, Branson, was using his Virgin Money company to follow suit and he too opened an Internet bank. And recessions do not stop technological advances and fierce competition.[22] For example, Google has been trying to undermine Microsoft's Internet Explorer by supporting the Firefox browser developed by Mozilla Foundation and also, in September 2008, it released a new browser called Chrome which could be downloaded free of charge on computers running Microsoft's Windows operating system.[23] Microsoft has tried to thwart this by investing billions in its own search engine and making an unsuccessful attempt to buy Yahoo. In May 2009, physicist Stephen Wolfram, CEO of Wolfram Research, announced the Wolfram Alpha computational knowledge system.[24] Some commentators dismissed it as a tool for mathematicians but others thought that it could revolutionize how we interact with the Internet. The point is that the same organizational reality revealed by stories of crunches, collapses and recessions is also revealed by the stories of growth, competition and technological advances that are going on at the same time. There is still the organizational reality of uncertainty and the same interplay of intentions making it impossible for anyone to choose what actually happens although they are all choosing what to do next.

Consider, then, a summary of aspects of the organizational reality I have been pointing to while going through the story of the last few years:

- Organizations are not actually existing things but patterns of interactions between people constituted in their responsive acts of communication with each other in which, amongst other things, they develop imaginative constructs of ideological 'wholes' such as 'Citigroup' and the 'market'. But this reality is covered over by the way we tell the story of what happened in abstract terms of impersonal forces and abstract institutions where real people are largely absent.
- People, who are the organization, are interdependent and in this interdependence they constrain and enable each other and since this is what power means, power is a central organizational reality which we also usually cover over.

- People and groups of people, who are the organization, make choices, form intentions and implement strategies but what happens is not simply determined by the choices, intentions and strategies of one group. What happens is determined by the interplay of all the intentions of all the groups and individuals. The stories of the last few years make this undeniably clear.
- No one in any organization can control the interplay of intentions, because they cannot control what everyone else in every other organization is choosing and doing. Consequently, no one can choose or be in control of what happens. The interplay of intentions produces emergent patterns, such as the one we call 'credit crunch', which often are not what anyone intended or wanted.
- The interplay of intentions easily escalates small local changes across entire national and international populations, generating widespread patterns of change of an uncertain kind, for example, the patterns we call globalization, recession, credit crunch and technological innovation.
- Since no one can control the interplay and small changes can escalate, uncertainty is a fundamental, irremovable organizational reality. Uncertainty means high levels of unpredictability so that no one knows with any confidence what will happen: all we can rely on is the fact that we will be surprised. It also means that no one is sure of what is going on now, and it could take a long time to find out what has been happening in the past and even then it will be open to different interpretations. But it is even more complex than that, because there is the paradox of the known-unknown: while we may not be able to predict and will be surprised at what happens we can speculate in the knowledge that there is some repetition in human affairs and we can recognize with hindsight what has happened. We can expect evolving repetition and so can know some things but never with certainty, because they will always be open to radical change. And we can understand more about what we actually do together in an uncertain world in which our intentions play into each other.
- The interplay of intentions takes the form of local interactions of communication, power relating and ideologically–based choosing which can be understood as the daily politics of organizational life.
- Executives and leaders play influential roles in the interplay of intentions and their visibility leaves them open to idealization and denigration. Far from being the simple 'heroes' of the dominant discourse, they and most other people in an organization, cover things over, 'game the system', cheat and act in their own interest as well as acting ethically in the interest of others.
- What happens, therefore, is cocreated by all the actors involved and one cannot simply blame bankers or politicians. Other actors such as borrowers who took on loans they could not repay also cocreated what happened. Most of these actors play their part without malignant intentions. But while each of us must still take responsibility for what we do, how are we to think about ethics in an uncertain world where no one can control the outcomes of their actions?
- Activities in organizations are characterized by many paradoxes: novelty and continuity; knowing and not knowing; forming patterns of interaction while being formed by them at the same time.

I am arguing that all of these aspects of organizational reality stand out as we review some of the key features of events over the last few years and, I argue, always do, whatever the period we take. I am arguing that the reality I have described is what people are actually doing in organizations and always have done. One would have thought that an explanation of what we are doing in organizations and what we might do next would be based on this organizational reality. However, this is not the case because executives, consultants, management teachers and researchers do not usually talk about what they are *actually doing*. Instead, they talk about what they *should be doing* and they do this largely within what I would call the dominant discourse. This takes remarkably little account of the organizational reality I have described and so does not help us much to understand what we are actually doing in an uncertain world. I would go further and argue that the collapse of investment capitalism, if that is what is happening, has revealed the poverty of the dominant discourse which I would say is largely a fantasy of rationality dangerously removed from the reality of organizational life. Surely, we must reflect on how we are thinking and how this might be a significant reason for the confusion we feel about the situation we are now facing. According to the dominant discourse, the events of the last few years should never have happened. I gave a very brief outline of what I understand to be the dominant discourse in the first paragraph of this chapter. I would now like to expand this outline a little further before going on to the question of an evidence base for its prescriptions.

The dominant management discourse of managers choosing

The discourse on organizations and their management has come to be dominated by a particular notion of what an organization is and how it changes. In claiming that a particular notion is dominant, I am not claiming that such a notion is the only one there is or that everyone accepts it. Instead, I use the term 'dominant' to identify the discourse about organizations which reflects the most powerful ideology displayed in organizational practice and research as well as management education. It is the ways of talking engaged in by practitioners and researchers that one repeatedly hears and reads about. It is repetitive forms of conversation which are unproblematically taken to be the truth. So, what is it that is being taken to be the truth?

It is now taken for granted in most communities of managers, consultants, and organizational teachers and researchers that an organization is a system, that is, a set of parts (individuals) that interact to form a whole (organization) that has a boundary separating it from an environment. The organization is thought to be a higher-level system than the individuals and groups of them who form it. An organization interacts with its environment which consists of other organizational systems, competing with some to supply goods and services to others as well as individual consumers, taking in supplies from yet other organizations, and negotiating with regulatory and other government bodies, also understood as systems. In their interaction, these organizational systems create industrial, economic, social and global supra-systems, which then affect them. It is thought that an organizational system can be designed in deliberate, rational ways, largely by the most powerful members of that organization. It is generally thought to be the role of the leaders of an organization to set its direction in the form of vision, purpose, objectives and targets and then apply monitoring forms of control to ensure that the vision is realized. It is also generally thought to be the role of an organization's leaders to shape its values or culture, understood to be the deep-seated assumptions governing the behavior of the individual members of an organization. One of the most influential writers on leadership and organizations, Schein,[25] said that the primary function of leadership was the manipulation of culture. An equally influential writer, Senge,[26] talks about the building of a vision, purpose and values as the 'governing ideas' of the organization. In successful companies, leaders deliberately construct values and teach their people in training sessions to act according to them. The leader forms a personal vision and builds it into a shared vision through ongoing dialogue in which people suspend their assumptions and listen to each other. In this way of thinking, then, an organization is treated as a thing, a system, which actually exists outside of the individuals who form it. The leaders play a significant role in designing this system, specifying its purpose and inspiring others to act according to values that will achieve this purpose. The organizational system so created unfolds the purpose and vision ascribed to it by leaders and, for this to happen, its individual members must share a commitment to act in a way that does unfold the ascribed vision and purpose. Pursuit of individual agendas should be avoided, because this is contrary to the good of the system which requires acting for the good of the whole if it is to function as a system – the requirement for systemic functioning is compliance.

The dominant theory of organizational development taught at business schools and expressed in the public discussions of managers and consultants in organizations is still what could be called 'Strategic Choice' theory. The fundamental premise of this theory is that it is the role of top executives to choose the future state of their organization, more or less, and to guide its development in the 'right' direction. This is believed to be possible, because it is thought that managers can usually make reasonably useful forecasts, which makes the implicit assumption of 'scientific' causality taking the form of 'if x . . . then y follows'. Control is understood to be secured by setting goals and then monitoring actual outcomes to identify the gap between target and actual outcomes so that the gap can be closed by appropriate action. The implicit assumption here is that an organization is a cybernetic system, an example of which is a central heating system, so that strategic choice theory is built on rather simple first order cybernetics. Uncertainty is to be dealt with by rational risk assessment. Mintzberg[27] has long been a critic of this view and has drawn a distinction between the deliberate strategy of the strategic choice school and what he calls emergent strategy.[28] Emergence here is equated with the effects of random chance events that could not be foreseen and calls for ongoing trial and error responses which amount to learning. The learning school of management therefore offers an addition to that of strategic choice and design. Senge[29] has significantly developed this approach in his work on the learning organization which he thinks of as non-linear systems of the systems dynamics type in which cause and effect are so distant that they often lead to unexpected outcomes. Nevertheless, it is held that managers can identify leverage points and so move the organization in an intended direction if they practice the disciplines of mastering the self, changing their mental models and those of others, building shared visions, encouraging team learning and engaging in systems thinking. Prescriptions for achieving learning organizations include empowering employees, decentralizing and practicing bottom up management, motivating people by providing fulfilling work and encouraging participation in teams, all reflecting the assumption that success requires stability and harmony. What I have been describing in the last few paragraphs can be called managerial capitalism which has also been imposed on the public sector over the past three decades.

However, since the late 1980s, despite the rhetoric of the empowered learning organization, managers have in fact conformed to the pressure to ignore stakeholders other than shareholders. The overriding management aim became that of maximizing share prices in the short term by developing strategies that add economic value which 'efficient capital markets' will reflect in share prices. It was thought that managers could be motivated to maximize share prices if they were awarded bonuses for achieving performance targets and if they came to feel like shareholders through being rewarded with share options. They would be able, so it was thought, to continue to deliver rising share prices by engaging in bigger and bigger and more and more mergers and acquisition. This whole way of thinking has come to be called investment capitalism, a narrowing of the managerial capitalism described in the last few paragraphs.

In this discourse of both managerial capitalism and its investment capitalism form, the focus of attention is on organizational change rather than continuity and such change is thought to come about when the powerful intentionally alter the system design in a planned way and then persuade others to implement the changed design, rolling it out, cascading it through the hierarchy and aligning parts, objectives and actions with each other. Organizational politics is usually regarded as an obstacle to change which can be overcome if values and culture are aligned with organizational objectives. This whole way of thinking focuses attention on the macro level, the global, the whole system, the 'big picture'. It also focuses attention on the strategic level and the long-term future, largely a rhetorical presentation, because action succumbs to the pressures to elevate the short-term share price increase above all else. People and the details of their ordinary, everyday activities in organizations receive very little attention indeed and are certainly not seen as central to either organizational continuity, change or share price increases. Just as medical practitioners may think of the human body as a system and themselves as objective observers who diagnose problems and make interventions to improve the health of the body, so the most powerful organizational practitioners think of an organization as a system and themselves as objective observes who define problem situations and make decisions on what interventions they need to make in order to improve organizational performance and above all increase the earnings expectations upon which share price increases depend.

The contrast between the dominant thinking and the organizational reality revealed by the stories of the past three years, summarized in the preceding section, is striking. While people and their ongoing messy daily political interaction are absent in the dominant discourse, or feature simply as obstacles, they are the central aspect of organizational reality in the stories. In the dominant discourse, uncertainty plays a very minor role and leaders know what is going on; in the organizational reality of the stories neither leaders nor anyone else really knows what is going on and few pay much attention to what they could know about, namely, what they are actually doing to live in uncertainty. I argue that in thinking in the dominant way, we are covering over the complexity and uncertainty we actually experience in our ordinary, everyday experience of life in organizations and we are positing capacities of foresight in leaders which they do not actually possess. The story of the last few years must surely raise questions about the validity of the dominant discourse. What happened to the rational decision making supposed to lead to success that this discourse prescribes? Were executives making irrational decisions or were they making rational decisions but the dynamics of the world economy were so unusual that the decisions did not produce what was hoped for? Either way it is clear that executives could not choose what happened to their organization. How are we to explain this? How are we to explain the dynamics of the economy that make it impossible for managers to know what is happening? But is the present 'debacle' really proof that there are real problems with the whole dominant discourse? Perhaps this is an unusual sequence of events, a crisis executives could not have been expected to deal with because they were caught in complex dynamics of world markets, but once the crisis is past, organizations can continue to be managed in ways prescribed in the dominant discourse. However, what is the evidence that dominant management prescriptions have been working before the obvious 'failure' of the past three or so years? Then, what are we to make of the claim that the dominant discourse about organizations and their management is based on science – organization science and management science? Fundamental to the scientific method is the subjection of hypotheses about some phenomena to empirical testing. Science is science because it is based on evidence. So an organization and management science can only be such if there is a reliable evidence base for its propositions and prescriptions. The next section explores the evidence base for the prescriptions of the dominant discourse, starting with the evidence for the prescription to increase share value through acquisitions and mergers.

The lack of a scientific evidence base for the prescriptions of the dominant discourse

Over the 1980s, 1990s and into the first decade of the twenty-first century, a particular management orthodoxy has dominated theories and practices of management. The orthodoxy is that corporate executives are the agents of their organization's shareholders, who are accorded much more importance than any other stakeholders such as employees or customers. This is supported by the well developed agency theory[30] taught at leading business schools in North America and Europe. The overriding aim of executives must therefore be the maximization of shareholder value and this happens when executives generate expectations of accelerating earnings growth which are immediately reflected in rising share prices in efficient capital markets. This view is also backed by the well developed theory of efficient markets[31] and capital asset pricing models[32] which are also taught at the leading business schools. The next proposition is that executives must be motivated to act in the best interests of the shareholders through ensuring that they gain and lose with the shareholders. This requires granting them large bonuses, including share options linked to share price growth or to some target for actions thought to drive up earnings expectations such as number of derivative sales. This too is backed by motivation theory[33] also taught at leading business schools. All of these prescriptions come together in the theory of Economic Value Added[34] taught at leading business schools and advocated by the large, powerful management consultancies. One widely advocated strategy for generating expectations of rapid growth is that of mergers and acquisitions, a key feature of the story of the last few years. This prescription is also backed by theory[35] taught at leading business schools. Many of the leading executives in financial corporations around the world have been to these business schools – for example, Sir Fred Goodwin, former CEO of the now nationalized Royal Bank of Scotland referred to earlier, went to Harvard Business School as did many other CEOs in the finance sector. All of these theories are not only taught at leading business schools and taken out into the world by their management graduates, but they are also propagated by the highly influential management consultancies and reinforced by the speeches of charismatic corporate leaders, such as the famous 1981 speech made by Jack Welch.[36] On the face of it, the story of the last few years strongly suggests that the whole edifice I have just outlined is fundamentally flawed and indeed this is now what many commentators are saying. But what about the research evidence? Have we only just found out that mergers and acquisitions generate problems? Surely in a profession that claims to be based on science, there must be a relevant evidence base? Well, there is some evidence although it is remarkably sparse and conflicting, and although some disagree, the consensus of studies conducted years ago seems to be that the only beneficiaries of mergers and acquisitions are the shareholders of target companies and that long-term performance is damaged by mergers and acquisitions. Despite this 'evidence', the 1990s and the first decade of this century have seen an acceleration of ever larger mergers and acquisitions. There is no sign that this will be abate once the credit crunch is over. The next section summarizes some of this evidence.

Evidence base for mergers and acquisitions

It seems appropriate in the light of the story of the past few years to start with the banks where some studies produce evidence backing bank mergers and acquisitions. For example, a study in 1997[37] found that large merged banks experienced a significant increase in profit and efficiency relative to other large banks, with most of the improvements coming from increasing revenues and shifts to higher value products. A later study[38] noted that mergers in the 1990s, in contrast to the 1980s, were mostly stock swaps prompted to a major extent by deregulation with very few hostile takeovers. Over the 1973–1998 period, this study showed that the stock market response was positive for both parties in mergers, suggesting that they create value for shareholders and also improve operating performance. On the other hand, a study in 1998[39] pointed to how little evidence there was on the success or failure of bank mergers, particularly given the major increase in merger activity following deregulation. It seems that while small banks might gain from mergers, large banks do not. The evidence for mergers and acquisitions of banks is sparse, contradictory and based on a few studies of small samples. The problem with 'evidence' relating to organizational actions is that it is highly context and time dependent. It is possible that a sample of banks engaging in mergers and acquisitions in a particular country may produce successful results for a short period only for it all to fall apart not long thereafter. I think we have to conclude that there is no reliable evidence to counter the clearly disastrous impact of large bank mergers and acquisition on the credit crunch. So what is the evidence more widely than just banks?

A paper in 1996[40] explored many studies of the impact on performance of mergers and acquisitions and concluded that these activities have a disappointing history. In 1997, researchers[41] analyzed the impact of acquisitions on the performance over a long period of a large sample of quoted companies in the UK and concluded that acquisitions have a detrimental impact on company performance and company growth. Growth through acquisition yielded a lower return than growth through internal investment. A 2001[42] analysis of 80 empirical merger studies concluded that no more than a quarter of mergers increased consumer welfare while another quarter increased profit at the cost of the consumer and half reduced the value of the firm. The shareholders of the merger target win out while those of the bidder break even upon announcement but lose out in the long term. In 2003, findings were published[43] showing that performance was not enhanced by acquisition activity in the USA and was negatively affected to a modest extent. A 2004 study[44] of 257 Canadian mergers and acquisitions between 1980 and 2000 showed that the acquirers significantly underperformed over the three-year post-event period. The study also found that cross-border deals performed poorly in the long run. Research published in 2007[45] pointed to the more than doubling of expenditure on acquisitions in the UK despite the consensus in the academic literature that this activity does not enhance performance. The authors drew on survey evidence from 146 of the UK's top 500 companies and concluded that large acquisitions do not enhance performance although small acquisitions might not suffer from the same problems as large ones and so might be performance enhancing. The authors of this study also conducted a survey of executive opinions on mergers and acquisitions and found that, despite any evidence to the contrary, the executives felt that their organization's performance was enhanced by acquisitions. The notion that managers are scientists looks extremely dubious. The continuing belief of executives that merger and acquisition activity enhances performance is surely an indication that actual management is far from scientific. The reality is that executives act on ideological bases, have their own agendas and pursue their own careers as part of trying to work toward success for the whole organization. But what of the evidence base for other management prescriptions?

More general information on evidence base

Over the last three years, some organizational researchers have been calling for an improvement in the management of organizations by adopting what they describe as *'evidence-based management'*.[46] Evidence-based management is defined as the translation of principles derived from research into management practices. Such principles are only credible if backed by clear research findings and the practices derived from them must suit the particular setting where they are to be applied to solve organizational problems. Evidence is defined as generalizable knowledge about cause-effect relationships derived from controlled testing and observation and the linking, measuring and analyzing of the causal variables. These researchers claim that this approach to management promises more consistent attainment of organizational goals, because it is based on empirical knowledge. Managers are called upon to act on the facts rather than on beliefs, personal experience or politicking, and to continually test, probe and experiment with their approaches to the organization. Although it is claimed that there is compulsive evidence that certain best practices based on research improve profitability, those writing about evidence-based management complain that there is unfortunately a poor uptake of practices shown by research to be effective, such as goal setting and performance feedback. Managers persist in practices which research shows to be largely ineffective, such as downsizing. However, some writers[47] who support evidence-based management also note that, although there is an enormous amount of evidence concerning best management practice, there is very little synthesis of different studies of the same issues and practices. By synthesis they mean far more than a literature search; they mean comprehensive accumulation, transparent analysis and reflective interpretation of all empirical studies pertinent to a particular question, which is what one would expect of an evidence base.

I am struck by how the evidence referred to by these writers relates to the nature of a particular problem situation and is concerned with whether a particular decision-making technique leads to the right answer or not. They are basically recommending that managers should gather information and base their decisions on an analysis of that information. This is hardly a novel notion. They do not ask why the uptake of this idea is so poor. They do not account for their conclusion that managers do not set goals nor do they produce much evidence to support this assertion – I cannot think of any managers in the modern world who are not setting and working to goals. If anything, the problem might be too much reliance on goals. The advocates of evidence-based management do not seem to be concerned with whether particular ways of thinking about the process of management are helpful or not. In particular, they produce no systematic synthesis of research evidence for their claim that evidence-based management leads to improvement. They simply restate the dominant discourse.

Another group of researchers are also much concerned with the question of an evidence base for management and describe their work as *implementation science*. These researchers are primarily concerned with the management of healthcare organizations, pointing to how medical practice is supposed to be evidence based but how management practices, which also affect patient care, seem to escape the need for an evidence base. A number of researchers concerned with the implementation of evidence-based medical guidelines have found that simply disseminating the evidence-based knowledge does not lead to automatic implementation. For example, recent evidence[48] from the USA and Netherlands indicates that 30–40 percent of patients do not receive care according to current scientific guidelines and that for 20 percent the care is not needed or is potentially dangerous. This has led a number of researchers to call for the development of an 'implementation science' which is a rigorous scientific study of what additional strategies need to be implemented to produce a greater uptake of best practice. They have established that organizational contexts and cultures play an important role in whether best practice is taken up or not. Therefore, just as they seek to provide evidence-based medical guidelines they are undertaking research to provide evidence-based organizational initiatives to bring about the necessary changes in practitioner behavior. However, they conclude that at present there is only limited evidence for claims of strategies that lead to improvement – they could not find any strategy where the effects could be predicted with much certainty and none of the improvement strategies produced consistent effects. The Centre for Quality of Care Research (WOK) in The Netherlands assessed 13 theories/models relating to implementing change including individual, group and organizational methods. The study concluded that there is still a lack of knowledge on the factors that are decisive in achieving particular types of changes, in particular target groups and settings and so implementation interventions are left to chance. Grimshaw & Eccles[49] recently conducted a systematic review of 235 studies of guideline dissemination and implementation strategies and found that while there was evidence of success in particular situations, there was little evidence that the particular implementation strategies associated with the success were generalizable to other behaviors and settings. They concluded that while there are many change management methodologies in general organizational settings, their applicability to healthcare professional and organizational behavior has yet to be established. It still requires the exercise of considerable judgment on the part of decision makers to select interventions likely to succeed so that any important improvements seem to be a result of 'gut feel' rather than any scientific basis.

Burgelman & Grove[50] refer to a 2001 study by Collins[51] which analyzed the results of companies in the USA in order to identify which of them could be classified as 'great' companies. He defined a company as great if after 15 years of continuous good results it produced another 15 years of great results. This excluded most high-technology companies from the sample, because they had not been in existence for 30 years. Of all companies that had been in existence for 30 years, Collins could find only 11 who qualified as great companies. He claimed that such greatness depended upon: a paradoxical blend of personal humility and professional will; people willing to confront the facts; pursuing a simple core business and achieving the number one position; feeling passionate about profit; a culture of discipline and entrepreneurship; and the use of carefully selected technologies. Great companies push relentlessly in one direction. This is of course immediately recognizable as a simple restatement of the dominant discourse and I find it remarkable that a major growing economy making all kinds of innovations contains only 11 great companies – surely, this is some kind of omnipotent fantasy. Indeed, Burgelman & Grove point out that since 2001, eight of the eleven members of the 'great' group have either been acquired or underperformed, leaving only three 'great' companies (Abott, Nucor and Walgreens) – what a weight they must bear!

This is reminiscent of earlier studies of the same type. In 1982, Peters & Waterman[52] published their famous and influential study of 43 excellent US companies which included names such as Disney, Boeing and Kodak. They argued that these companies were successful because they all had eight attributes: focus on a core business; close to the customer; productivity through people; autonomy and entrepreneurship; hands on, values driven; bias for action; simple form and lean staff; simultaneous loose-tight properties. Just as Collins was to do nearly twenty years later, Peters and Waterman produced a recognizable restatement of the dominant discourse. However, within five years, two thirds of the companies in the sample had slipped from the pinnacle, some to return later but others to disappear. Two years after the Peters & Waterman study, there was another,[53] this time of UK companies. The analysis produced a similar sample of excellent companies with much the same attributes and they suffered the same fate as their America counterparts. A Royal Dutch Shell study in 1988[54] found that the average life of the largest industrial corporations was 40 years. I am not aware of a more recent study but corporations certainly do not seem to be living any longer than that and no one has been able to identify what leads to their survival or demise. Clearly, the population of companies is a dynamically evolving one in which new ones are born and old ones die – in such a process looking for the excellent or great ones is bound to produce only short-lived examples.

The search over the last 30 years, therefore, has not been able to provide a reliable evidence base which would enable us to conclude that certain general approaches to organizing produce consistent success. Has there been any greater success in researching particular management techniques?

The evidence for particular management techniques

It has proved difficult to establish a link between *formal strategic planning* and superior performance. After a few abortive attempts in the mid 1980s,[55] this project seems to have been periodically taken up by researchers with much the same result. A survey[56] in 1990 showed that only 15 percent of UK companies actually used long-terms plans as control instruments and even those 15 percent monitored their plans against events such as building a factory rather than performance. From a brief literature search, I cannot find later examples of this kind of study and so it seems we have no idea whether formal strategic planning improves performance or not and yet most still do it.

Rather more research has been conducted on *Total Quality Management* (TQM) and *Business Process Re-engineering* (BPR). Some researchers[57] have used the award of prizes for the implementation of total quality management programs in industrial companies as a proxy for effective TQM. A sample of 400 such award winners between 1983 and 1993 in the USA was selected and then publicly available accounting data and stock prices were analyzed to test for changes in operating performance and income as a result of TQM and the consequent impact on long-run stock market performance. This analysis shows that the award winners produced operating income changes 48 percent above a control sample of other companies over a 10-year period (six years prior to the award and three years after the award). The award winners showed higher growth in both employment and total assets. There is also some evidence that award winners did better on sales growth and some weak evidence that they were more successful in controlling costs. In a 5-year post implementation period, the award winners outperformed the control sample in stock market price terms. Some other studies in the 1990s have produced similar results. However, another piece of research[58] analyzed the perceived success of TQM in a cohort of 109 firms over a 5-year period. Some 42, mainly small firms had discontinued their programs and the remaining 67 reported varying degrees of success. The conclusion from this data is that the size of the firm, the nature of its customer base, whether it holds ISO certification or not, all have no effect on TQM outcome. Boyne & Walker[59] point to how governments across the world are promoting TQM in public organizations but there are no empirical studies of the relationship between TQM and performance in public sector organizations. They conducted a critical review of 19 private sector studies of the relationship between TQM and performance and concluded that they do not provide comprehensive support for a positive impact of TQM on performance. Another study[60] of 150 successful organizational turnarounds in the USA concluded that typical TQM implementation strategies had limited impact. Analysis of a mail-based survey[61] of 150 organizations in the UK affiliated to the European Foundation for Quality Management concluded that quality improvement programs were perceived to be effective by managers. However, they also concluded that there was a major discrepancy between the rhetoric of these systems and the reliability of their practice. Surveyed organizations provide little evidence that they were developing a more strategic approach to managing the softer aspects of quality management.

It seems to me that there are repeated assertions in the literature that TQM has either succeeded or failed but few are actually backed with evidence and the evidence there is provides a rather conflicting picture. There is now a claim that Six Sigma is replacing TQM and is much more successful but again there is little evidence to support this claim. The story of Business Process Re-engineering is not any more promising, and it is now widely regarded as having been a failure. What is striking is how sparse and inconsistent the evidence is. It hardly provides a scientific evidence base.

There has been some research on the link between *human resource management* (HRM) practices and organizational performance[62] which is critical of the use of quantitative techniques[63] to demonstrate a link between the 'High Performance Work Practices' of HRM and a range of individual and organizational outcomes variables. These cross section studies rely on the answers of a single informant in each organization to questions on practices and performance. The author of this research, Truss, took a longitudinal case study of Hewlett-Packard over a two-year period, collecting data on many areas and conducting questionnaires and interviews with a number of people in the organization. She found that change takes place only slowly in HRM and those managing the change do not always get it right. The evidence on outcomes is conflicting and informal processes of networking often override the formal HRM processes. Truss claims that if she had simply used one cross section method she could easily have concluded that HRM practices produce successful outcomes at Hewlett-Packard, but the more varied methods and closer scrutiny over time reveals a much less clear picture in which it is difficult to find links between HRM practice and outcomes, not least because the HRM practices are often covers for what is actually happening informally. Another study[64] is instructive in this regard. It is an examination of the experience of managers at a plant in Northern England who sought to re-engineer working practices in response to corporate driven initiatives. They found this a very frustrating experience, because employees practice all manner of individual and collective acts of resistance. They give a show of cooperating, while behind the scenes they repeatedly undermine the initiatives. The employees were identified with the earlier work practices, and the new ones made little sense to them.

The difficulty of providing traditional scientific evidence in an uncertain world

Having reached the conclusion that there is no comprehensive, reliable scientific evidence base for currently dominant management prescriptions, I now want to consider some reasons why this might be so. The very notion of empirical evidence in the traditional scientific method is based on a particular understanding of causality as efficient causality having the structure of 'if x ... then y'. Thus, in Newton's laws of motion there is a cause, force applied to an object, and an effect, movement of the object. The relationship between the cause and the effect is linear, that is, proportional, so that *if*, in a vacuum, the force is doubled *then* the object moves twice as far. Such causal relationships are ahistorical; they are generalizations which apply at all times in all places. In other words, time and context are irrelevant. Empirical evidence is then provided by an accumulation of measurements and if they fail to falsify the prediction, the causal connection is taken to be a law of nature. However, the empirical evidence provided usually takes the form of identifying a statistical association between say winning a prize for TQM systems and higher profitability. However, this does not 'prove' a causal link. Perhaps prizes are won because higher profits make it possible for organizations to fund expensive TQM systems, not the other way around. In Chapter 3, I will be providing a brief summary of the development since the 1950s of what have come to be called the complexity sciences, where relationships between variables are nonlinear rather than linear so that the relationships are historical and so time and context dependent, in fact, events are unique. This makes the standard method of accumulating evidence highly problematic, because it is based on the assumption of repetitive events. Evidence is accumulated by observing repetitions in traditional science but rather different notions of evidence need to be developed for the complexity sciences.

The studies summarized in the previous section were all looking for links between a management action and some successful outcome and so they are all making the assumption that relationships are linear, or even when they are not, as in the learning organization, they can still be leveraged, and so the implied causality is still that of efficient cause.[65] However, if we develop explanations of organizational life that are informed by the complexity sciences, as I propose to suggest in later chapters, then we would consider the consequences of nonlinear, that is, nonproportional, relationships between variables. In this case, time and context will be important in understanding the relationship between one variable and another and we will have to confront the difficulties created by imperfectly repeated events. Any evidence provided will depend on the period selected and the place in which the events are occurring as well as other aspects of context. It follows that any relationship anyone identifies between a management action and an outcome could have far more to do with a particular time and place where the sample is selected than anything else. Evidence will always be very temporary and highly contested, particularly when other difficulties are added. Defining what performance, success and improvement all mean is very difficult and always reflects the ideology of the definer. So take events to do with particular techniques of facilitating a meeting. The facilitator's technique might foster the enactment of a concealed conflict. This would be a failure if one is informed by an ideology of appreciative enquiry but would be judged to be a success from the ideological perspective of valuing conflict, of knowledge arising in conflict as the movement of thought.[66]

In a linear world of equilibrium and predictability, the sparse research into an evidence base for management prescriptions and the confused findings it produces would be a sign of incompetence; it would not make much sense. Nevertheless, if organizations are actually patterns of nonlinear interaction between people; if small changes could produce widespread major consequences; if local interaction produces emergent global pattern; then it will not be possible to provide a reliable evidence base. In such a world, it makes no sense to conduct studies looking for simple causal relationships between an action and an outcome. I suggest that the story of the last few years strongly indicates that human action is nonlinear, that time and place matter a great deal, and that since this precludes simple evidence bases we do need to rethink the nature of organizations and the roles of managers and leaders in them. Moreover, the problem is wider than the banking system and the private corporate sector. It extends to the public sector too.

The spread of dominant thinking to the public sector despite the lack of evidence

Despite the lack of satisfactory evidence to support the explanations and prescriptions of the dominant management discourse, which has been developed primarily with private sector commercial and industrial companies in mind, the thinking has now become taken for granted in the public sector. Over the past two decades, there has been a growing orthodoxy in many countries on the form that public sector governance should take. For example, the trend in the United Kingdom, for two decades now, has been a movement away from a model of governance for public sector health and education which had persisted for more than half a century. This model had a number of key features. First, it was highly decentralized. Rather independent institutions delivered health and education services and their lines of accountability were to local bodies such as special statutory local area authorities or local government. These were basically funding bodies and the relatively independent institutions were accountable to them for the way in which they spent the funds allocated to them according to standard formulae. The delivering institutions were also accountable to validating bodies for what they did. Professional bodies, often of very long standing, represented professional standards and had certain disciplinary powers, often legitimized by statute. Professional regulation was thus, to a significant extent, a voluntary, self-governing affair. The role of central government was primarily one of allocating funds to the local funding agencies and also of nationally coordinating the activities of those bodies, as well as legitimizing the professional bodies. Central government had a policy role in allocating resources and establishing responsibility for the adequate provision of health and education. The central government also had a fiduciary role in ensuring transparent accountability for the expenditure of public funds.

Within this decentralized, rather loosely controlled framework, health and education services were delivered by institutions which were internally governed in a highly collegial manner. Professional groupings within any institution tended to govern themselves through collegial, and often very rivalrous, negotiation. Central management in these institutions was rather weak and often had great difficulty in exercising any form of detailed control over the professional groups. In other words, public sector governance was characterized by a particular figuration of power relations in which individual professional practitioners, and professional groups, had considerable freedom to make decisions about what they did, and how they did it, in the specific situations they operated in. In the health sector, clinical decisions were made by professionals in particular situations – in effect, they were making allocation decisions about how the scarce health resource should be distributed in specific cases. The result was considerable variation in health care across the country. The same applied to educational institutions. That power figuration was sustained by an ideology of vocation and professional freedom.

The form of governance just described was not without its problems. For example, it was difficult to remove professionals who were clearly not performing and periodically scandals concerning medical and educational errors hit the headlines. Not surprisingly then, this model came under considerable attack about three decades ago, particularly in the United Kingdom under the Thatcher government. The powerful professional bodies, such as the British Medical Council, were said to be outdated 'old boys' clubs incapable of reliably policing their professional groups. It was said that standards were too often low, even declining, and general government policies were not effective in rectifying this. Educational institutions were criticized for not matching their offerings to the needs of industry and the economy. The whole public sector was held to be inefficient, irresponsible, nonaccountable for quality delivery and far from innovative. Unfavorable comparisons were made with the private sector which was held up as an indubitably successful alternative to an approach to governance in the public sector, seen as a leftover from the Victorian era.

Policy makers responded by making attempts to mimic markets in the public sector, and managerialism, the private sector theory of management described in the preceding section, was imported and increasingly imposed by central government on the whole of the public sector. It was taken for granted that the supposed success of the private sector was caused by the method of governance practiced in commercial and industrial organizations in a market setting. This was thought to involve the setting of targets, the formulation and implementation of plans, the monitoring of achievement, or lack of it, of the targets and the punishment of those who failed to achieve targets by the forces of the market. The taken-for-granted efficiency of the market mechanism was reflected in the rhetoric of marketization – patients and students should be regarded as consumers of health care and education, which meant that they should have more choice, and funds should follow demand. The public sector was supposed to work as a market. In fact, however, this has proved to be impossible and behind the rhetoric of the market there has emerged its opposite, namely, heavy regulation directly from the central government. It is the ministers and their policy advisors who set the rapidly multiplying targets for health and education, and it is a proliferating number of central government bodies who monitor performance against the centrally set targets. The aim is to standardize health care and education across the country. To increase transparency, league tables are published showing how well or how badly institutions are doing in meeting their targets. Those who do not meet the targets, who do not comply, are publicly named and shamed, and if this does not work, the CEOs and senior managers of offending institutions are removed.

Therefore, what we now have is a highly centralized form of governance, involving detailed intervention from the centre – cabinet ministers may intervene in detailed local situations. The performance management regime, with its targets, plans, and league tables has resulted in a major increase in the number of public bodies whose role is to scrutinize what the delivering institutions are doing – the Modernization Agency, The Quality Assurance Agency, The Clinical Health Inspection Agency, to name but a few. Naturally, this has led to a dramatic increase in the number of people employed to manage and conduct the scrutinizing activities and a responding increase in numbers of managers and staff in the delivering institutions themselves whose role it is to manage the demands of the scrutinizing bodies. The result is a major change in the power figuration, such that power is heavily tilted to the scrutinizing bodies of central government and away from the delivering institutions. Within those institutions themselves, there has been a corresponding shift in the power figuration, with the power relations now tilted firmly towards the top of the hierarchy of managers and away from the professionals who actually deliver the service. The collegial form of public sector governance has all but vanished, or perhaps more accurately is still practiced to some extent in the shadow of the legitimate surveillance procedures. However, the particular form of power figuration which has emerged is sustained by a very different ideology to that which prevailed before. This is an ideology of efficiency, measurable quality and improvement. It is an ideology of managerial control to produce uniformity of service.

I think an examination of reports on the operation of public sectors under this regime, which I will present in Chapter 10, leads to the conclusion that while there may have been pockets of improvement, there is very little evidence indeed for overall improvement. In the face of this conclusion, it becomes important to ask why it is so hard to argue against this mode of governance. The first reason is that doing so amounts to challenging the dominant ideology and power figuration, so risking exclusion. The second reason is that the underlying way of thinking which supports the new model is so taken for granted, while an alternative way of thinking is not immediately apparent, that there seems to be no way out. After all, who can be against improvement and efficiency? But now we need to face the world after the collapse of investment capitalism and recognize that there is no evidence base for managerialist prescriptions. Surely, that calls for a radical reappraisal of public sector governance. The collapse of investment capitalism could have major implications not just for financial institutions but also for all organizations.

Conclusion

I find it difficult to see how we can continue to avoid questioning dominant thinking about organizations and their management in view of what has been happening in both the public and private sectors of our economies around the world. In the private sector, we have seen the collapse of investment capitalism and in the public sector the failure of managerialism and marketization. It is extraordinary both that this should have happened and that there is so little evidence that dominant management prescriptions achieve what they are supposed to, given the sheer volume of research on organizations and their management. By 2006, when I arbitrarily took up the story of the collapse of investment capitalism, there were probably more that 2,000 management and organizational research journals in the USA and Europe. This probably translates into at least

50,000 research papers per annum. A quick web search for 'management and organization' at Google Scholar and Amazon comes up with at least 4 million journal papers and books on management, organization, finance and leadership. With this volume of research findings about the functioning of organizations and how they should be designed, managed and led, it is amazing that private and public sector governance should have gone so badly wrong. The amazement increases when one remembers that the first business school was established at Wharton in the USA in 1881 and the numbers grew rapidly over the following years. The idea of business schools in research-based universities spread to Europe after World War II. There are now 1,200 MBA programs internationally. The number of MBA graduates in the USA reached 116,000 in 2000–2001 according to Department of Education figures. In the UK, about 117 business schools produce more than 10,000 MBAs annually and, in the rest of Europe, the numbers are similar. So in North America and Europe there are going on for 150,000 MBA graduates per annum from about 1,500 business schools which disseminate some of the huge volume of research mentioned earlier. The population of MBA holders must exceed two million by now. Surveys show that 70 percent of MBA graduates reach senior management positions and major companies recruit heavily from this population, so by now MBA holders must surely constitute the majority of executives in major companies, particularly financial institutions and management consultancies. Not only is there a huge volume of research, but also there is a large population of senior executives educated by business schools who disseminate the research and are advised by enormous numbers of management consultants, all mostly reinforcing the dominant discourse. How could the events of the past few years have occurred if this dominant discourse, backed by enormous research and expert consulting activities reflected organizational reality? I think this calls for enough humility to acknowledge that there are fundamental problems with how we are thinking about organizations and their management, which means that we cannot adequately explain either the crisis we face or how we nevertheless continue to get things done. It is important to hold in mind the fact that even in a state of crisis, most in the richer countries continue to have jobs, for most life goes on nearly as before, and executives and others in organizations continue to work in ways that produce 'good enough' outcomes. If the crisis has emerged in the interplay of many intentions, then the previous period of growth and technological innovation must also have emerged in the interplay of intentions and so will the responses to the crisis which will eventually lead to the emergence of yet another period of growth and development. Good times and bad times are not caused by overarching intention as the dominant discourse implies but by the interplay of many, many intentions. I think we can only make sense of this if we develop an alternative discourse, one close to the reality of life in organizations. I suggest that this requires us to reflect on the reality of our own, ordinary organizational experience.

What I think is required to move away from the magico-mythical thinking, dressed up in the rational sounding jargon of the dominant management discourse, is an approach to thinking about our lives in organizations in a way that involves taking our ordinary, everyday experience seriously. Taking seriously one's experience of what one is actually doing in local interactions with others, taking seriously our interdependence, leads to very different views on what is practical. Taking this route, we come to see that there are no mysterious social forces acting upon us, no abstract cultures that visionary leaders can move around at will. Instead, we see how we are taking up global patterns in our local interactions, so reproducing and potentially transforming those global patterns.

This call to focus on experience should not be mistaken for some utopian ideal for a 'return' to some primal harmony. By experience, I mean the actual experience of interaction in which we express hatred, aggression and greed as well as love, compassion and care.

Earlier on in this chapter, I pointed to the dominant organizational discourse in which an organization is understood to be a system, or at least a systemic concept in the mind, and how change comes about because powerful individual agents intentionally change this system by designing the change and then intervening in the system. This is an entirely abstract rational mode of thinking which removes us from our experience of locally interacting with each other, indeed rendering us rationally blind to the importance of ordinary everyday experience. So what do I mean by the term 'experience' and in what sense is it 'everyday'? Our experience is the experience of everyday, local interaction with each other. Interaction is local even when someone makes a gesture to a whole population, because the meaning will emerge in many, many local interactions. It is 'everyday' simply because it is what we are doing all the time, and it is local in the sense that we can only do anything in a specific place, at a specific time, with specific people dealing with each other on the basis of our and their life experiences in an evolving community. This experience may be humdrum and boring or it may be exciting, even terrifying. It may be very ordinary or in another sense, quite extraordinary. It may be the experience of relationships that are profoundly good or the experience of relationships which are cruel, distressing and downright evil. All of these aspects of experience are relevant for understanding the reality of organizational life.

However, to avoid facilely replacing one fantasy or one ideology with others, I want to take a more rigorous approach which starts by a reasonably careful inquiry into how the currently dominant discourse on organizations and their management has evolved as part of the history of Western thought. This chapter has argued that the dominant discourse provides an inadequate understanding of how organizations evolve and pointed to how this dominant discourse claims to be based on science, despite the lack of an evidence base for its prescriptions, including the prescribed roles of managers and leaders in organizations. I am intrigued by the way in which so many managers, consultants and academics ignore the lack of evidence and mostly continue to claim a scientific basis for what they are doing. How and why did the dominant discourse become so firmly linked to science? This is the matter to be explored in the next chapter as a step toward identifying and reflecting upon the taken-for-granted assumptions on which the dominant discourse is built.

Notes

1 For example, there was an article in *Business Week* on 15 June, 2006, by Michael Mandel, 'Bubble, Bubble, Who's in Trouble'.
2 *Observer*, 6 August, 2006, 'Fed admits US recession on cards', by Heather Stewart.
3 19 August, 2006, 'A Car-Sales Indicator Suggests a Recession is Near or Already Here' by Floyd Norris.
4 *TheStreet.com Real Money*, 17 August, 2006, 'Pause, Not a Recession' by John D. Markman.
5 *Herald Tribune*, 4 August, 2006, 'Investing: Mood's Rejects Crisis at Banks in Iceland' by Tasmeen Broger.
6 *The Washington Post*, 27 February, 2007, 'Greenspan Says Recession Is a Possibility By End of Year'.
7 *Herald Tribune*, 18 December, 2007, 'Column: Economists Say US Recession Could Loom, but Should We Believe Them?'
8 Elias, N. (1939) *The Civilizing Process*, Oxford: Blackwell.

9   *USA Today*, 15 March, 2007, 'Subprime mortgage troubles could still spread pain but probably not recession'.
10 Elias, N. (1939) *The Civilizing Process*, Oxford: Blackwell.
11 *The New York Times*, 2 February, 2008, 'White House Does Not See a Recession' by Edmund L. Andrews.
12 *The Times*, 2 February, 2008, 'Return of Megadeals Defies the Credit Crunch' by Siobhan Kennedy.
13 *Daily Mail*, 1 February, 2008, 'From Rogue Trader to Robin Hood: Why Jérôme Kerviel is a National Hero in France', by David Jones.
14 Scott, J. C. (1990) *Domination and the Arts of Resistance*: *Hidden Transcripts*, New Haven: Yale University Press.
15 *Herald Tribune*, 9 March, 2008, 'US Recession Appears Unavoidable' by David Leonhardt.
16 *The Washington Post*, 3 April, 2008, 'It Might Be a Recession, Fed Chief Tells Congress' by Neil Irwin and Renae Merle.
17 *BBC News*, 7 May, 2008, 'Paulson Sees End of Credit Crunch'.
18 *The Times*, 18 March, 2009, 'Corporate Governance Cries Out for Reform' by David Wrighton.
19 *The Times*, 17 April, 2009, 'The Goldman Sachs Rules for Mastering the Universe' by Mathew Syed.
20 *The Independent*, 12 March, 2009, 'Morrisons Reports Profit Hike'.
21 *The Wall Street Journal*, 29 March, 2009, 'Tesco to Open Bank Branches in 130 Stores by Year End'.
22 *The Observer*, 17 May, 2009, 'Branson Plans Launch of Virgin Internet Bank' by Richard Wachman.
23 *BBC News*, 13 May, 2009, 'Google Unveils "Smarter Search"' by Maggie Shiels.
24 *The Register*, 18 May, 2009, 'Taking a First Bite Out of Wolfram Alpha' by John Ozimek.
25 Schein, E. H. (1985) *Organizational Culture and Leadership*, San Francisco: Jossey-Bass.
26 Senge, P. M. (1990) *The Fifth Discipline*: *The Art and Practice of the Learning Organization*, New York: Doubleday.
27 Mintzberg, H. (1973) *The Nature of Managerial Work*, New York: Harper & Row; Mintzberg, H. (1994) *The Rise and Fall of Strategic Planning*, Hemel Hempstead: Prentice Hall.
28 Mintzberg, H. and Waters, J. A. (1985) 'Of Strategies Deliberate and Emergent', *Strategic Management Journal*, 6, 257–72.
29 Senge, P. M. (1990) *The Fifth Discipline*: *The Art and Practice of the Learning Organization*, New York: Doubleday.
30 Jensen, M. C. and Meckling, W. H. (1976) 'Theory of the Firm: Managerial Behavior, Agency Costs, and Ownership Structure', *Journal of Financial Economics*, 3, 303–60.
31 Jensen, M. C. and Smith, C. W. (eds) (1984) *The Modern Theory of Corporate Finance*, New York: McGraw-Hill.
32 Jensen, M. C. and Meckling, W. H. (1976) 'Theory of the Firm: Managerial Behavior, Agency Costs, and Ownership Structure', *Journal of Financial Economics*, 3, 303–60.
33 Ibid.
34 Rappaport, A. (1986) *Creating Shareholder Value*: *The New Standard for Business Performance*, Simon & Schuster.
35 Ibid.
36 Back in 19981, Jack Welch emphasised the need to increase share prices through better quarterly results but now says that it is dumb to focus on increasing quarterly results since this is the outcome of strategy not strategy itself. He now says that employees, customers and products are the main constituencies. *Financial Times*, 13 March, 2009, 'A need to reconnect'.
37 Akhavein, J. D., Berger, A. N. and Humphrey, D. B. (1997) 'The Effects of Megamergers on Efficiency and Prices: Evidence from a Bank Profit Function', *Review of Industrial Organization*, 12(1), 95–139.
38 Andrade, G., Mitchell, M. L. and Stafford, E. (2001) 'New Evidence and Perspectives on Mergers', *Harvard Business School Working Paper* No. 01–070.
39 Amihud, Y. and Miller, G. (1998) *Bank Mergers & Acquisitions*, Amsterdam: Kluwer Academic Publishers.
40 Cartwright, S. and Cooper C. L. (1996) *Managing Mergers, Acquisitions and Strategic Alliances*: *Integrating People and Cultures*, London: Butterworth-Heinemann.
41 Dickerson, A., Gibson, H. D. and Tsakalotos, E. (1997) 'The Impact of Acquisitions on Company Performance: Evidence from a Large Panel of UK Firms', *Oxford Economic Papers*, 49(3), 344–61.

42   Tichy, G. (2001) 'What Do We Know about Success and Failure of Mergers?', *Journal of Industry, Competition and Trade*, 1(4), 347–94.
43   King, D. R., Dalton, D. R., Daily, C. M. and Covin, J. G. (2003) 'Meta-analyses of Post-Acquisition Performance: Indications of Unidentified Moderators', *Strategic Management Journal*, 25(2), 187–200.
44   Andre, P., Kooli, M. and L'Her, J. (2004) 'The Long-Run Performance of Mergers and Acquisitions: Evidence from the Canadian Stock Market', *Financial Management*, 33(4), 15–25.
45   Ingham, H., Kran, I. and Lovestam, A (2007) 'Mergers and Profitability: A Managerial Success Story?', *Journal of Management Studies*, 29(2), 195–208.
46   Pfeffer, J. and Sutton, R. (2006) *Hard Facts, Dangerous Half-Truths and Total Nonsense: Profiting from Evidence-Based Management*, Boston: Harvard Business School Press; Rousseau, D. M. (2006) Is there such a thing as 'evidence-based management?', *Academy of Management Review*, 31(2), 256–69; Rousseau, D. M., Manning, J. and Denyer, D. (2008) 'Evidence in Management and Organizational Science: Assembling the Field's Full Weight of Scientific Knowledge through Synthesis', *Annals of the Academy of Management*, 2, 475–515.
47   Rousseau, D. M., Manning, J. and Denyer, D. (2008) 'Evidence in Management and Organizational Science: Assembling the Field's Full Weight of Scientific Knowledge through Synthesis', *Annals of the Academy of Management*, 2, 475–515.
48   Grol, R. and Wensing, M (2004) 'What Drives Change? Barriers to and Incentives for Achieving Evidence-Based Practice', *Medical Journal of Australia*, 180: 57–60.
49   Grimshaw J. M. and Eccles, M. (2004) 'Is Evidence-Based Implementation of Evidence-Based Care Possible?', *Medical Journal of Australia*, 180, 50–51.
50   Burgelman, R. A. and Grove, A. S. (2007) 'Let Chaos Reign, then Rein in Chaos – Repeatedly: Managing Strategic Dynamics for Corporate Longevity', *Strategic Management Journal*, 28, 965–79.
51   Collins, J. (2001) *Good to Great*, New York: Harper Business.
52   Peters, T. J. and Waterman, R. H. (1982) *In Search of Excellence*, New York: Harper & Row.
53   Goldsmith, W. and Clutterbuck, D. (1984) *The Winning Streak*, London: Weidenfeld & Nicholson.
54   de Geuss, A. (1988) 'Planning as Learning', *Harvard Business Review*, March-April, 70–74.
55   Greenley, G. E. (1986) 'Does Strategic Planning Improve Performance?', *Long Range Planning*, 19(2), 101–9.
56   Goold, M. and Quinn, J. J. (1990) *Strategic Control: Milestones for Long Term Performance*, London: Hutchinson.
57   Hendricks, K. B. and Singhal, V. (1997) 'Does Implementing an Effective TQM Program Actually Improve Operating Performance? Empirical Evidence from Firms That Have won Quality Awards', *Management Science*, 43(9), 1258–74; Hendricks, K. B. and Singhal, V. (2000) 'Firm Characteristics, Total Quality Management and Financial Performance', *Journal of Operations Management*, 238, 1–17; Hendricks, K. B. and Singhal, V. (2001) 'The Long run Stock Price Performance of Firms with Effective TQM Programs', *Management Science*, 47(3), 359–68.
58   Taylor, W. A. and Wright, G. H. (2002) 'A Longitudinal Study of TQM Implementation: Factors Influencing Success and Failure', *Omega*, 3(2), 97–111.
59   Boyne, A. G. and Walker, R. M. (2002) 'Total Quality Management and Performance: An Evaluation of the Evidence and Lessons for Research on Public Organizations', *Public Performance and Management Review*, 26(2), 111–30.
60   Eskildson, L. (2006) 'TQM's Role in Corporate Success: Analyzing the Evidence', *National Productivity Review*, 14(4), 25–38.
61   Soltani, E. and Pei-Chun Lai (2007) 'Approaches to Quality Management in the UK: Survey Evidence and Implications', *Benchmarking: An International Journal*, 14(4), 429–54.
62   Truss, C. (2001) 'Complexities and Controversies in Linking HRM with Organizational Outcomes', *Journal of Management Studies*, 38(8), 1121–49.
63   Huselid, M. A., Jackson, S. E. and Schuler, R. S. (1997) 'Technical and Strategic Human Resource Management Effectiveness as Determinants of Firm Performance', *Academy of Management Journal*, 40(1), 171–88.
64   Ezzamel, M., Willmott, H. and Worthington, F. (2001) 'Power, Control and Resistance in "The Factory that Time Forgot"', *Journal of Management Studies*, 38(8), 1054–79.
65   Mowles, C. (2009) 'Emerging Evidence' (to be published in *Development in Practice*).
66   Ibid.

2 How we came to believe that leaders and managers choose an organization's direction

Professional identification with the sciences of certainty

In the last chapter, I presented the case for a fundamental rethinking of the nature of organizations and the role of those who manage and lead them. That case rests firstly on the lack of persuasive evidence backing up the dominant explanations and prescriptions for organizing, managing and leading; and secondly, on the possible collapse of investment capitalism. In order to form a coherent idea of just what it is we are to rethink, we need, I believe, to understand how we have come to think about management and leadership as we now do, particularly how and why this thinking has come to be identified with science (as in the natural sciences), for it is through this identification that we have come to believe that leaders and managers choose what happens to an organization. This chapter will therefore provide a brief history of how the roles of manager and leader have evolved over the last century or so and what this means for how we now think about organizations. To start with, consider the origins of the words 'manage' and 'lead' in the English language and how the form of the modern corporation emerged.

Etymology of 'leading' and 'managing' and the origins of the modern corporation

Words both reflect and create ways of thinking in cultural contexts so that looking at the origins of words helps us to understand how people think; and looking at these origins in a particular culture gives us insights into the development of that culture.[1] So consider first the origins of the word 'leadership'.

Going back to the Greeks, we find that *archein* means to begin, or to lead, or to rule, while the verb *prattein* means to pass through, or to achieve, or to finish. The corresponding Latin verbs are *agere* meaning to set in motion or to lead and *gerere* meaning to bear.[2] This usage reflects an idea to be found in Plato differentiating leading and executing, so that knowing what to do and doing it are different performances requiring different talents and thus different words. This distinction is still to be found in modern organizational literature when some writers draw a distinction between leaders and managers. There is also the Latin verb *ducere* meaning to draw, drag or pull, and to lead, guide and conduct. This word thus reflects the coercive aspects of leading, which also feature in modern notions of leading. However, the origins of the English verb *lead* are not to be found in Greek or Latin but in the Anglo-Saxon Old English words *loedan* or *lithan,* meaning to travel. By 825AD, the word 'lead' was used to mean causing others to go along with oneself in the sense of taking a person or an animal to a place. It is interesting that this notion of leading is still to be found in modern times when we speak of a leader as one who sets the direction of an organization. By 1225AD, written records use the word *lead* to mean guiding actions and opinions by persuading or counselling others, conducting an argument to a conclusion and inducing something. Originally, then, leading meant the actual physical action of moving an animal or person from one place to another, then it became the actual political action of persuading through argument and then became a metaphor for moving an organization in a direction, a notion of leadership which is abstracted from the actual reality of physical and political actions of leaders who clearly are not actually moving an 'it' around in space. So the question is just how this abstraction occurred. By 1828, Webster's dictionary defines leading in terms of influence and domination and *leadership* as the state or condition of a leader.[3] This attachment of *–ship* to leader was, therefore, a recent phenomenon of around 1828. The leadership scholar, Grace,[4] argues that the appearance in the English language of the word 'leader' in the early thirteenth century reflects the emergence of a new political role in society as the 'divine right of kings' gradually faded away. The industrial revolution also brought new roles into society in the eighteenth and nineteenth centuries, including the role of leader in commercial and industrial organizations, and the word leadership emerged as the description of what these business leaders, as well as political leaders, actually did, namely, the politics of guiding and influencing the opinions and actions of others using persuasion and domination. It was really only in the late nineteenth and early twentieth centuries that the more detached metaphorical understanding of the role of leader took hold.

The word *manager* has French origins, denoting one who worked with, or handled, horses, and appears in the English language in the seventeenth century in relation to a role in the British parliament. By the early nineteenth century, it came to refer to working with and handling people, originally the poor housed in a workhouse. So, although the word 'leader' was used from the thirteenth century onwards in relation to government, the words 'leadership' and 'management' appear at about the same time in the nineteenth century, frequently in relation to commerce and industry where they described rather different activities, one elevated and the other rather lowly. However, by 1925, *leadership* and *management* were being used synonymously and related very much to roles in the modern commercial and industrial corporations in which leader-managers chose what an organization should be and do. It would be after the 1980s that leading and managing would come again to have different meanings for some people.

The roles of management/leadership just described enabled and shaped the form of the modern corporation while at the same time those roles were shaped by the modern corporation. The key feature of the modern corporation is the limited liability which it affords to its owners, the shareholders – this organizational form arose to limit the liability of investors so encouraging a greater flow of capital for the growth of enterprises. The earliest legal corporations in Europe were the dioceses and religious orders of the Roman Catholic Church and in medieval times some cities, charitable organizations such as hospitals, and craft and merchant guilds, were also legal corporations. This meant that they were regarded in law as legal persons with some collective liability for what was done in their names by their officers. It was also common in medieval times for ownership of ships to be divided into shares and these share owners provided finance for merchant voyages. These ideas of institutions as legal persons with liabilities and shareholders came together in the form of the joint stock company. Perhaps the first corporation to have the features of legal personality, shareholders with limited liability, transferable shares and a managerial hierarchy was the Russia Company, formed by a royal charter in England in 1557, giving it exclusive rights of trading with Russia.

This was copied in the Netherlands by the creation of the Dutch East India Company in 1580. In 1599, the English East India Company was established and the Bank of England was incorporated in 1694. However, the joint stock company aroused some hostility when monarchs used their right to grant and renegotiate charters to raise revenues. Then in the early eighteenth century, the stock of the South Sea Company was over-promoted through promising unrealistic dividends and this South Sea bubble collapsed, bankrupting many investors, and later on in that century Adam Smith expressed his disapproval of corporations. After many other speculative bubbles, recessions and booms, there was the significant collapse in 1886 of the bank Overend Gurney Limited with claims of fraud against its promoters and investors.[5] It all sounds strangely familiar to someone in the early twenty-first century! By 1844, the practice of granting charters had ended and the English Companies Act of that year created freedom of incorporation but, in return, corporations were required to report on earnings to their shareholders. In the United States, some of the states started granting charters in the early part of the nineteenth century and by 1860, most US states had adopted free incorporation with limited liability.[6]

So, by the second half of the nineteenth century, a corporate form was functioning in which shareholders could be pure investors able to trade in their shareholdings and the corporations were run by a new class of managers who were legally required to report on earnings to their shareholders. Over the nineteenth century, the separation between ownership and management became more and more common as entrepreneurial founders and their families retained ownership but passed the management function over to a growing class of managers. The development of new corporate forms also gave birth to new groups of external advisors. Accountancy firms such as Arthur Anderson were set up to assist and legitimize the required management reporting of corporate earnings and engineering consultancies provided not only engineering studies but also financial studies and reports on large investment projects managers were required to make decisions about.

Striving for a professional management identity on the basis of the reductionist sciences of certainty[7]

The role of the new class of managers became a social issue, with some questioning the contribution and legitimacy of non-owner managers. Serious conflicts arose between management and labor in the nineteenth century, resulting in managers being seen as the masters and oppressors of working people and this posed major obstacles to the legitimization of management. It became a matter of importance for these managers to develop some kind of recognized identity through establishing themselves as professionals along the same lines as lawyers and physicians. It was in the search for professional identity that management first became linked to science. During the nineteenth century in the USA, the practice of natural science changed from a private interest of some members of the richer families to a professional activity largely conducted in universities. Science developed into a public institution dedicated to the greater good, supported by organized private and public funding and involving the diffusion of experiments through scholarly journals and professional institutes. This was also the period in which the scientific method of the natural sciences was increasingly taken up in the study of human society which became known as the social sciences. As *scientists* scholars of society found that their standing and power in society increased, particularly when their expert advice was sought by policy makers. They too developed journals and professional institutes, creating an image of disinterested, apolitical, rational men concerned with solving the problems of society. The ideology of science was rooted in truth, service to the community, progress and improvement. A strategy emerged in the managerial class whereby managers sought to present themselves as science-based professionals along-side social scientists, lawyers and physicians. By developing management as a profession based on science, particularly engineering, managers could claim the moral authority of science and present themselves as the coordinators of labor rather than its masters. It is no surprise, then, that scientific management, arising first in the profession of engineering, began to develop the institutions upon which professionalization depends, namely, educational institutions, research activities, learned journals and professional societies with political standing and negotiating power.

Over the course of the nineteenth century there had been some development of management education which consisted mainly of specific commercial skills such as bookkeeping, office procedures and specific industry skills provided by commercial schools. Then, as a key aspect of professionalization, the first university-based business school was established in 1881 at the University of Pennsylvania with funds provided by industrialist John Wharton and so named the Wharton Business School. It was followed by the founding of the Tuck School of Administration and Finance at Dartmouth College and later by the Harvard Business School at Harvard University in 1907. Wealthy industrialists and bankers wanted to see the development of a well-respected profession of management and were prepared to found and fund business schools to this end. The number of business schools grew rapidly up to the entry of the USA into World War II. By this time, some 52 percent of large company executives had been to business schools, most obtaining the MBA.

The business schools, therefore, were established as a key institutional foundation of the profession of scientific management through providing education for managers so as to develop more significant and improved ways of managing. I think this development is of great importance, because it is still the basis of today's dominant discourse on organizations and their management. The identification with science was not simply some rational choice of the best way to perform the task of management but, more fundamentally, the identification with science was a social phenomenon to do with the development of identity and the establishment of patterns of power relations and ideology which favored the new managerial classes. The identification of management with science also represented the continuing expansion of the scientific method into the conduct of human affairs, thereby establishing not only a dominant way of thinking about the tasks of managing but also reinforcing a particularly individualistic way of thinking about managers themselves. If we are to understand the now taken-for-granted assumptions reflected in the dominant discourse on management, I think it is necessary to reflect on just what the early identification with science imported into the perception of management in the early twentieth century and as a basis for such reflection, the next section provides a brief description of some key movements in Western thought.

The scientific revolution and the age of reason

In medieval times, people thought that nature moved according to universal, unchanging laws that revealed the glory of God's creation, which they could only know through the authoritative revelation of the Holy Scriptures. Humans were unquestionably a part of nature, the pinnacle of God's creation, differing from other creatures in having souls which made them free to choose whether or not to act according to universal ethical laws, being divinely rewarded if they did and punished if they did not. There was no notion of the subject as a self in the modern sense and instead, subjectivity was experienced in relation to a cosmic order so that persons thought of themselves as coming most fully to themselves when they were in touch with that cosmic order, or to put it another way, when they were in union with God.[8] Individual identity was also related to one's position or role within the social hierarchy. The individual subject was thus defined by external authority in relation to an external social and cosmic world and the group or society consisted simply of a given hierarchical order which individual subjects fitted into. A particular theory of causality is implicit in this view of the world and the person and this is a dogmatic view that everything in the universe moves according to natural laws which reveal God's glory so that the cause of any change is God's grace.

The Scientific Revolution, extending over more than a century from the work of Copernicus in the early sixteenth century to that of Galileo, Bacon and Descartes in the early seventeenth century and maturing in the late seventeenth century in the work of Newton and Leibniz, represented a major departure from medieval thinking. A common assumption that united all these figures was their claim that the basis of knowledge lay in the human mind and its encounter with the real world. This real world could be observed, couched in the language of mathematics, and explained through reductionism and experimentation so that science could generate certain knowledge and truth. This was a realist belief that human minds could know what the real world actually was. There is nothing relative about knowing. The natural scientific method is one by which humans come to know the reality of both stability and change through careful observation, formulating hypotheses and then testing them empirically. For example, the movement of the planets was observed; hypotheses were formed about their movement and then tested by measuring the actual movement of those planets. The hypotheses suggested causal links between the action of a body and some aspect of its nature. For example, in the case of the planets, it was hypothesized that the gravitational attraction of a planet depended upon the mass of that planet. *If* the mass of one body increased *then* the gravitational attraction it exerted on others would increase in proportion. This kind of hypothesis immediately focuses attention on cause and effect links having an *efficient causal 'if-then' structure*. The method involves isolating linear causal links between fundamental entities in a reductionist approach which focuses attention on the parts of a phenomenon. Those parts were postulated to behave predictably according to efficient causality, while the interaction between them was accorded no significance. The interaction simply followed from the nature of each part. The testing step in the method required humans to stand outside the phenomenon of interest and observe and measure its behavior in an objective way in order to test the previously postulated causal links. The claim was that nature was entirely determined by necessary laws of this 'if-then' kind. The empirical approach began to question the dogmatic one, and it came to be thought that nature had laws of its own, but they were no longer necessarily a reflection of God's order. The causality of dogmatic natural law was replaced by *efficient causality* but what they had in common is the assumption that the laws of nature produced certainty and in the case of efficient cause enabled reasoning humans to predict and so control nature's movement. In importing science into thinking about organizations and management, we are therefore importing notions of reasoning individuals and efficient causality as the basis of rational control of organizational life based on certainty, the laws of which could be progressively uncovered through research.

The empiricist, Locke, a contemporary of Newton and Leibniz, differed from them in arguing that all knowledge of the world rested in sensory experience so that rational thought could be mere speculation, or even spurious. Reason had to be concerned with appearances in a procedure to uncover probable rather than absolute truths. By the late eighteenth century, intellectual challenges were mounted against the scientific method in the form of the radical skepticism of Hume and Berkley, who argued that what looked like causal links in nature were simply the association of one experience after another in a habit.

The German philosopher, Immanuel Kant,[9] countered the undermining of the scientific method by radical sceptics through developing a dualistic theory in which reality itself (noumena) could not be known by humans but the appearance of reality to the senses (phenomena) could be known because the human mind contains innate categories, such as time, space and cause-effect, which enable the ordering of appearances in a nonrelative way. Kant was proposing a transcendental logic where transcendental means knowing in advance the form that something will take. The forms of reason are given beforehand and knowing is then outside of the present experience itself and in that sense science is an abstraction concerned with appearances to our senses, the phenomenal. Kant's claim about the unknowabilty of reality in itself meant that while we could not claim to know constitutive ideas, that is, the principles by which nature was actually constituted, we could formulate regulative ideas because they are one of the categories of the human mind. Regulative ideas take the form of hypotheses about the purposive movement of nature – we are able to observe nature and understand it '*as if*' it were moving toward some end, which would be a mature state of itself. However, this purpose is not in nature itself but, rather, it is we, as objectively observing scientists, who can understand nature '*as if*' it were moving towards the end that we have postulated. Kant incorporated this notion of 'regulative ideas' into a systemic approach in which organisms in nature are understood as wholes consisting of parts and in the interaction of the parts, both those parts and the whole emerge. For example, the parts of a plant are its roots, stems, leaves and flowers, together forming the whole plant. The parts also emerge, as parts, through the internal interactions within the plant itself in a self-generating, self-organizing dynamic in a particular environmental context. Organisms develop in a 'purposive' movement from simple initial forms, such as a fertilized egg, into a mature adult form, all as part of an inner coherence expressed in the dynamic unity of the parts. A system of this kind reflects a particular notion of causality in that the cause of a form is the process of formation itself in which a mature version of the phenomenon is already present at the beginning and is unfolded through the formative process of maturing. We can call this *formative causality*. Kant, therefore, introduced a systems theory, with a distinctive notion of causality, into philosophy and science and this became the foundation of systems thinking which became prominent around the middle of the twentieth century.

So, in addition to understanding inanimate matter in nature as mechanism governed by efficient cause, as Newton had done, we can also understand organisms in nature as systems governed by formative cause. The move to linking organizations, management and leadership to science, therefore, brings with it both efficient causality expressed in scientific management and formative causality expressed in systems models of organizations. For example, in the organizational literature, direct comparisons have been made between mechanistic and organic types of organization. Formative causality underlies every description of phases of development in organizations and industries, for example, from simple to divisionalized structures of organizations.

Kant also dealt with another problem raised by the scientific revolution: humans are part of nature but if nature is governed by fixed mechanistic and systemic laws, then they cannot have any freedom to make their own choices. Kant presented another dualism in claiming that when action is directed by the passions of the body, it is subject to the laws of nature so that the person is not free, but when the action is based on reason then the person is free to make rational choices. Therefore, the body is subject to the fixed laws of nature but the mind is governed by the laws of reason, *rationalist causality*, and it is reason that makes us free. Kant was here formulating the theory of the autonomous, rational individual who chooses goals and the actions required to achieve them on the basis of reason. Kant then stressed that autonomous individuals could not be understood as parts of a whole because then they would be subject to the whole and so lose their autonomy. The notion of system could, therefore, not be applied to reasoning individuals and it would not be valid to regard society as a system whose parts were individuals. The question then became how an autonomous individual could know which acts to choose so that autonomous individuals could live together. In other words, the question was how autonomous individuals could know which choices were ethical and which were not. For mediaeval thinkers the answer was to follow the revealed dogma but Kant argued that ethical principles could also be identified by human reason on its own. Kant argued that the notion of the 'regulative idea' could be applied to human conduct just as it could to nature. This meant that in matters of ethics, just as in relation to nature, autonomous individuals as scientists could objectively observe their own conduct and ethical actions could be understood 'as if' they were actions that could be performed by everyone because then the principle behind the action would reflect a universal law. This is the categorical imperative. Therefore, an individual could formulate hypotheses about an ethical action, testing them against the regulative idea or categorical imperatives 'as if they could be performed by everyone'. As people proceed in this way, different formulations of the categorical imperative emerge, for example, 'treat others as you want them to treat you' and 'do not treat other people as means to an end since all people are ends in themselves'. These imperatives have the character of universals but they do not dictate what to do in any specific situation. In specific situations, people have to choose what to do, testing their actions against the categorical imperatives and using them to justify what they have done. In this way, just as we can progressively build up a body of knowledge about the timeless universal natural laws governing nature, so we can progressively build up a body of knowledge on timeless, ethical imperatives for human conduct.

Some philosophers objected to Kant's articulation of the rational, autonomous, moral individual because of the split it implied between mind and body and the split between man and nature. Particularly influential here was the work of the German philosopher, Herder, who took an expressivist approach. From this perspective, each individual has his or her own intrinsic way of being and to become anything other than this is a distortion or mutilation. The subject is then characterized by an inner force imposing itself on the world in a process of actualizing itself. It is this self-actualizing process that forms the subject so that the subject is constituted in its expression of feelings and aspirations to others and to itself. It is this expressive process that makes determinate what the subject feels and wants. The fullest expression of the subject is where he or she realizes and clarifies what he or she wants, so actualizing an essence or form which is not fully determinate before being fulfilled. Although the subject is still self-defining, it is no longer split off from nature, and mind is no longer split off from body because the subject is fundamentally embodied. The moral act is then the authentic expression in which the subject realizes what he or she potentially is. The expressivist perspective enhances the notion of freedom, that is, authentic self-expression, as a value. However, such freedom is not simply related to an individual body, because it implies a higher aspiration to the freedom and expression of the whole of nature including other human beings. The ultimate self-actualization lies in communion with nature and others. This view implies formative rather than rationalist causality in that the cause of change is formative processes of self-definition. The expressivist view was developed around the middle of the twentieth century as humanistic psychology and this too was imported into management thinking, clearly evident in some theories of leadership, Organizational Development and management training.

The theoretical underpinnings of management science

The identification of management with science, therefore, amounted to taking a particular view of the role of the manager as scientist and that meant as an autonomous, rational, moral individual whose task was that of objectively observing the organization, formulating hypotheses about its efficient functioning and making rational decisions about that functioning, so producing the empirical evidence to support or reject their hypotheses. The assumption was that managers behaved according to *rationalist causality*. Also in keeping with the scientific tradition, the scientist manager would need to understand the organization in reductionist terms as mechanism driven by *efficient causality* or as system driven by *formative causality*. Initially, management thinking relied on the reductionist mechanistic approach and, after the Second World War, this was extended to encompass the systems approach.

By the 1920s, the business schools based the education they provided on two theoretical approaches, one of these focusing on industrial efficiency and the other on the psychology of human motivation. With regards to industrial efficiency, Frederick Taylor[10] in the United States and Henri Fayol[11] in Europe, both engineers, were the founding figures of scientific management. Taylor's central concern was with the efficient performance of the physical activities required to achieve an organization's purpose. His method was that of meticulously observing the processes required to produce anything, splitting them into the smallest possible parts, identifying the skills required and measuring how long each part took to perform and what quantities were produced. His prescription was to provide standardized descriptions of every activity, specify the skills required, define the boundaries around each activity and fit the person to the job requirement. Individual performance was to be measured against the defined standards and rewarded through financial incentive schemes. He maintained that management was an objective science that could be defined by laws, rules and principles: if a task was clearly defined, and if those performing it were properly motivated, then that task would be efficiently performed. Fayol's approach to management was much the same. He split an organization into a number of distinct activities (for example, technical, commercial, accounting and management) and he defined management as the activity of forecasting, planning, organizing, cocoordinating and controlling through setting rules that others were to follow. Taylor argued that scientific management would curtail the harsh exercise of arbitrary power and bring about greater economic prosperity for all. He believed that science would establish a moral authority for managers that workers would accept.

Management science equates the manager with the scientist and the organization with the mechanistic phenomenon that the scientist is concerned with. The manager's main concern is with getting the right 'if-then' causal rules. There is a quite explicit assumption that there is some set of rules that are optimal, that is, that produce the most efficient global outcome of the actions of the parts, or members, of the organization. There is an important difference between the scientist concerned with nature and the analogous manager concerned with an organization. The scientist discovers the laws of nature while the manager, in the theory of management science, chooses the rules driving the behavior of the organization's members. In this way, there is rationalist causality, but it applies only to the manager who exercises the freedom of autonomous choice in the act of choosing the goals and designing the rules that the members of the organization are to follow in order to achieve the goals. Those members are assumed to be rule-following entities. The organizational reality, of course, is that members of an organization are not rule-following entities and they all do choose their own goals and actions to some extent. Not surprisingly, then, scientific management does not work as it is supposed to and given the lack of an evidence-base for its rules, it is surely a misnomer to use the term scientific in relation to management. Closely linked to this point about freedom is that of acting into the unknown. Kant argued that the choices humans make have unknown consequences. In scientific management, rationalist causality is stripped of the quality of the unknown and as it developed after Taylor, it was also stripped of the ethical limits within which action should take place. In fact, scientific management does what Kant argued against. It applies the scientific method in its most mechanistic form to human action, whereas Kant argued that it was inapplicable in any form simply because human freedom applies to all humans. Second, Kant's coupling of autonomous human action with universal ethical principles is absent in the way that the rationalist causality of management science was developed, which regarded human action as reflex-like responses to stimuli in accordance with the behaviorist psychology of its time.

The second theoretical approach common in the business schools of the early twentieth century was based on the work of Hugo Münsterberg in the industrial psychology of managing workers – a scientific psychology. Münsterberg believed that modern scientific psychology could be used to change the attitudes of workers and so resolve labor problems. In the 1930s, the Human Relations School, initially led by Mayo, developed out of Münsterberg's work.

Mayo,[12] a social psychologist, conducted experiments to identify what it was that motivated workers and what effect motivational factors had on their work. He pointed to how workers always formed themselves into groups that soon developed customs, duties, routines and rituals and argued that managers would only succeed if these groups accepted their authority and leadership. He concluded that it was a major role of the manager to organize teamwork and so sustain cooperation. Mayo did not abandon a scientific approach but, rather, sought to apply the scientific method to the study of motivation in groups. From the 1940s to the 1960s, behavioral scientists[13] continued this work and concluded that effective groups were those in which the values and goals of the group coincided with those of the individual members and where those individuals were loyal to the group and its leader. Efficiency was seen to depend upon individuals abiding by group values and goals, having high levels of trust and confidence in each other in a supportive and harmonious atmosphere. In extending freedom to all members of an organization and paying attention to motivational factors, the Human Relations School took up a fuller notion of rationalist causality but still also thought of an organizational whole driven by efficient causality toward an optimal state of harmony.

The primary motivation behind these two approaches taken together, scientific management and the psychology of motivation, was not simply industrial efficiency but also the reduction of labor strife, the violence of strikes and the power of the unions. The role of managers became one of developing a scientific form of decision-making and control to replace rules of thumb and personal whim. Interestingly, in view of later developments, economics played a minor role in early business school curricula, because neoclassical economics showed little interest in the internal structure and management of the firm and finance and accounting also did not occupy a central place at this time. Instead, the early curricula placed much greater emphasis on the newly emerging social and political sciences and the ethical dimension, not just expert knowledge, was important, indeed, the greater concern was the moral education of the manager as part of institutionalizing the profession of management and gaining respect for it. Management was regarded as a calling, like medicine and education, and managers were supposed to be stewards of society's resources. Of course, there were many who criticized the whole approach as too idealistic and they claimed that, anyway, management could not be taught. Moreover, as the years went by, the idealistic and ethical aspects of management were gradually submerged in the growing emphasis on rational decision-making.

Taking scientific management and the Human Relations School together, we have a theory in which stability is preserved by rules, including motivational rules, that govern the behavior of members of an organization (a mixture of rationalist and efficient causality). Change is brought about by managers when they choose to change the rules, which they should do in a way that respects and motivates others (rationalist causality) so that the designed set of rules will produce optimal outcomes (efficient causality). Because they are governed by efficient cause, organizations can function like machines to achieve given purposes deliberately chosen by their managers. Within the terms of this framework, change of a fundamental, radical kind cannot be explained. Such change is simply the result of rational choices made by managers and just how such choices emerge is not part of what this theory seeks to explain. The principles discussed in the foregoing section were developed a long time ago, and they have been subjected to heavy criticism over the years, but they still quite clearly form the basis of much management thinking. The result is a powerful way of thinking and managing when the goals and the tasks are clear, there is not much uncertainty and people are reasonably docile, but inadequate in other conditions. In other words, it is a way of thinking that is in serious conflict with the experience of organizational reality described in Chapter 1.

Research and consultancy

In parallel with the development of a scientific approach and ethical basis, the early business schools began to place importance on organizational research as another route to being recognized as professionals. In fact, this development would professionalize not only managers but also the teachers of management. By the 1920s, many management teachers at business schools were carrying out research, and this was reinforced by the establishment of more and more business schools at research-based universities.

Business-school teachers were looked down on by academics in the old established disciplines who claimed that organizational and management studies were not sciences and could not be regarded as academic disciplines. Business-school teachers had to struggle to form an identity for themselves that would bring them academic recognition and research was a route to this. It was also necessary to deal with the criticisms of practitioners that standards of management education were very low and varied greatly from business school to business school. There were about seven or eight elite business schools such as Wharton, Harvard, Stanford, Dartmouth College and Chicago, with all the others regarded as inferior and providers of lower standard education. By the time of the entry of the USA into World War II, there were nearly 100 business schools in research-based universities and they were producing nearly 20,000 bachelor graduates and over 1,000 MBAs per annum.

In terms of corporate form, this period up to the Second World War saw an increase in the large corporation and this raised questions about the social impact of such large enterprises which were expressed in antimonopoly policies. In 1933, Congress passed the Glass-Steagall Banking Act which was to have the unintended effect of promoting management consulting as a distinct profession.[14] Before the Act, commercial banks often supervised investigations into company reorganizations and investment projects conducted by accountants and engineers, but the Act made it illegal for banks to do this and also required the separation of underwriting and stock broking from commercial banks, so breaking commercial and investment banking apart. At the same time, the Securities Act of 1933 prescribed the carrying out of due diligence investigations prior to any corporate financing. The Securities and Exchange Commission also required that large accounting firms such as Arthur Andersen, founded in the late nineteenth century, should focus on corporate audits in order to maintain professionally independent accounts and avoid industrial and financial investigations because of the potential conflict of interests. For similar reasons, other professional groups, such as lawyers and engineers were prohibited from acting as consultants. The opportunity for rapid growth in independent management consulting firms, such as McKinsey and Booz Allen & Hamilton, founded in the 1920s, was created as all of the institutional and regulatory changes came together. Strict prohibition on companies sharing information with each other through industry associations also created an opportunity for management consultants to become primary sources of interorganizational knowledge. The origins of management consultancy were not so much in management science as in accounting and engineering studies and the growth came from changes in legislation.

Sustaining a professional management identity on the basis of the systemic sciences of certainty

During the war, the government had found it necessary to take seriously the techniques of management and administration because, to an important extent, the war was a contest of organizational strength and managerial competence. The US government turned to the business schools to address the difficulties of administering a war economy, including the tasks of collecting statistics and other information and developing techniques for coordinated decision-making across many different organizations. This led to the development of techniques such as linear programming, systems analysis, computer simulations, network analysis, queuing theory and cost accounting systems. There was progress in statistics and statistical sampling, as well as in survey methods and focus groups, under the pressures of assuring the quality of armaments. Engineers such as Norbert Wiener in the UK developed the theory of cybernetic systems[15] to improve the aim of antiaircraft guns and after the war servo-mechanical engineers developed the theory of systems dynamics.[16] Around the 1950s, these notions of systems were taken into sociology, psychology, economics and organizational management theory, as were the modelling and statistical techniques and methods developed during the war. Large organizations came to be viewed with less hostility after the war, because they were now seen as contributors to social goals and the support of democracy. Managers were now thought to play a critical role in society and business education became much more important. All of this called for a new and more rational conception of the managerial role using the modern techniques that had been developed during the war. Those who had done this work in the war were available in their thousands to work in business corporations and consulting firms, such as McKinsey, applied the new techniques to organizational problems. This was part of the move to systems thinking that spread through sociology and psychology too. In developing an identity for managers as systems scientists, further assumptions about the nature of an organization were being introduced and it is important in understanding today's dominant discourse to reflect on what they were.

Systems thinking

During the 1930s and 1940s, a number of scholars were working in related areas, very much in conversation with each other, culminating in the publication of some important papers around 1950. The related areas covered systems of control, systems of communication, the development of computer language, and the development of a new science of mind in reaction to behaviorism, namely, cognitivism.[17] These ways of thinking amounted to a new paradigm in which the whole came to be thought of as a system and the parts as subsystems within it. A system in turn was thought to be part of a larger supra system. The parts were now not simply additive in that they affected each other. The focus of attention shifted from understanding the parts, or entities, of which the whole was composed as in mechanistic reductionist science, to the interaction of subsystems to form a system and of systems to form a supra system. The new systems theories developed along three pathways over much the same period: general systems theory,[18] cybernetics[19] and systems dynamics.[20] All three of these strands began to attract a great deal of attention in many disciplines from around 1950, as did the new cognitivist psychology, and of course, computers. Engineers, bringing with them their notion of control, took the lead in developing the theories of cybernetic systems and systems dynamics, while biologists, concerned with biological control mechanisms, developed general systems theory. This systems movement, particularly in the form of cybernetics, has come to form the foundation of today's dominant management discourse, so importing the engineer's notion of control into understanding human activity. Some brief remarks are made on each of these stands of development in systems thinking before looking at the theories of causality underlying them.

The central concept in general systems theory is that of homeostasis, which means that systems have a strong tendency to move towards a state of order and stability, or adapted equilibrium. They can only do this if they have permeable boundaries that are open to interactions with other systems. Such systems display the property of equifinality, which means that they can reach homeostasis from a number of different starting points along a number of different paths. It follows that history and context are unimportant.

All that matters is a system's current state in terms of boundaries and how systems are relating to each other across these boundaries. Disorder is corrected at all levels by boundary and role definitions and change takes place through change in boundaries. It is easy to see how these notions lead, in organizational theories, to emphasis on clarity of roles and task definition and equation of management with a controlling role at the boundary.[21]

Cybernetic systems are self-regulating, goal-directed systems adapting to their environment, a simple example being the central heating system in a building. Here, the resident of a room sets a target temperature and a regulator at the boundary of the heating system detects a gap between that target and the actual temperature. This gap triggers the heating system to switch on or off, so maintaining the chosen target through a process of negative feedback operation. All planning and budgeting systems in organizations are cybernetic in that quantified targets are set for performance at some point in the future, the time path towards the target is forecast, and then actual outcomes are measured and compared with forecasts, with the variance fed back to determine what adjustments are required to bring performance back to target. All quality management systems take the same form as do all incentive schemes, performance appraisal and reward systems. The same point applies to change management and culture change programs. Total Quality Management and Business Process Re-engineering projects are also fundamentally cybernetic in nature. The thinking and talking of both managers and organizational researchers, therefore, tends to be dominated by cybernetic notions. It is easy to see the consistency of this way of thinking with that of scientific management, despite the shift to a 'systemic' perspective and just as easy to see its problematic relationship with organizational reality.

The third form of systems theory was also developed largely by engineers who turned their attention to economics and industrial management problems. In systems dynamics, mathematical models of a system are constructed, consisting of recursive, nonlinear equations that specify how the system changes states over time. One important difference from the other two systems theories is the recognition of amplifying, or positive, feedback as well as negative feedback. Another is the introduction of nonlinear responses into a chain of circular causality that could lead to unexpected and unintended outcomes, which means that it can no longer be assumed that the system will move to equilibrium. The system is then no longer self-regulating but it is self-influencing: it may be self-sustaining or self-destructive. Systems dynamics originally had little impact on management thinking but more recently, it has attracted much interest as a central concept in the notion of the learning organization, particularly in the influential writings of Senge.[22] Here, instead of thinking of a system moving toward an equilibrium state, it is thought of as following a small number of typical patterns or archetypes. Effective management requires the recognition of these archetypes and the identification of leverage points at which action can be taken to change from one to another and so stay in control of an organization, in effect controlling its dynamics.

Systems theories hold that the internal dynamics of a system, the form of the system, plays a major role in determining its behavior. This formative causal link, however, is thought of in linear terms in that the form, or internal dynamic, causes the behavior but that behavior does not cause the form, or internal dynamic. The internal dynamic is a given. In the theories of cybernetics and general systems, there is also linear causality of an efficient kind. For both, if there is a change in the environment, then the system will adapt. It is a gap between environment and internal state that triggers a change back to an equilibrium state in a straightforward linear manner. History here is unimportant since change toward equilibrium is triggered only by the current gap between environmental conditions and internal state. In the systems dynamics strand, as well as formative causality, there is also efficient causality but this time it takes a circular nonlinear form. The behavior produced by a system in one period feeds back through the system to determine behavior in the next period. In systems dynamics, history does, therefore, play a part. However, with this one difference we can say that, in all three strands of systems thinking, the notion of efficient cause is expressed as a feedback process and linked to formative causality. The manager designs, controls or leverages the system to achieve the chosen goals. This too is efficient causality in that if the manager chooses the right design then the system will move in the predetermined direction desired.

Consider how this systems thinking compares with the earlier framework of scientific management. The manager continues to be equated with the natural scientist, the objective observer, and just as the scientist is concerned with a natural phenomenon, so the manager is concerned with an organization. Now, however, the organization is understood, not as parts adding to a whole, but as a system in which the interactions between its parts are of primary importance. The manager understands the organization to be a self-regulating or a self-influencing system, and it is the formative process of self-regulation or self-influence (formative cause) that is organizing the pattern of behavior that can be observed. In the case of general systems and cybernetics, that pattern is movement toward a chosen goal, an optimally efficient state, and the pattern of behavior is held close to this goal/state when the system is operating effectively. In the case of systems dynamics, the form toward which the system moves is a typical pattern or archetype enfolded in the system, which the manager can alter by operating at leverage points. In all of these systems theories, therefore, the state towards which the system tends is a state already enfolded, as it were, in the rules (efficient cause) governing the way the parts interact (formative cause). The goal is set outside the system but its own internal formative process determines its movement toward the goal.

In management science, the manager is the objective observer who designs rules of individual behavior to do with task performance and motivation. In cybernetics and general systems perspectives, however, the manager is the objective observer who designs the whole system, including the rules of interaction between members that drive it. In systems dynamics, the manager is the objective observer who detects system archetypes and operates at leverage points to alter them. In early systems thinking, the freedom was located in the manager to choose the system or to choose changes in it. The rationalist causality of management science continued as before and the first wave of system thinking about organizations as systems paid as little attention as management science did to ethics, ordinary human freedom and the unknown nature of the final state toward which human action tends. However, as I will return to in Chapter 4, some more recent developments of second order systems thinking in the 1980s and 1990s actively took up the issues of participation and ethics.

A narrower focus for management

Before the war, management practice had been strongly influenced by both the scientific method and the human relations school of management which drew on insights of social psychology, anthropology, sociology and psychoanalysis. In the postwar period, the conception of management moved away from the ideas and the ideals of the prewar human relations approach and focused much more narrowly on the scientific manager who used models and analytical techniques and designed and manipulated systems. Cybernetic systems came to be expressed in the design of quality assurance, budgeting and planning systems and, indeed, the organization as a whole came to be thought of as a cybernetic system and then later in terms of systems dynamics as the learning organization. The tenor of the managerial discourse changed as theorists looked for an orderly body of general knowledge about organizations and their management that applied in all contexts and in all periods. Management was equated with setting objectives, designing systems for meeting them, planning, forecasting and controlling. Managers were described as 'systems designers', 'information processors' and 'programmers' regulating the interface of the organization and its environment in accordance with cybernetic systems theory. The rise of the conglomerate was characterized by a multiplicity of managers removed from the grass roots of the organization's activities and they felt the need for models, maps and techniques that would enable them to exert control from a distance. This need for techniques enabling the taking of a generalized macro view from a distance in order to apply some degree of control had already been faced over a century before by tax collectors and other administrators of the business of the modern state.[23] The approaches they took were also those of modelling, mapping and measuring. This is a development I will be exploring in more detail in the next chapter, but it is worth mentioning here because it presents an administrative background and history to what commercial and industrial managers now found themselves doing. It was not simply the importation of systems ideas from science but also of systemic practice from public administration.

The period from the end of the Second World War to the economic crisis of the early 1970s saw the firm establishment of managerialism in American society[24] and also in Europe. This was a period of more or less sustained growth and economic prosperity. Immediately after the war, returning military were provided with free education. This, together with the gradual increase in prosperity, created a huge demand for business education. By 1956, there were nearly 50 percent more business schools and the competition for competent teachers increased. Not surprisingly, the quality of business school teaching was rather low, except at the few elite schools. During the 1950s, despite pressures from the American Association of Colleges and Schools of Business to improve the quality of education, academics at business schools were poorly trained with few having doctorates or even rudimentary training in research methods and so research was largely superficial. Many of the students were also not of the top grade. The postwar period saw the emergence and domination of the large diversified conglomerate form of business corporation and the growth of large government agencies. There was also an increase in the number of philanthropic foundations, such as the Carnegie Foundation and the Ford Foundation, which funded business schools and so came to have an important impact on how they developed. They pressed for better-qualified faculty and it became more and more a requirement that faculty should have a doctorate and engage in research.

The much-changed conception of the management role brought with it a complete orientation toward profit. The distant manager's primary role was to perform the tasks required to maximize profits. It was believed that the new management techniques could be applied in any organization of any size so that experience in a particular industry was not necessary – expertise in decision-making and control was all that was needed. But at the top of the hierarchy there was a CEO who many have described, in this period, as a kind of industrial statesman who worked closely with outside bodies such as government ministers, politicians and regulatory authorities, while managers lower down in the hierarchy were simply technicians applying the techniques of decision-making and control that would maximize profits. The postwar period can, therefore, be described as a period of relationship capitalism[25] where the major concern was with relationships between big corporations and the government and a move away from the simpler kind of managerial capitalism of the prewar period. In prewar managerialism, the managers were thought of as more rounded professionals, as stewards of society's resources, a role they could carry out by using scientific decision-making and science-based motivation of labor all the time with a strong emphasis on ethical responsibility for what they did. However, in the postwar period managerialism was affected by an internal split of role with those lower down in the hierarchy using a much greater range of scientific techniques to make decision and exercise control – instead of being more rounded professionals, managers were now more like technicians. Managers at the top of the hierarchy, however, had a different role in response to much greater government intervention after the war. Competition was controlled by regulatory authorities and large conglomerate CEOs had to deal with these and politicians to get the best for their corporation. They had to specialize in relationships.

There were, of course reactions against the narrowing focus on profit and technical decision-making with people understood in behaviorist terms. This took the form of the humanistic psychology developed by Herzberg[26] and also Maslow.[27] Their theories of motivation emphasized the need for higher motivators such as work that enables self-actualization. This richer view of human beings and their motivations became an important foundation of the later development of the discipline of Organization Development, executive coaching and some forms of management development.

Business schools had to seek government accreditation to get government funds but at least as important was the funding provided by the Foundations. The Foundations were driving for a more mechanized, capital-intensive process of educating the large numbers attracted to business schools by the government funding of GIs returning from the war. The Foundations wanted to raise the academic standards of the business schools by getting teachers at business schools to focus on solving real, complex problems using quantitative methods. Economic analysis now became more prominent, because it also provided analytical tools. This was supplemented by some emphasis on organizational behavior and on the relationship between business and society. The Ford Foundation was strongly of the view that there was now a science of management which enabled managers to make decisions solely on rational grounds using techniques such as decision analysis and game theory, making any appeal to intuition and judgment unnecessary. It was believed that this management science could be taught at business schools by a faculty expert in these techniques. Not surprisingly with managers being regarded as technicians, the role of the faculty at the business schools was that of transferring to managers the decision-making and control techniques that they would need. Since little importance was attached to experience, it did not seem at all strange that business school faculty were largely academics with no experience of managing in industry and commerce. The core curriculum came to be standardized and this approach was reflected in the increasingly important research activities of business schools. By 1956 there were 587 business schools in the USA which were awarding 40,000 bachelor degrees and over 4,000 MBAs per annum and there was further rapid growth to the 1970s.

The number of government employees rose rapidly after the end of the War and legislative amendments sought to curb this growth. President Truman and his successors changed the composition of federal government employment so that the majority of those employed consisted of temporary contractors. This created an opportunity for independent management consultants who became very important in government administration and advice by the 1970s. Legislative antitrust regulation in the 1950s led to IBM and other computer manufacturers being prohibited from offering computer-consulting advice, so creating an opportunity this time for the large accounting firms such as Arthur Andersen who set up information technology consultancies.[28] In the 1960s, specialist strategy consultants such as the Boston Consulting Group and Bain & Company grew rapidly. Consultants also found a lucrative market in advising first universities, then religious institutions and then hospitals on their organizational structures. During this period, management consultants successfully established themselves as a profession with its own institutions. During this period, too, there was a major export of the American model of consulting to other countries.

The emergence of investment capitalism and the mathematics of certainty

The Ford Foundation had played a large part in business school reforms of the postwar period so that, by the 1960s, one could say that the business schools provided professional education for what had become an institutionalized profession of managers. Science-based professionalism was founded on the view that there was a scientific body of knowledge, acquisition of which was essential for the professional manager. At first, this postwar professionalism also rested on a code of ethics, a code of conduct and an ideal of service. Although the reforms pressed for by the Foundations tended to erode the code of conduct aspect there was, nevertheless, still room for some notion of stewardship. The post 1970 period, however, was to see the sweeping away of notions of managers as stewards or indeed professionals. Over this period, the numbers of business schools and business students in the USA rose markedly. By 1980 there were more than 600 MBA programs producing 57,000 graduates per annum. On average, 26 new business schools were established each year and total enrollments, including undergraduates, were around 300,000 per year. This was also the time of the spread of business schools across Europe.

In the 1970s, the elite business schools were still focused on producing general managers – rational decision makers and problem solvers. The CEO was still seen as an enlightened statesman, a pillar of managerialism and relational capitalism. However, after the 1970s, there was a marked shift in power relations from the general managers of major corporations producing goods and services to the CEOs and executives of banks and investment houses. This was the development of investment capitalism which dominated the world until the credit crunch of 2008 to 2009.[29] The year 1970 is a watershed year, because through the 1970s, the economies of the USA and other industrialized countries experienced oil price crises and consequent recessions and industrial unrest. This continued into the deep recession of 1980–82. As unemployment rose and old industries went into serious decline, there was a major shift in Western economies from industrial products to service providers. This was accompanied by a shift in how government was conceptualized with a move to reduce the size of government and its intrusion into the economy. Managers were blamed for the recession and business schools were criticized for producing ineffectual managers. Abernathy and Hayes[30] wrote a famous paper called *'Managing our way to economic decline'* putting the blame on managers, particularly on the analytical techniques they had learned at business schools and the short-term perspectives this had led to. They called for a 'back to basics' approach in which experience-based judgment would be more important. Others, mainly economists and policy makers, criticized relationship capitalism and called for the imposition of the free market system. They called for the maximization of corporate value, measured by share price and justified mergers and acquisitions as the route to increasing share prices. Market discipline was intended to counter the lax control provide by managers. Institutional investors and other shareholders came to be viewed as more trustworthy than managers. The election of Thatcher in 1979 as Prime Minister of the UK and of Reagan in 1980 as President of the USA brought political weight to support this view. Government and old-fashioned CEOs were the problem. Regulation was relaxed and corporate raiders thrived, acquiring large slow moving corporations in the interests of raising shareholder value. This new ideology of shareholder primacy absolved managers from any responsibility other than maximizing the return to shareholders.

Over the 1970s and 1980s, the field of strategy emerged as a separate field of study, indeed as a particular form of management. Economics and econometrics became more important and finance also became a very important part of the curriculum at business schools. The analytical methods of economics were applied to finance in developing sophisticated mathematical models such as Capital Asset Pricing Models and eventually expressed as the Efficient Market hypothesis.[31] According to this hypothesis, markets, operating all on their own, seeking their own self interest untrammelled by government intervention, are efficient in the sense of always immediately reflecting all public information in share price valuations. According to this hypothesis, market prices are the best reflectors of fundamental asset values – the mathematics provides certainty. These developments in the field of finance revolutionized teaching at elite business schools who now trained not general managers but professional investors and financial engineers for the investment banks, private equity and hedge funds, and management consultants. Agency theory[32] became the most respected theory of the firm. This theory focuses on the difficulties of monitoring managers when ownership is widely dispersed, arguing that managers were effectively out of control, because they did not have to bear the financial consequences of bad decisions. This could be overcome by regarding managers as agents of shareholders and rewarding them with a part of the shareholding so that they would come to have the same motivation as shareholders. Business school lecturers, at least at the elite schools, increasingly had little contact with managers in industrial or service enterprises, becoming more and more concerned with strategy and finance. Agency theory justified mergers and acquisitions and the leveraging of corporations with debt while minimizing the importance of other stakeholders and dismissing any social function for managers. Business policy courses on MBAs became strategic management modules strongly rooted in industrial economics.

By 2004 there were 955 business schools in the USA with another 300 or so in Europe. They were probably churning out more than 1.5 million business graduates per annum with the elite graduates going primarily into finance and management consulting. By this time, the large majority of senior managers in corporations of any size must have had some kind of business education. The ideas of economists came to dominate not just finance but international business, production, strategy and human resources. The system of ranking MBA programs and business schools has generally commercialized the MBA so that business schools must now think of themselves as operating in a market which requires them to develop a value proposition. The value proposition now seems to have more to do with image and networking than with education.

By the time we get to the first decade of the twenty-first century, the pre-1970s notion that managers were fundamentally the stewards of society's resources and acted on behalf of all stakeholders (the managerial/relational capitalism) gave way after 1970 to a notion of managers as agents for shareholders (agency theory) whose prime function was to maximize shareholder value. Managerialism as a scientific approach to decision-making and control has continued in much the same form as that which it took in the postwar period but managerial capitalism as an ideology evolved into investment capitalism in the 1980s and has continued as the dominant ideology until very recently. Now, of course, investment capitalism has been revealed to be deeply flawed, with the extended risk-taking of investment bankers, the collapse of financial markets and the evolving recession. The development of investment capitalism was reinforced by the elite business schools of the USA and the development of investment capitalism has altered the fundamental purpose of business schools.[33] In the prewar period, their primary purpose was to support the professionalization of managers, emphasizing their social role. Under investment capitalism, the role of manager shrank to that of simply maximizing shareholder returns. They were subjected to the demands of investment fund managers and investment bankers to provide short-term growth often through mergers and acquisitions. The role of the business schools was reduced to preparing managers for this role, largely by training them in the rational (mathematical) techniques required for their profit maximizing tasks.

These developments meant that the role of the business schools was potentially diminished with impoverished academic content threatening their standing in research-based universities where, after years of struggling, they had finally been accepted and indeed started to affect the very concept of university. To compensate for the inadvertent discrediting of managers by investment capitalism, business schools seized on a renewed purpose and identity which has become popular since the early 1990s under the name of leadership.[34] The role of the business schools became the development of leaders. In 1977, Zaleznik published a paper[35] drawing a distinction between managers and leaders. Managers are affected most by 'initiation of structures'. According to Zaleznick, they differ in motivation from leaders and in how they think and act – they emphasize rationality, control, problem solving, goals, etc. They coordinate and balance conflicting views and get people to accept solutions. They are tactical and bureaucratic. Leaders work in an opposite way. Instead of limiting choices, they develop fresh approaches and open up new issues. They project their ideas into images that excite people. Later writers made much the same distinction between transactional and transformative leadership. The distinction now being made between managers as traditional and rational while true leaders are charismatic is an idealization which glorifies change itself and the individual change agents with visions and missions. This resurrection of the hero myth was widely taken up by motivational speakers, consultants and corporate trainers as well as aspiring CEOs, who sought to emulate charismatic leaders such as Lee Iacocca and Jack Welsh. A leadership ideology had thus been added to the managerialist ideology in business and, with something of a lag, it replaced the public administration ethic in the public sector. However, in both private and public sectors, the prescriptions on how to manage continued to be those scientific techniques brought in after the war.

Also in the 1990s banking regulators largely eliminated the Glass-Steagall Act of 1933, making it possible for bankers to take on both commercial and investment banking functions as well as provide management-consulting advice. Management consultants played an increasingly important role in popularizing particular management concepts. During the 1980s and 1990s, consultancies such as McKinsey popularized the concept of 'corporate culture'. Two former McKinsey consultants published the highly popular book *In search of Excellence* in 1982, and this had an enormous impact on management thinking around the world, making concepts such as vision, mission and charismatic leader commonplace in management-speak.[36] Such concepts became commoditized and marketed by the consultancies. Then in 2000, the Enron scandal broke out, and it emerged that Arthur Andersen had earned huge fees both for providing management consultancy advice to Enron and from acting as its auditor. This was once again seen as a conflict of interest and accounting firms were barred from offering consultancy advice to any company they audited. Rapid growth in management consultancy, however, continued into the twenty-first century.

The story of the evolution of the roles of managers and leaders in organizations and how they are thought about brings us to the present time of another financial collapse and recession, and there can be little doubt that the roles of managers will continue to evolve, probably in ways that will surprise us. The organizational reality is that no one has planned or is planning the evolution of roles, rather, that have been and still are emerging in the interplay of powerful institutional actions which are shaping and at the same time being shaped by various management, leadership, consultancy, research and educational roles.

The problematic continuing role of the sciences of certainty and notions of systems

For over three hundred years now, the evolving global economy has experienced periods of expansion followed by periods of crisis eventually succeed by further periods of expansion. Some of these crises have been mentioned in the brief account of the evolution of management roles given in this chapter, namely, those of the 1720s, the 1860s, the 1930s, the 1970s and the 2000s. At present, no one knows what the next stage of evolution will be like. Each crisis provokes anxiety and blame with the hostility directed at politicians but even more at the managers, often managers of banks, who are believed to have caused the crisis. And this blaming and questioning usually produces a call for regulation of markets and attempts to encourage growth. Less noticeably, however, the crises also prompt changes in the concept of capitalism and as an inevitable consequence, changes in the roles of managers and leaders. In other words, each crisis provokes the rethinking of how organizations should be governed and what it means to manage and lead. While much attention is focused on measures to stimulate economies and regulate organizations, the rethinking and the changing roles of managers and leaders proceed much less visibly.

What strikes me about the lead up to the current crisis is that, despite changes in the thinking about organizations, leaders and managers, there seems to be one constant theme running unquestioned through the story since the end of the nineteenth century, namely, the insistence, later taken for granted, that management is a science in some sense and in the postwar period this science is very much developed around the notion of system. The management and leadership textbooks continue to present, as the central aspect of management, the rational, analytical techniques developed in the last war, the business schools still have curricula which reflect this and organizational research still largely claims to be scientific. Yet, as the last chapter showed, an essential aspect of the scientific method is lacking, namely, an empirical evidence base for hypotheses made. Furthermore, nothing like the certainty traditional science seeks to produce has so far materialized in our research on organizations. Indeed, we are currently experiencing economic consequences that make dramatically clear just how uncertain these consequences and their further development are. If we are to rethink the roles of managers and leaders, then we need to understand what we are conceptually importing into our thinking about organizations when we appeal to the natural sciences, traditionally the sciences of certainty.

Concepts imported with science into understanding organizations

In identifying management with science, we have imported three very important concepts which we now take so for granted that we hardly notice them. First, there is the taken-for-granted assumption of the autonomous, rational individual. The conception of the individual mind as split off from the body, of individuals as split off from each other and the natural world goes hand in hand with an atomistic view of society and the objectification and control of nature. The natural and social worlds, as objects of control, confirm man's self-defining identity. As mentioned in the foregoing section, this view of the autonomous individual continues to exist in some tension with the expressivist view which denies the splits of mind and body, human nature. This too has been imported into management thinking. It is useful to note at this point that there is a disjuncture between the reality of human interdependence and the interplay of human actions identified in the last chapter and the highly individualistic views of human beings in both the autonomous and the expressivist perspectives. The assumption of the rational autonomous individual carries with it the implication of the masterful individual who can be in control. In a subsequent chapter, I will explore the problems for thinking about organizations which is caused by the conflict between organizational reality and dominant theories of the individual.

The second concept imported from science into management is that of the objective observer who identifies and isolates causality in nature and then tests hypotheses based on these identifications. The objective observer is detached from the phenomenon being studied, avoiding any subjective involvement so as not to influence or affect the formulating and testing of hypotheses. When the notion of the objective observer is imported into theories of organization, the manager and the leader are identified with the objective observer and they are supposed to act upon rationally formulated and tested hypotheses about organizational life. This does not accord with the organizational reality of highly emotional involvement, the pursuit of personal agendas, neurotic forms of leadership, politics and significant elements of subjectivity. This too creates problems for making sense of the actual experience of what managers and leaders do.

Thirdly, the following concepts of causality have been imported in the identification of management with science:

* Mechanistic, efficient cause producing stable movement over time and change that is predetermined and entirely predictable. Time is irrelevant and interaction between parts plays no essential role in the explanation. There is, therefore, no notion of emergence or novelty and organization is continuity of a perfect, optimal kind.

- Organic, formative cause producing movement to an already given mature state contained, as it were, within the formative process. A pre-given, mature state emerges through developmental stages in the formative interaction of the parts of a system and change is confined to regular movement from one form, say infant, to another, say child, leading to the final state, mature adult. Contextual differences produce small variations in mature form but these do not alter the identity of the system. Organization is continuity of form with small variations, all enfolded so that genuine novelty is not possible.
- Rationalist cause producing autonomously chosen goals and the strategies to achieve them. Both stability and change are human choices without any notion of emergence. Organization exists by human choices and designs and this could include the rational design of the truly novel. Figure 2.1 gives a summary of the key features of these different causalities.

There are a number of important points to note about these notions of causality. First, they are all causalities of certainty with outcomes that are known in advance. They do not encompass uncertainty which was identified in the last chapter as key to organizational reality. Therefore, in importing science into management thinking, we have imported notions of causality which exclude unique uncertainty and with it the unknowable, the unexpected and the surprising. In later chapters, I will be suggesting that there is a fundamental problem with theories built on these notions of causality, as dominant management thinking is, and the experience of the unknowable as an organizational reality.

The causalities of certainty:

	1. Efficient	2. Rationalist	3. Formative
Movement toward a future that is:	a repetition of the past.	a goal chosen by reasoning autonomous humans.	an unfolding of a mature form already enfolded from the beginning.
Movement in order to:	reveal or discover hidden order/realize an optimal state.	realize chosen goals.	reveal, realize a mature form already given.
Process of movement/ cause is:	universal, timeless laws of 'if-then' kind.	human reason within ethical universals.	unfolding a whole already enfolded in the rules of interaction.
Nature of variation/change:	corrective/fitting.	Design/choice to get it right.	shift from one given form to another in stages of development.
Freedom/constraint:	conforming to natural laws.	through reason constrained by ethical universals.	no freedom only constraint by given forms.

Figure 2.1 Summary of the key features of different causalities.

Thirdly, identification of science with management thinking imports dualistic 'both/ and' thinking introduced by Kant which eliminates the organizational reality of paradox identified in the last chapter. There is both determinism and freedom, but separately located in nature (including human bodies) and in human action. There is both stability and change but the end point of change is given in nature and not given in relation to human action since autonomous individuals can choose to change. It is important to notice this because Kant's 'both/and' resolution of conflicting arguments is still widely employed in thinking about organizations. For example, conditions in which it is appropriate to apply mechanistic approaches to management are identified and then different conditions are set out in which an organic approach should be adopted. This preserves a place for both the mechanistic and the organic by confining them to separate areas of action. In this way, contradictions are resolved, conflict is ignored and paradox plays no important part so that there is little motivation to look for alternative explanations.

This dualistic thinking with its elimination of paradox is clearly evident in the application of the scientific concept of system to an organization – there is *both* the formative causality of the system *and* the rationalist causality of the autonomous individual manager who objectively observes and designs the organizational system. The act of observing or designing a system is immediately an act of applying formative causality, because the act of observing or designing points to, or sets up, interactions in which the patterns of behavior they will produce are already there in the identified or designed rules of interaction. The system can only do what it is designed to do. When humans are regarded as parts of a system they are subject to formative cause, but when they are regarded as objective observers and designers of such systems they exercise rationalist causality. Human interaction becomes objectified as a system which subjugates human choice to the formative causality of the system leaving reasoned choice to the objective observer outside the system. Therefore, humans regarded as parts of a system in dominant discourse on organizations and management are no longer autonomous and this is why Kant held that human action could not be thought of as a system. Furthermore, as soon as one thinks of a human organization as a system that can be identified or designed by the managers or leader taking the role of objective observer outside the system, one immediately encounters the problem that the identifier or the designer is also part of the system. Modern second order systems thinkers[37] attempt to overcome this difficulty by redrawing the boundary of the system so that it includes the objective observer. These redrawn boundaries, however, also presuppose an objective observer who has to be outside to do the redrawing. The result is an infinite regress. The dominant management discourse tends to be based on first order[38] systems thinking and the hypothetical 'as . . . if' nature of the system concept tends to slip out of awareness so that people in an organization, and many researching it, talk about it as an actually existing system, so reifying it, turning a concept into a thing. The organization as system is a spatial metaphor and forgetting the metaphorical nature of the construct, managers talk frequently about steering the organization, giving it a direction, moving it forward, moving its culture from one state to another, and so on and on. Once again, there is a conflict between this way of thinking and the organizational reality of being unable to 'move the system around'.

Conclusion

This chapter has told the story of how management was identified with the sciences of certainty as a move to legitimize the professional status of managers. This led to the development of scientific management and a corresponding understanding of human relations. It also led a theory of organizations as systems. The chapter also briefly told the story of some significant developments in Western thought which point to what concepts have been imported into thinking about organizations and management in the move to science. Three important, now taken for granted concepts entered management thinking along with science. First, there is the conception of human beings as autonomous individuals who act rationally to stay in control of the organization as a system understood, sometimes as mechanism driven by efficient cause and sometimes as organism driven by formative cause. Second, managers in essence take the role of scientist, the objective observer standing outside the system, designing it to unfold a chosen purpose, expressing rationalist causality. Third, the concept of system has been imported and applied directly to human action and this brings a number of problems with it. Taken together these imports create conflicts with organizational reality. In organizational life, we find ourselves moving into the unknown but there is no place for this or for essentially linked novelty in the dominant way of thinking about organizations. In organizational life, the reality is of managers subjectively engaged in what they do, not simply standing outside as objective observers. The organizational reality is one in which no one is really in control of what happens but the imported way of thinking and its ideological basis is all about control. Finally, the organizational reality is often one of corruption and greed which the imported way of thinking is ill equipped to deal with, because it largely ignores ethics and when it does recognize ethics, it does so in a dualistic way in which blame for wrong doing is directed at 'the system' and a few powerful scapegoats.

Reflection on the history of the evolution of the dominant discourse reveals an irony: the rationality of science would lead one to expect that it became the basis of the dominant discourse simply because science offers the most rational, the best way of governing organizations but the reality is that the identification with science came about as an important element of the professionalization of the managing classes. The identification with science had relatively little to do with whether the science-based prescriptions work or not and a great deal to do with matters of power, identity and ideology. Moreover, how the discourse on organization continues to evolve will no doubt have just as much to do with power, identity and ideology. The question now is whether the identification of the organizational discourse with science should, or even could, be ended or whether it is the way in which science has been taken up that is the problem. The dominant discourse is clearly built on what we might call the sciences of uncertainty but there are now sciences of uncertainty and this immediately suggests a scientific basis more in accord with organizational reality. The next chapter will therefore inquire into what the sciences of uncertainty are.

Notes

1 Grace, M. (2003) 'Origins of Leadership: The Etymology of Leadership', *Selected Proceedings from 2003 Conference of the International Leadership Association*, 1–15.
2 Arendt, H. (1958) *The Human Condition*, Chicago: University of Chicago Press.
3 Rost, J. C. (1991) *Leadership for the Twenty First Century*, New York: Praeger.
4 Grace, M. (2003) 'Origins of Leadership: The Etymology of Leadership', *Selected Proceedings from 2003 Conference of the International Leadership Association*.
5 Barnes, P. A. (2003) The origins of Limited Liability in Britain, The First 'Panic', and their Implications for Limited Liability and Corporate Governance Today, Available at SSRN: http://ssm.com/abstract+488703.

6 Hickson, C. R. and Turner, J. D. (2005) 'Corporation or Limited Liability Company' in McCusker, J. J., Engerman, S., Fischer, L. R., Hancock, D. J. and Pomeranz, K. L. (eds) (2005) *Encyclopaedia of World Trade Since 1450*, New York: Macmillan.

7 Khurana, in his book *From Higher Aims to Hired Hands: The Social Transformation of American Business Schools and the Unfulfilled Promise of Management as a Profession*, Princeton NJ: Princeton University Press, explores the intertwined development of organizational forms, roles of managers and the development of management education in the United States and in doing so provides an insightful view of the evolution of the roles of managers and leaders, which is as applicable in Europe as it is in North America and indeed more widely than that. He distinguishes between three phases in the evolution of management and leadership roles: what he calls managerial capitalism running from the late nineteenth century to the entry of the USA into World War II in 1941; relationship form of managerial capitalism from 1941 to 1970; and investment capitalism from the 1970s on. This and the following two sections keeps to these periods and draws much of the material from this book.

8 Taylor, C. (1975) *Hegel*, Cambridge: Cambridge University Press.

9 Kant, I. (1790) *Critique of Judgement*, trans. W. S. Pluhar, Indianapolis: Hackett (1987).

10 Taylor, F. ([1911] 1967) *Scientific Management*, New York: Harper Brothers.

11 Fayol, H. ([1916] 1948) *Industrial and General Administration*, London: Pitman.

12 Mayo, E. (1945) *The Social Problems of an Industrial Civilization*, Cambridge, MA: Harvard University Press.

13 For example, Likert, R. (1961) *New Patterns of Management*, New York: McGraw-Hill.

14 McKenna. C. D. (2006) *The World's Newest Profession: Management Consulting in the Twentieth Century*, Cambridge: Cambridge University Press.

15 Cybernetic systems are explained later in this chapter.

16 Systems dynamics is also explained later in this chapter.

17 McCulloch, W. S. and Pitts, W. (1943) 'A Logical Calculus of Ideas Imminent in Nervous Activity', *Bulletin of Mathematical Biophysics*, 5, 115–33.

18 Bertalanffy, L. von (1968) *General Systems Theory: Foundations, Development, Applications*, New York: George Braziller; Boulding, K. E. (1956) 'General Systems Theory: The Skeleton of Science', *Management Science*, 2, 97–108.

19 Ashby, W. R. (1945) 'The Effect of Controls on Stability', *Natura*, 155, 242–43; Ashby, W. R. (1952) *Design for a Brain*, New York: Wiley; Ashby, W. R. (1956) *Introduction to Cybernetics*, New York: Wiley; Beer, S. ([1959] 1967) *Cybernetics and Management*, London: English Universities Press; Beer, S. (1966) *Decision and Control: The Meaning of Operational Research and Management Cybernetics*, London: Wiley; Beer, S. (1979) *The Heart of the Enterprise*, Chichester: Wiley; Beer, S. (1981) *The Brain of the Firm*, Chichester: Wiley; Wiener, N. (1948) *Cybernetics: Or Control and Communication in the Animal and the Machine*, Cambridge, MA: MIT Press.

20 Goodwin, R. M. (1951) 'Econometrics in Business-Style Analysis', in Hansen, A. H. (ed.) *Business Cycles and National Income*, New York: W. W. Norton; Tustin, A. (1953) *The Mechanism of Economic Systems*, Cambridge, MA: Harvard University Press; Forrester, J. (1958) 'Industrial Dynamics: A Major Breakthrough for Decision Making', *Harvard Business Review*, 36, 4, 37–66; Forrester, J. (1961) *Industrial Dynamics*, Cambridge, MA: MIT Press; Forrester, J. (1969) *The Principles of Systems*, Cambridge, MA: Wright-Allen Press.

21 Miller, E. J. and Rice, A. K. (1967) *Systems of Organization: The Control of Task and Sentient Boundaries*, London: Tavistock.

22 Senge, P. M. (1990) *The Fifth Discipline: The Art and Practice of the Learning Organization*, New York: Doubleday.

23 Scott, J. C. (1998) *Seeing Like a State: How Certain Schemes to Improve the Human Condition Have Failed*, New Haven: Yale University Press.

24 Khurana, R. (2007) *From Higher Aims to Hired Hands: The Social Transformation of Business Schools and the Unfulfilled Promise of Management as a Profession*, Princeton NJ: Princeton University Press.

25 Ibid.

26 Hertzberg, F. (1966) *Work and the Nature of Man*, Cleveland, OH: World.

27 Maslow, A. (1954) *Motivation and Personality*, New York: Harper Brothers.

28 McKenna. C. D. (2006) *The World's Newest Profession: Management Consulting in the Twentieth Century*, Cambridge: Cambridge University Press.

29 Khurana, R. (2007) *From Higher Aims to Hired Hands*: *The Social Transformation of Business Schools and the Unfulfilled Promise of Management as a Profession*, Princeton, NJ: Princeton University Press.

30 Abernathy, W. J. and Hayes, R. (1980) Managing our Way to Economic Decline, *Harvard Business Review*, July-August, 67–77.

31 Jensen, M. C. and Meckling, W. H. (1976) Theory of the Firm: Managerial Behavior, Agency Costs, and Ownership Structure, *Journal of Financial Economics*, 3, 303–60.

32 Ibid.

33 Khurana, R. (2007) *From Higher Aims to Hired Hands*: *The Social Transformation of Business Schools and the Unfulfilled Promise of Management as a Profession*, Princeton, NJ: Princeton University Press.

34 Ibid.

35 Zaleznik, A. (1977) 'Managers and Leaders: Are They Different?', *Harvard Business Review*, 70(2), 126–35.

36 Peters, T. J. and Waterman, R. H. (1982) *In Search of Excellence*, New York: Harper & Row.

37 Flood, R. L. (1990) 'Liberating Systems Theory: Towards Critical Systems Thinking', *Human Relations*, 43, 49–75; Jackson, M. C. (2000) *Systems Approaches to Management*, New York: Kluwer; Midgley, G. (2000) *Systemic Intervention*: *Philosophy, Methodology, and Practice*, New York: Kluwer.

38 First-order systems, sometimes referred to as hard systems thinking, are those developed in general systems, cybernetics and systems dynamics around the 1950s. Second order and critical systems thinking seeks to include the observer of the system in the system and to bring in matters of culture and ethics.

3 Complexity and the sciences of uncertainty

The importance of local interaction in the emergence of population-wide patterns of continuity and change

The review of the economic events of the last three years in Chapter 1 made it undeniably obvious that a key aspect of organizational reality is uncertainty. This means that executives of organizations do not know what the outcomes of their chosen actions will be and that in fact, they are not in control of the evolution of their organizations, although they are forming plans and making choices and can know what they are actually doing. This reality of uncertainty is strongly linked to other obvious aspects of organizational reality, namely, the interdependence of people in their own and other organizations so that what happens arises in the interplay of their actions, which is why they cannot choose outcomes although they can choose their next action. However, as Chapter 2 shows, in linking management to the natural sciences as a way of legitimizing the professional status of managers in society, organization and management science was developed on the basis of the natural sciences of certainty. Furthermore, in so doing, management thinking imported key concepts of the masterful, rational autonomous individual who could choose not only the goals of action and the outcomes but could also select the rules, provide the motivation and design the system that would deliver predetermined organizational outcomes. In all these respects, therefore, organization and management science has been based on theoretical foundations quite contrary to the experience of organizational reality. It seems to me that this must then lead to an inadequate and confused understanding of what people in organizations are doing and how they have managed to produce the crises of the last three years and at the same time continuing technological achievements and prosperity for some, just as in the years before this they managed to produce growth and innovation, also accompanied by crises. However, there are what might be called the sciences of uncertainty, first in Darwin's theory of evolution developed in the mid-nineteenth century and then in the sciences of complexity which appeared after the middle of the twentieth century. This chapter will explore some key concepts in these sciences of uncertainty to see if they can provide a theoretical basis more in keeping with organizational reality than the classic sciences of certainty. Then Chapter 4 will take up how writers on organization and management are linking the sciences of uncertainty to their theorizing. The next section provides a brief review of the theory of evolution and the section after that will do the same for the sciences of complexity.

Chance and adaptation: Darwin's evolutionary theory

Darwin[1] argued that the motive force for change in organisms was the struggle for survival in which they developed biological variations that were more or less adapted to their environment, which included other organisms. The more adapted organisms survived and their numbers increased, while the less adapted perished. A species consists of a number of organisms with much the same body parts, that is, mode of survival and species change through small variations at the level of the individual organism, some of which enhance its chances of survival, and thus reproductive success, in a changed environment, while other variations do not enhance survival chances and so disappear from the species. The more adapted changes, arising by chance, spread through the species so that it gradually changes toward more adapted forms. If groups of the species are separated from each other by, for example, geographic barriers, then those groups are likely to change in different ways, with each becoming more and more adapted to their separate local environments through the competitive sifting of more from less adapted changes, that is, through the process of natural selection. Eventually, the difference becomes so great that one could say that the divergent groups constitute new species. Novelty, therefore, arises through a gradual process of chance changes sifted by natural selection, the struggle for survival, so that the most adapted forms survive to constitute a new species. Darwin, however, could not explain how these individual chance changes were passed from one generation to the next so as to spread through the population. An answer to this question was provided by Mendel who explained the genetic basis of inheritance. The combination of Mendel and Darwin became the neo-Darwinian synthesis, to be described at the end of this section.

In Darwin's theory, cumulative adaptations result in completely new species, new forms that had not existed before and were in no sense already there, as was the case in Kant's formative process of development. Kant's theory of development produces phases of predictable change that are movements into the known while Darwin's evolution produces unpredictable change of a truly novel kind as movement into the unknown. Causality in Kant's theory of development is formative cause but Darwin's theory of evolution expresses what we might call adaptionist cause. Darwin's argument, then, was that novelty arises through a gradual process of divergence in small chance variations naturally selected for their adaptive functions, and it is hard to say just when the novelty occurs. What Darwin was proposing was a transformative process of variation, selection and retention at the level of whole organisms in which truly new species emerged. There is clearly come similarity between this kind of biological evolution and the evolution of economies through processes of competitive selection. However, even in Darwin's time, there were dissenting voices.

For example, Lamarck[2] believed that an organism passed on to its offspring the adaptive changes it made during its life and that evolution followed a predetermined plan. Darwin's theory rejects both of these points. Thomas Huxley[3] argued that novelty emerged in a sudden discontinuous fashion before natural selection exerted its influence of refining the newly emergent species. However, he could not explain how this occurred. Around the beginning of the twentieth century, when Mendel's explanation of the genetic basis of inheritance began to attract increasing attention, William Bateson[4] argued that mutations typically arose as small changes in genes in their recessive state where they were shielded from natural selection until they spread through the population and suddenly became dominant. Natural selection and adaptation to an environment were thus seen to be far less important in the origin of new species than Darwin thought. Others[5] developed this idea in rather different ways and later views of this kind were expressed in the idea of genetic drift where random variation might lead to less fit species surviving as more fit ones were eliminated. Some species might survive contrary to selection, or for reasons that had nothing to do with selection, such as a disaster that wiped out the more fit species. Later, in the 1970s and 1980s, Eldridge and Gould[6] took up this kind of argument and suggested that new species arise in discontinuous jumps (punctuated equilibrium) in a way not due to natural selection. Another line of disagreement has to do with whether natural selection operated at the level of the individual or the group.[7] The latter pointed to the particular role of regulating genes that control other genes in a move that gives more emphasis to interaction between genes rather than a simple focus on chance variation in individual genes. However, these dissenting voices have never come to occupy the dominant position, as the neo-Darwinian synthesis did.

According to the neo-Darwinian perspective,[8] variations take place in the process of reproduction. One cause of variation is the errors arising as genetic material is copied (random mutation) and the other cause is the somewhat random mixing of genetic material in sexual reproduction so that the explanation of variation shifts from the level of the organism to the level of the gene. New varieties of organism, therefore, appear by chance and accident lies at the heart of the process. The explanation is reduced to the level of the individual gene and interaction between genes is unimportant. Natural selection, that is, competition for survival, then sifts out for further reproduction those variations that adapt most effectively in the competitive environment constituted by other species of organisms. The result is an adaptionist form of causality which is summarized in Figure 3.1.

Some organizational theorists[9] and evolutionary or institutionalist economists[10] base their views on the kind of evolutionary theory just outlined. The writers in the organizational evolution tradition[11] questioned the ability of managers to choose the state of their organization in any way. They took a neo-Darwinian view and held that organizations changed through random events that were then selected for survival by competition.

Institutional economics, which focuses on the behavior of organizations as entities seeking legitimacy rather than simply competitive advantage, has been taken up in organizational theory.[12] These writers seek to understand organizations in terms of routines, norms and rules. In the evolutionary theories taken up in the organizational literature, chance variations in routines and other actions are held to create novel forms of behavior which are then competitively selected for survival. A key question in evolutionary theories of organizations has to do with whether traits can be inherited only through intergenerational processes, as held by social Darwinists or whether traits can be inherited within a generation through cultural evolution, mimicry and learning. Organizational evolution, imported directly from biology to constitute a theory of organizational development, implies adaptionist causality. The cause of change is chance, which is adapted to an environment through the process of competitive selection so that very little, if any, room is allowed for human agency and organizational evolution is primarily due to chance and competition. The evolutionary approach has never had

Movement toward a future that is:	unknown and dependent on chance.
Movement in order to:	survive as a species.
The process of movement/cause is:	random variation in individual entities/natural selection.
Nature of variation/change:	small chance variations.
Freedom/constraint:	freedom arising by chance, constrained by competition.

Figure 3.1 Adaptionist causality.

much impact on the dominant discourse and, for me, does not reflect organizational reality. While the dominant discourse unrealistically elevates the possibility of deliberate managerial change, the evolutionary approach reduces it almost to insignificance, but the experience of organizational reality suggests that managers do have significant influence on what happens, although in much more complex ways than the dominant discourse contemplates. So are the complexity sciences any more promising?

The complexity sciences

There is as yet no single science of complexity but, rather, a number of different strands comprising what might be called the complexity sciences. What they all have in common is a concern with nonlinear interactions. The models of classical science assume that the laws of nature can be represented by linear equations in which entities as causes are related in a linear fashion to entities that are effects. This means that the relationship between the two is assumed to be proportional and that one cause has one perfectly predictable effect if the equation correctly expresses the law. Key figures in this way of thinking knew, of course, that nature was nonlinear, meaning that relationships were not proportional so that doubling of a cause could more than double the effect or less than double it and there could be more than one cause for an effect and more than one effect from a cause. However, the problem with models consisting of nonlinear equations is that they cannot be solved and models with no solution did not seem to be very useful. Therefore, although they knew that nature was nonlinear, Newton and Leibnitz developed the mathematical method of the calculus which enables nonlinear relationships to be simplified and expressed as linear equations. It was assumed that this small simplification would have a small impact on the model's predictive capacity and indeed this was the case for many phenomena such as planetary movements. All the branches of the complexity sciences move away from this assumption of linear relationships and build models of nonlinear relationships, accepting that although they cannot be solved they can be iterated on powerful computers and these simulations allow the scientist to observe and explore patterns of movement in space and through time – the dynamics of a system. Moreover, it turns out that dropping the assumption of nonlinearity has a major rather than a minor consequence for the models of most phenomena in nature. The big difference is that linear relationships yield models of certainty while some nonlinear ones are models of uncertainty. This immediately resonates with the primary organizational reality of uncertainty.

At the beginning of his last book, called *The End of Certainty*, the Nobel Prize winning chemist and leading figure in the complexity sciences, Prigogine,[13] poses what he sees as a central question: 'Is the future given, or is it under perpetual construction?' His answer to the question is very clear: he sees the future for every level of the universe as under perpetual construction and he suggests that the process of perpetual construction, at all levels, can be understood in nonlinear, non equilibrium terms, where instabilities, or fluctuations, break symmetries, particularly the symmetry of time so that new order emerges in disorder. He says that nature is about the creation of unpredictable novelty where the possible is richer than the real. When he moves from focused models and laboratory experiments to think about the wider questions of evolution, a move that many scientists would question, he sees life as an unstable system with an unknowable future in which the irreversibility of time plays a constitutive role. He sees evolution as encountering bifurcation points and taking paths at these points that depend on the micro details of interaction at those points. Prigogine sees evolution at all levels in terms of instabilities with humans and their creativity as a part of it. For him, human creativity is essentially the same process as nature's creativity and this is the basis for his call for 'a new dialogue with nature' which moves away from domination and control. These features, unknowable futures emerging in here-and-now disorderly interactions, present a paradoxical form of causality which can be defined as *transformative causality*. The paradox here is that entities are *forming patterns* of interaction and *at the same time*, they are *being formed by these patterns* of interaction. If we were to think of human organizations and societies in these terms, it would mean that interdependent individual agents are forming patterns of organization/society in the interplay of their intentional acts while, at the same time, those individuals are being formed by the patterns they are creating where what is being formed is personal identity, including ways of thinking. This is the causality of the perpetual construction of the future as movement into the unknown. For me the resonance with the experience of organizational reality is very powerful.

Central to Prigogine's approach, at all levels, is the distinction between individual entities and populations, or ensembles, consisting of those entities. He points to how classical physics, within which he includes relativity and quantum mechanics, takes the trajectories of individual entities as the fundamental unit of analysis. He then argues that individual trajectories cannot be specified for complex systems, not simply because humans are unable to measure with infinite precision but for the intrinsic reason that interaction between particles produces resonance, that is, amplified frequencies of motion, which makes it impossible to identify individual trajectories. Resonance, an intrinsic property of matter, therefore introduces uncertainty and breaks time symmetry, making the future unknowable.

Since individual trajectories cannot be identified for intrinsic reasons, Prigogine takes the ensemble as fundamental and argues that changes in whole ensembles emerge over long periods through the amplification of slight variations in individual entities, that is, the variability of individuals in the case of organisms or microscopic collisions in the case of matter. It is this variability that is amplified to reach bifurcation points where a system spontaneously self organizes to take completely unpredictable paths into the future. He sees whole populations, or ensembles, changing at bifurcation points in processes of self-organization. Prigogine is arguing, therefore, that at the most fundamental levels of matter, it is the individual variability of entities and the interactions between them that lead to change in populations or ensembles. Again, the resonance with organizational reality is powerful and certainly warrants the attention and consideration of those who are interested in a better understanding of organizational life.

Key aspects of the transformative causality of the perpetual construction of the future are summarized in Figure 3.2.

The rest of this chapter will be exploring some of the key features of the complexity sciences and the next chapter will take a look at how they being used by writers on organization and management.

Types of scientific model

Both classical science and the complexity sciences do their work through the use of mathematical and statistical models of the reality they are trying to understand. The method involves solving equations in the former case and running simulations on

Movement toward a future that is:	perpetually constructed by the movement itself as continuity and transformation, the known and the unknown, all at the same time.
Movement in order to:	express continuity and transformation of individual and collective identity.
The process of movement/cause is:	local interaction forming and being formed by population-wide patterns.
Nature of variation/change:	diverse micro interaction and escalation of small changes.
freedom/constraint:	both freedom and constraint arise in diversity of micro interactions under conflicting constraints.

Figure 3.2 Transformative causality.

computers in the latter case. The kind of model used depends upon the assumptions made about the world. Allen[14] usefully identifies five key assumptions which modellers make and the consequent differences in the models that this produces. He distinguishes, as Kant did, between reality which cannot be known in itself and the models scientists construct to represent our experience of this reality, stressing that models of systems and boundaries are all simplifications, in a sense figments of our imagination. He distinguishes between mathematical models where a set of equations models a system as a whole and multi-agent models which try to model the distinct elements and their interactions in detail. He is particularly interested in multi-agent models in which the agents learn over time. For him, thinking is a form of modelling limited by language and experience, and modellers use models as an extension of thinking to try out ideas. Allen identifies five fundamental assumptions made when constructing a model:

1. A boundary can be defined separating a system from its environment. This distinguishes between the parts of the world we want to understand and the rest which we then exclude.
2. Rules for classifying objects, often developed intuitively, which provide a typology of elements identifying the main features of the elements in a system.
3. The elements or components are assumed to be homogenous in that they have no structure, or are made of identical subunits, or are made up of subunits whose diversity is distributed normally around an average. The components are fixed stereotypes which cannot change over time. Such a model, therefore, cannot represent evolution or learning.
4. The individual behavior of the components can be described by their average interaction parameters. This eliminates luck, randomness and noise.
5. The reality being modelled is that of stability or equilibrium.

Equilibrium models: controllable futures

A model, making all of these five assumptions, will predict the future of the model perfectly as in the equilibrium models of neoclassical economics and the cybernetic and general systems models. These assumptions make it possible to construct a mechanistic model of reality, that is, a set of deterministic equations describing the dynamics of the model, which produce stable, predictable outcomes in accordance with efficient and formative causality. However, the conclusions drawn when one takes an equilibrium perspective on organizations are seriously defective, because equilibrium models ignore the importance of time in the development of dynamic patterns of interaction and because they ignore the obviously complex dynamics of interaction at the level of microscopic events and entities found in real life. These models are the central models of the sciences of certainty and the most basic foundation on which the dominant management discourse is built, but they are of very limited use.

Models of chaos: unfolding an enfolded future

When assumption 5 to do with equilibrium is dropped, we get nonlinear dynamical models of the systems dynamics type[15] and of mathematical chaos. Now, equilibrium is a special case but, in addition, there are much more complex patterns of behavior: different possible stationary states, different cyclic states, or mathematical chaos. This is formative causality and because the assumptions about average events and entities at the microscopic level are retained, the model does not reproduce the internal capacity to move from one state to another or evolve to completely new, novel states. When one thinks within the systems dynamics/chaos theory frameworks, therefore, one ignores both how patterns of behavior change of their own accord, that is, without outside intervention, and how those patterns evolve and so produce novelty.

Chaos theory[16] provides an explanation of the behavior of a system that can be modelled by deterministic nonlinear equations in which the output of one calculation is taken as the input of the next. In other words, the equations are recursive, or iterative, taking exactly the same form as those used in the systems dynamics strand of systems thinking. Chaos theory shows how particular control parameters cause its behavior to move according to a particular pattern called an attractor. Attractors are global patterns of behavior displayed by a system. For example, the control parameter might be the speed of energy or information flow through the system. At low rates of energy or information flow, the system follows a point attractor in which it displays only one form of behavior, namely, a stable, equilibrium pattern. At higher rates of energy or information flow, the system may switch to a periodic attractor. This too is a stable equilibrium pattern in which behavior cycles between two forms. Then, at very high rates of energy or information flow, the system displays patterns of explosive growth or even random behavior. In other words, behavior takes on highly unstable forms in which the system may disintegrate. Furthermore, at some critical level of the control parameter, between levels that lead to equilibrium attractors and those that lead to unstable attractors, behavior displays strange attractors, reflected in patterns, that is, shapes in space or movements over time, which are never exactly repeated but are always similar to each other. A strange attractor displays a recognizable pattern in space or over time but that pattern is irregular. In other words, strange attractors are paradoxically regular and irregular, stable and unstable, predictable and unpredictable at the same time. They are neither equilibrium nor random patterns but, rather, an inseparable interplay of both at the same time: within any stable space or time sequence, there is instability and within any unstable space or time sequence, there is stability. Another term used to describe patterns of this kind is 'fractal'. It is the identification of strange attractors, or fractals, which distinguishes chaos theory from systems dynamics, indeed, from all of the systems theories discussed in the last chapter. We can begin here to understand that complexity is a dynamic, a pattern of movement which is a paradox of stable instability or unstable stability, of predictable unpredictability or unpredictable predictability.

The weather is usually used as an example of a system that displays patterns typical of a strange attractor. The abstract representation of the weather system's attractor has a shape rather like a butterfly, in which patterns of air pressure, temperature, and so on, swirl around one wing and then shift abruptly to the other wing, never ever exactly repeating the same movement. The heartbeat of a healthy human also follows a strange attractor reflected in temporal rhythms.[17] Although heartbeats are regular when averaged over a particular period, movements within that average display a regular irregularity. A failing heart is characterized by a loss of complexity in which it moves to a periodic attractor and, of course, the ultimate stability is a point attractor – the straight line.

Strange attractors, also referred to as mathematical chaos, have important implications for predictability.[18] The precise parametric conditions required to produce a strange attractor for a given mathematical model are predictable. Once revealed by iteration, the spatial shapes and time contours of the strange attractor are also predictable, because a given equation, or set of equations, can produce one and only one strange attractor for given parametric conditions. It is as if the equation enfolds an implicit, or hidden, order that is revealed by iteration. For example, the strange attractor followed by the weather system has the characteristic shape already referred to and any deviation from it is soon drawn back into it. The shape of the attractor bounds the movement of the system in space and time, that is, it establishes the limits of the behavior that it is possible for the system to produce. The overall shape of weather movements can therefore be predicted. It is possible to predict the limits within which temperature will vary over a particular season in a particular geographical area, for example. Furthermore, the specific behavior displayed by the system within these limits is reasonably predictable over short ranges in space and short periods, because it takes time for small changes to be escalated into completely different patterns. However, over long ranges in space and long periods, the specific behavior of a system following a strange attractor cannot be predicted. This is due to the system's sensitivity to initial conditions, more popularly known as the butterfly effect, which means that the long-term trajectory of the system is highly sensitive to its starting point. The usual example is that of a butterfly flapping its wings in Sao Paulo which alters the air pressure by a minute amount that could be escalated into a major hurricane over Miami. Long-term predictability would then require the detection of every tiny change and the measurement of each to an infinite degree of precision. Since this is a human impossibility, the specific long-term pathway is unpredictable for all practical purposes. The long-term behavior of such a system, therefore, is as much determined by small changes as it is by the deterministic laws governing it. Deterministic laws can therefore produce indeterminate outcomes, at least as far as any possible human experience is concerned.

This, then, is one branch of the sciences of uncertainty – clear mathematical models demonstrating that nonlinear relationships can, in definable circumstances, produce predictable unpredictability in which it is impossible to make long-term predictions but only provide qualitative, general, macro descriptions of limiting patterns. If human relationships are nonlinear, and they certainly seem to be, then we will not be able to make long-term predictions of organizational futures, and this means that failure to do so is not due to human incompetence but to the inescapable dynamics of our interactions. However, chaos models are of rather limited use for understanding organizations, because they do not have the capacity to move of their own accord from one attractor to another. They can only move if some external agent changes the parameters. In other words, chaos theory does not model internal or intrinsic creativity, a point that applies equally to the systems theories, discussed in the last chapter, that underlie the dominant management discourse. Instead, chaos models display the unfolding of patterns already enfolded in the specification of the model. As for the models in systems dynamic systems, therefore, the underlying causality is that of formative cause. What is distinctive about chaos theory, compared to the other systems theories, however, is the clear identification of the limits to predictability. In doing this, chaos theory challenges the manner in which systems dynamics is used in organizational theory because, while systems dynamics points to the likelihood of nonequilibrium behavior, the way in which it is used continues to equate success with attraction to a state that is as close as possible to equilibrium. From a chaos perspective, this move towards the simplicity of equilibrium could be interpreted as a move towards failure, while health and success are strange attractors in which long-term predictability of specific trajectories is impossible. For systems dynamics thinkers, the aim is to identify leverage points for interventions that will enable them to identify where, when and how to initiate change and so stay in control. However, the ability to do this in a system that is sensitive to tiny changes is called into question. That obviously has serious implications for the human ability to stay 'in control'.

Why does this matter? It matters because dominant ways of thinking and talking about management are based on the sciences of certainty with their rationalist, efficient and formative causality according to which good enough long-term prediction is possible. The efficacy of the whole process of choosing aims, goals, visions and actions to realize them in order to be 'in control' depends on this foundation of predictability. If a system's specific long-term behavior is unpredictable, however, then specific goals can of course still be set, but there is little certainty that the actions taken will realize them. If chaos theory were to indicate anything at all about human action, then currently dominant ways of thinking about management would be undermined. In the end, however, both systems dynamics and its extension to include chaos theory cannot be applied directly to human action. This is because human interaction is not deterministic while the models of systems dynamics and chaos theory are. The equations in these models are fixed, while the principles of human interaction change through learning. Chaos theory might provide a loose metaphor for the unpredictability of action but it can do no more. Even then, the inability to model processes of learning and creativity severely restricts even the metaphorical use of chaos theory for understanding management. Therefore, chaos theory cannot apply directly to human interaction but its insights to do with strange attractors and unpredictability could present a challenge at the level of metaphor.

Models of dissipative structures: spontaneously moving from one given pattern to another

Continuing with the survey of what happens to scientific models as fundamental assumptions are dropped, when assumption 4 is dropped we get self-organizing dynamics, the kind of model developed by Prigogine for physical systems.[19] Assumption 4 says that microscopic events occur at their average rate and when this is dropped it means that fluctuations are introduced into the model, usually in the form of 'noise', so that events of different probabilities, which occur in reality, are incorporated. The resulting model exhibits self-organizing behavior in that movement from one attractor to another does take place entirely due to the internal dynamics of the model. Instead of moving according to a trajectory, this kind of model displays collective adaptive capacity in that it can spontaneously reorganize itself due to the presence of fluctuations. In other words, a different form of order can emerge in the presence of fluctuations, noise or chaos. Shifting one's thinking from systems dynamics and chaos frameworks to a self organizing one, therefore, increases one's understanding of how a system can shift spontaneously from one pattern of behavior to another but the underlying theory of formative causality remains the same since the system can only jump from one already given attractor to another that is also already given. This kind of model also ignores the possibility that the elements of the system could be internally affected by their experiences and by the collective structure of which they are parts. There can, therefore, be no transformed future for such models.

An example of a dissipative structure, which is sometimes referred to by management complexity writers, is that of convection which is the basis of the circulation of the atmosphere and oceans that determine weather changes. A laboratory experiment may be used to explore the complexity of the phenomenon of convection, which involves taking a thin layer of liquid and observing its behavior as increasing heat is applied to its base. At thermodynamic equilibrium, the temperature of this liquid is uniform throughout and it is consequently in a state of rest at a macro level in the sense that there are no bulk movements in it. However, at the micro level, the positions and movements of the molecules are random and hence independent of each other. They fluctuate without correlations, patterns or connections and there is therefore symmetry in the sense that no point in the liquid differs from any other point. However, as heat is applied to the base of the liquid it sets up fluctuations that are amplified through the liquid so that molecules at the base stop moving randomly and begin to move upward, displacing those at the top which then move down to the base of the liquid. The molecules display bulk movement in the form of a convection roll. Consequently, the symmetry of the liquid is broken in that one position in it is different from some others. At some points in the liquid, molecules are moving up and at other points, they are moving down. There is now diversity at the micro level and motion at the macro level. When a critical temperature point is reached, a bifurcation occurs and a new structure emerges in the liquid in a process of self-organization. Molecules move in a regular direction, setting up hexagonal cells, some turning clockwise and others turning anticlockwise. The result is long-range coherence where molecular movements are correlated with each other. The direction of each cell's movement is unpredictable and cannot be determined by the experimenter. The direction taken by any one cell depends upon small differences in the conditions that existed as the cell was formed. This unpredictability is not due simply to practical difficulties; it is intrinsic. Although a change is imposed from outside this experimental system, its response is determined by its own internal dynamic. The emergent pattern is called a dissipative structure, because it maintains pattern by dissipating energy. As further heat is applied to the liquid, the symmetry of the cellular pattern is broken and other patterns emerge. Eventually the liquid reaches a turbulent state of evaporation. There is movement from one state, characterized by perfect order at the macro level and perfect symmetry at the micro level, to other states of more complex order and this occurs through a destabilizing process at bifurcation points. The system is pushed away from stable equilibrium in the form of a point attractor, through bifurcations to other attractors, such as the periodic attractor of convection rolls, and on to deterministic chaos. There is unpredictability at each bifurcation point in the sense that no subsequent state is simply deducible from the previous one. The system displays the capacity to move from one attractor to another but the causality is still formative in that the pathways available for selection are already given in the model or experiment.

Currently, dominant ways of talking and thinking about organizational change, based on the engineer's notion of control, make the implicit assumption that successful change occurs when people are persuaded to hold the same beliefs. Those who give a central role to conflict are rare[20] and the call is usually for strongly shared cultures and harmonious teamwork. Managers seek to remove or suppress the conflicts that arise when people differ, seeing such conflict as disruptions to orderly processes of change. The work of Prigogine, in focusing on a notion of formative causality incorporating difference, challenges this perspective, suggesting that the very difference managers seek so strenuously to remove is the source of spontaneous, potentially creative change. However, the dissipative structure model cannot be directly applied to human action because these models do not evolve or produce genuine novelty. So consider what happens when a further fundamental assumption is dropped.

Complex evolutionary models: constructing an unknowable future

When assumption 3, to do with homogeneous elements or components of the system, is dropped, we get evolutionary models with outcomes that are necessarily uncertain and novel. Now, in addition to possessing the capacity to move from one existing attractor to another, the model can evolve in novel ways. The possibility of the evolution of novelty depends critically on the presence of microscopic diversity. When individual entities are the same, that is, when they do not have any incentive to alter their strategies for interacting with each other, the model displays stability. When individual entities are different and thus do have incentives to change their strategies of interaction with each other, the model displays change of a genuinely novel kind. The 'openness' of the individual entities to the possible, through some 'error-making' or search process, leads to a continuing dialogue between novel individual 'experiments' and (almost certainly) unanticipated collective effects. Since this kind of possibility will out-compete an equivalent system without it, the process might be described as an 'evolutionary drive'.[21] The collective system conditions the response that any particular new behavior will receive, and this then leads to a characteristic restructuring of the collective system. The model takes on a life of its own, in which its future is under perpetual construction through the micro interactions of the diverse entities comprising it. New forms continually emerge in an unpredictable way as the system moves into the unknown. However, there is nothing mysterious or esoteric about this and it is not due to chance or accident as is the case in adaptionist causality. What emerges does so because of the transformative cause of the process of the micro interactions in which small individual differences can be amplified into population-wide changes.[22] Micro interactions transform global patterns and themselves in a paradox of forming while being formed and an explanation of what is happening requires an understanding of these micro interactions. Such models provide a science of uncertainty, with the potential for evolution and creative novelty indicative of transformative causality, which resonates strongly with the organizational reality identified in Chapter 1. I want to describe these properties a little further by taking a particular example of complex evolutionary models, namely, complex adaptive systems.[23]

Models of complex adaptive systems: a life of their own

A complex adaptive system consists of a large number of agents, each of which interacts with some of the others according to its own evolved principles of local interaction. No individual agent, or group of them, determines the local interaction principles of others and there is no centralized direction of either the patterns of behavior of the system as a whole or of the evolution of those patterns. This local interaction is technically called self organization, and it is this which produces emergent coherence in patterns of interaction across the whole population of agents. Local dynamics produce diversity of agent behavior in which there emerges evolving global behavior. Complex systems do not obey simple, fixed laws. Instead, individual agents respond to their own particular local contexts and even though there is no explicit coordination of the interaction, it leads to the emergence of collective order.[24] For example, some neuroscientists[25] think of the human brain as a complex adaptive system which consists of a very large number of neurons, perhaps ten billion, each of which can be thought of as an agent. The neurons are agents, because they do something, namely, discharge electrochemical energy. Each neuron agent is connected to only a small number of other agents, perhaps around 15,000, and through the experience of the body a pattern of impact of one neuron agent on other neuron agents has evolved and continues to evolve. The result is that if neuron A is taken to start with, it may be that when this neuron fires it triggers the firing of neurons X, Y and Z, while inhibiting the firing of neurons L, M and N. The firing of X, Y and Z will, of course, trigger the firing of others that they are connected to and A only fired in the first place, because it was triggered by some other neuron. So what is happening is the responsive interaction of neuron agents which is local in character, because each agent is connected to only a tiny fraction of the total population, its local connections, and each is interacting with others according to its own locally evolved 'rules'. The result of all this local activity is the continuous patterning of activity across the whole population of neurons which must be coherent and orderly otherwise we would not be able to function. However, these population-wide patterns emerge without any pattern, blueprint or program for the collective pattern.

It is easy to misunderstand the meaning of self-organization and the emergent collective order it produces. In the context of a human organization, people tend to equate self-organization with empowerment or worse a free-for-all in which anyone can do anything, leading to anarchy. The example of the interaction of neurons, however, shows that self-organization is not a free-for-all, in fact, it is the opposite of a free-for-all. Agent neurons are constrained to respond to others in the particular ways their evolution has brought them to – they cannot do just anything: they must respond and they must do so in particular ways so that the agents are constraining and enabling each other at the same time. This immediately resonates with the organizational reality of interdependence. Human agents can never simply do whatever they like, because they will be excluded if they do. In their local interaction, human agents constrain and enable each, which is what power means, and these patterns of power constitute social control and order. Furthermore, emergence is usually immediately understood as a pattern which just happens and this produces a kind of despair in managers who think that if it is going to just happen then there is nothing for them to do. In fact, emergence means the exact opposite of 'just happening anyway'. The patterns that emerge do so only because of what every agent is doing and not doing. There is no chance in emergence; it is precisely the product of many, many local interactions. Creative-destructive, evolving and repetitively stuck, surprising and familiar, predictable and unpredictable patterns emerge across a population of agents because of what all the agents are doing and not doing in their local interactions. For me the resonance with the organizational reality of power and the interplay of deliberate actions is very powerful. Moreover, the consequence of taking this view is profound, because instead of being determined by a prior plan, organizational change will be emerging in the local interactions of many, many people. If this is the case, it is not at all surprising that there is no scientific evidence that planned culture change produces changing culture. The change can only happen in many, many local interactions. It is worth, therefore, exploring a little further just what complex adaptive systems are.

Other examples of phenomena whose behavior is being modelled as complex adaptive systems are termites constructing large structures, ants signalling food locations and birds flocking. The population-wide patterns produced in local interaction – large structures, flows, patterns of movement – display a similar paradoxical dynamic as that produced by mathematical chaos, namely, regular irregularity, predicable unpredictability which in complex adaptive system theory is known as the dynamics at the 'edge of chaos'. Nevertheless, whether a pattern at the edge of chaos can evolve or not depends on diversity, as Allen argued so clearly in an earlier section. One type of complex adaptive system assumes that each agent follows the same small number of simple rules. For example, three simple rules are sufficient to simulate the flocking behavior of birds.[26] Here, each agent is the same as every other agent and there is no variation in the way that they interact with each other. Consequently, they can only display one pattern of behavior and cannot evolve. It is important to stress this point because, as Chapter 4 will show, many of those using complexity theories to write about organizations propose that if people follow simple rules then they will produce complex behavior. They may do, but it will certainly never be novel or capable of evolving. Complex adaptive system models of this type display formative causality which means that interacting according to simple rules will simply unfold forms that are already there, enfolded in the simple rules. However, other simulations of complex adaptive systems do take account of differences amongst agents, or classes of agents, and different ways of interacting.[27] They do, therefore, display the capacity to move spontaneously from one attractor to another and so they evolve into the unknown. In this case, causality is transformative in that the local rules of interaction between agents evolve at the same time as population-wide patterns are evolving. These models therefore produce evolutionary possibilities. They are all models that take on a life of their own, producing surprising, unexpected patterns which means that they cannot yield predictions of what will happen in the model or in the phenomenon it is trying to model but such models may enable us to gain deeper insight into the dynamics. Returning to organizational reality the implication is that even though we cannot predict what will emerge in the interplay of our intentions, we can understand more than we currently do about the dynamics involved in such interplay. We can pay attention to the local dynamics of the diversity of human behavior. If it turns out that diversity is an absolute requirement for evolution, change, creativity and destruction then the dominant management discourse is once more turned on its head, because it emphasizes harmony, fit, sharing and sameness in the mistaken belief that this leads to success. Instead, we will have to understand that conflict and hotly contested difference lie at the centre of organizational progress and decline.

Causality: certainty and uncertainty

In the previous chapter in talking about the work of Kant, I pointed to three notions of causality all of which produce certainty as far as outcomes are concerned, arguing that these notions of causality are the foundations on which the dominant management discourse is built. These are:

1. Efficient cause where a cause leads to an effect in a straightforward linear way. Concepts of self-organization and emergence do not feature at all and there is no change, other than movement to the perfect, optimal state.
2. Rationalist causality in which rationally chosen goals are achieved by following rationally chosen strategies. There are no particular implications for self-organization and change is the consequence of deliberate human choice rather than any form of emergence.
3. Formative causality which implies a form of self-organization that reproduces stable forms without any significant transformation, slight variations emerge in mature states as a result of contextual differences.

Then, in this chapter, two kinds of causality were identified which yield uncertain outcomes over the long run:

1. Adaptionist causality, which implies a chance-based competitive search for optimal adaptation to an environment which produces new forms.
2. Transformative causality, in which local interaction (self-organization) between diverse agents forms population-wide patterns (emergence) while at the same time being formed by those patterns.

One of Kant's main contributions was to suggest that different causal frameworks applied to nature (efficient and formative causality) and to human action (rationalist causality). This Kantian split is manifested in the dominant discourse on management where organizations are understood to be like natural phenomena in that one causal framework (efficient cause in the case of scientific management and formative cause in the case of systems theories) applies to 'the organization' and another (rationalist causality) applies to the individual choices of 'the managers'. The same procedure is evident when organizational theorists use some kind of neo-Darwinian theory (adaptionist causality) to explain the evolution of populations of organizations, within which 'the managers' make choices to shape the evolution according to another causal framework (usually rationalist). The next chapters will explore how complexity management writers sustain much the same split causality and look at the consequences this has.

A comparison of the five frameworks for thinking about causality is given in Figure 3.3.

Conclusion

The main difference between the sciences of uncertainty and the sciences of certainty lies at the most fundamental level in the different causal frameworks they are built upon. When the sciences of certainty are taken up in understanding organizations and management, there is always a duality of causal framework in which the choosing human agent,

	The causalities of certainty:			The causalities of uncertainty:	
	1. Efficient	2. Rationalist	3. Formative	1. Adaptionist	2. Transformative
Movement toward future that is:	a repetition of the past.	a goal chosen by reasoning autonomous humans.	an unfolding of mature form enfolded at the beginning.	unknown and dependent on chance.	perpetually constructed by the movement itself as continuity and transformation, the known and the unknown, at the same time.
Movement in order to:	reveal hidden order/ realize optimal state.	realize chosen goals.	realize a mature form already given.	survive as a species.	express continuity and transformation of individual and collective identity.
Process of movement/cause is:	universal, timeless laws, of 'if-then' kind.	human reason within ethical universals.	unfolding a whole already enfolded in rules of interaction.	random variation in individual entities/ natural selection.	local interaction forming and being formed by population-wide patterns.
Nature of variation/change:	corrective/fitting/ aligning.	designed by rational choice to get it right.	shift from one given form to another in stages of development.	small chance variations.	diverse micro interactions and escalation of small changes.
Freedom/constraints:	freedom through conforming to constraint of natural laws.	through reason constrained by ethical universals.	no freedom, only constraint by given forms.	freedom arising by chance, constrained by competition.	both freedom and constraint arise in spontaneity and diversity of micro interactions.

Figure 3.3 The causalities of certainty and uncertainty.

that is, the manager or leader, is governed by rationalist cause and the object whose form is being chosen, the organization, is governed either by formative or efficient cause or both. In other words, the rational manager or leader is choosing (rationalist cause) a particular design or structure for the organizational system which will unfold (formative cause) the chosen goal of the manager. The choice of one system rather than another in order to realize a given goal is clearly efficient cause: *if* I choose system design A *then* it will yield behavior Y and *if* I chose system design B *then* it will yield behavior X. However, this causal foundation of the dominant discourse cannot explain the organizational reality of uncertainty and the undoubted current experience across the world of the inability of managers and leaders to choose what happens to their organizations. No one has chosen the undoubted collapse of investment capitalism and yet it is happening. It is this complete disjuncture between our experience of uncertainty and the dominant explanations of management and the prescriptions for its conduct that call for a fundamental rethink of management and leadership.

This fundamental rethink must involve a radical reappraisal of the causal framework on which we build our explanations, and if they are to resonate with our experience of uncertainty then they must be built on the causal frameworks to be found in the sciences of uncertainty. One could turn to the adaptionist causal framework of neo-Darwinian evolution and, indeed, some organizational theorists have done just that.[28] However, this leads to an approach which tends to deny managers and leaders of much influence and bases its explanations ultimately on chance. I do not think that this resonates with my experience of the powerful impact of managers and leaders on what happens even though it falls far short of the ability to choose the future. Managers and leaders play highly influential roles in processes of continuity and change, in creative and very destructive outcomes. The question is about what the roles are and just how their influence is exerted. For this reason, I am drawn to explore the possibility of explanations of organizational life based on the causal framework of transformative causality. I think that it is a move to theories based on this causal framework that offer the potential for a radical rethink of management and leadership. Transformative causality presents a radical challenge to the dominant management discourse because it points to:

1. *Severe limitations on the predictability of organizational evolution.* Although short-term developments are predictable, new forms emerge unpredictably over the long term. Emergent creative and destructive developments can be articulated and understood only as they emerge and cannot be predicted in advance. Creativity-destructiveness and uncertainty are thus inextricably linked and if organizations are to change in novel ways then managers have no alternative but to act continually into the unknown without being able to reliably say in advance whether the outcome of their actions will be creative or destructive. The invitation is for managers to seriously reflect upon how they do this because they are already doing it and by understanding it more explicitly, they might be able to identify how to act in more helpful ways. Such a perspective departs from the dominant paradigm in which the role of managers is thought to be the reduction of uncertainty rather than the capacity to operate creatively within it. This uncertainty and unpredictability is undeniably a central reality of the situation we currently find ourselves in.
2. *The centrality of local interaction in the emergence of the ongoing patterns of organizational life.* This puts cooperative-competitive interaction and the enabling, conflicting constraints that relationship imposes, right at the centre of the creative-destructive

processes of organizational development. Since power is enabling constraint, this perspective places power, politics and conflict at the center of the cooperative-competitive, conflictual social process through which joint action is taken. Novel organizational developments, good and bad, are caused by the political, social and psychological nature of human relationships. This departs from the dominant discourse on management in which the role of the manager is one of removing ambiguity and conflict to secure consensus. Power is thought of as unpleasant and its importance is made undiscussable, while politics is a process that is to be minimized. In the now collapsed investment capitalism, cooperation was thought to be subservient to the overriding importance of competitive advantage and competitive survival.

3. *The limits to individual choice.* If novel organizational patterns emerge in power relations between people, and if those emergent patterns are largely unpredictable, then the notion that individuals, or small groups of them, can choose creative futures for their organization falls away. The outcomes of organizational interaction, indeed, the very dynamics of that interaction, are not within the power of any single organization to choose. Both outcomes and dynamics producing those outcomes emerge from the interaction between people in organizations, with none being able individually or collectively to choose them. The dominant management discourse is built firmly on the notion that small groups of powerful managers can and should choose the future states of their organization, almost as if other organizations play no part in what happens. However, the organizational reality is that they are unable to realize their choices.

4. *The sources of stability.* Stability emerges in relationships, because relationships are enabling, conflicting constraints, that is, power. Individuals cannot do just what they please, precisely because they cannot survive outside of relationships and relationships constrain. At the edge of chaos, destruction, which is an inevitable companion of the emergent new, is controlled because of the power law in which large extinction events are few and most extinction events are small in size. In other words, organizational life is controlled because of the dynamics of relating at the edge of chaos, although no individual or group of individuals can be 'in control' of the whole system. This departs from the dominant discourse in which the only alternative to an individual being 'in control' is thought to be anarchy. However, it resonates with the organizational reality of activity being orderly despite no one being in control.

5. *The importance of diversity and difference.* Complex systems evolve when there is micro diversity, or fluctuations. In human terms, this means that there can be no novel organizational developments without differences between the people who comprise it. It follows that deviance and eccentricity, the difficult search for understanding in misunderstanding and conflict are prerequisites for novel change. This departs from the dominant management discourse emphasis on harmony and consensus, now seen to be inimical to creativity. But once again the resonance with the organizational reality of resistance and deviance is strong.

6. *Limits to the ability to design and plan.* Complex systems have the internal capacity to change spontaneously in unpredictable ways that cannot be described as optimizing anything. Their creative-destructive development cannot be designed, planned or controlled. This departs from the dominant discourse in which designing and planning for maximal or optimal outcomes are seen as the very essence of

the management role. The sciences of uncertainty, however, connect with the organizational reality of unplanned financial collapse and unplanned technological development.

7. *Potential success as the paradox of stable instability.* This means that organizations have the potential to succeed in that they possess the capacity for novel change only when they display patterns of behavior combining stability and instability. This is a potential not a guarantee because of the destructive as well as the creative nature of evolution. This differs from the dominant discourse in which success is equated with stability alone, so ignoring the inevitability of conflict and destruction. Moving from this aspect of the dominant discourse to complexity theories offers us a way of understanding the reality of the collapse of investment capitalism. Nevertheless, it resonates with the reality of how groups such as managers create professional identities, for example, by linking themselves to highly regarded scientists

8. *The centrality of the expression of identity and thus difference.* This means, in relation to organizations, that the movement of stability and change in human organizations arises in the human need to express identity, both individually and collectively at the same time. Goals to do with competitive survival and profit are then seen to be subservient to this overriding need. This departs from dominant management views that elevate performance to the level of all-important motivating force, the outcome of which, as we can now see, is the collapse of investment capitalism.

9. *Interdependent people rather than autonomous individuals.* While the dominant discourse is built firmly on the assumption of autonomous, rational individuals the complex interactions described in this chapter demonstrate the clash between this notion and the organizational reality of interdependent agents and the interplay of their actions.

The conclusion, then, is that there are views within the complexity sciences that do challenge the dominant discourse in important ways and so sustain the claim that the complexity sciences may offer a new way of thinking about life in organizations. There are also, however, views that are probably reflective of the majority of complexity scientists, which do not form the basis of any significant challenge to currently dominant ways of thinking and talking about management. The question now is just how those who write about complexity in human organizations are taking up the insights of the complexity sciences. It is to this question that the next chapter turns.

Notes

1 Darwin, C. (1859) *The Origin of Species by Means of Natural Selection or, The Preservation of Favoured Races in the Struggle for Life*, London: John Murray; Darwin, C. (1871) *The Descent of Man*, London: John Murray.

2 Lamarck, J. B. (1984) *Zoological Philosophy: An Exposition with Regard to the Natural History of Animals,* Chicago: University of Chicago Press.

3 Huxley, T. (1863) *Man's Place in Nature*, New York: D. Appleton.

4 Bateson, W. (1851) *Materials for the Study of Variation, Treated with Special Regard to Discontinuity in the Origin of Species*, New York: Robert Schalkenbach Foundation (1970).

5 Fisher, R. A. (1930) *The Genetic Theory of Natural Selection*, Oxford: Oxford University Press; Haldane, J. B. S. (1932) *The Causes of Evolution*, New York: Harper Brothers; Wright, S. (1931) Evolution in Mendelian populations, *Genetics,* 16, 97–159; Wright, S. (1940) 'Breeding Structures of Populations in Relation to Speciation', *American Naturalist,* 74, 232–48.

6 Eldridge, N. and Gould, J. (1972) 'Punctuated Equilibria: An Alternative to Phyletic Gradualism', in Schopf, T. J. M. (ed.) *Models in Paleobiology*, San Francisco: Freeman, Cooper and Co.

7 Lewontin, R. C. (1974) *The Genetic Basis of Evolutionary Change*, New York: Columbia University Press.

8 Dawkins, R. (1976) *The Selfish Gene*, New York: Oxford University Press.

9 Hannan, M. T. and Freeman, W. J. (1989) *Organizational Ecology*, Cambridge MA: Harvard University Press.

10 Hodgson, G. M. (199a) *Evolution and Institutions: On Evolutionary Economics and the Evolution of Economics*, Cheltenham: Edward Elgar; Hodgson, G. M. (1999b) Structures and Institutions: Reflections on Institutionalism, Structuration Theory and Critical Realism, Paper for the 'Realism and Economics' Workshop, King's College, January; Veblen, T. B. (1899) *The Theory of the Leisure Class: An Economic Study in the Evolution of Institutions,* New York: Charles Scribeners; Veblen, T. B. (1934) *Essays on our Changing Order*, Ardzrooni (ed.) New York: The Viking Press.

11 Hannan, M. T. and Freeman, J. (1989) *Organizational Ecology*, Cambridge MA: Harvard University Press; Aldrich, H. (1979) *Organizations and Environments*, Englewood Cliffs, NJ: Prentice-Hall.

12 DiMaggio, P. J. and Powell, W. W. (1991) Introduction, in Powell, W. W. and DiMaggio P. J. (eds) *New Institutionalism in Organizational Analysis*, Chicago: Chicago University Press, 1–38; Tolbert, P. S. and Zuckner, L. G. (1996) The Institutionalization of Institutional Theory, in Clegg, S. R., Hardy, C. and Nord, W. R. (eds) *A Handbook of Organization Studies*, London: Sage.

13 Prigogine, I. (1997) *The End of Certainty: Time, Chaos and the New Laws of Nature*, New York: The Free Press.

14 Allen, P. M. (2000) 'Knowledge, Ignorance and Learning', *Emergence, Complexity & Organization*, 2(4), 78–103; Allen, P. M. (2001) 'What is Complexity Science? Knowledge of the Limits of Knowledge', *Emergence, Complexity & Organization*, 3(1), 24–42.

15 These were mentioned in Chapter 2.

16 Gleick, J. (1988) *Chaos: The Making of a New Science*, London: William Heinemann Limited; Stewart, I. (1989) *Does God Play Dice*, Oxford: Blackwell.

17 Goldberger, A. L. (1997) 'Fractal Variability Versus Pathological Periodicity: Complexity Loss and Stereotypy in Disease', *Perspectives in Biology and Medicine,* 40(4), 553–61.

18 Stewart, I. (1989) *Does God Play Dice*, Oxford: Blackwell.

19 Prigogine, I. and Allen, P. M. (1982) 'The Challenge of Complexity', in Schieve, W. C. and Allen, P. M. (eds) (1982) *Self-Organization and Dissipative Structures: Applications in the Physical and Social Sciences*, Austin, Texas: University of Texas Press; Prigogine, I. and Stengers, I. (1984) *Order Out of Chaos: Man's New Dialogue with Nature*, New York: Bantam Books; Nicolis, G. and Prigogine, I. (1989) *Exploring Complexity: An Introduction*, New York: W. H. Freeman and Company.

20 Pascale, R. T. (1999) 'Surfing the Edge of Chaos', *Sloan Management Review,* 40(3), 83–95; Pascale, R. T., Millemann, M. and Gioja, L. (2000) *Surfing the Edge of Chaos: The Laws of Nature and the New Laws of Business*, New York: Crown Business.

21 Allen, P. M. (2000) 'Knowledge, Ignorance and Learning', *Emergence, Complexity & Organization*, 2(4), 78–103; Allen, P. M. (2001) 'What is Complexity Science? Knowledge of the Limits of Knowledge', *Emergence, Complexity & Organization,* 3(1), 24–42.

22 Prigogine and Stengers say 'We believe that models inspired by the concept of "order through fluctuations" will help . . . to give more precise formulation to the complex interplay between individual and collective aspects of behavior . . . . This involves a distinction between states of the system in which individual initiative is doomed to insignificance on the one hand, and on the other, bifurcation regions in which an individual, idea or behavior can upset the global state. Even in those regions, amplification obviously does not occur with just any individual, idea, or behavior, but only those that are "dangerous" – that is, those that can exploit to their advantage the nonlinear relations guaranteeing the stability of the preceding regime. Thus we are led to conclude *the same* nonlinearities may produce an order out of the chaos of elementary processes and still, under different circumstances, be responsible for the destruction of this same order, eventually producing a new coherence beyond another bifurcation.' (Prigogine, I. and Stengers, I. (1984) *Order Out of Chaos: Man's new dialogue with nature*, New York: Bantam Books, p. 206).

23 Lewin, R. (1993) *Complexity: Life at the Edge of Chaos*, London: J. M. Dent; Waldrop, M.M. (1992) *Complexity: The Emerging Science at the Edge of Order and Chaos,* London: Penguin.
24 Maguire, S. and McKelvey, B. (1999) 'Complexity and Management: Moving from Fad to Firm foundations', *Emergence,* 1(2), 19–61.
25 Freeman, W. J. (1994) 'Role of Chaotic Dynamics in Neural Plasticity', in van Pelt, J, Corner, M. A., Uylings, H. B. M., and Lopes da Silva, F. H. (eds) *Progress in Brain Research*, 102, Amsterdam: Elsevier Science BV; Freeman, W. J. (1995) *Societies of Brains: A Study in the Neuroscience of Love and Hate*, Hillsdale, NJ: Lawrence Earlsbaum Associates Publishers; Freeman, W. J. and Schneider, W. (1982) 'Changes in the Spatial Patterns of Rabbit Olfactory EEG with Conditioning to Odors', *Psychophysiology*, 19, 45–56; Freeman, W. J. and Barrie J. M. (1994) 'Chaotic Oscillations and the Genesis of Meaning in Cerebral Cortex', in Buzsaki, G., Llinas, R. Singer, W., Berthoz, A. and Christen, Y. (eds) *Temporal Coding in the Brain*, Berlin: Springer.
26 Reynolds, C. W. (1987) 'Flocks, Herds and Schools: A Distributed Behaviour Model', Proceedings of Siggraph '87, *Computer Graphics*, 21(4), 25–34.
27 For example, Ray, T. S. (1992) 'An Approach to the Synthesis of Life', in Langton, G. C., Taylor, C., Doyne-Farmer, J. and Rasmussen, S. (eds) *Artificial life II, Santa Fe Institute, Studies in the Sciences of Complexity, Volume 10,* Reading, MA: Addison-Wesley.
28 Aldrich, H. (1979) *Organizations and Environments*, Englewood Cliffs, NJ: Prentice-Hall; Hannan, M. T. and Freeman, J. (1989) *Organizational Ecology*, Cambridge, MA: Harvard University Press.

4 Complexity and what writers on organizations do with it

Obscuring local interaction and mostly re-presenting the dominant discourse

The interpretation of the complexity sciences in organizational terms usually takes the form of the direct application to organizations of the concepts developed by the natural complexity scientists, sometimes also using their modelling techniques. I will call this the *scientific approach*. For some, this scientific modelling approach represents an addition to the techniques available for the prediction, or at least better understanding, of organizational development and so offers prospects of more effective control and greater success. For others adopting this approach, complexity implies significant unpredictability so that the contribution from the models is a deeper understanding of organizational dynamics which can point to counterintuitive strategies. Although many taking the scientific approach would disagree that the natural scientific method reflects an implicit ideology to do with progress and control, others argue that it does and are critical of the abstract, quantitative nature of scientific models when applied to organizational life because recognizable human individuals disappear. Instead, they turn to the natural complexity sciences as providers of metaphors leading to the *metaphorical approach*. Here, the attributes of complex phenomena are used to make claims about the nature of organizations and provide prescriptions for their effective management. There is a rapid move to equating organizational life with chaos, or the edge of chaos, for example, in which order emerges from the bottom up. This can quickly lead to prescriptions of empowerment, decentralized control and facilitating forms of leadership. The reflection of the writers' ideologies tends to be much more obvious in this approach, if still often unacknowledged. The metaphorical approach also lends itself to some rather mystical interpretations of the ideal for life in organizations.

Yet others in the field recognize the importance of the scientific approach in generating insight into abstract relationships between entities comprising phenomena but argue that this approach faces severe limitations when it comes to understanding the ordinary daily activities of people in organizations. Managers do not employ formal models as they go about their ordinary, everyday activities, and they are greatly affected in what they do by power, politics, ideology, culture, social habitus and psychology. Some of those taking this line of argument are also, however, dissatisfied with the metaphorical approach and the idealized, even mystical, directions in which it also seems to lead away from understanding actual ordinary daily life. This leads to a third approach in which the natural complexity sciences serve as a source domain for analogy – *the analogical approach*. Here, the natural complexity sciences provide abstract insights into the implications and consequences of micro interaction between large numbers of agents. However, such analogies must be interpreted in terms of the important attributes of human agents. Human agents are conscious and self-conscious; they feel emotion and often spontaneously improvise; they exercise imagination and spin fantasies; they experience and act upon values and on societal norms; they conflict with each other and often seek to deceive and manipulate each other; they negotiate with each other in the ordinary politics of daily life; they act out their neuroses and psychoses in leadership and other roles they take up; and they are essentially interdependent. Furthermore, they are capable of desiring idealized macro patterns and offering some articulation of the macro patterns they feel themselves involved in and how this affects how they act. The method in this approach is the reflexive, reflective narrative accounting of organizational practitioners.

This chapter will be concerned with the scientific and metaphorical approaches, by far the most frequently adopted interpretations, and Chapter 6 will take up an analogical interpretation. The question for all the approaches is whether they add anything to, or challenge, the dominant discourse or whether they simply re-present the dominant discourse in new jargon.

The application of complexity science to industries: unpredictability and the importance of deviant behavior

This application approach involves either or both of the following:

*   Constructing computer simulation models of industries to produce indications of how strategies are formed and what strategies might be more effective.
*   Directly applying the insights provided by computer simulations primarily from the natural sciences to organizations.

Some following this scientific application path hold that organizations are in reality complex adaptive systems – they exist as real complex systems.[1] Others avoid this simple form of realism and hold that we cannot experience reality in itself so that any representation of a complex system must be an incomplete, provisional abstraction.[2] This means that there are multiple, potentially contradictory, representations of complex systems calling for a pluralist position which denies one overarching valid representation. Although there is no unified theory of complexity, the plurality is coherent, because we are forced to view reality through categorical frameworks. This view can be expressed as *critical pluralism*[3] which requires organizational members to approach organizations in a critical way from a number of perspectives. McKelvey[4] rejects the extremes of both positivism and relativism in arguing for *Campbellian realism* which combines model-centered realism (reflecting positivism) and an evolutionary realism (highlighted by relativism). Phenomena and model idealizations of them are separate entities and the point of the model is to predict the movement over time of the model idealization while real world phenomena provide the criteria against which model representations are to be tested for accuracy. Theory is tested by the model and the model is tested against the ontology of the phenomena. This approach requires multiple models, which are necessary because human agents are heterogeneous and fit the postmodernist assumptions of probabilistic, idiosyncratic behavior. The result is a postmodern ontology and a realist scientific epistemology. McKelvey argues that the study of organizations will only become scientific when dysfunctional ideologies and parochial perspectives are dropped and the method outlined in the preceding section is adopted. Those who avoid simple realism, therefore, restate Kantian transcendental idealism and so avoid radical skepticism as well as the romantic idealism of Hegel and others which regard all knowledge as culture- and history-dependent.

In applying complexity as science to organizations, some writers are concerned with industry level dynamics. They model populations of organizations and draw conclusions about the nature of their evolution. This perspective stresses the changeable nature of industries and organizations, the radical unpredictability of, and the limited ability to control that change and the importance of difference in the process of change. Two examples of this level of thinking are provided by the work of Allen and the work of Marion.

The importance of deviant behavior

Allen[5] first develops an equilibrium (cybernetic) model of the fishing industry and shows how it produces a policy recommendation to constrain fishing effort at, or just below, the maximum that yields a sustainable fish population. He then shows how the dynamics of fish populations and fish markets rapidly render any selected sustainable level of fishing highly inaccurate. So, second, he takes a systems dynamics model of the fishing industry and demonstrates that it generates more complex patterns of variation in fish populations and in economic conditions similar to those found in the real industry. However, because the model uses average data for all of these factors, it generates a long-term tendency towards stationary states that are not found in data on the fishing industry. In reality, there are large and continuing fluctuations in fish populations around the average, related to unpredictable factors such as movements in currents of warmer water, which the systems dynamics models do not incorporate. Furthermore, because the assumptions about average events and entities at the microscopic level are retained, the model cannot explain how the pattern of industrial activity changes. Third, he develops what he calls a self organizing model of the fishing industry, introducing 'noise' into the model's equations to represent random fluctuations in the spatial distribution of the fish population and he introduces the possibility of internally determined variations in factors such as responses to fish availability, levels of technology and price responsiveness. The model produces boom and bust oscillations in fishing fleet catches, reflecting patterns that can be observed in the real fishing industry, and then a spontaneously emergent small high-priced niche where fish becomes a luxury food. This model increases understanding of how an industry can shift spontaneously from one pattern of activity to another. Finally, he constructs what he calls an evolutionary complex model which distinguishes between fleets that follow rational strategies of moving to areas of highest catch and others that move more randomly in the hope of identifying new catch areas. If a fleet pursues a failing strategy it is removed by the programmer and replaced by a fleet with new, randomly chosen strategies.

Allen has introduced differences in the entities comprising the model, incorporating different levels of information acquired by each fishing fleet, different attitudes to risk, different degrees of attraction to particular fishing areas and different extents to which they spy on and copy each other. By running the program, the programmer 'learns' about more viable fishing strategies. The model demonstrates how effective strategies are reinforced and come to dominate the rest and how those fleets pursuing losing strategies explore and search for different ones through changing behavioral parameters. In this way, genuinely new strategies emerge and the program learns about them. Allen is able to show that being diverse is what builds a rich, sustainable system. Having and building on idiosyncrasies is the key to creating and maintaining an ecology of behaviors. If one shifts one's perspective from self-organizing to evolutionary complex thinking, therefore, one can acquire a greater understanding of the processes underlying the creative changes of strategic direction pursued by different organizations in an industry and how they come to fit together in compatible clusters. In relation to this fourth, preferred model, Allen repeatedly stresses the amplification of difference, that is, the eccentric, deviant behavior of the entities comprising the system. It is this behavior that destabilizes population identity and so leads to change. Allen also stresses radical unpredictability and the inevitability of uncertainty, arguing that even those models displaying the capacity to evolve will not necessarily do so as reality does. He thinks that evolving reality is radically unpredictable but that models may assist in thinking about the nature of the dynamic and the kind of possibilities it might imply. Such a view has major implications for how one thinks about government policies for industries and what view one takes on the possibility of individual organizations within an industry choosing their realized strategies. The emphasis on instability and the importance of eccentricity and deviance also represents a significant challenge to the dominant management emphasis on stability and group harmony.

However, there are important limitations inherent in the activity of model building itself and in the focusing of attention at a macro level. As soon as one draws a conceptual boundary around particular human interactions and regards them as a system with a life of its own, one objectifies that human interaction. The interaction is then thought of as an objective phenomenon consisting of interacting entities. It is this way of thinking about human interaction that makes it possible to formulate a model of it. The immediate consequence, however, is the rather strong possibility of proceeding as if humans were like entities in the natural sciences, assuming away the essential human quality of freedom. In the evolutionary models, individual choice is not specified by the model designer but introduced as statistical noise, probability distributions or diffusion equations. Clearly, this is a proxy for, rather than an explanation of, choice and decision making. Building macro models of human interactions, therefore, inevitably loses the quality of human freedom. Furthermore, there is a powerful tendency to think of the model, even a model with a life of its own, as an aid to human choice in relation to the objectified phenomenon of interacting entities. Human choice is then located in the model builder, and by analogy in the managers of organizations, who stand outside the system of interactions and make choices about it, as if this phenomenon did not itself consist of human choices. In other words, thinking in terms of macro models, of an industry or an organization, implicitly produces a split between the system and the human chooser. The system is assumed to behave according to one kind of causal framework and the model designer, or manager using the model, is implicitly assumed to be behaving according to another causal framework. This dual causality is the same as that found in the dominant discourse, limiting the challenge to that discourse. Surely, it is problematic to think of human choice in terms of rationalist causality and the object in terms of formative/transformative causality when that object is itself choosing humans. If rationalist causality does explain the human action of choosing system designs, why do we use some other causal framework to explain the human action of fishing? We seem to be caught in an intellectual process of regarding the human interactions we are trying to explain as equivalent to natural phenomena and then using one causal framework for the explanation of human action and another for how we might use the explanation, that use also being human action. This problem is also demonstrated in the work of Marion.

The constraints on management choice

Marion[6] describes the development of the microcomputer industry and uses it to illustrate his perspective on organizational complexity. Mainframe computers became commercially available in 1952 and in the mid 1960s, microprocessors were developed and incorporated in hand held calculators. Small packets of technology were, therefore, emerging in a moderately coupled network of industries over the 1950s and 1960s. Then in 1975, MICS produced the first microcomputer, the Altair, which was cheaper and more accessible to a wider market than main frames. Micros had a different architecture to mainframes and calculators and during the initial stage of market development, competition in the micro sector had more to do with architectures than anything else. There were, and still are, two architectures. One is based on the Intel chip and the other on the Motorola processor. A number of operating systems were built around these chips: CP/M; the Apple system; IBM DOS; and systems for the Commodore, Tandy, Texas Instruments (TI), NCR, NEC, Olivetti, Wang and Xerox microcomputers. The early market niche for micros was thus crowded with architectures and operating systems when, in 1981, IBM entered the micro market. The entry of IBM immediately put the fastest growing operating system, CP/M, out of business. By the mid-1980s, IBM's architecture was dominant and others adopted it in order to survive. At the same time, Apple introduced the Mac, which was not as cumbersome and difficult to learn as DOS. Later, Microsoft brought some simplicity to DOS, but it is still not able to match the elegance and simplicity of the Mac. During this period, microprocessor technology was also developing: the earliest processors were 4 bits and were soon replaced by 8 and then 16-bit processors. By the mid 1990s, 32-bit technology was dominant. Therefore, there were a few people dreaming of microcomputers in 1974, a great many people wanting one by 1976 and explosive growth in the ensuing two decades. It looked as if microcomputers had suddenly appeared out of nowhere. However, the pieces were coming together long before microcomputers were ever envisioned: microcircuits, microprocessors, ROM and RAM memory chips were being used in calculators, while computer language logic was being documented in mainframes. The microcomputer was built from these pieces.

Marion argued that the microcomputer is an example of how an industrial network evolves through its own internal dynamic to the edge of chaos. He emphasized the radical unpredictability of such evolution and the continuing unpredictability when a network operates at the edge of chaos. He draws on three characteristics of the edge of chaos to reach this conclusion. The first is sensitive dependence on initial conditions, the butterfly effect, which he argues can be seen in the sensitivity of human interaction to small events. Unpredictability here is due to human inability to monitor and observe infinite detail. Second, he refers to Prigogine's work to argue that intrinsic unpredictability is also a feature of complex systems. Third, he brings in the power law to argue that despite its great stability and robustness, a network at the edge of chaos will be subject to many small, and a few large extinction events and that these are impossible to predict. He argues that all of these factors are sources of radical unpredictability in the evolution of human networks that makes it impossible for an individual to be in control of such a network. In other words, no single organization in the industrial network chooses the future direction of the industry, and this means that it cannot choose its own evolution either. Furthermore, no single organization can choose the dynamics of the industry as a whole and therefore no organization can choose its own dynamic either. In the early stages of the micro industry development, the dynamics were chaotic because of the large number of simply structured competitors, loosely connected to each other. None of them chose this. It flowed from the nature of the interaction between them. The entry of IBM was a deliberate choice but the reduction in the number of competitors and the increase in the range of competitive interaction between the survivors was not simply IBM's choice. It depended upon what the others did too. The evolution from chaos to the dynamic at the edge of chaos was cocreated through the interaction of the organizations, not chosen by one in isolation. Outcomes and dynamics continued to change in unpredictable ways, outside the power of individual organizations to choose, as the number of micro producers increased and Microsoft gained greater power over the market. Marion is making an important point here, because many who take up complexity theory in relation to organizations may accept that organizations cannot choose future outcomes but then claim that they can deliberately choose the dynamic in which they operate. As Marion makes clear, this is not a conclusion that is in any way consistent with the properties of complex systems.

Marion also repeatedly stresses that unpredictability does not lead to the conclusion that there is no control. Attractors at the edge of chaos are bounded and demonstrate a family-like similarity. Therefore, it is not possible for just anything to happen. He also argues that the power law is itself a form of control because, at the edge of chaos, the numbers of extinction events both large and small are smaller than they are in the dynamics of stability, on the one hand, and chaos, on the other. Because of the relatively small number of large extinction events, change spreads through a network in a controlled manner. In the other dynamics, change spreads through the network in a highly destructive, continuous manner. The central argument, then, is that change at the edge of chaos is controlled by the very nature of the dynamic, making it unnecessary, as well as impossible, for individuals to take control. This is an understanding of control that is very different indeed to the assumption made in the dominant management discourse where control means simply that someone is 'in control' and so ensures survival. The notion that there may be a form of control that imparts stability to a whole network of networks, but no guarantee whatsoever for the survival of any individual part of the network, is a concept quite foreign to ideas of control in the dominant management discourse. Shifting the focus of attention from individuals who are in 'control' to control as a characteristic of a particular system-wide dynamic, implying periodic destruction of parts of the whole network, has potentially significant implications for how one thinks about the nature of management which resonates strongly with the organizational reality described in Chapter 1.

However, I think there are also problems with what Marion does. He focuses at a macro level and talks about a population of impersonal organizations (IBM and Apple, for example) interacting with each other in a self-organizing manner, driven by an urge to survive. He is talking about this population and the organizations of which it consists as if they were no different from a population of organisms. However, what are these organizations? They are not organisms, or anything like organisms, but, rather, patterns of joint human action. Marion reifies organizations and treats them as if they were things, or organisms, apart from, or outside of humans, interacting according to principles that apply to them at a macro level, split off from the humans that constitute them.

The principles governing these systems are taken to be the same as those governing nonhuman systems. To this, Marion adds the deliberate causality of human beings, by which he means what I have been calling rationalist causality. The result is that humans, acting according to rationalist causality, find themselves having to act within a system that is somehow independent of them, operating according to the causal principles of self-organization, which I would call formative causality which considerably restricts human choice. Patterns in human action, then, emerge as the 'both/and' paradigm of both human choice and a system with a life of its own without any recognition of paradox.

Therefore, Marion's approach encounters much the same difficulty as the work of Allen did. Both focus their attention at the level of a population of organizations, regard those organizations as independent entities having a life of their own, and implicitly assume some split between the macro system, to be explained according to one causal structure, and human action to be explained according to another. The difficulty with this is that both levels are about human action and one would, therefore, expect the same causal structure to apply to both. The problem with the macro approaches so far reviewed is that while they reach very important and challenging conclusions about the nature of management, they leave the management process itself largely unexplored. Many other management complexity writers, however, do focus specifically on the management process and it is to these that I now turn.

The application of complexity science to organizations: re-presenting the dominant management discourse in new jargon

I now want to look at how those taking a simple realist or some kind of critical realist position see the key concepts of self-organization and emergence and what prescriptions they provide for managing organizations.

Self-organization

Self-organization is a concept frequently used by writers on management complexity[7] who generally take it to be a special process or force in organizations, even a new form in our era, which tends to be linked to self-determination by individual members of the organization. Most writers say that self-organization is a form of organization in which there is no central controller within the organization and no external controller either. Self-organizing agents behave in exploratory and experimental ways and do not have complete knowledge of the circumstances surrounding their actions. This is contrasted with deliberate control exercised through formal and informal power, through the authority and feedback processes of bureaucracy, and through the work routines which discipline human interaction. Too much deliberate control is held to be counterproductive and the emphasis should be shifted to self-organization. Instead of regarding self-organization as a threat to order, it should be seen as a creative force which must not be suppressed but harnessed and used for the good of the organization. Self-organization, defined as the opposite of central control, is equated with self-governance, empowerment, teamwork in which individuals manage themselves within clear boundaries and bottom up decision making, all of which must be balanced with top down control to avoid chaos. Network organizations are the preferred form and organizations have to find the right dynamic mix of collaboration and competition.

Therefore, on the one hand, these writers are identifying self-organization as an impersonal force which must be harnessed and used, and then, on the other hand, they equate this with empowerment and looser forms of organization. Furthermore, the force of self-organization, according to these writers, only produces creative good outcomes. However, in the science, self-organization is not a force at all – it simply refers to local interaction and calling it a force immediately obscures this local interaction behind a kind of mysterious global force. This then means that we have lost the invitation to explore the organizational reality of local interaction. Since the prescriptions of empowerment and loose organizational forms can be found in the dominant discourse, there is no need to look anywhere else for explanation or justification. In fact, the conceptualization of self-organization as a force or an alternative form of organization simply re-presents the dominant discourse in new jargon. The 'both . . . and' structure of the dominant discourse is retained as both top down control and bottom up decision making, the problem being one of balance with no hint of paradox. This all makes no addition or challenge to the dominant discourse.

Emergence

Another popular concept among complexity writers is that of emergence. For some writers,[8] emergence is the unpredictable arising of global, higher level, properties from lower level self-organization which is understood in terms of simple rules of agent behavior. This view is taken to justify a new model of an organization which focuses on utilizing emergent dynamics as opposed to hierarchical direction and control.[9] This new model takes the form of a shared decision making process governed by organization-wide principles and intentions with managers acting as catalysts for emergence at all levels. Emergent strategy, practiced by entrepreneurial organizations, is understood to be distinct from formal planning processes. Such emergent strategy requires the management of context and the creation of conditions which foster emergence, such as steadfast relationships, rewards for communication at all levels, allowing multiple representations, encouraging the telling of stories and risk taking. These are the conditions that encourage spontaneous self-organization within which strategies may emerge. However, although the outcomes that emerge from the dynamic interplay of networks and groups can only be partially planned, it is held that clear and consistent underlying principles, shared and aligned at all levels, make it possible to achieve intended patterns and avoid chaos. Such organizations are said to operate at the edge of chaos, a state which can be intentionally achieved. Others[10] present yet another variation on this theme, appealing to the notion of dissipative structures which are said to rely on deep structure for the order they display. This deep structure is a quasi-permanent, invisible substructure that remains largely intact while manifest, observable structures break down at bifurcation points. Deep structure is equated with a few simple rules in organizations that define business logic and operate as organizing principles. Change occurs in an organization when these hidden simple rules are surfaced, reframed and then enacted during the chaotic transformation characteristic of a bifurcation point. The role of managers is to manage this deep structure and in doing so, they condition the emergence of new deep structures. By operating on deep structures, managers can have a limited influence on the outcomes of self-organization rather than simply relying on the spontaneous, random and unpredictable self-organization of systems in nature.

Richardson[11] holds that it is too simple to say that emergence is a process in which macroscopic properties of the whole emerge from microscopic properties of the parts.

Instead, he claims that emergence is the production of novel wholes and that this is a process in which we are abstracting (filtering information) away from descriptions in terms of parts and interactions to a new description in terms of entities/concepts quite different from the constituent parts we started from, for example, regarding an organization as interacting departments rather than interacting people. These new entities have novel properties in relation to the parts, for example, whole department do not behave like individuals. What emerges through our acts of abstraction is the existence of stable abstractions which themselves bring about properties different to the parts. The new abstractions can interact with the parts from which they have emerged – the operation of downward causation.

Again, emergence is regarded as some kind of force to be deliberately brought about by managers by creating the right conditions. It is striking, how in these developments of the notion of emergence, people and their ordinary activities simply disappear. In my understanding, emergence does not refer to a force that someone can operate on or a process that someone can use another process to shape or condition. As I understand it, emergence refers to a pattern arising across a population that is not the realization of a prior design or plan for that population-wide pattern but flows from many, many local interactions. This notion of emergence is completely nullified in the writing of most who apply the concept of emergence to organizations. As a result, they simply re-present the dominant discourse in a different language. We are back to someone choosing macro events, which is in direct contradiction of the current reality of global credit crunch and recession.

A complexity view of leadership

Notions of self-organization and emergence raise questions about the nature of leadership. Some[12] distinguish leadership from leaders. They move away from the notion of leaders who act 'on' an organization to achieve their objectives and from a focus on the symbolic, motivational and charismatic actions of leaders. They argue that leadership is not in or done by leaders but is rather an emergent outcome of relational interactions between agents. Leadership is the expediting of processes which combine interdependent actions of agents into a collective venture. Leadership is a systems phenomenon transcending individuals and relationships are not defined in terms of hierarchies but in terms of interaction between heterogeneous agents across a network. Individuals and groups are said to 'resonate' with each other in the sense of sharing common interests, knowledge, goals, worldviews and histories. Agents respond to pressures from leaders and others and struggle with conflicting needs. These tensions generate system-wide emergent learning, the conditions for which can be enabled by leaders. A distinction is drawn between leadership as the product of interactive dynamics in which knowledge, preferences and behaviors change and leaders who influence the process of dynamic interaction. Interactions are thought to be governed by rules and mechanisms for changing the rules, one of which is leadership events which produce a new identity. They recommend the use of computational modelling to better understand the dynamic of leadership, arguing that complexity leadership theory expands the potential for creativity and positive change. Complexity leadership is more than simplistic notions of empowerment. Instead, complexity leadership encourages all members to be leaders and 'own' their leadership to evoke greater responses from everyone. Complexity leadership theory provides an unambiguous pathway for driving responsibility downward, setting off self-organization and innovation. This removes a significant pressure from formal leaders, allowing them to attend more directly to identifying strategic opportunities.

Complexity leadership creates new managerial strategies, such as the introduction of low levels of tension to create adaptive change. Complexity theory calls for much greater attention to be paid to relationships.

This view of leadership still presents the highly idealized notions to be found in the dominant discourse, even though it is cast in relational terms. Leaders enable the learning of others, they influence the process of dynamic interaction, they encourage all to be leaders and they drive responsibility down the hierarchy. These quite conventional prescriptions, it seems to me, have no clear link with complexity sciences or with what self-organization and emergence mean. The leaders are still supposed to use one process, such as influencing and driving, to operate on another process, the learning of others and their dynamic interaction as self-organization and emergence.

Other complexity writers[13] continue within the dominant discourse when they identify generative leaders as visionary and charismatic people who promote clear and effective communication, and limit signal noise so as to reduce and absorb complexity. They help to evolve a language all can understand and they ensure goals are specified and interactions aligned to system goals. Generative leaders are open to collaboration; they adopt modular organizational systems and foster problem solving and innovation. They evolve and enforce rules that govern the system's dynamic by fostering and sustaining generative relationships through structuring situations and managing interactions. Effective leadership creates a system which brings together appropriate individuals and knowledge and allows them to interact with minimal friction. The focus must be on the process, because outcomes are uncertain and leadership affects the simple, local rules governing agent interaction. Innovation flows from how interactions are managed and regulated. The steps managers can take are the partitioning of tasks to allow effort to be structured within a confined context rather than allowing attention to be distracted. Generative leaders promote information flow and feedback and they distribute problem-solving efforts more widely. Innovation can be institutionalized in the form of simple rules which operate locally to solve problems. Interactions must be regulated to prevent a complexity catastrophe. This is simply a restatement of the empowerment strand of the dominant discourse in the jargon taken from the complexity sciences and gets no closer to the organizational reality described in Chapter 1.

Yet, others[14] model an organization as a complex adaptive system using a multiagent network model. They recognize a paradox of organizations needing to stimulate emergent collective action but also needing to use bureaucracies to control outcomes for exploitation. Emergence is here set up as the opposite of control. Postmodern leadership accommodates the paradox by combining managerial, adaptive and enabling leadership roles. Complexity leadership theory focuses on the latter two. Adaptive leaders shape the overall communication structure and help advance the coevolution of human and social capital. Human capital appreciation takes the form of knowledge flows in informal networks of social interactions in the conditions created by enabling leadership. It all sounds very familiar and very distant from organizational reality.

Common prescriptions

The main aim of most of those applying complexity as science to organizations is that of providing prescriptions and tools for improved decision-making and management. However, Richardson[15] describes this as a neoreductionist search for general principles of complex systems as simple mathematical rules which does not bring about any change in worldview. So, for some of those applying the science, the main aim is to generate a different worldview in which complexity science, as agent-based models, is used to forecast the dynamics of success and leverage gains. For example, Chiles and Meyer[16] propose macro-entrepreneurship as a form of creating and strategically managing clusters of interrelated firms where the effect of this clustering is to generate increasing returns as they support and create competitive advantage for each other. They are concerned with catalyzing and guiding the emergence of these clusters.

There are widespread prescriptions for fostering the conditions for emergence, moving the organization to the edge of chaos and allowing/unleashing the power of self-organization. These views of self-organization and emergence are taken to justify the rejection of hierarchical, command and control organizational structures and their replacement with more fluid network structures based on simple rules.[17] However, those presenting such views are usually quick to explain that this does not mean abandoning control. For example, Meek, De Ladurantey and Newell,[18] researching complex metropolitan administrative systems, subscribe to another widely expressed prescription calling for simple design principles, said to underlie self-organizing systems, which involve keeping routines and rules few and simple: '. . . those responsible for working with complex systems need not throw up their hands either, totally abandoning control for self-organization and top down for bottom up decision making . . . [because] complex systems lie between . . . complicated and chaotic systems . . . Managers of complex systems must pay attention to the inherent needs of the systems as well as their needs of the system.'[19] Policy-makers should choreograph the interrelation between the varieties of elements of concern to them.[20] Agent-based models of a banking network[21] have been used to explore the distinction between deliberate and emergent strategy. The simulations indicate that a stay still (deliberate) strategy provides little benefit, while following a leader (deliberate) strategy is beneficial when customers are very responsive, but when the environment is turbulent, the best strategy is customer-centric (emergent). It is not at all clear to me why a customer-centric strategy is emergent while following a leader is deliberate or how this use of the terms differs from the way they are used in mainstream strategic management literature. Allen, Strathern and Baldwin[22] summarize the insights provided by the simulation, described in the foregoing section, of the fisheries industry in Canada. The simulation shows that fleets behaving according to economic rationality do not win; instead, profit is generated by behavior that does not seek to maximize profits. Success flows not simply from efficient exploitation but also from some mix of exploitation and exploration. Ability to learn (exploration) is more important than ability to exploit (efficiency). There is no such thing as an 'optimal strategy'.

A number of writers applying the complexity sciences to organizations adopt a contingency approach.[23] The claim is that since it is possible to make predictions in stable environments and repetitive businesses, it follows that standard planning and rule-abiding strategic actions and processes are applicable. But in situations where technology and the environment are changing rapidly, it is not possible to predict and then rule-changing strategies of experimenting, developing agility, adaptability and coevolution are called for in organizational forms of decentralization, networks, project teams, empowerment and innovation. It is pointed out that it will normally be impossible to predict shifts from rule-abiding to rule-changing strategies which means that managers must maintain a mental state of constant alertness. However, even in turbulent environments intention, as commonly owned visions for the future, is said to be central because, even if not realized, intention provides fast feedback.

Sword[24] argues that uncoordinated self-organization destabilizes systems since even tiny conflicts can set off a cascade that destabilizes the system. She argues that avoiding or resolving conflict too early may prevent system adaptation while, by tipping the system into chaos and then back to the edge of chaos, conflict can stimulate innovation and information exchange which allow change to flourish.

Throughout these prescriptions, there is the clear notion of the manager making rational decisions and acting on forces of emergence and self-organization, designing loose structures and encouraging interaction. The language is a little different in that managers are now said to choreograph and create conditions but in the end the leaders are still making choices which they can still realize, as in the dominant discourse, if they follow what are called 'complexity principles'. For me, it is doubtful whether any of this is the application of science at all and even if it is, I cannot see what it adds to the dominant discourse.

The complexity sciences as metaphor: justifying existing ideological positions

I now come to a group of writers who do not construct mathematical models or computer simulations and do not claim to be applying the science but take a loose metaphorical approach instead. This work tends to point to unpredictability but then retains predictability in some form and so continues to assume that individuals can stay 'in control' of organizations in important ways.

A number of organizational complexity writers[25] claim that organizations are living systems. They say that it is the role of managers to move the organization to the edge of chaos where it can be a *creative living system*. Appealing to the metaphor of birds following simple rules to produce complex emergent flocking behavior, they claim that managers need to find the few simple structures that will generate enormously complex adaptive behavior. Some[26] believe that the complexity sciences call for a return to ancient mythological wisdom to do with participating in a higher-level whole which is an overriding system that assures the emergence of order. This can be presented as a concern with the individual's soul being allowed to be present in the workplace and with the emergence of the collective soul of the organization. The simple rules governing human interactions have to do with ensuring caring relationships. Others,[27] however, focus not on universal harmony but on conflict as the most important quality of relationship in looking at the organization as a complex adaptive system. The leader judges how much the system needs to be disturbed and then disturbs it by communicating the urgency of the challenge, keeping up the stress until guerrilla leaders come forward with solutions. Leaders intentionally generate anxiety and tension. Some[28] interpret the metaphor of complexity in terms of rapid change and aggressive competition. It is the role of managers to balance the organizational structure between stability and chaos at the edge where semicoherent strategy is allowed to emerge. The prescriptions for moving to the edge are to: foster frequent change in the context of a few strict rules; keep activity loosely structured but at the same time rely on targets and deadlines; and create channels for real-time, fact-based communication within and across groups. One firm outperforms another if it is adept at rapidly and repeatedly disrupting the current situation to create a novel basis for competing. Successful strategies rely on surveillance, interpretation, initiative, opportunism and improvization. The use of the notion of simple rules is so frequent that it warrants further exploration.

Simple rules and hidden order

Almost all of the writers who use the complexity sciences primarily as a source of metaphor, emphasize how large numbers of agents interacting with each other according to a few simple rules can produce global, emergent patterns of coherent behavior. However, none of them comments on the underlying assumption of formative causality as a causal structure which is clear as soon as rules are specified for interactions. The rules enfold a pattern which is unfolded by their operation so that there is no possibility of novelty, a key feature these writers are proposing to install in organizations.

Wheatley[29] makes the call for simple rules one of the foundations of her exposition. She holds that the 'New Sciences' reveal how order is created by a few guiding principles rather than complex controls. This, she says, makes us aware of how we share our yearning for simplicity with nature and proposes that simple rules provide the basis of a simpler, more caring way of running organizations. She formulates this into an inspirational call for a return to a more natural way of managing human affairs. Wheatley talks about the need to understand the deeper reality, the hidden order, of organizational life and life in general, one that ideas from complexity can help to uncover. For me, this resonates with somewhat 'New Age' views about ancient wisdom and connection to deep levels of primal reality. This view, that there is something essential, fundamental or deep lying behind or underneath behavior and causing it, is clearly formative causality. The form that emerges is already enfolded, already there, in these deep, primitive levels. This is not a transformative view in which behavior, including potentially novel behavior that is in no sense already there, emerges in the interaction of the entities.

The approach adopted by Lewin and Regine[30] has much in common with that of Wheatley. They point to the central concern of the complexity sciences, namely interaction, or relationship. They claim that human systems are complex adaptive systems and they equate interactions between abstract entities in complexity models with human relationships without any justification for doing so. Human relationships are then equated with 'caring' and the notion of 'soul' is imported from a completely different discourse to that of complexity, again without any justification. The simple rules idea is then brought to play to explain how human systems of caring, with soul, can be brought about. It seems that, here, the complexity sciences are being used as a rhetorical device to support an already held ideological position, rather as Wheatley does.

Brown and Eisenhardt[31] give a more detailed account of the importance of simple rules. They talk about a few simple rules generating very complex adaptive behavior in the flocking of birds as shown in some of the computer simulations. They extend this notion to the resilience of democratic government and the successful performance of corporations, without, however, providing any justification for such an extension. In doing this, they ignore the fact that flocking is one attractor for bird behavior, one that already exists. The few simple rules that produce it will not produce spontaneous jumps to new attractors. If success for corporations over the long term requires a move to new attractors, then the metaphor of flocking birds is not well chosen. However, the authors proceed, much as Wheatley does, to prescriptions for improvising while relying on a few key rules.

By now it should be evident that the causal framework that all of these writers are implicitly using is that of formative cause, governing a system about which humans can make choices, that is rationalist cause. This is the same causal framework as that underlying the dominant discourse on management. For example, simple rules as formative cause can be chosen and their implementation guided by managers' choices. If they choose correctly then they get what they want. This amounts to a negation of self-organization and emergence. If managers are choosing what 'emerges', then it is not emerging. If they have a blueprint guiding self-organization then it is not self-organization, that is, it is not agents acting on the basis of their own local organizing principles, but rather on the basis of simple rules chosen for them. Emergence is relegated to the level of the superficial while managers remain in control of the fundamentals. There is an unrecognized contradiction between the loss of freedom that this choice of simple rules implies for the many and the call for caring relationships. Freedom here is interpreted, not as freedom to choose one's own next step, but to choose the state of the whole system and as such it is confined to a few powerful and stripped from the rest, on the one hand, or equated with democracy on the other. Neither of these positions needs the complexity sciences to justify them. Furthermore, the emphasis on a few simple rules driving the behavior of all agents in an organization completely misses the fundamental importance of fluctuation and diversity.

The result is an approach that has nothing new to say about the generation of the truly novel. The way in which the concept of causality is used, therefore, has very important consequences. When causality is implicitly used as it is by those who emphasize a few simple rules, the consequence is the closing down of further thinking about the nature of control in organizations, on the one hand, and the nature of creative processes in organizations, on the other. The simple rules idea adds nothing, other than new terminology, to the dominant discourse. At least as popular as the simple rules idea is that of the dynamic at the edge of chaos.

The edge of chaos

The use of this metaphor ranges from the highly simplistic to the somewhat more sophisticated. An example taken from the highly simplistic end of the spectrum[32] interprets the edge of chaos in organizations as formal systems characterized by neither too little nor too much structure. Organizations at the edge of chaos are those that are only partially structured in formal terms. This interpretation of the 'edge' metaphor immediately loses the paradoxical quality of the edge of chaos. Partial structure is not a state of contradictory forces that can never be resolved but, rather, a simple balance: too much structure produces stability and too little produces chaos, while a balance between the two produces the dynamics of the edge of chaos. When an organization is at the edge, its managers *allow* a semicoherent strategy to emerge, that is, one that is neither too fixed nor too fluid. This approach completely loses the sophisticated concept of self-organizing criticality in which a system evolves to the edge of chaos through its own internal dynamic, where self-organization produces potentially novel strategies, again through the system's own internal dynamic, where extinction events occur again through its own internal dynamic. Instead, managers are 'allowing' strategies to emerge. Managers can choose to install just enough structure to move their organization to the edge of chaos where it can experience relentless change. Managers should identify whether they are at the edge of chaos or trapped in one of the other dynamics, in which case they should move the organization to the edge not only by fostering frequent change in the context of a few strict rules and loosely structuring activity but also by relying on targets and deadlines. They should create channels for real-time, fact-based communication within and across groups. Complexity may mean that managers cannot choose detailed outcomes, but according to this simplistic view of the dynamics at the edge of chaos, they certainly can choose the dynamic of their system.

This move completely ignores a key feature of the edge of chaos, namely, the power law. The small numbers of large extinction events and the large numbers of small extinctions that occur periodically mean that there is no guarantee of survival at the edge of chaos, only the possibility of new forms emerging that might survive. Managers cannot choose these extinction events, nor can they avoid them since they are a property of the internal dynamic of a complex system. Nowhere do the authors mention this power law. Instead, they make a simplistic equation between being at the edge of chaos and success. Because they implicitly think within a framework of formative and rationalist causality, they miss the constraints in self-organization. As Marion convincingly argues, managers in a single organization cannot choose the dynamic for their industry or their organization, because the dynamic emerges from the interaction within the whole population of organizations in an industry. Also conspicuously absent in the argument is the importance of fluctuations and diversity so often emphasized by Allen.

Others describe the edge of chaos in much more threatening terms, emphasizing the need to relentlessly promote change.[33] For them, the comfortable notion of equilibrium yields to a view of organizational life that is hectic and pressured. Many other writers[34] equate the edge of chaos with crisis and a state in which managers are stretched and stressed. They then recommend that managers should create crisis and stretch/stress conditions in order to push their system to the edge where it can be creative. Yet others retain the notion of equilibrium to some extent by describing system change in terms of a cycle. For example, the evolution of a complex system is understood in terms of punctuated equilibrium, in which stable states are interrupted by significant discontinuous change before moving to other stable states. When the dynamics of change is described in these terms, the paradox of stability and instability is also lost, this time by proposing a sequential process incorporating *both* stability *and* instability that follow each other *sequentially*. It seems to be very difficult to hold the paradox of both stability and instability simultaneously in order to grapple with what it might mean for making sense of life in organizations.

It is evident from the foregoing review that the writers referred to are claiming to use the 'edge' as a metaphor but in ignoring the importance of the internal dynamic, they are in fact not using it at all. Their metaphors may be useful, although I clearly doubt it, but it is certainly misleading to claim that they are derived from concepts of the edge of chaos.

Predictability

Almost everybody who uses insights from the nonlinear sciences refers to the problem of predictability but usually with enormous ambivalence. For example, Connor[35] states that it makes no sense to maintain a sense of balance by foreseeing distinct events in an unstable environment. However, he is adamant that this should not stop managers trying to guess what will happen, because they might just be right and claims that success becomes a matter of guesswork and taking bets with long odds. In other passages, however, he talks about how important predictability and personal sense of control are. He talks about a continuum from predictability to instability, viewing the later as a temporary and rather unfortunate phenomenon to be dealt with by reliance on responsive processes. In this way, the 'nimble' organization secures a sense of control.

Beinhocker[36] also points to the limits to predictability and concludes that reliance on a single strategy is inappropriate. Instead, managers should develop a population of strategies so that at least some of them will turn out to be successful.

Those who do recognize radical forms of unpredictability, and therefore the limitations of strategic planning, nevertheless emphasize the need for vision. They usually explain that by this, they do not mean a picture of a future state, or a destination, but clarity about purpose and direction. Wheatley, for example, sees vision as an invisible field that permeates an organization and shapes desired behaviors. For many, vision is the formulation by an individual of a transcendent, over the horizon, goal for an organization. Yet, others make even more unsuccessful attempts to deal with the recognized problem of unpredictability in nonlinear systems. For example, Sanders[37] claims that pictures of strange attractors allow one to see the order hidden in disorder, ignoring the fact that strange attractors are abstract mathematical concepts, not 'real' pictures. She says that it is possible to identify a system's initial conditions, because it is deterministic, but that it is difficult to predict its future state, because it is nonlinear. Of course, this statement is wrong, because it is impossible to forecast the long-term state of a nonlinear deterministic system precisely because it is not possible to identify the initial conditions to the infinite exactness required. Determinism is a theory of causality and implies nothing whatsoever about the ability to measure initial conditions. However, she proceeds to argue that despite an inability to make predictions of long-term states, it is possible to provide qualitative descriptions of whole system behavior over time. This may be true, but only for the attractor that the system is currently drawn to. It would not be possible to describe any new attractor that some system was capable of spontaneously jumping to, until the jump occurred. Sanders tries to get around this by saying that it is possible to identify what she calls 'perking' information. This is the new initial condition to which a system may be sensitive, that is, changes or developments that are already taking shape just below the surface. It takes peripheral vision, or well-developed foresight skills, to recognize a system's initial conditions as they are emerging. This enables one to see change coming and so influence it to one's advantage. Recognizing these conditions before they emerge is the new leverage point. This attempt runs into the same problem as before. It is not possible to identify all of the initial conditions and measure all of them with infinite accuracy. So, how can you have foresight if you cannot predict? What is peripheral vision? Unpredictability is mentioned and then, in effect, ignored.

The ambivalence about the unpredictable nature of complex systems is, of course, tightly coupled with the concern about control. If one holds the paradox of predictability and unpredictability, it requires a continuing exploration of what control means in such situations. What it is unlikely to mean, of course, is that powerful individuals can be 'in control' of their organization. This is at least unpalatable to many and raises anxiety for most, both leaders and led. The result is talking about unpredictability in a manner that never leaves the dominant discourse, because it stays within the split causality of formative system and a chooser governed by rationalist cause. Those who use the complexity sciences primarily as a source of loose metaphor for organizations, select elements of thinking in the natural sciences of complexity in a way that preserves the implicit assumptions about causality underlying the dominant discourse on management. They preserve intact the framework of formative causality. All of these writers, implicitly or explicitly, point to the limitations of the notion of efficient causality but continue to rely on formative causality in their interpretation of what the complexity sciences might mean for organizations.

An interpretive approach

Some regard complexity science as a useful metaphor for understanding the contextualized and emergent discourse in organizations as members interpret and reinterpret, negotiate and renegotiate their discourse.[38] Meaning occurs in the interplay between people in which new systems of organizational discourse are continually emerging. Evoking discourse becomes the key prescription. Tsoukas and Hatch[39] draw a distinction between first and second order complexity where the latter involves a consideration of the modes of thought being used to theorize about complex systems. They argue that complex thinking is best accomplished in a narrative mode of thinking rather than the propositional thinking of the traditional scientific method. They claim that complexity theory itself supports the use of a narrative mode of thought, because both involve recursiveness, nonlinearity, sensitive dependency on initial conditions, indeterminacy, unpredictability and emergence. They point out how most of those taking a complexity approach to organizations do so within the tradition of cybernetics which involves looking at the social world in the same way as the natural world. This calls for modelling organizational systems in much the same way as biological ones to yield generalized propositions which apply irrespective of context. Taking a narrative approach falls within the interpretive traditions of the social sciences with their sociological-historical-anthropological orientation. Here the social science offers an account of organizations which does not necessarily rely on the natural sciences, although chaos and complexity do offer new metaphors positing new connections and so draw our attention to new phenomena. These authors advocate a move from the scientific orthodoxy of complexity theories applied to organizations to a narrative perspective that draws on complexity as metaphor. For me, this kind of approach is much more consistent with organizational reality.

More critical views

There are, of course, also those who take a highly critical view of how the complexity sciences are being used by organizational theorists. For example, Zhu[40] reviews a number of the more common prescriptions made by complexity writers and asks just how radical and practical they are compared with the old paradigm they claim to be replacing. He argues that prescriptions for specifying simple rules and moving organizations to the edge of chaos imply that rules and edges exist in hidden form waiting to be discerned. Prescriptions for identifying initial conditions, guessing what is likely to occur and formulating a population of strategies imply that managers can still be in control. If rules are specifiable and imposable they are not genuinely emerging, and if organizations can be moved to and positioned at the edge of chaos they are then subject to intentional maneuver and so not self-organising. Having said that the future is unpredictable, complexity writers immediately call for anticipation and foresight; having said that design-and-control is not appropriate, they immediately urge for interventionist restructuring, targets and deadlines; having questioned the effectiveness and revealed the ritual nature of strategy, they demand more strategies. More damaging, when management writers promote 'just enough structure' and the like, they turn complexity sciences into a mysterious enterprise. If we take unpredictability seriously, it is impossible to know in advance what 'balance' is. Without the 'new sciences', managers already knew from experience that predictability is problematic and control is difficult. With the 'new' prescriptions, managers are simply told to do basically the same thing, just do it more, faster and harder. The old paradigm re-emerges as new jargon, with messier logic and poorer consistency.

For Chia,[41] the complexity sciences are a program of simplification with a thoroughly reductionist intent. He argues that truly complex understanding is provided by narrative knowledge, not propositional knowledge, which is always reductionist and intrinsically unable to deal with the complex at its own level of articulation. He holds that there is a fundamental difference between human social systems and natural systems and while the complexity sciences may offer useful explanations of inert systems, vital, human systems require complex thinking inspired by philosophy, literature, art and the humanities. In particular, he draws on Bergson and Whitehead to establish the essence, or fundamental nature, of human experience. Human experience is continuous in time, with the past, present and future flowing seamlessly into each other as undifferentiated flux and flow. Raw, lived human experience is irreducibly dynamic and complex, an amorphous, vague, unwieldy, shapeless mass and unorganized process of continuously becoming. The constraints on this formless essence of human experience are socially constructed and the human intellect chops experience up into discrete moments of time, differentiating, puncturing, isolating, classifying and punctuating it. The purpose of this intellectual activity is to center and stabilize experience to enable action, but in so doing, it alienates people from their true experience. For Chia, it is an oxymoron to talk about organizations as complex. It is lived experience that is complex and intellect and organization are about simplification and this applies to the complexity sciences as much as it does to any other science. In Chia's argument, society and organization are essentially context dependent and historically determined, while real experience seems to be timeless and context free. The former is simple and the latter is complex so that science can say nothing about the reality of complex dynamical experience. It can only operate in the realm of simplifying intellect and organization, phenomena that are inert and static.

Conclusion

It is sometimes claimed that there has been an enormous increase in interest in complexity theories in both the academic and organizational practitioner worlds. But is this so? A rough Google Scholar search of journal papers concerned with complexity, management and organizations indicates that roughly 100 journal papers appeared between 1992 and 2000. For the period 2000 to 2008, this number increased to nearly 1,000. Taking some leading Journals, we find that the number of papers in the Academy of Management Journal increased from 10 in 1992–2000 to over 50 in 2000–2008 and for the Strategic Management Journal, the number fell from 12 to 5. In Organization Science, there were 16 papers over the last decade, with 10 of these to be found in a 1999 Special Issue. As far as books, including edited volumes, are concerned, a search of Amazon and other sources suggests that the number is not much above 100 over the past decade compared to a handful in the previous decade. While there has been a large percentage increase, therefore, the number remains a very tiny fraction of the enormous output of books on management and organizations generally, where over 2,000 journals must be producing at least 50,000 papers per annum. While there has been an increase in annual conferences devoted to complexity, they represent a tiny fraction of the number of conferences on management and organization generally. In my experience, there is relatively little attention paid to complexity theory in both undergraduate and post-graduate programs at Business Schools, apart from a small number of more critical postgraduate programs in Europe and North America. Also in my experience, notions from the complexity sciences do not feature at all in the ordinary everyday discourse of managers in organizations in Europe and North America. Despite crises and growing awareness of uncertainty, the management discourse continues to be dominated by the ideologies of control and improvement and the conversation is conducted in terms of visions, shared values, positive diversity, conflict resolution, targets and monitoring, and major change initiatives. The dominant discourse continues as before, with a public science-based rhetoric despite the lack of any reliable scientific evidence that any of the dominant prescriptions really deliver what they promise. It seems that we must conclude that after nearly two decades, interest in complexity remains at the fringes of academic activity and as far as other organizations are concerned, it is usually only taken up explicitly in some in-house management development programs seeking to present innovative perspectives which end up having little impact if they stray from the dominant discourse.

Why is it that in a world of clearly experienced uncertainty, the sciences of uncertainty and complexity make no headway against the sciences of certainty? While agreeing that complexity research has not yet entered the mainstream, some say that the reason is that the research has not produced practical tools.[42] Others[43] hold that organizational complexity will simply be a fad unless it takes the form of rigorous, scientific modelling. Yet, others[44] argue that the application of science to human organizations is fundamentally misguided, while some take the view that organizational complexity writers have simply repackaged the dominant discourse in new jargon.[45] In my view, the key features of the dominant discourse, particularly those of learning organization theory, are remarkably similar to those of the applied science and the complexity metaphor.

Applications of the science and the use of complexity metaphors by most management complexity writers seem to me to lead to conclusions that can be stated without any recourse to the complexity sciences, indeed, they are mostly already to be found in the mainstream literature. Most complexity writers are simply not presenting a challenge to the dominant discourse. But, one might ask whether an interpretation of the complexity sciences which is more congruent with organizational reality, one which presented a radical challenge to the dominant discourse rather than a repackaging of it in new jargon, would fare any better. Surely, a way of thinking that resonated more strongly with the organizational reality we experience would rapidly replace the dominant discourse. To believe that it would, amounts to ignoring the very organizational reality we are trying to explore. I think the account in Chapter 2 makes it clear that the identification of management, management consultancy, management research and management education with science was itself complex responsive processes of social organization, struggles for recognition and identity, rather than a simple, rational, scientific choice. The identification of management with the sciences of certainty had fundamentally to do with the development of professional identity as essential to the forming of power figurations reflecting ideologies favorable to managers, consultants and academics. Moreover, the identification of management with science has indeed enhanced the power of management and leadership roles, as well as the power of consultants and particularly the power of business schools within universities. Pointing out the shaky basis of this claim to science and describing the lack of an evidence base for the prescriptions of the dominant discourse is to do far more than conduct an argument, engage in a rational debate or present a view. A challenge to the dominant discourse amounts to a challenge to widespread power figurations, professional identities and ideologies.

The response is, therefore, bound to be a brushing aside of points about evidence bases and reality congruence and the denial that there is anything radical in the challenge. Given patterns of power relations and institutionalized career paths dependent on recognized research, it is not at all surprising that different ideas would mostly surface in forms that are consistent with the dominant discourse.

I do not think that it is too sweeping to say that instead of provoking new thinking, the sciences of complexity have been used in ways that simply justify existing ideologies, preserve without any questioning the taken-for-granted underlying assumptions of causality to be found the dominant discourse and so simply re-present that discourse in strange jargon. Furthermore, it is striking how in the dominant discourse and its re-presentation in the vocabulary of complexity, the organizational reality of ordinary people acting in ordinary, everyday ways to get things done together, disappears completely from the scene. Instead, we have forces, wholes, systems, abstract entities such as 'the organization' which intends and does. Organizations interact with each other and ordinary people are simply their resources. What we seem to be stuck in is an abstract way of thinking which distances us from our experience of being immersed in the experience of daily life in real activities of organizing. If we are to slowly develop a more promising way of rethinking management then it seems to me that it is important to understand the split in our thinking between abstract reasoning about organizations and immersed experience of daily organizational life. I argue that rethinking management would require a more paradoxical way of thinking than that provided by a split between abstraction and immersion. The next chapter will explore how we have come to think in highly abstract ways and just what I mean by abstract thinking and immersed thinking.

Notes

1 Campbell-Hunt, C. (2007) 'Complexity in Practice', *Human Relations*, 60(5), 793–823; Carlisle, Y. and McMillan, E. (2006) 'Innovation in Organizations from a Complex Adaptive Systems Perspective', *Emergence, Complexity & Organization*, 8(1), 2–9.
2 Allen, P. M. (2000) 'Knowledge, Ignorance and Learning', *Emergence, Complexity & Organization*, 2(4), 78–103; Allen, P. M. (2001) 'What is Complexity Science? Knowledge of the Limits of Knowledge', *Emergence, Complexity & Organization*, 3(1), 24–42; Richardson, K. A. (2008) 'Managing Complex Organizations: Complexity Thinking and the Science and Art of Management', *Emergence, Complexity & Organization*, 10(2), 13–27; McKelvey, B. (2003) 'From Fields to Science: Can Organization Studies make the Transition?', in Westwood, R. and Clegg, S., *Point/Counterpoint: Central debates in Organization Theory*, Oxford: Blackwell; Cilliers, P. (1998) *Complexity and Postmodernism: Understanding complex systems*, London: Routledge, 1998.
3 Richardson, K. A. (2008) 'Managing Complex Organizations: Complexity Thinking and the Science and Art of Management', *Emergence, Complexity & Organization*, 10(2), 13–27.
4 McKelvey, B. (2003) 'From Fields to Science: Can Organization Studies make the Transition?', in Westwood, R. and Clegg, S., *Point/Counterpoint: Central Debates in Organization Theory*, Oxford: Blackwell.
5 Allen, P. M. (1998a) 'Evolving Complexity in Social Science', in Altman, G. and Koch, W. A. (eds) *Systems: New Paradigms for the Human Sciences*, New York: Walter de Gruyter; Allen, P. M. (1998b) 'Modeling Complex Economic Evolution', in Schweitzer, F and Silverberg, G. (eds) *Selbstorganization*, Berlin: Dunker and Humbolt; Allen, P. M. (2000) 'Knowledge, Ignorance and Learning', *Emergence, Complexity & Organization*, 2(4), 78–103; Allen, P. M. (2001) What is Complexity Science? Knowledge of the Limits of Knowledge, *Emergence, Complexity & Organization*, 3(1), 24–42.
6 Marion (1999) Marion, R. (1999) *The Edge of Organization: Chaos and Complexity Theories of Formal Social Systems*, Thousand Oaks, CA: Sage.

7   Haynes, P. (2003) Managing Complexity in the Public Services, Maidenhead, Berkshire: Open University Press (McGraw-Hill Education); Carlisle, Y. and McMillan, E. (2006) 'Innovation in Organizations from a Complex Adaptive Systems Perspective', *Emergence, Complexity & Organization*, 8(1), 2–9; Coleman, H. J. (1999) 'What Enables Self-Organizing Behavior in Business', *Emergence*, 1(1), 33–48; Meek, J. W., De Ladurantey, J. and Newell, W. (2007) 'Complex Systems, Governance and Policy Administration Consequences', *Emergence, Complexity & Organization*, 9(1–2), 24–36.

8   Robertson, D. A. and Caldart, A. A. (2008) 'Natural Science Models in Management: Opportunities and Challenges', *Emergence, Complexity & Organization*, 10(2), 49–61; Anderson, P. (1999) 'Application of Complexity Theory to Organization Science', *Organization Science*, 10(3), 216–32. Cilliers, P. (1998) *Complexity and Postmodernism: Understanding Complex Systems*, London: Routledge, 1998.

9   Twomey, D. F. (2006) 'Designed Emergence as a Path to Enterprise Sustainability' *Emergence, Complexity & Organization*, 8(3), 12–23; Downs, A., Durant, R. and Carr, A. N. (2003) 'Emergent Strategy Development for Organizations', *Emergence*, 5(2), 5–28; Campbell-Hunt, C. (2007) 'Complexity in Practice, Human Relations, 60(5), 793–823; Gershenson, C. and Heylighen, F (2003) 'When Can We Call a System Self-organizing?', in Banzhaf, W., Christaller, T., Dittrich, P., Kim, J. T. and Ziegler, J. (eds) *Advances in Artificial Life*; Goldstein, J. A., Hazy, J. K. and Silberstang, J. (2008) 'Complexity and Social Entrepreneurship: A Fortuitous Meeting', *Emergence, Complexity & Organization*, 10(3), 3, vi–x; Hodge, B. and Coronado, G. (2007) 'Understanding Change in Organizations in a Far-from-Equilibrium World, *Emergence, Complexity & Organization*, 9(3), 3–15; Mitleton-Kelly, E. (2006) Co-evolutionary Integration: The Co-Creation of a New Organizational Form Following a Merger and Acquisition, *Emergence, Complexity & Organization*, 8(2); Anderson, C. and McMillan, E. (2003) 'Of Ants and Men: Self Organized Teams in Human and Insect Organizations', *Emergence*, 5(2), 29–41.

10 Pascale, R. T., Millemann, M. and Gioja, L. (2000, *Surfing the Edge of Chaos: The Laws of Nature and the New Laws of Business*, New York: Crown Business; MacIntosh, R. and MacLean, D. (1999) 'Conditioned Emergence: A Dissipative Structures Approach to Transformation', *Strategic Management Journal*, 20(4), 297–316; Sanders, T. I. (1998) *Strategic Thinking and the New Science: Planning in the Midst of Chaos, Complexity and Change*, New York: The Free Press; Wheatley, M. J. (1999) *Leadership and the New Science*, revised edition, San Francisco: Berrett and Koehler; Lewin, R. and Regine, B. (2000) *The Soul at Work*, London: Orion Business Books.

11 Richardson, K. A. (2008) 'Managing Complex Organizations: Complexity Thinking and the Science and Art of Management', *Emergence, Complexity & Organization*, 10(2), 13–27.

12 Lichtenstein, B. B., Uhl-Bien, Marion, R., Seers, A., Orton, J. D. and Schreiber, C. (2006) 'Complexity Leadership Theory: An Interactive Perspective On Leading in Complex Adaptive Systems', *Emergence, Complexity & Organization*, 8(4), 22–12.

13 Surie, G. and Hazy, J. K. (2006) 'Generative Leadership: Nurturing Innovation in Complex Systems', *Emergence, Complexity & Organization*, 8(4), 13–26.

14 Schreiber, C. and Carley, K. M. (2006) 'Leadership Style as an Enabler of Organizational Complex Functioning', *Emergence, Complexity & Organization*, 8(4), 61–76.

15 Richardson, K. A. (2008) 'Managing Complex Organizations: Complexity Thinking and the Science and Art of Management', *Emergence, Complexity & Organization*, 10(2), 13–27.

16 Chiles, T. D. and Meyer, A. D. (2001) 'Managing the Emergence of Clusters: An Increasing Returns Approach to Strategic Change', *Emergence*, 3(3), 58–89.

17 Ashmos, D. P., Duchon, D., McDaniel, R. R. and Huonker, J. W. (2002) 'What a Mess! Participation as a Simple Managerial rule to 'Complexify' Organizations', *Journal of Management Studies*, 39(2), 189–206.

18 Meek, J. W., De Ladurantey, J. and Newell, W. (2007) 'Complex Systems, Governance and Policy Administration Consequences', *Emergence, Complexity & Organization*, 9(1–2), 24–36.

19 See note 18, p 30.

20 Edelenbos, J, Gerrits, L. and Gils, M. (2008) 'The Co-evolutionary Relation Between Dutch Mainport Policies and the Development of the Seaport Rotterdam', *Emergence, Complexity & Organization*, 10(2), 49–61.

21 Robertson, D. A. (2003) 'Agent-Base Models of a Banking Network as an Example of a Turbulent Environment: The Deliberate vs. Emergent Strategy Debate Revisited', *Emergence, Complexity &*

Organization, 5(2), 56–71; Tsai, S. D., Hong-quei, C. and Valentine, S. (2003) 'An Integrated Model for Strategic Management in Dynamic Industries: Qualitative Research from Taiwan's Passive-component Industry', *Emergence, Complexity & Organization*, 5(4), 34–56; van Dyck, W. and Allen, P. M. (2006) 'Pharmaceutical Discovery as a Complex System of Decisions: The Case of Front-Loaded Experimentation', *Emergence, Complexity & Organization*, 8(3), 40–56; Varga, L. and Allen, P. M. (2006) 'A Case-Study of the Three Largest Aerospace Manufacturing Organizations: An Exploration of Organizational Strategy, Innovation and Evolution', *Emergence, Complexity & Organization*, 8(2), 48–64.

22 Allen, P. M., Strathern, M. and Baldwin, J. S. (2006) 'Evolutionary Drive: New Understandings of Change in Socio-Economic Systems', *Emergence, Complexity & Organization*, 8, 2.

23 Allen, P. M., Strathern, M. and Baldwin, J. S. (2006) 'Evolutionary Drive: New Understandings of Change in Socio-Economic Systems', *Emergence, Complexity & Organization*, 8, 2; Boisot, M. (2000) 'Is There a Complexity Beyond the Reach of Strategy?', *Emergence, Complexity & Organization*, 2(1), 114–34. Burgelman, R. A. and Grove, A. S. (2007) 'Let Chaos Reign, then Rein in Chaos – Repeatedly: Managing Strategic Dynamics for Corporate Longevity', *Strategic Management Journal*, 28, 965–79; Sommer, S. C., Loch, C. H. and Dong, J. (2009) 'Managing Complexity and Unforeseeable Uncertainty in Startup Companies: An empirical Study', *Organization Science*, 20(1), 188–133.

24 Sword, L. D. (2007) 'Complexity science conflict analysis of power and protest', *Emergence, Complexity & Organization*, 9(3), 47–61.

25 Wheatley, M. J. (1999) *Leadership and the New Science*, revised edition, San Francisco: Berrett and Koehler; Lewin, R. and Regine, B. (2000) *The Soul at Work*, London: Orion Business Books; Pascale, R. T., Millemann, M. and Gioja, L. (2000) *Surfing the Edge of Chaos: The Laws of Nature and the New Laws of Business*, New York: Crown Business.

26 Wheatley, M. J. (1999) *Leadership and the New Science*, revised edition, San Francisco: Berrett and Koehler; Lewin, R. and Regine, B. (2000) *The Soul at Work*, London: Orion Business Books.

27 Pascale, R. T., Millemann, M. and Gioja, L. (2000) *Surfing the Edge of Chaos: The Laws of Nature and the New Laws of Business*, New York: Crown Business.

28 Brown, S. L. and Eisenhardt, K. (1998) *Competing on the Edge: Strategy as Structured Chaos*, Boston, MA: Harvard Business School Press.

29 Wheatley, M. J. (1999) *Leadership and the New Science*, revised edition, San Francisco: Berrett and Koehler.

30 Lewin, R. and Regine, B. (2000) *The Soul at Work*, London: Orion Business Books.

31 Brown, S. L. and Eisenhardt, K. (1998) *Competing on the Edge: Strategy as Structured Chaos*, Boston, MA: Harvard Business School Press.

32 Brown, S. L. and Eisenhardt, K. (1998) *Competing on the Edge: Strategy as Structured Chaos*, Boston, MA: Harvard Business School Press.

33 For example, Connor (Connor, D. R. (1998) *Leading at the Edge of Chaos: How to Create the Nimble Organization*, New York: John Wiley & Sons), talks about this, as do Sanders (Sanders, T. I. (1998) *Strategic Thinking and the New Science: Planning in the Midst of Chaos, Complexity and Change*, New York: The Free Press) and Brown and Eisenhardt (Brown, S. L. and Eisenhardt, K. (1998) *Competing on the Edge: Strategy as Structured Chaos*, Boston, MA: Harvard Business School Press).

34 The following writers use Prigogine's phases of development far-from-equilibrium to posit a cycle of change in organizations that moves from stability, or normal equilibrium, through a bifurcation that is described in terms of crisis and chaos and a period of experimentation, out of which emerges a new order: Nonaka, I. and Takeuchi, H. (1995) *The Knowledge Creating Company*, New York: Oxford University Press; Pascale, R. T., Millemann, M. and Gioja, L. (2000) *Surfing the Edge of Chaos: The Laws of Nature and the New Laws of Business*, New York: Crown Business; Beinhocker, E. D. (1999) 'Robust adaptive strategies', *Sloan Management Review*, Spring, 95–106; MacIntosh, R. and MacLean, D. (1999) 'Conditioned Emergence: A Dissipative Structures Approach to Transformation', *Strategic Management Journal*, 20(4), 297–316.

35 Connor, D. R. (1998) *Leading at the Edge of Chaos: How to Create the Nimble Organization*, New York: John Wiley & Sons.

36 Beinhocker, E. D. (1999) 'Robust Adaptive Strategies', *Sloan Management Review*, Spring, 95–106.

37 Sanders, T. I. (1998) *Strategic Thinking and the New Science: Planning in the Midst of Chaos, Complexity and Change*, New York: The Free Press.

38 Luhman, J. T. and Boje, D. M. (2001) 'What is Complexity Science? A Possible Answer from Narrative Research', *Emergence*, 3(1), 158–68; Luhman, J. T. (2005) 'Narrative Processes in Organizational Discourse', *Emergence, Complexity & Organization*, 7(3–4), 15–22.

39 Tsoukas, H. and Hatch, M. J. (2001) 'Complex Thinking, Complex Practice: The Case for a Narrative Approach to Organizational Complexity', *Human Relations*, 54(8), 879–1013.

40 Zhu, Zhichang (2007) 'Complexity Science, Systems Thinking and Pragmatic Sensibility', *Systems Research and Behavioral Science*, July.

41 Chia, R. (1998) 'From Complexity Science to Complex Thinking: Organization as Simple Location', *Organization*, 5(3), 341–69. Houchin, K. and MacLean, D. (2005) 'Complexity Theory and Strategic Change: An Empirically Informed Critique', *British Journal of Management*, 16(2), 149–66.

42 Others, for example, Tait, A and Richardson, K.A. (2008) 'Confronting Complexity', *Emergence, Complexity & Organization*, 10(2), 27–41, conclude that while organizational complexity researchers have made considerable advances, their views have not moved from the margins.

43 Maguire, S. and McKelvey, B. (1999) 'Complexity and Management: Moving from Fad to Firm foundations', *Emergence*, 1(2), 19–61; McKelvey, B. (1999) Complexity Theory in Organization Science, Emergence: Seizing the Promise or Becoming a Fad, Emergence, 1(1), 5–31; McKelvey, B. (2002) Postmodernism vs. Truth in Management Theory, in Locke, E., *Post: Modernism & Management: Pros, Cons and Alternatives*, Amsterdam: Elsevier; McKelvey, B. (2003) 'From Fields to Science: Can Organization Studies make the Transition?', in Westwood, R. and Clegg, S. *Point/Counterpoint: Central debates in Organization Theory*, Oxford: Blackwell.

44 Tsoukas, H. and Hatch, M. J. (2001) 'Complex Thinking, Complex Practice: The Case for a Narrative Approach to Organizational Complexity', *Human Relations*, 54(8), 879–1013; Chia, R. (1998) 'From Complexity Science to Complex Thinking: Organization as Simple Location', *Organization*, 5(3), 341–69.

45 (Zhu, 2007) Zhu, Zhichang (2007) 'Complexity Science, Systems Thinking and Pragmatic Sensibility', *Systems Research and Behavioral Science*, July.

5 Understanding organizations as games we are pre-occupied in

Finding ourselves immersed in local interaction and using abstract management tools at the same time

> For what I really wish to work out is *a science of singularity*; that is to say, a science of the relationship that links everyday pursuits to particular circumstance. And only in the *local* network of labor and recreation can one grasp how, within a grid of socioeconomic constraints, these pursuits unfailingly establish relational tactics (a struggle for life), artistic creations (an aesthetic), and autonomous initiatives (an ethic). The characteristically subtle logic of the 'ordinary' activities comes to light only in the details.[1]

I concluded the last chapter by pointing to how the application of the complexity sciences to organizations has yielded some challenging insights but that it has mostly collapsed into a re-presentation of the dominant discourse in a new jargon or loosely used to justify ideologies of some kind of holism or mysticism. I suggested that it was striking how interdependent, ordinary people in all their conflictual and cooperative relationships were absent from the explanations and exhortations. The theories, explanations and research are split off from the actual experience of everyday organizational reality. I am interested in exploring how we might develop alternative ways of thinking that try to avoid the split between explanation and experience and I believe that this attempt is aided by reflecting on the history of how we have come to think in these split terms and how we might adopt more paradoxical modes of thought. I am convinced that it is when we reflect on the historical evolution of ways of thinking that we become aware of the taken-for-granted assumptions upon which they are built and what entailments they have, most of which have slipped from our view.

Placing actual human bodies and their ordinary, everyday activities at the center of explanations of organizations and their management amounts to a reversal of the focus of attention from the 'macro' to the 'micro', from 'global wholes' to the everyday, local interactions or more accurately the focus of attention shifts to the simultaneous experience of population-wide patterns in local interaction. I think that the key notions here are 'experience' and 'everyday interaction'. All we can actually experience in a direct social sense is our everyday, local interaction with each other – we cannot directly experience a 'global whole' such as British Airways, but we can experience interactions with staff employed by that organization. And that interaction is local where acting locally means interacting with only a tiny proportion of a total population and doing so on the basis not of directly and simply applied diktats from a central authority but on the basis of thematic narrative patterns that have emerged historically in our community and our own lives and continue to be sustained and transformed in our interaction with others. Even when there are central diktats, what they mean is interpreted in local interaction. Even when some powerful person addresses thousands, even millions, the meaning of what they say or do only emerges in the many, many local interactions in which there is a response. And we engage in such interaction with each other in complex ways that have evolved in our own lives in the evolving history of the community we live in, that is, in the social habitus we dwell in which cannot be reduced to rules. Such interaction is 'everyday' simply because it is what we are doing all the time, and it is local in the sense that we can only do anything in a specific place, at a specific time, with specific people dealing with each other on the basis of our and their life experiences in an evolving community. This experience may be humdrum and boring or it may be exciting, even terrifying. It may be very ordinary or in another sense quite extraordinary. It may be the experience of relationships that are profoundly good or the experience of relationships which are cruel, distressing and downright evil. All of these aspects of experience are relevant for understanding and explaining the reality of organizational life. So how have we, in our thinking about organizations, become distanced from the reality of our experience of everyday life? To answer this question I want to go over some of the ground already mentioned in Chapter 2 but to do so now in a little more detail.

From porous selves in an enchanted world to buffered selves in a disenchanted world

In order to identify the key changes in how Western people now experience themselves and think about the society they live in, Charles Taylor[2] makes a comparison between the modernity in which we now live and the Western world some 500 years ago. At that time, almost everyone believed that the natural world reflected divine action and that events in the natural world, the cosmos, were acts of God. The social order was also believed to be grounded in God so that people encountered God, the creator-designer, everywhere. Any change in the social order was only justified if it reflected more closely the will of God. The purpose of any change ought to be that of bringing human life into greater conformity with the will of God. Nevertheless, this is a highly simplified description and Taylor carefully describes how these beliefs were aspects of a wider experience of 'living in' an 'enchanted' world of spirits, demons, saints and moral forces. Consequently, for people five centuries ago, meaning lay not in individual minds but in extra human agencies and power actually resided in things like relics so that meaning was also in things. The causes of change, both natural and social, lay in extra human forces and things in the natural world infused with supernatural powers.

Furthermore, people did not experience a clear boundary between mind and world. For example, people fell under spells cast by supernatural forces. In other words, the boundary between extra human agency and individual human agency was not clearly drawn. The boundary was porous and Taylor refers to this way of experiencing a self as the 'porous self' where there is no split between subject and object which are instead fused. Porous individuals fear being taken over by demons and they have little notion of distancing themselves from the world including the world of their feelings. Therefore, at the time we are talking about, people experienced their world as *enchanted* and themselves as *porous individuals* very much *immersed* in the enchanted world. There was no clear notion of individual agency, let alone an individual agency which could design changes in both the natural and social worlds. On the contrary, the sense of risk and fear in the enchanted world created enormous pressure on people to embrace orthodoxy and condemn diversity and difference as heresy which had to be punished and stamped out.

Over the past 500 years, this mode of experience came to be replaced by the experience of a 'disenchanted' natural world in which nature moves according to impersonal laws having mostly the efficient causal structure of 'if x . . . then y'. It is now quite possible, although not compulsory, to believe that natural phenomena have nothing to do with God, spirits or demons and that in fact there is no God, nor are there spirits or any other kind of extra human agencies. Instead, natural phenomena are held to evolve gradually over very long periods through chance variations and competitive selection. These beliefs and experiences of the world and society would have been quite literally inconceivable to almost everyone 500 years ago. The social world today is also 'disenchanted' in that it is possible to believe that it too has nothing to do with God, spirits or demons but has everything to do with human plans and actions. Naturally, the experience of living in a disenchanted world is also a very different experience of the self. Meaning is no longer located 'outside' in things and extra-human agencies but is now entirely located 'inside' in the mind as the only locus of thought and feeling. The porous individual has evolved into what Taylor calls the 'buffered' individual. The buffer takes the form of a clear boundary between the mind inside the individual and the world outside. Buffered selves have learned to disengage and distance themselves from everything outside the mind including the body and its feelings. It came to be believed possible for human beings to find the highest fulfilment for themselves in what Taylor calls radical humanism without any appeal to God. Human beings are then thought to be able to actualize themselves, even engineer changes in their thinking and behavior. As mentioned in Chapter 2, this notion of individual agency was powerfully expressed by Kant's notion of rational, autonomous, moral individuals and Leibnitz's idea of individuals as monads. The monadic, rational-autonomous, buffered self makes clear distinctions between subjects and objects and other boundaries too move from porous to sharp, creating numerous dualities: self and other; laws of physical science and the meaning things have for us; thought and action; thought and feeling; physical and moral; planning and implementing.

This enormous shift in experience is also an enormous shift in our understanding of agency. If, as moderns came to believe, the natural world moves according to causal laws, to which there are no exceptions, then the movement of nature can be predicted. It is this that enables individual human agents to intervene in the operation of nature and control at least important aspects of it in an instrumental way. Moreover, this scientific approach to nature has afforded modern people enormous control over natural phenomena and enabled the development of quite amazing technologies. However, we are now increasingly encountering limits to our ability to control nature and becoming increasingly worried about the unexpected consequences of these attempts. Furthermore, we have something of a problem in thinking in the same 'scientific' way about the social world. For, although we build models and conduct research to identify the natural laws governing social evolution, we experience strongly the agency of the individual who can make exceptions. So, from this perspective, the social is not really moving according to impersonal laws but rather according to exceptional individual efforts of will, charismatic persuasion and skill in leading and managing. We have come to believe that special individuals can have an enormous impact on the social order and far from bolstering its stability, they should be changing it to improve it. But then sometimes in conducting research into, and making prescriptions for, organizations we do think that organizations are systems moving according to impersonal laws. As I have said before, we have developed a dualistic way of thinking about the individual and the social.

The sociologist, Norbert Elias,[3] provided detailed research on how this experience of self and agency in a disenchanted world was inseparable from the development of much more disciplined society characterized by 'civility'. Civility is a mode of behavior that separates an elite from the rest according to their more refined behavior not characterized by rowdiness, random violence and unsophisticated ways of exercising bodily functions. It is a taming of our wilder natures and accords superiority to the elite. It is this disciplined behavior that is essential to a mode of government which is orderly and subject to the rule of law. Elias showed how this civility was imitated by groups outside the elite and so over the years came to characterize whole populations. He pointed to the role of rising barriers of shame and disgust in exercising a powerful form of control over people. Civility also depends upon legitimate authorities exercising a monopoly of violence. Self-restraint and self-control brought about by the evolution of civility, as well as greater anticipation of the consequences of one's actions, were all essential requirements to support the growing chains of interdependence between people, brought about by the division of labour and economic growth. Like Taylor, Elias also describes how our thinking about nature and society has evolved and he does this by distinguishing between what he calls involved and detached thinking.

Involved and detached thinking

In thinking about the evolution of society, Elias drew attention to the impact on our emotional experience of developing scientific ideas about nature: he describes this as movement from an involved to a detached way of thinking.[4] He pointed out how, centuries ago, people experienced much higher levels of anxiety and fear when confronted by nature, because they had rather low levels of control over their natural environment. They tended to see threatening natural events in terms of spirits and gods in a form of magico-mythical thinking having a high level of fantasy and a low level of reality congruence: their thinking was highly involved in their everyday experience in which they were confronted with a double bind. This took the form of fear and anxiety which led them to think in involved ways but since this had little reality congruence, it did not lead to any improved control and so simply provoked more involved thinking, trapping people in a double bind. Highly involved thinkers lose distance and are caught up in the situation and the feelings this arouses, losing awareness of the distinction between self and other which leads them to perceive their own characteristics as belonging to the other. However, the development of a fund of knowledge about the functioning of nature led to greater ability to control it, and in order to develop such a fund of knowledge, people had to think in more detached ways and as such thinking brought about greater reality congruence so their control over nature increased and they felt less fear and anxiety. This enabled them to think in even more detached terms. Elias talked about obtaining more reality congruent knowledge by means of a detour via detachment. Detached thinking requires self-regulation and self-distancing. It is synoptic and involves the extraction of regularities in a situation. The detached thinker is able to step back and take a calmer, more objective view of the situation, one less dominated by his own feelings.

Elias then pointed out how the scientific method has not brought about a similarly large fund of knowledge of the social world. He thought that the difficulty people had in taking a detached view of society had to do with their own irremovable involvement in social processes, which had become increasingly interconnected, complex and tightly coupled: 'It is as if first thousands, then millions, then more millions walked through this world with their hands and feet chained together by invisible ties. No one is in charge. No one stands outside. Some want to go this way, others that. They fall upon each other and, vanquishing or defeated, still remain chained to each other. No one can regulate the movements of the whole unless a great part of them are able to understand, to see as it were, from the outside, the whole patterns they form together. And they are not able to visualize themselves as part of the larger patterns because, being hemmed in and moved uncomprehendingly hither and thither in ways which none of them intended, they cannot help being preoccupied with urgent, narrow and parochial problems which each of them has to face . . . . They are too deeply involved to look at themselves from without. Thus what is formed of nothing but human acts upon each of them, and is experienced by many as an alien external force not unlike the forces of nature'.[5] The incomprehension arouses the fear that keeps people trapped in involved, magico-mythical thinking about the social which traps them in a double bind. Perhaps, the currently dominant discourse about organizations and their management, with its emphasis on forces and highly abstract wholes, is a major example of the kind of magico-mythical thinking that Elias is talking about with its consequent poor reality congruence. Yet the dominant discourse is, or is claimed to be, the clearly detached thinking of science.

Elias is clear that involved and detached thinking are never found in pure form but always exist together. He thinks of thinking and acting always lying along a continuum between involved and detached and argues that the balance can shift. So, hundreds of years ago, thinking about nature and the social was more involved than detached. It has now come to be more detached than involved, significantly so with regard to nature but much less so with regards to the social despite all our attempts to be scientific in understanding the social.

Elias' notion of involved thinking is much the same as Taylor's notion of the porous self experiencing an 'enchanted world'. Taylor also traces the evolution of Western society from this position to that of a buffered self in a 'disenchanted world' which is much the same as Elias' notion of detached thinking. The modern experience of a disenchanted world with a social order consisting of disciplined, distanced, autonomous selves capable of exercising rational agency is an outcome of the economic development and eventual industrialization of the West as well as the scientific revolution, the Age of Enlightenment, the Reformation and the development of the modern state with its culture of civility. The eighteenth century saw the beginnings of the notion that civility should be imposed on the wider population. An ideology developed of improving the social order through education and the development of effective government structures. It was thought that the social order could be designed by individual agency, indeed it was the moral duty of leaders to do this in the interest of improvement. Later in this chapter, I will describe research by James Scott[6] on how the modern state and action upon the ideology of control and improvement were all made possible by state simplification of highly complex local interaction which was generated and imposed from the center. He described this as a form of thinking that was rational, detached and abstract. However, the local interaction which is being simplified for state control purposes continues in its complexity which is not necessarily rational and unlikely to be detached or abstract, even though it is affected by the state simplification. This makes the state simplification's functioning far from straightforward and the imposition of dominating abstractions provokes resistance.[7]

Therefore, Taylor, Elias and Scott are all saying something similar but there are also important differences. Elias distinguishes between involved, short-term thinking which is not fact oriented, on the one hand, and detached, long-term thinking which is fact oriented, on the other hand. He claims that since medieval times the balance has shifted from involved to detached thinking although both have always been present. To me this notion of balance between opposite poles implies a duality rather than a strong sense of paradox, in which opposite modes are present at the same time in continuous tension with each other out of which some new form emerges. The duality, rather than the paradox, is further evidenced by the split Elias makes between fantasy and reality congruence. He argues that involved thinking is prompted by high levels of anxiety and fear and he equates such involved thinking with fantasy or magico-mythical thinking having little reality congruence. As levels of anxiety and fear decline, Elias claims, people are able to think in detached ways which he equates with greater reality congruence. Elias says that detachment gets to the facts while involvement does not because it is an inability to distance ourselves from traditional attitudes. He says social scientists should separate their scientific and nonscientific knowledge to prevent emotional spillage and calls for reality congruent social models which he insists cannot be the same as the models in the natural sciences.

However, he does not really explore these distinctions. For example, he does not develop in any detail just what involved and detached thinking consists of, nor does he point to any problems that might be created by detachment. For example, it is quite possible that we will respond to high levels of anxiety by using detached intellectualizations as defences against the anxiety and ways of ignoring uncomfortable feelings. Such detached thinking could quite easily produce fantasies of rationality. Similarly, emotionally involved thinking could actually produce greater reality congruence. For example, psychotherapists work by being highly emotionally involved in the experience of interacting with patients; they use affect, including their own anxiety, as information. Therefore, the therapist is involved but at the same time, in making some kind of interpretation, he or she is detached, even more so than normally. The therapist's thinking is not less reality congruent, because it is involved – I would claim that it is more reality congruent, because it is involved in the emotion of the other. However, such thinking is also detached at the same time. The activities of reflecting on one's thought and behavior, the activities of reflexivity, requires involvement and detachment at the same time. I can reflect on my involvement, as I am involved so that involvement and detachment together constitute reflection. Furthermore, Elias does not indicate how we can say one thought is fantasy and another reality congruent. It sounds like he is talking unproblematically about objectivity and evidence, or at least I think I can now understand how some would take what he is saying in this way. However, what is fantasy and what is reality will always be contested in local interaction, because they are socially constructed – indeed my repeated appeal to newspaper articles to identify what I am calling organizational reality will be contested by many who are reading what I write. Also, there is the matter of the values and norms constituting ideology which will be discussed in Chapter 9. This makes our thinking much more complex than a simple juxtaposition of fantasy and reality would suggest. Ideology, the habitus of belief, which we live in, plays a large part in determining what we choose, collectively, to call fantasy and what we choose to call reality. The involved thinking of porous individuals reflects some ideology and detached thinking is no less a reflection of a different ideology. Humans can do no other than live in habits of belief that is ideology. So, when I review newspaper articles on events over the past three years, I am, of course selecting and interpreting them in a way conditioned by habits of belief which are more than my own idiosyncrasies. In the community in which we live, I can point to patterns of events called 'credit crunch' as a reality no one chose and call this a 'fact'. And I say this from the habit of believing which I believe others share that no one is mad enough to choose a 'credit crunch' and if they were then no one is powerful enough to realize the choice.

Scott presents a more paradoxical picture than Elias does of the simultaneous interplay of thinking in the complexity of local interaction and thinking in the form of state simplification which is socially constructing the subjective-objective reality of experience. The next section outlines what Scott has to say in his book '*Seeing Like a State*'.[8]

Taking an overview from the center

The modern state with its monopoly of violence within its borders, establishing a pacified and peaceful environment for its citizens, was an essential requirement for economic growth, technological developments and industrialization. Armies and navies were needed not just to protect the state from other states but also to build economic empires and control the transport routes upon which profitable international trade depended. All of this naturally cost a great deal of money which had to be financed from taxes and since medieval systems of tax collection were highly inefficient, reform of tax collection systems was another essential aspect of the evolution of highly interdependent Western societies and the sense of self as a buffered, rational, autonomous agent able to change whole societies. Hundreds of years ago, kings raised revenues by imposing on their subjects excise duties, tariffs, tolls, market dues, licensing fees and taxes based on landed wealth. These taxes were collected for the king by his nobles who in turn used tax collectors to gather in the revenue. Tax collecting was rather arbitrary, often involving force, and the lack of control over the system meant that peasants could cheat and at each level from the tax collector up, parts of the taxes raised were siphoned off for the benefit of the collector. Seen from the level of the king, increasingly understood as the state, this system of tax collection was extremely inefficient. Without reform, the modern state could not develop, because it would not be possible to finance the monopoly of violence or more widespread education and welfare. The principal problem of reforming the most important of the taxes at the time, the tax on land wealth, was that the practices of land tenure were extremely intricate and varied considerably from one local context to another – very different tenure arrangements could be encountered geographically very close to each other. Detailed local knowledge was required in order to know what it was possible to collect and the local tax collector, of course, had this knowledge but any attempt to rationalize and centralize tax collection would founder on the impossibility of those at the center gaining knowledge on all the varieties of tenure arrangements. The locals would always be able to conceal the real situation from uninformed central tax collectors. In Scott's terms, the property owning system was illegible to the state. A centralizing state could only succeed if it could impose a legible property system. This meant that economic activities and all landed wealth had to be identified, measured and attached to some individual or group of individuals. Measuring wealth and changing tenure arrangements was a major political act. It would be necessary to impose the reforms, because a simplified, unified and transparent property system would profoundly shift existing patterns of power relations and so, naturally, any reforms would be resisted.

An important move in the reform of the property systems of Europe occurred first in Holland, Denmark and France around the Napoleonic era: cadastral maps of rural areas were prepared. A cadastral survey is one on a scale sufficiently large to accurately show the extent and measurement of every field or other block of land, so accurately identifying land boundaries. However, accurate measurement of the immense variations across small areas was not possible. The maps had to be simplifications of some kind and the more orderly the actual land tenure practices the more useful the maps would be. Surveyors then pressed locals to consolidate their disparate holding of strips of land into neater farms which could be measured. Therefore, the act of measuring was producing patterns of tenure that could be measured. Measuring was more than a detached scientific act; it was a social, political act as are all acts of measuring human activity. Simplified tenure, of course, was the ideal but what actually happened in each local situation still varied as 'the reformers were generally thwarted, despite tremendous pressure to produce integral farms. There were unauthorized consolidations, although they were forbidden; there were also "paper consolidations" in which the new farmers continued to farm their strips as before'.[9] However, although not accurate, the maps did serve some useful purposes: 'The value of the cadastral map to the state lies in its abstraction and universality. In principle, at least, the same objective standard can be applied throughout the nation, regardless of local context, to provide a complete and unambiguous map of all landed property. The completeness of the cadastral map depends, in a curious way, on its abstract sketchiness, its lack of detail – its thinness. Taken alone, it is essentially a geometric representation of the borders or frontiers between parcels of land. What lies inside the parcel is left blank – unspecified – since it is not germane to the map plotting itself'.[10]

The cadastral map therefore makes local conditions legible to the state but only in a highly simplified way. The actual wealth and its taxable capacity depend not just on the size of the plot but also on its detailed production capacity and the locals need no map to know this, which, however, still remains illegible to outsiders. Scott describes the cadastral map as a still photograph of an ever-moving picture as land boundaries and soil conditions change. To get a more accurate picture, surveyors can then grade land by soil class and average yield. However, 'these state simplifications, like all state simplifications, are always far more static and schematic than the actual social phenomena they presume to typify. The farmer rarely experiences an average crop, an average rainfall or an average process for his crops. Much of the long history of rural tax revolts in early modern Europe and elsewhere can be illuminated by the lack of fit between an unyielding fiscal claim, on one hand, and an often wildly fluctuating capacity of the rural population to meet that claim, on the other. And yet, even the most equitable, well intentioned cadastral system cannot be uniformly administered except on the basis of stable units of measurement and calculation. It . . . [cannot] . . . reflect the actual complexity of the farmer's experience'.[11]

Scott emphasizes how what seems to be an objective, scientific, value free activity of measuring and classifying established new institutions administering title deeds, fees, applications and other matters. The maps were changing the world in many respects to accord with what could be measured and in doing so they were shifting patterns of power relations in which administrators became more powerful and cultivators less so. This early application of measuring, standardizing, establishing a property system provides us with important insights into what we are still doing today in the dominant discourse. The dominant discourse lays great emphasis on simplifying and abstracting in an attempt to bring about the uniformity which enables some control from a distance. Attempts at centralized control do require some imposition of uniformity and in so doing shifts patterns of power relations and has an effect on shaping behavior. As an example, take the government targets for the National Health Service in the UK. In the 1990s, the government imposed waiting time targets on all hospitals in England and Wales and some ten years later, most hospitals were indeed meeting those targets. Apparently, the setting of uniform targets does shape behavior.

Local resistance

However, going back to changes in the tax system, Scott then emphasizes the capacity of the locals to block, subvert and countermand the categories that state simplifications impose on them. In another book, *'Domination and the Arts of Resistance: Hidden Transcripts'*,[12] he explores just how locals do resist state simplifications. Scott is interested in how subordinate groups of people often have to adopt a strategic pose when dealing with the more powerful but how they also find other ways amongst themselves of expressing what they think and feel. He refers to the latter as 'hidden transcripts' and argues that contradictions and tensions expressed in the hidden transcripts and between them and the strategic pose have a major impact on what happens. In other words, it is vital to understand the nature of local political interactions if one is to understand the wider social evolution. The problem with studying the hidden transcripts is that they are usually clandestine and so closed to outsiders. However, they are frequently expressed more publicly in disguised form as rumors, gossip, folktales and jokes. Scott argues that these apparently innocuous and anonymous forms of discourse are disguised ideological insubordination which provides a reasonably safe critique of power. Civility requires us to smile and exchange routine pleasantries, especially when the other has the power to harm or reward us, even if we privately despise that other. Especially, in the face of domination, people will express themselves in their public transcripts in ways which are ritualized and stereotypical. The public transcript will be a performance, masking the hidden transcripts which will often irrupt in ways that catch the more powerful off guard. Eventually, the hidden transcripts may be expressed publicly and Scott argues that when this happens, it is often experienced as a breach of etiquette, even a symbolic declaration of war. The frontier between public and hidden transcripts is a constant struggle between the dominant and the subordinate.

We can see this distinction between public and hidden transcripts quite clearly at play in the modern National Health Service in the UK. The public transcript is cast in terms of targets, visions, values, strategies and the implementation of plans to achieve the targets, keeping the organization on message going forward. Managers and others in the service strike a strategic pose in which they subscribe to the public transcript. However, in private, the hidden transcript comes out as people try to work out how to achieve targets given resource constraints. Waiting times are met by occasional 'massaging' of the figures, by discharging people early, and by cancelling follow up appointments. The forms of resistance identified by Scott are much in evidence for those who look – the gossip, the jokes about leaders and so on. These hidden transcripts and the forms of resistance they embody are having just as much effect on the delivery of health care to the public as the public transcript is having. What happens does so in the interplay of public and hidden transcripts or what previously I have called the legitimate and the shadow themes organizing our experience of being together in organizations.[13]

The purpose of the public transcript is to provide an appearance of unanimity and of keeping discord out of sight while the hidden transcripts are forms of resistance. The strategies of resistance all involve some form of concealment, disguise and anonymity and they take the form of: gossip, sometimes taking the form of stories designed to ruin the reputation of others; rumor as a kind of magical aggression; deferential performances covering over hidden acts of aggression; euphemisms concealing what is actually being done; grumbling; expressing disguised bits of the hidden transcript publicly.

Scott mentions a number of other aspects of state simplification which were necessary for the evolution of the modern nation state. For example, standardization of family names allowed births, deaths and tax capacity to be registered and was also the basis for organizing the distribution of benefits and the provision of education and public health. Models of cities made it possible to carry out engineering projects for sanitation and water as well as redesigns of whole areas to make state control easier. Indeed, they made possible the kind of utopian large projects aimed at societal transformation that Taylor emphasized in the foregoing section. However, alongside these grand macro, state developments there is always the local interaction that both supports and potentially subverts those projects so that they often have unexpected and sometimes even disastrous outcomes. Much the same happens today. We adopt the public transcript of thinking that an organization is a system and this does enable a higher degree of uniformity and control from the center upon which continuity and stability depend. Nevertheless, when it comes to the change aspect of the ongoing iteration of organizational interactions, ignoring the hidden transcripts leads to unexpected and sometime disastrous change. Therefore, in organizations today, attempts to produce uniformity through punishing deviants may well have the effect of suppressing the local interaction, removing the flexibility upon which the ongoing functioning of the organizations depends. However local interaction and resistance is not simply good either and may take the form of greed, evidenced in current financial instability.

Scott argues that state projects produce disasters when three factors combine. The first is the aspirations of High Modernity to order nature and society, to control and improve. Scott identifies this utopian ideology of control and improvement with engineers, planners, politicians, high-level administrators, architects, scientists and visionaries. This ideology in itself is, of course, not simply the cause of disaster, because it has also been the source of enormous beneficial change. So when does the ideology produce beneficial change and when does it produce human tragedy or simply expensive failure? Scott argues that when the ideology is combined with the unrestrained use of power to achieve the aspirations and when this power blots out the local interaction which could resist or adapt the plans, then disaster is likely. He gives examples in history where these three elements have been present as in the disastrous famines in Soviet Russia following Stalin's agricultural collectivization and China's Great Leap Forward. There are also numerous examples of Western aid projects to the developing world which have actually made conditions worse rather than better.

Therefore, we can now see how the dominant discourse on organizational change reflects the evolution of socially constructed notions of agency and ideologies of control. The example of the reform of the tax system also draws our attention to the way that the exercise of modern notions of agency depends upon measuring, standardizing, establishing a property system providing us with important insights into what we are still doing today in the dominant discourse. The dominant discourse, or public transcript, lays great emphasis on simplifying and abstracting in an attempt to bring about the uniformity which enables control. Centralized control does require some imposition of uniformity and in so doing shifts patterns of power relations and has an effect on shaping behavior. However, to take a polarizing critical position on central control and call for its replacement with local control, as some management complexity writers do, is to ignore organizational reality. What is called for, instead, is recognition that central control efforts are too important to be replaced but cannot be understood apart from local interaction and its hidden transcripts or shadow themes. What may be of most help is the effort to try to hold onto the paradox of the central and the local, the strategic pose and the hidden transcript.

So, there are problems when we build theories of organizational change on assumptions of masterful individual agents and abstractions across populations – we lose sight of human beings and their local interactions, both good and bad, which have an enormous impact on what the state simplifications actually produce. But is there an alternative way of thinking?

Pre-occupation in the game

I have been drawing on the analyses of Taylor, Elias and Scott to identify key aspects of how the experience of self and society has shifted over the last hundreds of years characterized by the development of the scientific method, political revolutions in North America, France, Britain and many other European countries, the Reformation, the development of technology, industrialization and global trade, the emergence of the nation state supported by administrative procedures based on standardization, measurement, mapping and modelling. This movement has changed perceptions of the world and self from an experience of an enchanted world, often to be feared, and a porous self not sharply distinguished from this world, to an experience of an impersonal, disenchanted world following laws without exceptions and a buffered, disengaged, autonomous, rational self with a powerful sense of agency and ability to change the world. This distinction between medieval and modern selves is extremely helpful in drawing our attention to how modern conceptions of individual agency have evolved as socially constructed reality reflecting assumptions that we now take for granted. However, I want to argue that we need to avoid taking the distinction between porous and buffered selves too literally.

Bordieu[14] offers an alternative way of thinking which has strong resonances with other writers, such as Elias and Mead, for example. He makes a distinction between modes of experience and thought. According to one view, human agents do not do just anything but always act on the basis of reasons: they engage in reasonable forms of behavior. Once we find the reason for the coherent set of principles governing a series of actions we are able to see the pattern in what might have looked like random actions. If agents act unreasonably or randomly then it might be argued that the social sciences can have nothing to say about what such agents are doing. It seems to me that this particular view of the reasonable agent is close to Elias' detached way of thinking about the actions of agents. Bourdieu contrasts this notion of the reasonable agent with one in which agents act on the basis of interests. He relates this to the notion that in their ordinary activities, agents are engaged in a game which they take seriously and in which they are invested. They act on the basis that playing the game is worth the effort, because they have an interest in it. It is in their interest to participate in the game, recognizing the game and the stakes. They are pre-occupied by the game rather than acting rationally to achieve goals. Bourdieu relates the game to the habitus in which people live, that is, the habitual social customs and ways of thinking into which they are born. We acquire our interest in particular social games through our living in the society we are born into. Our minds are structured by this social experience which is imprinted in our bodies as a feel for the game. Here Bourdieu is saying much the same thing as Elias in his major works on sociology[15] where he too talks about habitus in much the same sense. Bourdieu talks about agents 'being invested . . . in the stakes existing in a certain game, through the effect of competition, and which only exists for people who being caught up in that game and possessing the dispositions to recognize the stakes at play, are ready to die for the stakes which, conversely, are devoid of interest for those who are not tied to that game and which leave them indifferent'.[16] Of course, much of this is unconscious as agents embody schemes of perception on the basis of which they act rather than setting objectives for what they do. Agents 'are not like *subjects* faced with an object (or, even less, a problem) that will be constituted as such by an intellectual act of cognition; they are, as it is said, absorbed in their affairs (one could also say their doing): they are present at the coming moment, the doing, the deed . . . which is not posed as an object of thought, as a possible aimed for in a project, but which is inscribed in the present of the game'.[17] He explains how having a feel for the game, embodying it, based on a sense of history and skill in anticipating the moves of others, allows us some mastery over the unfolding game. 'It is true that most human behaviors take place within playing fields; thus they do not have as a principle a strategic intention such as that postulated in game theory. In other words, social agents have "strategies" which only rarely have a true strategic intention as a principle'.[18]

Bourdieu poses an opposition between a preoccupation as anticipation immediately present although not yet perceived and a plan as a design for the future requiring the mobilization of actions to bring this future about. This is directly relevant to the dominant discourse on change in organizations which focuses attention almost entirely on the design and the plan, so encouraging us to ignore how we are actually pre-occupied by the organizational game. We are absorbed in the affairs of the organization in our local interactions, conducting skilful performances which give us some mastery of organizational continuity and change. However, we could be covering over the limitations to such mastery by focusing attention only on the design. Bourdieu's analysis suggests that while the buffered individual with the capacity for powerful individual agency exercised in a rational, detached way is what is publicly presented, the reality of ordinary interaction is that of participating, largely unconsciously, in games, in the habitus in which we live.

Therefore, Taylor, Scott, Elias and Bourdieu are all contrasting some kind of abstract, rational thinking about human action with the ordinary practices of action. Elias talks about the difficulty of detached thinking in relation to the experience of interconnection with others. Scott talks about state simplifications and local practices, Bourdieu contrasts rational planning and pre-occupation with the game. Taylor talks about the buffered individual compared to the porous self. They are all contrasting an abstracted prior design (intention, strategy) with participation in ordinary everyday interactions: Scott identifies the important advantages of the rational planned approach but also identifies its dangers while Bourdieu, on the other hand seems to imply that the rational planned approach is what is publicly proclaimed while agents actually do something else. Bourdieu's notion of pre-occupation in the game seems close to Elias' involved thinking and Bourdieu's reference to rational planning seems close to Elias' detached thinking.

Nevertheless, Bourdieu dismisses the rational planning and focuses on pre-occupation, so taking the opposite view to Elias. However, in most of his other work Elias argues in terms of interdependence and habitus where reality congruence is a problematic notion. It seems to me that Elias presents a duality of involved and detached thinking and regards a move toward the detached pole as desirable while Bourdieu proposes a similar duality with the preoccupied mode at one pole and the rational planned mode at the other pole, his preference being for the former. Neither presents a strong paradox where both involved-preoccupied and detached-planned are practiced at the same time: after all people do make plans and at the same time, they are preoccupied in the game, acting out the habitus in which they live.

I am interested, therefore, in a more paradoxical take in making an analytical distinction between immersing in and abstracting from local interaction. Immersion can be characterized by both involved and detached thinking, as can abstracting, and this problematizes any sharp distinction between them. The next sections explore the paradoxical activities of immersing in the experience of local interaction and abstracting from it at the same time.

The activities of generalizing/idealizing and particularizing in local interaction

We can only interact with each other locally and that local interaction always reflects population-wide generalizations, idealizations most of which we are not conscious of. In other words, in our local interaction, we are normally pre-occupied in Bourdieu's sense and we are always reflecting the habitus in which we live. I want to use the term *immersing* to describe what we are doing as we act locally in ways which unconsciously reflect the generalizations and idealizations, the habitus of our society. However, we also have the capacity to become aware of our pre-occupation with the game, to reflect upon our practical action, which expresses the habitus in which we live, in an effort to make conscious sense of what we are doing.

Centuries ago, people also articulated generalizations/idealizations of their experience, as people have always done everywhere, and I suggest that such articulations took two forms. First, people made sense of the population-wide patterns of interaction they lived in through the stories they told and the myths they recited from generation to generation. Bourdieu particularly makes clear, as does Elias in most of his work, that this mode of articulating and reflecting upon our experience of local interaction remains important to this day. We still articulate the general/ideal in stories, rumors, and fantasies about distant powerful figures despite social and individual evolution of the past centuries. The point about the narrative forms of our articulations of the generalizations and idealizations of our practical everyday activity is that they stay close to our experience of local interaction in that they provide descriptions and accounts of that local interaction itself, even in mythical form. Articulations of these generalizations and idealizations in narrative form involve selecting and simplifying and in that sense, *abstracting* from experience. However, the selection is not only simplification but also elaboration. Narrative articulations of experience require interpretation in particular contingent situations. Their aim is not simplicity, standardization and uniformity, as it was with the mapping abstraction described earlier, but rather their aim is the opening up of accounts of experience for greater exploration in order to develop deeper understanding. However, the conscious simplifying generalization of narrative does amount to abstracting from, that is, simplifying and generalizing, the detail of each uniquely experienced situation.

The second form of simplification and generalization, that is, abstracting from, the detail of experience is that of categorizing. Thought is essentially an act of categorizing and generalizing. So people do not think entirely in terms of specific objects such as this table or that table but instead they think in terms of a general and so abstract category of tables. There were always philosophers and theologians who articulated formal simplifications, generalizations and categories of experience concerned with perceiving, knowing and acting ethically. Metaphysics involved abstracting from unique experience to signify hidden causes. Philosophy sought to explain the experience of perception, of knowing and relating in abstract modes that opened up exploration and interpretation, so elaborating further reflection on experience. Human thought, therefore, has always been paradoxical acts of immersing and abstracting at the same time.

However, Taylor, Elias and Scott all point to the emergence of the modern, rational, calculating and planning individual agent. They all point out that a central feature of such modern individuals is their capacity to reflect and to think in objective, simplifying, rational ways. This amounts, I suggest, to the emergence of a kind of generalizing about our experience which was not available to premodern individuals. What the modern agent developed was the kind of simplification that Scott identifies so well: forms of simplification which made it possible for powerful figures at the centre of the state to 'read' and control much of what happens locally. What emerged we could say was a particularly rigorous form of simplification taking a stronger form of *abstracting* from the experience of local interaction than before. For now, in addition to generalizing through the identification of categories of experience, which we might call first order abstracting, there was an added generalization expressed in the mapping and modelling of relationships between the categories, which we might call second order abstracting. This, it seems to me, was a new form of simplification by abstraction in that it was manipulating the categories of first order abstractions and was therefore operating at yet another remove from direct experience. This abstraction from the abstraction of categories of experience would make it easier to split the second order abstraction off from the experience through reification and so lose the sense of the paradox of immersing and abstracting at the same time. The second order abstracting activity that Taylor and Scott describe as emerging in the development of Western society sought to simplify, standardize and measure so reducing elaboration, multiple interpretations and mystery.

I am arguing that in our ordinary, everyday local interaction with each other, in which we accomplish all our activities, we always have been and still are *immersing* ourselves in the experience of such interaction and at the same time we are *abstracting* from that experience by simplifying, generalizing and categorizing in the forms of narrative and philosophy as *first order abstracting*. However, in the modern world we also frequently articulate generalizations/idealizations of the categories of experience as maps and models which can be described as *second order abstracting*. Local interaction in the modern world, therefore, necessarily includes the formulation and interpretation of second order abstractions as one aspect of what we are doing together in organizations. Certainly, to be included in groups of managers one must be a skilled participant in the dominant discourse conducted in terms of second order abstractions. In our immersion, our pre-occupation in the game of ordinary, everyday organizational life, we are together meaningfully patterning our interactions by drawing upon both the first and second order abstractions which have evolved in our community and in so doing we are together changing the abstractions in our local interaction. We are largely unconscious of how we are relying upon abstractions and find it difficult to notice just how readily we reify second order abstractions that covers over how we are particularizing them in our pre-occupation in the game.

We can now compare more formally the meaning of the terms abstracting and immersing, as I want to use them in understanding organizational continuity and change. The most common understanding of abstract is that it denotes theory as the opposite of something practical. However, the word 'abstract' comes from the Latin preposition 'ab' meaning 'away' and the verb 'trahere' meaning 'to draw' so that 'abstrahere' means to 'draw away from'. Therefore, in this original sense, the meaning of 'to abstract' is 'to draw away from, to separate from'. All forms of thinking about experience necessarily involve a first order abstracting or drawing away from that experience. However, what Scott describes in the state simplifications required for the control of the modern state is a further second order abstraction, a further drawing away from local experience. What Taylor describes as the buffered, detached individual separated from the world, including the body, is also clearly an abstraction, a drawing away from ordinary, everyday felt, bodily experience. Looked at in this way, it makes little sense to contrast abstract as theory with an opposite of practical, because you might say that it is quite practical to draw a map even though the map is abstract in that it draws away from the terrain it maps. Instead, the opposite of abstract in the sense I am using it is 'immersed'.

The word 'immerse' comes from the Latin 'immergere' where 'mergere' means 'to plunge or dip' and 'in' means into. Therefore, the word 'immerse' means to be absorbed in some interest or situation. The words 'infuse', meaning 'to pour into' or instil, and the word 'absorb', meaning to 'swallow up the identity of', to be 'engrossed', are also candidates for opposition to 'abstract' but I think 'immerse' better describes what I am trying to get at. Immerse then means devoting oneself fully to some interest or situation, to thrust or throw oneself into that situation, to be swallowed up by or to be enveloped by that situation, and to engage others to be so immersed. It has the meaning of engaging deeply, engrossing the attention of, involving, overwhelming and has a strong connotation of unconscious processes. The porous self and the early forms of tax collection can all be understood as the experience of immersion in local interactions and situations. Nevertheless, to live simply immersed in this way would be to live a life devoid of all thought, reflection or meaning making. Since humans have always sought to make meaning they must also always have been paradoxically immersing and abstracting from experience in explorative forms of reflecting on the generalization and idealization of experience and articulating them in narrative and philosophy as first order abstraction. In using the term immersing, I am not engaging in a nostalgic return to some kind of artificially enchanted world but rather signalling an exploration of what being immersed in our experience of interaction means in an irretrievably disenchanted modern world. Furthermore, I am not suggesting that there is a more primitive, more authentic experience that we have lost and must return to. I am also explicitly not holding up the activity of immersing in experience without thought as somehow superior. I am trying to point to the paradoxical activity in which there is no meaning without abstraction and nothing for meaning to be about without immersion. I am also not arguing that there is something regrettable about second order abstraction because without it there could be no modern states or modern science. What I am inviting is the paying of attention to the consequence we so easily slip into of splitting second order abstractions off from our experience of immersing in local interaction and what that leads to by further elaborating on what the activities of abstracting and immersing involve.

Abstracting from the experience of local interaction

The activity of abstracting is basically a form of interaction between people in which they simplify the complexity of their own ordinary, everyday interactions and also that of others some distance from them, in an effort to make meaning of what they are doing and also of what more distant others are doing. This involves generalizing across many unique experiences through forming categories and so constitutes abstracting, because it is taking away the micro diversity, the specific context, of ordinary local interaction in ordinary, local physical situations. First order abstracting is the activity of creating mental categories of experience, including the experience of objects, through narrative and through philosophic propositions. Abstracting is an activity that requires some detachment and a focus on phenomena in imagination from the outside, often positing 'hidden mechanisms'. This is the imaginative construction of a unity of experience as a 'whole' and because this is the activity of imagination it is quite different to the notion of the objective observer. So I would define first order abstracting as interaction between people in which they are articulating, as categories of experience, some simplification, some generalization/idealization, of what is emerging across the larger population that they are part of. They may well be using narratives, myths and philosophical frameworks to exercise control over others from a distance. Second order abstracting, however, is an activity of more precise categorizing, measuring and deliberately operating on the categories to construct models. The intention is explicitly that of exerting some form of control. This also extends to simplifying the local interactions of others with whom they are not involved but want to exercise control over from a distance or resist the attempts those others are making to exert control.

This activity of second order abstracting involves:

- *Objectifying* and categorizing. Here phenomena from celestial bodies down to social patterns, modes of thinking and individual human feelings are placed in well-defined bounded 'spaces' where differences within categories are obliterated and all difference is located at the boundary.
- *Measuring* the quantitative aspects of these categories (and nowadays the qualitative too by means of quantitative proxies) using *standardized* measures.
- *Averaging* out differences within categories and interactions between categories.
- *Analyzing* the data so produced using mathematical, statistical and other analytical techniques.
- Selecting regularities and stabilities and forming hypotheses about relationships between entities, particularly *causal connections* often involving, by deduction, some hidden mechanism or whole.
- *Modelling*, forecasting, specifying probabilities with given distributions of variances, mapping, articulating rules and schemas.
- *Prescribing rules*, laws and moral norms.
- *Setting targets*, planning, monitoring and envisioning.

The scientific method is of course the paradigmatic example of the activity of second order abstracting but as we have seen earlier, such abstracting is also an essential activity for governing the modern state and listing the aforementioned activities involved makes it immediately clear that the governance of modern organizations also depends very much on the activity of second order abstracting. In all these cases, the mode removes diversity, indeed, that is its aim. Modelling inevitably leaves behind real people, replacing them with simplified averages. Even complex evolutionary models[19] which do introduce some diversity still simplify in a second order abstracting manner. Therefore, the activity of second order abstracting produces articulations of generalizations and idealizations in relation to hypothetical wholes which have the effect of focusing on what is believed to be important across a whole population, and this could and often does render invisible the experience of local interaction. This is by no means a criticism, because without the activity of second order abstracting there could be no modern state or policies of improvement. Nevertheless, this comes at a cost which a more complex, paradoxical way of thinking may make more evident. In reflecting an ideology of order, rationality, harmony, design, control and improvement, the activity of second abstracting does change the world and is essential for the kind of lives we live in modernity. The question is just how such abstracting changes the world. Furthermore, second order abstracting does render rationally invisible the disorder, diversity, deviance, conflict, compromise, manipulation, cheating, trickery, power plays, concealing and revealing of ordinary everyday experience which also change the world and so also need to be understood.

Immersing in local interaction

We can contrast the activity of first and second order abstracting with that of immersing which is an activity of bringing together, filling in, expanding, elaborating, complexifying and taking into account greater detail and diversity. In other words, it is what Bourdieu calls our pre-occupation with the game, our experience of the habitus in which we live, our direct involvement in our ordinary, everyday local interactions. Such activity, essentially ideology-based acts of choice, inevitably generates conflict. Immersing, therefore, refers to activities taking the form of:

- The ordinary, everyday politics of life. This is our ongoing negotiation with others, including our attempts to persuade and manipulate those others using techniques ranging from the use of rhetorical ploys to the use of emotional blackmail and the techniques of domination. Second order abstractions, especially those claiming to accord with science, are very powerful rhetorical ploys in the modern world and can certainly be used as techniques of domination but they do also create greater 'visibility' from a distance and so make some forms of improvement possible.
- The patterning of the power relations between people. Patterns of power relations between people reflect the dynamics of ideologically based group inclusion and exclusion which establish individual and collective identities. The ability to express and utilize second order abstractions, which reflect powerful modern ideologies of control and improvement, is of major importance in the inclusion-exclusion dynamics of modern organizations.
- Acts of politeness and face-saving. Analysis of the microinteractions of individuals in a workplace reveals how politeness is a fundamental aspect of power relations.[20]

Politeness is essential to maintaining good social relations and takes the form of political acts required to gain the cooperation of others, especially powerful others. Civility requires us to smile and exchange routine pleasantries, especially when the other has the power to harm or reward us, even if we privately despise that other. In local interaction, people are testing, challenging, supporting and undermining so as to shift or sustain patterns of power relations. Mostly, we do this by avoiding direct confrontational challenges but use instead socially acceptable, polite ways involving humour, irony, sarcasm and social banter. How to do this will depend upon the evolved habitus, the generalizations and abstractions across a population.

- Practicing the arts of resistance. Subordinate groups of people in organizations often have to adopt a strategic pose when dealing with the more powerful in which they express compliance in the 'public transcripts' (legitimate themes in the dominant discourse) couched in terms of abstractions. But they also find other ways of expressing what they think and feel amongst themselves in 'hidden transcripts' (shadow themes) in which they block, subvert and countermand the abstract categories imposed upon them. The contradictions and tensions expressed in the hidden transcripts, and between them and the strategic pose, have a major impact on what happens.
- Denial, scapegoating and blaming as defensive ways of living with the anxieties of ordinary, everyday life. Talking in terms of second order abstractions may serve the purpose of providing social defences against anxiety in organizations.
- The spontaneity and improvisation required of us if we are to respond appropriately in the unique contingent situations we so often face.
- The attachment to others, as well as the empathy with, and trust in, those others, which enables us to find fulfilment in what we do and also aggression, competition, rivalry, mistrust and hatred.
- The creative imagination of alternative ways of living and doing and the inevitable destruction of others' ways of living.
- Altruism and generosity as well as selfishness and meanness.

So, in the local interaction of making the general specific and the ideal functional in conversation with each other, people are negotiating their next actions in ways that have emerged and continue to emerge and evolve as patterns of power, identity and ideology. Furthermore, it is in local interaction that people perform acts of both first and second order abstraction, and it is in such local interaction that the meaning of these abstractions emerges.

It is in the interplay of the intended and unintended actions, taking all of the aforementioned forms, that we perpetually construct our future. It is in the interplay of all of these activities that the narrative and propositional themes of organizational life emerge and are both sustained and transformed at the same time. I now want to explore how one might think about both first and second order abstracting as activities performed in local interaction and finding their meaning in that interaction.

Local interaction and the production of abstractions

While first/second order abstracting and immersing can be understood as opposites for purpose of analysis, they can never be separated in our experience of life and, for modern people, this includes second order abstracting. For example, second order abstracting as described earlier is an activity that people engage in together in ordinary local interaction: scientists, administrators, managers, policy makers, and analysts are interacting daily in their own local communities to produce standards, measures, models, forecasts, targets, plans and monitoring reports. Second order abstracting is itself one pattern of local interaction, one way of immersing in local interaction as suggested in the preceding section. In addition, those engaging in the activity of abstracting are not simply adopting a distanced, analytical attitude – they are also deeply immersed in their worlds of abstraction. Richard Dawkins, the popularizing scientist of evolution, provides a dramatic example in his latest books and documentary films in which he displays enormous passion for the scientific abstraction of evolutionary theory and righteous anger at those who contest it. Scientists are immersed in their science and the ideology of that science. They are also immersed in the politics of funding their work. In fact, abstractions are not only emerging in local interaction in one group, but they come to have meaning in how they are taken up in the local interactions of other groups. Abstractions, by their very nature as generalizations and simplifications, can only be reflected in conduct through the ways in which people are interpreting them in their own contingent, local interactions. They have to be particularized or functionalized. So a chief executive who, after the local interaction of discussion with colleagues, announces a new vision will discover what this means in how others take it up, or not, in many other local interactions.

The activity of second order abstracting necessarily involves the postulating of an entity outside of our local experience and we easily come to believe that it actually exists, that we can be outside of it, observe it and then 'move' it around. This kind of belief in second order abstractions is the foundation of today's dominant discourse about organizations and management. What is striking about such formulations is just how thoroughly people disappear from view. For example, I recently made a contribution to a program aimed at developing the strategy competence of senior managers at a major international corporation. I listened to the session just before I was due to talk. The session took the form of a report back by small groups on their discussion of a number of case studies of strategic success and failure in other large companies. The conversation ran entirely in terms of abstract entities. *Toyota* was said to have decided to enter the Chinese market and an intense discussion followed on why *Toyota* had done this, what *China* expected in return and whether it had been the 'right' strategy or not. The whole discussion was purely speculative since none of the discussants, including the presenter, had any involvement with *Toyota* and few if any had actually been to China. When a particular decision looked puzzling, discussants looked for rational reasons for *Toyota* having made it and if they could find none they concluded that it had been a mistake. No one ever suggested that we might need to understand the figuration of power relations amongst senior groups of managers at *Toyota* or that the special interests and private agendas of senior managers and their Chinese counterparts might have had something to do with the decisions. It took only a few minutes discussion at the start of my session for participants to see just how abstract their discussion had been and how totally absent human beings had been.

Second order abstracting is a major activity in organizations today. It is also a major aspect of organizational research and management education. Economic, industrial, and organizational trends are abstractions. Strategy discussions are abstraction. Vision and mission statements are not only abstract generalizations but also idealizations of those abstractions. Targets set for public sector organizations, or any other organization for that matter, are abstractions. However, to label as second order abstractions so many of the activities that take up people's time in any organization is not to denigrate or dismiss such activities. Scott[21] strongly makes the point that large-scale change and improvement does require second order abstraction. However, he also insists that the state simplification, or abstraction, taken on its own cannot accomplish change or improvement. The second order abstraction must be interpreted in terms of local contingent situations in the everyday practical activities of people in local situations if they are to have the potential for beneficial effect. Many organizations create climates of fear which suppress local interaction. We have a tendency to become so immersed in the abstractions of models and plans that we collapse the practical art of local interaction into a stereotypical activity called 'implementation' and as a result, we lose sight of what is happening until it is too late. It is not difficult to see the strength of this point in modern corporations. For example, major banks do have systems of regulation and control which should prevent rogue traders taking financial positions which jeopardize the whole organization. However, these regulations can easily be reinterpreted, ignored or circumvented as we repeatedly see. To think that it is enough to set up an abstract system is to be in constant danger of unpleasant surprises. What is called for then is a renewed attention to everyday forms of experience and how particular first and second order abstractions are being taken up in ways which might be helpful but also in ways which might be harmful. Shifting the focus to local interaction will open up the possibility of reflecting on the usefulness or otherwise of the abstracting activity we now so blindly undertake in completely taken-for-granted ways.

Conclusion

The dominant organizational discourse is based on the view that an organization is a systemic whole which changes when powerful individual agents objectively observe it, intentionally redesign it and then intervene in it to implement the redesign. In the terms I have used in this chapter, this is a way of thinking entirely in terms of second order abstractions which removes us from our experience of locally interacting with each other, indeed rendering us rationally blind to the importance of ordinary everyday experience. There is almost no attempt to hold these second order abstractions in some kind of paradoxical tension with the activity of immersing in local interaction which always reflects the habitus, the game. It is in local interaction that the generalized second order abstractions have any effect as reflected in specific actions. It is in local interaction that both the first and second order abstractions are sustained and have meaning, so to be blind to it is to block the meaning of the abstractions. When we publicly pronounce on organizations, management and leadership, we do so in the terms of the dominant discourse, the public transcript, which actually blocks awareness of our immersion in local interaction and its hidden transcripts. However, when we go about the ordinary daily business of managing and leading we are always pre-occupied in the game and rarely reflect upon this pre-occupation or try to articulate it in some general form. To do so would be to engage in both first and second order abstracting. Therefore, on the one hand, we examine what we are doing in abstract ways that cover over what we are actually doing and when we are immersed in what we are actually doing, we avoid the activity of abstracting through which we might understand it. A key question then becomes how we might focus our attention on immersing in local interaction in a manner that brings to it the abstracting activity of thought. For example, in reflection, how am I to make sense of the activities of goal setting, planning, envisioning and stating values?

First, the argument of this chapter is that they are all activities of second order abstraction which reflect widespread ideologies of control and improvement. Second, far from simply carrying out the scientific rationality of analysis and calculation, people are highly immersed in organizational abstracting activity. This activity is carried out in local interaction characterized by everyday politics and power plays as described in the preceding sections. People tend to become so immersed in the activity of second order abstracting that they do not take a reflexive, reflective attitude to what they are doing. They may well be using the abstractions primarily as ways of saving face, defending against anxiety and practicing domination and oppression. Nevertheless, some of the abstractions are simplifications which are essential to modern corporate governance. However, the abstractions are always articulations of the general and the ideal and they must therefore be particularized in local interaction if they are to have any impact. In addition, of course, those formulating the abstraction are making a gesture whose meaning can only emerge in many, many local interactions.

So what is the implication? When we understand that what we are doing when we are planning and controlling an organization is the activity of abstracting, this immediately generates a much more reflective approach to what we are doing. We can have important conversations where we explore how the abstractions we are proposing might be taken up in local interactions. We can ask whether the abstraction will be harmful, because it could provoke very undesirable local responses. We might come to see that local acts of deviance and resistance are part of how organizations are sustained and at the same time transformed. However, such conversational activity will never be easy, because in questioning particular abstractions we are threatening current ideologies and patterns of power relations, peoples' very identities. There can be no universal, utopian prescriptions of being more open.

Notes

1   de Certeau, M. (1988) *The Practice of Everyday Life*, Berkeley, CA: University of California Press, p. ix.
2   Taylor, C. (2007) *A Secular Age*, Cambridge MA: The Belknap Press of Harvard University Press.
3   Elias, N. (1939/2000) *The Civilizing Process*, Oxford: Blackwell.
4   Elias, N. (1953/1987) *Involvement and Detachment*, London: Blackwell.
5   Ibid. p. 10.
6   Scott, J. C. (1998) *Seeing Like a State*: *How Certain Schemes to Improve the Human Condition Have Failed*, New Haven: Yale University Press.
7   Scott, J. C. (1990) *Domination and the Arts of Resistance*: *Hidden Transcripts*, New Haven: Yale University Press.
8   Scott, J. C. (1998) *Seeing Like a State*: *How Certain Schemes to Improve the Human Condition Have Failed*, New Haven: Yale University Press.
9   Ibid. p. 44.
10 Ibid. p. 44.
11 Ibid, p. 46.
12 Scott, J. C. (1990) *Domination and the Arts of Resistance*: *Hidden Transcripts*, New Haven: Yale University Press.
13 Stacey, R. D. (2001) *Complex Responsive Processes in Organizations*: *Learning and Knowledge Creation*, London: Routledge; Stacey, R. (2003) *Complexity and Group Processes*: *A Radically Social Understanding of Individuals*, London: Brunner-Routledge; Stacey, R. D. (2007) *Strategic Management and Organisational Dynamics*: *The Challenge of Complexity*, 5th ed., London: Pearson Education.
14 Bourdieu, P. (1998) *Practical Reason*: *On the Theory of Action*, Cambridge: Polity Press.

15 Elias, N. (1939/2000) *The Civilizing Process*, Oxford: Blackwell; Elias, N. (1970) *What is Sociology?*, New York: Columbia University Press; Elias, N. (1989) *The Symbol Theory*, London: Sage Publications.
16 Bourdieu, P. (1998) *Practical Reason*: *On the Theory of Action*, Cambridge: Polity Press, pp. 77–78.
17 Ibid. p. 80.
18 Ibid. p. 81.
19 Allen, P. M. (2000) 'Knowledge, Ignorance and Learning', *Emergence, Complexity & Organization*, 2(4), 78–103; Allen, P. M. (2001) 'What is Complexity Science? Knowledge of the Limits of Knowledge', *Emergence, Complexity & Organization*, 3(1), 24–42.
20 Holmes, J. and Stube, M. (2003) *Power and Politeness in the Workplace*: *A Sociolinguistic Analysis of Talk at Work*, London: Pearson Education.
21 Scott, J. C. (1998) *Seeing Like a State*: *How Certain Schemes to Improve the Human Condition Have Failed*, New Haven: Yale University Press.

6   Understanding organizations as social processes

The interplay of abstracting and
immersing producing outcomes
no one chooses

In the last chapter, I pointed to how Western thinking evolved from a mode that took the
form of a tension between immersing in experience and abstracting from that experience
through categorizing it (first order abstracting) to a mode that focused increasingly on
second order abstracting in which the first order categories of experience were used to
map and model not just the natural world but also the social world. This increasingly
drew even further away from the local interaction of immersing in experience itself.
Thought came to focus so heavily on second order abstractions of systems and models,
understood as science, that when it was applied to human organizations, the ordinary
reality of the experience of local interaction between actual human bodies disappeared
from view as attention was focused on objectively operating on abstractions as if they
were reality. I suggested that it was this movement in thought to second order abstraction, split off from immersion in local interaction, that led to the belief that organizations
could be designed and manipulated by objective observers. The result is an inadequate
way of thinking about organization and management that covers over the simple organizational reality of local interacting and leaves us without satisfying ways of understanding what is currently happening to organizations. In Chapter 4, I reviewed the application
of the complexity sciences as science or as metaphor and concluded that these applications have generated some insight into the dynamics of organizations but have primarily
simply reproduced the prescriptions of the dominant discourse in somewhat more esoteric language. This is not surprising when one notices how those applying complexity
sciences both as science and as metaphor focus their attention on the second order
abstraction of system or on somewhat mystical wholes and in doing so banish ordinary,
bodily human activity from view. It seems to me that there is a pressing need to develop
modes of thought in which there is a tension between immersing in ordinary daily experience of local interaction and abstracting (first and second order) from that experience,
also itself understood as emerging in local interaction, in order to understand what we
are doing.

In thinking about the dominant discourse on organizations and management, Chapter 2
traced how the professionalization of management involved identification with the
scientist in the position of an objective observer of some phenomenon. I pointed to how
when this mode is applied to organizations we get a rationalist causality which applies
to the objectively observing manager making choices about an object called the organizational system which is subjected to formative causality. The difficulty is that, unlike
natural scientists, who are dealing with natural phenomena quite distinct from themselves, managers trying to take a similarly objective position are in fact observing the
human interactions in which they are themselves inextricably involved. The strange

result of the dual causality is that sometimes a manager is thought of as the objective observer, standing outside the system making rational choices about the system, and sometimes the same person is thought of as a part of a system and so subject to its formative cause in which there can be no choice in the role of part. This difficulty was recognized a long time ago in the development of second order systems thinking.[1] So while first order, or hard, systems thinking regarded the split between observer and human system as unproblematic and simply took for granted the real existence of the system, the second order, or soft, systems thinkers suggested redrawing the boundary of the system to include the observer. It was recognized that this led to infinite regress, because there always had to be something outside the system doing the boundary drawing. This problem was usually brushed aside as practically unimportant.[2] However, the more recent development of second order systems thinking does represent an attempt to address the organizational reality of decision-making in complex uncertain problem situations. So how does it help us to understand what we are doing in local interaction?

Second order systems thinking

Second-order systems thinking is built on the understanding that human beings determine the world they experience (constructivist psychology) and this requires that managers and others should reflect upon how they operate as perceiving and knowing 'observers' in a continual attempt to be aware of their own frameworks of understanding.[3] Obstructions to change lie in the minds of the members of an organization, that is, in their mental models, but some systems thinkers believe that it is not practically feasible to surface these mental models and change them, as many learning organization theorists believe. Instead, they argue that members of an organization should participate in formulating an idealized design of the future they desire and create ways of achieving it.[4] This represents a shift in ideology from 'command and control' to teamwork and democratic participation. It is argued that human systems are best understood as systems of meaning (ideas, concepts and values) and learning which are purposeful because of a decision maker who can produce change in performance measures, a designer whose design influences the decision maker, a design aimed at maximizing value and a built-in guarantee that the purpose can be achieved.[5] Great importance is also placed on ethics, and it was held that the aim of systems thinking was to emancipate people from domination so that they could participate on a free and equal basis in the process of system design, that is, in the design of their own thinking. The way in which particular views are privileged over others was to be identified[6] and exposed so that people could be liberated from dominant worldviews. What this move does is substitute a democratic group for the individual designer of the system. The understanding of a system or the design of a system is now a task for a team in dialogue with each other. Therefore, the idea of human systems as systems of meaning is closely linked to an emphasis on participation as equality and an idealized, democratic freedom as prescriptions for better ways to manage human affairs.

Checkland,[7] in developing his soft systems methodology (SSM), also regarded systems as mental constructs of observers in the process of enquiry, meaning and intention. SSM approaches a problem situation on the basis that people possess free will rather than being subjected to forces beyond their control and because of this, they must be involved in any changes to the systems they create. The aim of the methodology is to integrate multiple viewpoints of free participants in order to assist them *to predict and control the changes to their systems* in vague situations in which there are no agreed goals. The initial phase of analysis should *not* be pursued in systems terms but should build up what Checkland calls a 'rich picture' of the problem situation. This is to avoid jumping too rapidly to conclusions about representing the situation in systemic terms. In the next phase, a number of systems are drawn from the 'rich picture'. These are systems regarded as relevant to improving the problem situation and each system represents a particular viewpoint, because it is not obvious which system design is appropriate to the particular problem situation. The third phase is the construction of a number of system models which are not blueprints for the design of an objective system but conceptual models contributing to a debate about change. SSM has strands: a cultural strand taking a cultural view of the social systems, roles, norms and values, as well as the politics and sources of power; and a logical analytic strand. Checkland, therefore, advocated an interpretive approach to systems in which account is taken of the social rules and practices of participants in a problem situation. Intertwined with designed intervention is an investigation of the process of designing the intervention itself and the culture and politics this process involves. In short, people are being advised to think of their interaction with each other as creating a system of values, culture, ideas, power interests, social relations and so on. SSM helps to *manage relationships by orchestrating a process* through which organizational actors can learn about accommodations to each other that are feasible and desirable. Managers are supposed to step out of the hurly-burly of ongoing events to make sense of these events and apply structured, systemic thinking to them. The use of systems models is meant to facilitate social processes of inquiry in which social reality is constructed.

More recently, the earlier approaches to second order systems thinking have been critiqued in what has come to be called critical systems thinking.[8] They are concerned with problem situations faced by people and how they may be assisted by systems thinkers to deal more rationally with those problem situations, understood in terms of wholes. It is assumed that people are facing a systemic problem or issue to which they must find a solution or answer in order to act. Systems thinkers seek to be as comprehensive as possible in their analyses but, because everything is connected to everything else, it is impossible to be totally comprehensive, making it essential to form boundary judgments. Boundaries are social and personal constructs that define the limits of the knowledge to be taken as pertinent (first-order system) and the people who may legitimately be considered as decision makers or stakeholders (second-order system). It is the inclusion of stakeholders that yields the second-order system, and this means that there are no experts and that far from being comprehensive, systems thinking highlights the bounded nature of understanding. However, systems thinkers need to widen boundaries so as to sweep in more information, because, even though understanding will never be comprehensive, it can be greater than what we currently have. Since everything is connected to everything, there are multiple realities. It is therefore necessary to make many different boundary judgments in any situation and this requires using many different theories and methodologies, which means tailoring a mix of systems methods to the situation and varying them during the work of systemic intervention. Systemic intervention is always purposive and the purpose is improvement, that is, the realization of a desired consequence that can be sustained indefinitely. Systems thinking is a holistic way of thinking that respects profound interconnectedness and pays attention to emergent properties in reaction to the reductionism of positivist science. It puts people, with their different beliefs, purposes, evaluations and conflicts, at the center of its concerns so that the essence of critical systems thinking is critical and social awareness.[9] Systems thinkers use models to try to learn about behavior. The essentials of critical systems thinking are commitment, pluralism and emancipation or improvement. It aims to help individuals realize their potential.

Soft and critical thinkers, then, use the notion of system as a description of how people might effectively think about their problems and opportunities as wholes, so paying attention to interconnections. The aim of doing this is to make better decisions, improve the lives of people and free them from oppression. To the extent that they see the notional systems as tools and techniques which interdependent humans could use to make better decisions, they escape Kant's stricture against understanding individuals as parts of a system and therefore lacking any freedom. Thinking about organizations as first order systems and individuals as parts of them is what Kant argued against.

However, there are also problems, I think, with the approaches of soft and critical systems thinkers. The belief is that decision-making processes in groups, organizations and societies can be greatly improved if those involved avoid commitment to a particular perspective. Instead, they should engage in dialogues, hold their assumptions in abeyance and explore with each other different ways of understanding their situation. I would argue that this is a highly idealized notion and I do not think that it is possible for people to follow this advice. The perspective we take on the world is intimately tied up with our very identities and we cannot easily change who we are as if our identities were simply interchangeable lenses. If the way we together make sense of our world is so much a part of who we are, is in fact a vital aspect of our identities, then putting on one lens after another would mean frequently changing identities, and pluralism implies that this is as easy as changing our spectacles. This is an idealized way out of conflict. People do not simply alter perspectives as if they did not matter – they kill each other for them, because they are aspects of collective identity. Despite the concern with the social, with political action, power and freedom, the second order systemic way of looking at these does not accommodate their ordinary conflictual nature, and it retains the primacy of the individual.

Second order systems thinkers seek to include the observer in the system but preserve a dualistic causal framework. Rational observers are to define problem situations, draw boundaries, and develop solutions. These thinkers do deal with power and ethics in very particular ideologically based ways. None of the soft or critical systems thinkers explain how people actually do go about dealing with ordinary life in organizations in which it is very unusual to make decisions using the procedures of second order systems thinkers. Instead, they present prescriptions for dealing more effectively with problem situations. This heavily prescriptive rather than descriptive stance points to the underlying ideology to do with participation and the validation of alternative viewpoints. The causal duality is a characteristic of all of the soft and critical systems thinking and this can be seen when they write about someone choosing an appropriate systems-based methodology. This immediately implies autonomous individuals subject to rationalist causality. The person(s) choosing between different types of systems thinking are exercising some kind of choice based on their observation of context and systems methodologies. Someone, the researcher, consultant or manager, has to form a judgment about the nature of the context of a problem situation and select the appropriate methodology. However, once the person has selected a methodology, that methodology is then applied to interacting humans, including the person(s) choosing the methodology. They are then subject to the formative causality of the system they have chosen. This is the dual causality and 'both . . . and' thinking that eliminates paradox. For me, even the move to second order systems thinking does not help to understand what people are actually doing in their daily lives in organizations, although the approaches to problem situations developed by second order systems thinkers represent a major improvement, in that this thinking focuses attention on connections between situations and people. In their daily lives, people may sometimes talk about problem situations and good ways of making rational decisions but mostly they are pre-occupied in organizational games.

Different ways in which the term 'system' is used

I reach the conclusion that even second order systems thinking does not do the work I have in mind in exploring and understanding ordinary, everyday local interaction people actually engage in. I am interested in what we are actually already doing rather than what we should be doing to make improvements. So just what is it that I want to move toward and what is it that I want to move away from? I want to present a temporal responsive processes perspective on ordinary local interaction which does not appeal to the notion that an organization is a system because of the split off abstracting this involves. As a first step in making such a move I want to specify what I understand to be the meanings of the term 'systems' and which of those meanings are central to the designed view of change that I wish to contest. I want to do this to avoid a view that simply dismisses all systemic notions in a wholesale manner. The word system can be used as:

1. A coherent, systematic whole of thought. For example, Hegel[10] referred to his philosophy of the nature of thought and of the historical and social development of humans as his system.
2. A regulative idea or hypothesis about the nature of the development of phenomena in nature. For example, Kant[11] held that it was useful to think of living phenomena *as if* they were wholes formed by interacting parts to develop a mature form of that nature already present at its inception. He held that this way of thinking could not be applied to human action because human actors are rational, autonomous individuals who cannot therefore be subject to, a part of, any system without losing their rational autonomy, their very selves.
3. A particular kind of conceptual model as in first order, hard systems thinking with its general systems theory, cybernetic and systems dynamics models of human groupings as systems which came to be regarded as actually existing.[12] Individuals came to be understood as parts of organizational and social systems.
4. A way of thinking about individual mind as information processing devices.[13] For example, cognitivist psychology[14] is very much based on this systemic idea.
5. A way of thinking about human communication as a cybernetic system of transmission consisting of senders and receivers.[15]
6. A living system. For example, Senge[16] and Burke[17] both prescribe thinking about an organization as a system that is actually living.
7. A particular kind of conceptual model as in second order, soft, and critical systems thinking where the systems model is understood to be in the mind of the observer who thinks of organizations as if they were systems.[18]
8. A complex system in which self-organization at the level of the agents produces emergent order at the global level.[19]

9. A tool or technique specifying rational sequential steps which observers and decision makers should use to structure and shape the problem situations facing them, find rational solutions and make rational decisions. I have in mind here the aspects of soft and critical systems thinking that focus attention on tools and techniques for rational problem solving by free agents, rather than thinking of organizations 'as if' they were systems. For example, these tools should be used by facilitators to facilitate rational discussion by groups of stakeholders to identity a plurality of ways in which problem situations can be understood as systems.[20]
10. A bureaucracy and hierarchy, that is as a comprehensive, interlocking set of procedures and actions. For example, there are accounting systems, quality assurance systems, legal systems, property systems, health systems and transport systems.

In the rest of this chapter and in the ones following it, when I refer to systems thinking I am referring to meanings 3, 6, 7 and 8 which, although each is different to some extent, together present a way of thinking about the nature of an organization as a system that is now completely taken for granted by most organizational practitioners and researchers. I am identifying systems thinking with a particular way of positing or thinking about an organization as an organization. I also include meanings 4 and 5 which provide a completely compatible theory of the mental functioning of individual humans and this naturally includes how they function as members of organizations, as well as a compatible theory of communication. Meanings 3 to 8 have a number of important features in common. They provide coherent ways of modelling organizations as whole, global phenomena, which enable powerful members at an organization's center to 'read' the situation at the macro level across the whole organization and make decisions in a rational manner, so ensuring some form of central control. However, all models regard human beings as agents in, or parts of, a system which are simplifications taking the form of averages, probabilities and regularities. Such simplifications remove difference and abstract from the detail of contingent situations and the complex detail of local interactions, which indeed are made rationally invisible by the focusing of attention on the abstraction. This is true even of the models found in the complexity sciences (meaning 8) which do introduce diversity and difference to model complex evolution[21] but cannot model the detail of ordinary human interaction. They all regard rational, cognizing individuals as parts of the organizational whole. Process is understood as the interaction between parts to form the whole which is then often thought of as exerting downward causal forces on the individuals. They all involve a split between observer and organization, between problem and solution, between sender and receiver, and between decision and outcome. They all take for granted the rational designed and planned view of organizational change and in doing so they all constitute second order abstractions which draw attention away from the first order abstraction of categorizing the experience of immersing in the local interaction of ordinary daily life in organizations. They split the world of second order abstractions off from the experience of ordinary bodily interaction. I am interested in developing a way of thinking about organizations which does not appeal in any way to an understanding of organization, which consists of people as agents, as a system with human parts but rather to think of organization as ongoing local interactions of an ordinary kind in which population-wide patterns of organizing emerge. The objection is to thinking about human beings in abstract (second order) ways as parts of a system split off from ordinary experience, which is not an objection to the activity of second order abstracting itself.

Meaning 1, a system of thought, and meaning 2, a hypothesis about systems in the natural sciences, are not meanings with which I am concerned when discussing organizations. When I refer to systems thinking I am also not referring to meaning 10 about hierarchy and bureaucracy since they are formal patterns of relationships and explicit generalized procedures. While the concept of system contained in all of the meanings 3 to 8 has come to occupy a dominant place in the conceptualization of the nature of organization, this has not been accompanied, perhaps surprisingly, by the widespread use of the tools and techniques (meaning 9) developed by communities of systems thinkers in academia and the consulting world. At a recent conference of such practitioners in the UK, they were asked to vote on the importance of their offerings and their conclusion was that while their work had not had zero impact, it also had not spread widely to become a method of making decisions and solving problems, despite its claims to rationality. People in organizations do not normally follow the steps proposed by systems practitioners nor do they follow 'rational' decision making where rational is understood in a technical way. Instead, the organizational reality is that they engage in daily conversation, gossip, political negotiations, power plays, acts of resistance and pursuit of personal agendas: in short local interaction. Moreover, the powerful are hardly likely to enthusiastically back the use of techniques reflecting the ideology of freedom, democracy and emancipation of the people from oppression. Perhaps those presenting the techniques are not taking enough account of the patterns of power relations. However, systemic tools and techniques are often used on special occasions such as strategy 'away days' or when large numbers are involved in highly visible problems. On these special occasions, the tools and techniques (meaning 9) may be useful when they stimulate conversation, local interaction, but in my view, they do run the risk of getting thought stuck at the abstract level of systems which avoids reflection on the messy reality of local interaction.

Systems thinking can be very fruitfully used to design flows of work. The system here is a tool that people use in their communicative interaction as a way of cocoordinating and accomplishing their work. In this view of system, the agent, the part of the system, is an activity not a person For example, although Seddon[22] very occasionally refers to the organization as a system, he devotes most of his book to understanding the system as the way work is designed and managed and holds that this system governs performance. Therefore, he sees customers and the organization's staff using the system to do their work. He distinguishes between value work, meeting the needs of the customer and failure work which is created when customers complain about the failure to meet their needs. He shows how one system design, one based on targets which are always arbitrary numbers, produces increasing levels of failure work. The design problem is to redesign the system to reduce failure work and focus on value work. Instead of targets, which he says should be scrapped, he measures the actual meeting of customer needs. Attending to this can lead to a failure to meet the targets but satisfy the customers. Managing by targets leads to achieving the targets but failing the customers. We have here a system – the parts are tasks interacting with each other to produce the whole task of the organization and performance; there is a boundary as customer demand flows in from outside the task system and customer service flows out. This is a very effective way of thinking about largely predictable but nevertheless highly variable work.

Therefore, I am not arguing against thinking of work-flows as designed systems – to think like this brings a great improvement over ways of thinking that fail to see linkages. I am arguing against thinking of the organization, as organization, consisting of individual people as parts that produce the whole called the organization. I am arguing that an organization is an evolving pattern of interaction, of activity between people and they very frequently employ tools to accomplish this interaction – tools which they design and the design of which can provide a greatly improved understanding of the way tasks are connected as a system to produce purpose. Nevertheless, people are not a system – people employ a system in their action. This is important because otherwise we tend to focus on the tool and ignore the people. Seddon shows clearly how the current system of organizing work generates cheating. Therefore, he is taking account of the people, staff and customers, but does not write about them as being parts of a system, although this may well be what he thinks. For Seddon, taking a systems approach involves managers seeing work-flows as a system. He says they need to think in flow terms of what is flowing from the outside into the system. This means starting with a study of demand to see what is working for customers now, for example, why customers call a local authority. Many work-flow designs separate front and back offices (parts) and so involve transferring pieces of work from one to another. The call comes into the front office and is dealt with by the back office. Seddon says this design blocks and slows down work-flow. I think all of this is certainly very helpful. I am therefore not particularly engaged in a critique of system meanings 9 and 10.

It is the forms 3 to 8 that I want to characterize as systems thinking and challenge by suggesting an alternative complex responsive processes way of thinking which I will cover in the remaining chapters of this book. Before doing that, however, I want to look at three important differences between systems thinking as I have defined it and complex responsive process thinking and these relate to the metaphor of space, the inclusion of the body and the view taken of time.

The spatial metaphor in systems thinking

Systems thinking is fundamentally based on a spatial metaphor. This is clear when we think of an organization as a system that can be given a direction by a leader, which can be steered, intervened in and operated on. All forms of individual psychology that I am aware of, for example, psychoanalysis, humanistic psychology and cognitivism, postulate a mind that is separate from but located in a body. Thinking is said to take place in the mind. The spatial metaphor is so ubiquitous that it is no longer even recognized that when we think in this way we are thinking in terms of a spatial metaphor. The use of the metaphor has now come to constitute common sense, and it seems ludicrous to imagine that we can think in any other way; after all, we live in space, don't we? I think it is important, however, to make a distinction between the actual space in which human bodies live and act and the use of the notion of space as a metaphor for thinking about the nature of actual human bodily acting, particularly in relation to those forms of bodily acting that we call mind and society. Clearly, human bodies live in space and time and the actions of human bodies, as in thinking (mind) and in interacting with others (social), are movements through space over time. This is our experience. Therefore, when I talk to you, I make a sound as the action of my body which takes the form of waves that move through space and over time. When I talk silently to myself, electrochemical changes occur over time across the space of my brain. Here space is actually there in experience. However, when it comes to talking about the nature of those actions of the body that constitute mind and society we are not saying that mind itself or society itself is an actual space somewhere. If we try to say this, then we immediately come up against the problem of identifying just where they are and no one can point to where they are. We can say that the artifacts associated with society, such as buildings, works of art, procedure manuals, books and many others are spaces that exist within spaces, because we can actually point to where they are. However, we cannot point to where society itself is. We can point to the artifacts of institutions, but we cannot point to where the habits/routines constituting social structure are in space, because they only exist in the interactions of bodies.

How then are we to think about the nature of mind and society? We could use space as a metaphor and say that mind is a metaphorical space inside an individual, which contains representations of objects outside that individual. Society is then a metaphorical space outside an individual. However, in thinking in this metaphorical way about mind and society, we are abstracting from our experience of the direct interaction between bodies and of bodies with themselves by postulating the existence of spaces outside that direct interaction. There is the inside space of mind (containing 'the unconscious') and the outside space of society and each of these is then thought to exercise causal powers over the direct interaction between bodies. In other words, the explanations of interaction, the causes of interaction, are to be found in notional, abstracted entities outside that interaction as second order abstractions. It also follows that immediately we think in this way, we are thinking about individual mind and society as different levels and we then have to ask where these levels, again spatial metaphors, actually are in our experience and I, for one, cannot find them.

If we want to stay with the phenomenology of our immediate experience of direct interaction between us and with ourselves, if we want to argue, as I will in subsequent chapters, that individual and social are the singular and plural of the same phenomenon, then we have to avoid thinking about them in terms of spatial metaphors. This does not dismiss the actuality of the space in which we live, but does dismiss the metaphor of space as a way of understanding mind and society. If we want to stay with the phenomenology of the experience of our direct interaction then we can think of mind and society as both being aspects of the same iterative processes of interaction between bodies, and this is essentially temporal rather than spatial movement. However, if we do this, then we have a problem, because now we are not able to appeal to a mind inside and a society outside of us as the causes of our actions. If we have abandoned such causes, how can we then explain how interaction between human bodies is patterned in coherent ways? If we abandon the spatial, systemic way of thinking, we have to look for another way of explaining the coherent patterning of our experience. This is where we need the insights of the complexity sciences to explain just how it is that local interactions produce widespread population-wide coherence over space and time. The complexity sciences demonstrate that iterative, nonlinear interaction can pattern itself in widespread coherent ways without any need to appeal to some cause outside that interaction.

I argue against the use of spatial metaphors in thinking about mind and society, because such metaphors generate unhelpful second order abstractions from our direct experience and because they are ultimately incompatible with thinking of mind and society as human action. Finally, I argue against using such metaphors, because in the light of local interaction between people producing emergent patterns across a population, they are unnecessary. This in no way, however, sidelines the actual space into which we act and within which we bodily live. I have mentioned the need to incorporate into our thinking about organizations our ordinary daily lives and this must mean the actions of our bodies. As I have said before, second order abstractions of systems based on spatial metaphors split off actually bodily action and this has led to a call from a number of thinkers to bring back the body and they talk about embodiment. I think it is important in building the foundations of an alternative way of thinking to look at this notion of embodiment and how the notion of body I want to take up is different.

The notion of 'embodiment'

The term embodiment refers to physical expressions and postures that arise in interacting with the world. If we turn to the dictionary we find that 'to embody' means to give a bodily form to something as in 'the painting (something tangible) embodies (represents) a feeling (something intangible)'; or to represent something in bodily or material form, for example, 'he embodies evil'; or to incorporate in the sense of making something a part of a system or whole. This is consistent with the literature concerned with 'embodiment' where it is taken to be physical movements, actions or states of human bodies that give a form to, or represent, something else, something other than the bodily movement, action or state itself.[23] As soon as we use the term 'embodiment', therefore, it seems to me that we have to be thinking in some kind of dualism to do with, on the one hand, some thing and, on the other hand, the bodily representation of that thing. Questions for me then become: What is it that is being given a form or is being represented by the body? What is the process of bodily forming or representing? What is the nature of the representation or form in the body? I am also interested in why these questions are being explored: What are they a response to, or refutation of? How are these explorations located in the history of thought?

With these questions in mind, I was struck by discussions of the role of embodiment in perception located in the literature on embodied cognition which immediately implies that perception is some wider process in which bodily movements, actions or states play only a part. If we are to say that 'embodiment' plays a role in perception then we are saying that there are other processes which also play a role; we are saying that perception also involves something abstract or nebulous which is not concretely represented or given form as bodily action or physical state. This something abstract is usually taken to be cognition, consciousness and language and these abstractions are contrasted with emotion, pre-reflection and direct bodily communication not involving language, which are taken to be concrete or real in some sense. Therefore, the body and the mind, real emotional experience and intellect, practice and theory, are split off from each other and set up as opposites.[24] Once this is done, an appeal can be made to give more importance to the body.

Discussion of embodiment in the sociology literature[25] talks about a somatic sector of social life, implying that there is some other sector which is not somatic. Cognition is thought to be disembodied and that marginalizes emotion which is embodied. When one abandons dualisms then embodiment makes no sense as a distinct category – all perceiving, thinking, feeling, speaking and doing are the actions of bodies; there is nothing else. There is only a need to stress the role of the body if you have a view of mind and language as abstract processes. As soon as you abandon that view, then talking about embodiment does not make much sense, at least to me. Others[26] refer to the body's 'knowing' in the sense of its finding its way around the environment without, or prior to, conscious direction. Bodies can understand their worlds without recourse to the symbolic (language) or objectifying functions of consciousness. Instead of being directed by consciousness, the intelligent body's movement is directed by connections with the world.

It is the body rather than consciousness that understands the world. What is said here is an equation of the pre-reflective, the pre-discursive, and the unconscious with the body, on the one hand, and consciousness and rationality with something abstract and not of the body, on the other hand. I think this kind of splitting and dualism is typical of the discussions of 'embodiment' that I have come across and it simply sustains the Cartesian duality of mind and body, while confusingly claiming to dissolve it, and then seeks to shift the emphasis from the mind to the body in order to grant the body some kind of special status or agency. In contrast, I will be exploring the writings of those who avoid any such split by regarding all perception, all thinking, all speaking and listening, including silent speaking and listening to oneself, all emotion and feeling, as actions of a body and so involving physical states.

I was then curious about the reasons for elevating one kind of bodily action (emotion, prereflection and nonverbal) above another kind of bodily action (reason, consciousness and language). A literature search for papers on embodiment quickly produces another area in which the term is popular, and this is in feminist studies, some forms of humanistic psychology and New Age spirituality. 'The body' is sometimes seen as the instrument for getting in touch with the true self, true being the self uncluttered by abstract rationality and theorizing. Therefore, the advice is that 'you need to get in touch with your body'; 'you need to listen to your body'; 'you are too much stuck in your head'. The implication is that there is some 'you' separate from 'the body' and that the body 'knows' best. This is a process that is not conscious and the wise agency attribute to the body differs from the cunning agency of the 'the unconscious' only in that the latter is a cauldron of nasty instincts while the former is noble and nice, in touch with more ancient and wiser ways of knowing. I think this is in the tradition of the Romantic idealists such as Herder and also of Rousseau who tended to idealize nature and the expressive function of the body.

Time

The past may be thought of as real events that are independent of any present so that any investigation of the past is a reconstruction of real events that unquestionably occurred in the past. This past is then the background for, the constraint on, dealing with the issues we face in the present. We refer to a given past out of which the issues we are now dealing with have arisen. However, George Herbert Mead[27] argued that we know that a particular reconstruction of the past is questioned and reinterpreted at some later date – each generation rewrites history, indeed each of us tends to reinterpret our own past from time to time. Any present interpretation of the past is therefore open to doubt. This means that the past is not a given to be discovered but is a meaning to be formulated anew in the present. In other words, we know the past through the present. Furthermore, the future is implicated in that the knowledge we gain of the past, the hypotheses we form about the past, depend upon the viewpoint of the present, which will change in the future. In other words, the future will change the meaning of the past. In this way, we construct different pasts and one past displaces and abrogates another. There are coincidences and events that are relatively permanent and this makes possible a translation from one historical account to another but these coincidences are not the object of our knowledge. Each present has a different past in that in each present we interpret the past differently, because we have a different viewpoint and so construct different meanings of past events. The reality of the past that gets into our experience is thus different depending upon our present standpoint. The past can only reach us though our own current frame of reference within which we are interpreting our own present and determining our future. There is a time structure of the present in which the movement of present experience is that of forming and being formed by our reconstruction of the past while forming and being formed by our expectation of the future, all at the same time in the present. We might say that it is the nonlinear nature of this iteration that makes possible both continuity and potential transformation at the same time.

Clearly, human experience is also the experience of what Prigogine[28] called the arrow of time, in the sense that we all know that what has been said cannot be unsaid, and what has been done cannot be undone. We cannot go back in time and unsay or undo. We can only go forward in time and elaborate on what we have said or done. It is also our experience that interacting with each other in one way immediately precludes all alternative ways of interacting and that what happens next will be different from what might have been if we had interacted in one of those alternative ways. It is because the past is not a given but a perpetual construction in the present that we cannot go back to the past. It is because of the potential for small differences to escalate that we cannot retrace our steps. In other words, it is because time has the structure of the living present that we also experience the arrow of time.

Complex adaptive systems as a source domain for analogies of human acting: the theory of complex responsive processes

I have been arguing for a move toward ways of understanding and explaining the reality of our experience of ordinary local interaction in organizations which avoids splitting second order abstractions off from lived experience and focusing attention exclusively on them as I claim is done in systems thinking. Instead, I am pointing to how we need to move from thinking in terms of the spatial metaphor of systems thinking and develop an explanation of the temporal responsive processes of ordinary interactions between human bodies which do not continue any split between body and mind and so do not elevate either intellectual or prereflective, emotional activities to some more fundamental, more real position. The move to temporal responsive processes also means taking a particular view of time which avoids the linear view in which the present is simply a dot separating the past from the future and, instead, takes a nonlinear view of the living present, the present we live in. The question now is how to do this and I want to return to the complexity sciences not as science to be directly applied to human interaction or as metaphor but as source domain for analogies.

One way of transferring knowledge from one domain to another is the use of metaphor, which involves transferring the attributes of an object and the relationships between those attributes from a source domain to a target domain. For example, when one says that wine is like water one is referring to attributes such as wetness and to the chemical structure. When management complexity writers say that an organization is, or is like, a complex adaptive system, they transfer, from the science to organizations, attributes of the scientific models such as large numbers of agents and the relationships between them, such as simple rules of interaction. However, the use of metaphor could be no more than the mere matching of appearance in which there is a transfer of only the attributes of an object in the source domain to an object in the target domain, for example, describing water as being as clear as glass. This device of metaphorical transfer is used in literature, but natural scientists also use it when they employ intuitive insights in model construction. However, having done this, the scientist leaves the original metaphor behind and constructs abstract (second order) models informed by the metaphor. Analogy is often used as a synonym for metaphor but, more precisely,[29] an analogy transfers a relationship, but not the attributes, in the source domain to a similar relationship in the target domain. For example, parts of a machine functioning together to produce integrated motion could be an analogy for departments in an organization functioning together to produce collective action. What is being transferred here is an explanatory structure. Management complexity writers do this when they transfer notions of self-organization as formative cause from the complexity sciences to the human domain. This differs from the metaphor in that it is the relationships without the attributes that are transferred. The analogical transfer, therefore, requires an act of interpreting the attributes of the entities in the relationship. This non-transfer of attributes and the consequent need for careful translation is what distinguishes the analogical from the metaphorical transfer.

In the case of a source domain that is a second order abstract relational structure containing only abstract principles and generalized entities, as in mathematical and computer models, what is transferred from the source to the target domain is this second order abstract set of relational principles without any attributes of the objects. This is done, for example, when notions of causality are transferred from scientific models to the phenomenal target domain. The careful interpretation required to bring in the attributes of the objects in the target domain is done when the mathematical equations, computer simulations and laboratory experiments of the complexity sciences are translated in terms of the features of physical, chemical and biological phenomena in their natural locations. There is no reason why social scientists should not adopt a similar approach, provided that a careful interpretation is made to incorporate the distinctive attributes of human beings. The procedure I intend to follow is one in which the abstract relationships in the theories and the models are taken from the complexity sciences and then interpreted in terms of the phenomena of human organizing and managing. In other words, the approach is to make a translation in terms of human sociology, psychology and philosophy with the purpose of seeing whether this procedure illuminates the experience of the reality of life in organizations.

So what are the models of complexity? The models I am taking as source domain are those of complex adaptive systems which are explored using computer simulations, in which each agent is a computer program, that is, a set of interaction rules expressed as computer instructions. Since each instruction is a bit string, a sequence of symbols taking the form of 0s and 1s, it follows that an agent is a sequence of symbols, arranged in a particular pattern specifying a number of algorithms. These algorithms determine how the agent will interact with other agents, which are also arrangements of symbols. In other words, the model is simply a large number of symbol patterns arranged so that they interact with each other. It is this local interaction between symbols patterns that organizes the pattern of interaction across the whole population of agents since there is no set of instructions organizing that global pattern. The programmer specifies the initial rules, that is, symbol patterns, then the computer program is run, or iterated, and the patterns of interaction across the system, the attractors, are observed. Simulations of this kind of local interaction repeatedly produce population-wide patterns of behavior. In other words, the models are a demonstration of the possibility of the hypotheses that local interaction produces a global pattern. They provide a 'proof' of existence in the medium of digital symbols arranged into algorithmic rules.

For example, in his Tierra simulation, Ray[30] designed one bit string, one symbol pattern, consisting of eighty instructions specifying how the bit string was to copy itself. He introduced random mutation into the bit string replication and limited computer time available for replicating as a selection criterion. In this way, he introduced instability into the replicating process and imposed conditions that both enable and constrain that process. This instability within constraints made it possible for the system to generate different kinds of agents and this diversity generated novel attractors – the model evolved spontaneously without external instruction or centralized control or direction from within. The first attractor was that of exponentially increasing numbers, which eventually imposed a constraint on further replication so that the global pattern was a move from sparse occupation of the computer memory to overcrowding. However, during this process, the bit strings were gradually changing through random bit flipping, so coming to differ from each other. Eventually, distinctively different kinds of bit strings emerged, namely, long ones and short ones. The constraints on computer time favored smaller ones so that the global pattern shifted from one of exponential increase in numbers of long-bit strings, to one of decline in long strings accompanied by an increase in short ones. The model spontaneously produced a new attractor, one that had not been programmed in. In other words, new forms of individual bit string and new overall global patterns emerged at the same time for there can be no global pattern of increase and decline without simultaneous change in the length of individual bit strings and there can be no sustained change in individual bit-string lengths without the overall pattern of increase and decline. Individual bit-string patterns, and the overall pattern of the system, are forming and being formed by each other, at the same time. To repeat, the new attractor is evident both for the whole population and for the individual bit strings themselves at the same time. Furthermore, the new attractors are not designed but emerge in local interaction, technically known as self-organization, so that the individual agents are together forming the global pattern of interaction while at the same time being formed by these global patterns. No individual bit string can change in a coherent fashion on its own since random mutation in an isolated bit string would eventually lead to a completely random one. In interaction with other bit strings, however, advantageous mutations are selected and the others are weeded out.

One could make a conceptual separation between the agents as systems at one level and the global pattern as a system at a higher level. This has two important consequences. First, the separation immediately makes it easy to think in terms of a causal dualism in that at the lower level, the individual agents could be said to be determined by efficient cause – if the computer memory space becomes crowded shorten the bit string – while causality at the higher level of the global pattern could be thought of as formative. Second, there is an immediate tendency to focus attention on the global level and develop propositions about general regularities of macro behavior as second order abstractions split off from local interaction. This is what happens in the 'both . . . and' structure of the dominant discourse on organizations, including the way in which complexity sciences are applied as science or metaphor, and it is this that I have been arguing generates modes of thinking about organizations which distance us from the reality of our own experience of local interaction. The paradox of local and population-wide patterning and transformative cause is then lost. The kind of explanation I am trying to put forward is one that avoids the spatial metaphor of levels and so avoids splitting agent interaction and emergent patterns into levels, making possible a mode of thought based on transformative cause.

Returning to Ray's simulation, he is clearly an objective observer external to the simulated system who observes the patterns of behavior it produces and then interprets the changes in symbol patterns in his simulation in terms of biology, in particular, the evolution of life. Using the model as an analogy, he argues that that life has evolved in a similar, self-organizing and emergent manner. Other simulations have been used to suggest that this kind of emerging new attractor occurs only at the edge of chaos where there is a critical combination of both stability and instability and that the evolution of the system is only possible if the agents are diverse, that is heterogeneous rather than homogeneous. The computer simulations thus demonstrate the possibility of the theory's hypotheses in the medium of digital symbols arranged as algorithmic rules. Digital symbols can quite clearly self organize in the dynamics at the edge of chaos to produce emergent attractors of a novel kind, provided that those symbol patterns are richly connected and diverse enough. Natural scientists at the Santa Fe institute and elsewhere then use this demonstration of possibility in the medium of digital symbols as a source of analogy to provide explanations of phenomena in particular areas of interest such as biology. There is no reason I can see why the same procedure should not be adopted in understanding human interaction, particularly given the importance of symbols in that interaction, provided that we make a careful interpretation of the human characteristics of human agents. My argument is that the abstract, nonlinear, iterative relationships of heterogeneous complexity models are analogous to the interactive processes of social evolution.

I suggest the following analogies as the basis for what needs to be interpreted in human terms in the rest of this book.

• *There is **no** analogy between the programmer of the complex adaptive system model and anything in human interaction.* There is no possibility of standing outside human interaction to design a program for it since we are all participants in that interaction and cannot control the interplay of our deliberate actions. When Ray and others use a model of complex adaptive systems to simulate life, they are quite clearly trying to simulate evolutionary processes where there is no outside programmer or designer. They are trying to model self-organizing and emergent phenomena in nature, that is, phenomena that evolve without prior centralized design. Since, they are using a model for this purpose, they naturally have to design the model, at least initially. However, they do not propose any analogy in nature for the modeller of the system – on the contrary, they argue that there is no designer outside nature. If one is trying to understand human organizations as self-organizing and emergent phenomena then one cannot find an analogy for the programmer – it negates the science if the manager is equated with the objectively observing programmer as many management complexity writers do.

• Furthermore, I suggest that *there is **no** analogy between systems and individual humans or their interactions.* This is based on the argument that thinking of human interaction in systems terms involves focusing attention entirely on second order abstractions which distance us from our experience of the reality of local interaction between human bodies. As soon as we cast individuals as parts in a system, we conceptually reify what are ongoing processes and ascribe a causality to human action that does not take account of individual capacities to choose actions which could play into each other to produce novel emergent forms. Furthermore, the simulations of heterogeneous complexity models begin to pose problems for systems thinking. Heterogeneous complexity models take on a life of their own, that is, they evolve in unpredictable and novel ways. It follows that the 'whole' is not there until it has emerged and since it is always evolving, it is never complete. One then has to talk about incomplete or absent wholes and this begins to undermine the usefulness of the very concept of the whole itself. The explanation for unpredictability and novelty has nothing to do with the 'whole'. It lies in the *intrinsic properties of the process of interaction between diverse entities*. The notion of a model that takes on a life of its own also creates problems for the use of the models. If one is modelling a phenomenon with a life of its own then the phenomenon and the model will soon diverge from each other. The usefulness of the model is then restricted to the insight it gives into the general nature of the dynamics. The foregoing points I have been making apply to all systems, whether one thinks of a system as mechanistic or as a living organism. These points apply to hard systems taken to actually exist and to 'as if' systems.

- With regard to human action, the *analogy begins with the individual agent.* The abstract agents in the form of computer instructions on how to relate to other agents are taken by analogy to the human domain by interpreting the concept of the human agent in terms of the human characteristics of consciousness, self-consciousness, emotion, desire, anxiety, capacity for imagination, excitement and spontaneity and ability to choose within limits.

- Central to understanding the agent is the *interaction* of agents in the complexity models which is analogous to the interdependence of individuals and the interplay of individual human intentions and plans described by Elias.[31]

- Furthermore, the *digital symbols of the complexity models are taken as analogies* for the symbols humans use to interact with each other. In other words, it is the aspects of responsive processes in the complex adaptive system models that I suggest provide analogies for human interaction, not the systemic aspects of those models. From a responsive processes point of view *there are no levels of operation*, only degrees of detail in which the phenomenon of interest is examined.

- *The patterns that emerge across a population* of digital agents are analogous to the population-wide patterns (social) which emerge in local interaction in organizations. Chapter 7 will explore processes of societies forming individual minds while being formed by them at the same time, which is analogous to populations of algorithms forming individual algorithms while being formed by them.

- Finally, the *transformative causality* displayed by interaction between heterogeneous entities in the complexity model is analogous to the transformative causality that a number of writers posit in relation to interaction between people – also matters to be dealt with in Chapter 7. This represents a move away from the dual causality of the dominant discourse to the paradoxical transformative causality of 'forming and being formed by at the same time' that will be the basis of the theory developed in the subsequent chapters of this book.

So, instead of talking about complex adaptive systems I will talk about complex responsive processes. Since humans do not always adapt to, or fit in, with each other, it is useful to think of human relating not as adaptive but as responsive and not as system but as temporal process. I therefore claim that the human analogues for complex adaptive systems in the simulations are *complex responsive processes* of relating in organizations. What is to be gained by drawing analogies between complex adaptive systems and human interaction is a clearer understanding of self-organization and emergence and a strong argument that coherent, population-wide patterns can emerge from many, many local interactions. Other insights of importance have to do with unpredictability, the importance of diversity and conflicting constraints and the paradoxical dynamics in which novelty can emerge. In the rest of this book, I want to explore what happens when organizational analogies are sought for in simulations in which there is agent diversity and hence the spontaneous capacity to change. Instead of thinking about the manager or leaders as the analogue of the programmer, I would like to consider the consequences of the manager/leader participating in the complex responsive processes of interacting with others.

We now need to clothe the abstract relationships drawn by analogy from the simulation of complex adaptive systems with the attribute of human agency. This means a turn to philosophy, sociology and psychology. If we want to capture the causality of forming and being formed at the same time, then we must look for an alternative to Kant and his dualisms, individual, individual autonomy and given mental categories and this leads us to Hegel's reaction to Kant's philosophy.

Hegel and the social process

In Kant's transcendental idealism human beings are born with innate forms of thought which order their experience of the world – patterns of thought do not fundamentally depend upon experience and so avoid any accusation of relativism. In the late eighteenth and early nineteenth centuries, some philosophers reacted against this philosophy of inherited ways of knowing and developed romantic idealism, which basically argued that we are born into a society or culture and come to acquire the ways of knowing of that society though our experience of living in it so that knowing is not through inherited universal forms but through ideas that arise in our experience. Romantic idealism moves to focusing on experience itself as a historical process of social consciousness and self-consciousness. In doing this, it represents a powerful break with the notion of the autonomous individual. Hegel's[32] philosophy is a philosophy of evolution, that is, of a living process that takes on successively different forms. These different forms arise in the differences we experience in the world and conflict, contradiction and paradox are the processes through which thought develops: the world of our experience is the world we are creating in our thought. How this way of thinking encompasses cultural relativity but avoids extreme relativism will be described in the following section.

Hegel held that one could not begin, as Kant had done, with an isolated individual subject experiencing the world and then ask how a world of objective experience gets built up out of the inner world of purely subjective experience. Rather, one must begin with an already shared world of subjects making judgments in the light of possible judgments by others. Hegel emphasized the idea of mutual recognition arising in desire, particularly the desire for desire of the other, and argued that there was an intersubjective unity of mutually recognizing agents in the natural world, in which patterns of entitlements of, and commitments to, each other constitute ethical conduct. Human knowing is not simply the result of natural process and does not arise from the causal powers of any kind of separate realm outside of experience.[33] In other words, there is no notion of a system lying outside experience and causing it. This is emphasizing the cooperative aspects of society, although power and competition were also central to Hegel's view. He argued that there were always elements of inequality in relationships so that some have more power than what others have. Without the right kind of social mediation, therefore, there will not be complete mutuality of recognition but rather relations of domination, which he explored as follows. In their encounter with each other, each self-conscious agent makes his own judgment about his right to have his desires fulfilled in accordance with his life project. He seeks to confirm these norms of his behavior and so requires the other to recognize this. The demand for recognition becomes a struggle to death when one party decides that his own self-conception is more important than life itself. One party then submits to the authority of the other and both enter into a relationship of master and slave. Taking as an example the relationship between master and slave, Hegel says that the master imposes his norms on the slave and the slave allows this. The master's project for his own life determines the project of the slave. However, the claim to superiority of the master's viewpoint is compulsion and the slave comes to understand that his submission is contingent on passions, luck and uses of personal power. This realization undermines his allegiance to the principles set by the master. In addition, the master comes to realize that the slave does not really recognize him but is simply submitting. This undermines his own allegiance to the principles of the relationship. The relationship cannot provide the free recognition he requires and the internal contradictions of the relationship lead to its transformation. Hegel held that modern life is the culmination of the dialectic of mastery and servitude, tracing this historically from Greek times. What counts as rational emerges within mutual dependency of a particular historically located type.

Mind or consciousness is thus manifested in social institutions, that is, ways of life, which give identities, self-concepts, to individuals. Each person is self-consciously, purposively directing himself but each is also dependent on the other. The self maintains and leads a life and so discriminates experience, objectively tied to the real properties of the world but also necessarily relational. How we come to understand our own desires, interpret their intensity and priority, how we categorize objects to satisfy our desires is not fixed or determined by our natures or the real world but depends on the concepts we employ which are historically developed in the society we live in. Some object that these notions of romantic idealism mean that all thought and all ethical action is relative, because they depend not on anything absolute and eternally universal but on the historical evolution of a society and the individual's experience of that society. Of course, this does make meaning culturally relative but does not mean that it could be anything. Thinking, acting and meaning are constrained by the culture and the physical world we live in – the 'anything goes' of radical scepticism and the extremes of postmodernism do not apply to romantic idealism. Indeed, Hegel regarded societies as reflections of Absolute Spirit, a metaphysical position one can reject without also rejecting Hegel's social way of understanding meaning. For me, the cultural relativism implied by romantic idealism resonates with the reality of organizational life in which people have to depend on each other and negotiate the meaning of what they are doing. Hegel argued that individual autonomy could only be achieved in a social context. For him, individuals are fundamentally social in that everything one does is formed by social practices but this does not render individuals subservient to society, because what they do also depends on their own responses to their social context. Social practitioners cannot exist without social practices, and there can be no social practices without social practitioners. In contrast to Kantian thinking, where there is a duality of the individual and the social, Hegel presents a perspective in which they cannot be separated. Indeed, individuals arise in the social, which they are simultaneously constructing. This is clearly a paradoxical or dialectical perspective in which individuals are simultaneously forming and being formed by the social as transformative cause.

Conclusion

There are a number of important consequences of taking this view of individual and society which will be explored in the chapters that follow. Here I want to emphasize that the Hegelian social approach makes it impossible to think of anyone who is an objective observer outside of social phenomena. Everyone, no matter how powerful, is a participant and organizational life therefore has to be thought about in terms of processes of participation. In the dominant discourse, the manager is regarded in some sense as objective observer outside the organizational system who designs that system, directs its movement and chooses where it is going. The objective observer is using one process, reason, to operate on another process the interaction of parts of a system. Those writing about organizations from a complexity perspective mostly do the same thing: they talk about processes of designing, constraining or influencing other processes called self-organization or emergence. Abandoning the assumptions of the autonomous individual, the objective observer and the system means abandoning this doubling of process: there are only the processes of human interaction which simply create further processes of human interaction. Any designing, constraining, directing or influencing can only be particular examples of social interaction. Any influence anyone exerts is through processes of participating in interaction with others – indeed, it is in this participation that each of us is playing some part, no matter how small, in the perpetual construction of the unknowable future.

Hegel's thought exerted a powerful influence on James and the school of American pragmatism which include Mead and Dewey. Mead rejected Hegel's metaphysics but particularly took up his dialectic of social process and developed social behaviorism. Elias rejected all philosophers but is closer in thought to Hegel, also shorn of any metaphysics, than Kant who he explicitly rejected. The chapters to follow will draw on the work of Mead, James, Dewey and Elias to present a theory of local interaction in organizations which colleagues and I have called complex responsive processes[34] taking the form of communication, power, the dynamics of inclusion and exclusion, identity formation, ideologically-based choices and the interplay of deliberate actions to produce emergent patterns across a population.

Notes

1   Bateson, G. (1973) *Steps to an Ecology of Mind*, St Albans: Paladin.
2   Midgley, G. (2000) *Systemic Intervention*: *Philosophy, Methodology, and Practice*, New York: Kluwer.
3   von Foerster, H. (1984) 'On Constructing Reality', in von Foerster, H. (ed.) *Observing Systems*, Seaside, CA: Intersystems; von Glasersfeld, E. (1991) 'Knowing without Metaphysics: Aspects of the Radical Constructivist Position', in Steier, F. (ed.) *Research and Reflexivity*, London: Sage.
4   Ackoff, R. L. (1981) *Creating the Corporate Future*, New York: Wiley; Ackoff, R. L. (1994) *The Democratic Organization*, New York: Oxford University Press.
5   Churchman, C. West (1968) *The Systems Approach*, New York: Delacorte Press; Churchman, C. West (1970) *The Systems Approach and its Enemies*, New York: Basic Books.
6   Flood, R. L. (1990) 'Liberating Systems Theory: Towards Critical Systems Thinking', *Human Relations*, 43, 49–75.

7 Checkland, P. B. (1981) *Systems Thinking, Systems Practice*, Chichester: Wiley; Checkland, P. B. and Schles, J. (1990) *Soft Systems Methodology in Action*, Chichester: Wiley.

8 Jackson, M. C. (2000) *Systems Approaches to Management*, New York: Kluwer; Flood, R. L. (1990) 'Liberating Systems Theory: Towards Critical Systems Thinking', *Human Relations*, 43, 49–75; Midgley, G. (2000) *Systemic Intervention: Philosophy, Methodology, and Practice*, New York: Kluwer.

9 Jackson, M. C. (2000) *Systems Approaches to Management*, New York: Kluwer.

10 Hegel, G.W.F. (1807) *The Phenomenology of the Spirit*, Bamberg: Joseph Anton Goebhardt, trans. A. V. Miller, Oxford: Oxford University Press.

11 Kant, I. (1790) *Critique of Judgement*, trans. W. S. Pluhar, Indianapolis: Hackett (1987).

12 Ashby, W. R. (1945) 'The Effects of Control on Stability', *Natura*, 155, 242–43; Ashby, W. R. (1952) *Design for a Brain*, New York: Wiley; Ashby, W. R. (1956) *Introduction to Cybernetics*, New York: Wiley; Beer, S. (1966) *Decision and Control: The Meanings of Operational Research and Management Cybernetics*, London: Wiley; Beer, S. (1979) *The Heart of the Enterprise*, Chichester: Wiley; Beer, S. (1981) *The Brain of the Firm*, Chichester: Wiley; Beer, S. (1994) *Beyond Dispute: The Invention of Team Syntegrity*, New York: Wiley; Bertalanffy, L. von (1968) *General Systems Theory: Foundations, Development, Applications*, New York: George Braziller; Boulding, K. E. (1956) 'General Systems Theory: The Skeleton of Science', *Management Science*, 2, 197–108; Philips, A. W. (1950) 'Mechanical Models in Economic Dynamics', *Econometrica*, 17, 283–305; Tustin, A. (1953) *The Mechanism of Economic Systems*, Cambridge, MA: Harvard University Press; Wiener, N. (1948) *Cybernetics: or Control and Communication in the Animal and the Machine*, Cambridge, MA: MIT Press.

13 Shannon, C. and Weaver, W. (1949) *The Mathematical Theory of Communication*, Urbana, IL: University of Illinois Press.

14 Gardner, H. (1985) *The Mind's New Science: A History of the Cognitive Revolution*, New York: Basic Books.

15 Shannon, C. and Weaver, W. (1949) *The Mathematical Theory of Communication*, Urbana, IL: University of Illinois Press.

16 Senge, P. M. (1990) *The Fifth Discipline: The Art and Practice of the Learning Organization*, New York: Doubleday.

17 Burke, W.W. (2008/1982) *Organization Change: The Theory and Practice*, Thousand Islands, CA: Sage Publications Inc.

18 Ackoff, R. L. (1981) *Creating the Corporate Future*, New York: Wiley; Ackoff, R. L. (1994) *The Democratic Organization*, New York: Oxford University Press; Churchman, C. West (1968) *The Systems Approach*, New York: Delacorte Press; Churchman, C. West (1970) *The Systems Approach and its Enemies*, New York: Basic Books; Flood, R. L. (1990) 'Liberating Systems Theory: Towards Critical Systems Thinking', *Human Relations*, 43, 49–75; Jackson, M. C. (2000) *Systems Approaches to Management*, New York: Kluwer; Midgley, G. (2000) *Systemic Intervention: Philosophy, Methodology, and Practice*, New York: Kluwer.

19 For example, Allen, P. M., Strathern, M. and Baldwin, J. S. (2006) 'Evolutionary Drive: New Understandings of Change in Socio-Economic Systems Emergence', *Complexity & Organization*, 8, 2; Goodwin, B. (1994) *How the Leopard Changed its Spots*, London: Weidenfeld and Nicholson; Holland, J. (1998) *Emergence from Chaos to Order*, New York: Oxford University Press; Kauffman, S. (1995) *At Home in the Universe: The Search for the Laws of Complexity*, London: Viking; McKelvey, B. (2003) 'From Fields to Science: Can Organization Studies make the Transition?', in Westwood, R. and Clegg, S., *Point/Counterpoint: Central Debates in Organization Theory*, Oxford: Blackwell; Gell-Mann, M. (1994) *The Quark and the Jaguar*, New York: Freeman & Co; Prigogine, I. and Stengers, I. (1984) *Order Out of Chaos: Man's New Dialogue with Nature*, New York: Bantam Books.

20 Checkland, P. B. (1981) *Systems Thinking, Systems Practice*, Chichester: Wiley; Checkland, P. B. and Schles, J. (1990) *Soft Systems Methodology in Action*, Chichester: Wiley; Flood, R. L. (1990) 'Liberating Systems Theory: Towards Critical Systems Thinking', *Human Relations*, 43, 49–75; Jackson, M. C. (2000) *Systems Approaches to Management*, New York: Kluwer; Midgley, G. (2000) *Systemic Intervention: Philosophy, Methodology, and Practice*, New York: Kluwer.

21 Allen, P. M., Strathern, M. and Baldwin, J. S. (2006) Evolutionary Drive: New Understandings of Change in Socio-Economic Systems, *Emergence, Complexity & Organization*, 8, 2.

22 Seddon, J. (2008) *Systems Thinking in the Public Sector: The Failure of the Reform Regime and a Manifesto for a Better Way*, Axminster: Triachy Press.
23 For example, Effron, D., Niedenthal, P. M., Gil, S., and Droit-Violet, S. (2006) 'Embodied Temporal Perception of Emotion', *American Psychological Association*, 6, 1; O'Loughlin, M. (1995) 'Intelligent Bodies and Ecological Subjectivism: Merleau-Ponty's Corrective to Postmodernism's "Subjects" of Education', *Philosophy of Education*; Shilling, S. (1999) 'Towards an Embodied Understanding of the Structure/Agency Relationship', *British Journal of Sociology*, 50, 4.
24 Effron, D., Niedenthal, P. M., Gil, S., and Droit-Violet, S. (2006) 'Embodied Temporal Perception of Emotion', *American Psychological Association*, 6, 1.
25 Shilling, S. (1999) 'Towards an Embodied Understanding of the Structure/Agency Relationship', *British Journal of Sociology*, 50, 4.
26 O'Loughlin, M. (1995) 'Intelligent Bodies and Ecological Subjectivism: Merleau-Ponty's Corrective to Postmodernism' "Subjects" of Education', *Philosophy of Education*.
27 Mead, G. H. (1932) *The Philosophy of the Present*, Chicago: University of Chicago Press.
28 Prigogine, I. (1997) *The End of Certainty*, New York: The Free Press.
29 Tsoukas, H. (1993) 'Analogical Reasoning and Knowledge Generation in Organization Theory', *Organization Studies*, 14(3), 323–46.
30 Ray, T. S. (1992) 'An Approach to the Synthesis of Life', in Langton, G. C., Taylor, C., Doyne-Farmer, J. and Rasmussen, S. (eds) *Artificial Life II, Santa Fe Institute, Studies in the Sciences of Complexity, Volume 10*, Reading, MA: Addison-Wesley.
31 Elias, N. (1939) *The Civilizing Process*, Blackwell, Oxford.
32 Hegel, G. W. F. (1807) *The Phenomenology of the Spirit*, Bamberg: Joseph Anton Goebhardt, trans. A. V. Miller, Oxford: Oxford University Press: Beiser, F. C. (ed.) (1993) *The Cambridge Companion to Hegel*, Cambridge: Cambridge University Press.
33 Pinkard, T. (2000a) *Hegel: A Biography*, Cambridge: University of Cambridge Press; Pinkard, T. (2000b) 'Hegel's Phenomenology and Logic: An Overview', in Ameriks, K. (ed) (2002) *The Cambridge Companion to German Idealism*, Cambridge: Cambridge University Press; Westphal, K. (1993) 'The Basic Context and Structure of Hegel's *Philosophy of Right*', in Beiser, F. C. (ed.) (1993) *The Cambridge Companion to Hegel*, Cambridge: Cambridge University Press.
34 Griffin, D. (2001) *The Emergence of Leadership: Linking Self-Organization and Ethics*, London: Routledge; Stacey, R., Griffin and Shaw (2000) *Complexity and Management: Fad or Radical Challenge to Systems Thinking?* London: Routledge; Stacey, R. (2001) *Complex Responsive Processes in Organizations: Learning and Knowledge Creation*, London: Routledge; Stacey, R. (2007 *Strategic Management and Organisational Dynamics: The Challenge of Complexity*, London: Pearson Education, (5th edn); Stacey, R. and Griffin, D. (2005) *Taking Experience Seriously: A Complexity Perspective on Researching Organizations*, London: Routledge; Stacey, R. (2005) *Experiencing Emergence in Organizations: Local Interaction and the Emergence of Global Pattern*, London: Routledge; Shaw, P. (2002) *Changing Conversation in Organizations*, London: Routledge.

7 Managers accomplish whatever they accomplish in processes of communication

In the last chapter, I proposed that the complexity sciences could serve as a productive domain from which we could take some abstract relationships to serve as analogies for relationships in organizations, with the intention of providing ways of thinking that are more in accordance with organizational reality than the currently dominant discourse. I claimed that potentially the most fruitful analogy was that of individual digital agents interacting locally with each other in the medium of digital symbols to produce emergent population-wide patterns. The process is one of transformative causality in which agents form population-wide patterns while at the same time being formed by them. This analogy is particularly important because it demonstrates that local interaction can produce coherent, emergent population-wide patterns which at the same time form that local interaction. If, in the human domain, it turned out that population-wide, that is social, patterns emerge without design in local interaction between individual human agents who form the social patterns while individually being formed by them, then the logic of the dominant discourse will be turned on its head. The dominant discourse is built on the assumption that global, population-wide, patterns of organizations and societies can only change through global plans and redesigns which are to be implemented by individual human agents. If the analogy from the complexity models were to apply to humans then it would not be possible to change human social patterns in a chosen way simply by implementing plans, because actual global change would be emerging in the interplay of intentions in local interaction. Furthermore, many management disciplines, such as Organization Development, would lose their fundamental basis. Clearly, then, I am talking about much more than some fine theoretical point – there are major practical consequences in what I am claiming.

Turning back to the use of analogy, I also made the point in the last chapter that the relationships explored in abstract digital terms in the complexity models would have to be interpreted in the human domain, and argued that the most insightful way of doing this would be to turn to Hegel's ideas on social processes. Basically, he presented social processes as acts of mutual recognition between interdependent people in which individual consciousness and self-consciousness emerge in historically evolved social patterns, institutions, which are at the same time formed by those conscious and self-conscious individuals. The models of the complexity sciences are valuable because they show how there is nothing mysterious about the emergence of population-wide pattern in local interaction and that such emergent pattern is an intrinsic property of nonlinear interaction between diverse agents. This provides a solid scientific foundation for the kind of social process theory proposed by Hegel. This chapter begins the work of developing a detailed exposition of social processes of local interaction in which wider social patterns emerge by turning to the thought of two writers influenced by Hegel's ideas of social process. First, I will look at the ideas of the process sociologist already referred to in previous chapters, Norbert Elias, and then the work of the American pragmatist philosopher and sociologist, George Herbert Mead. I will be using the work of Elias to explore how the nature of the modern human agent emerged, and the work of Mead to understand the underlying communicative processes in emerging, evolving human interaction.

The civilizing process and the personality structure of modern human agents

In *The Civilizing Process*, published in 1939, Elias[1] argued that as Western society evolved, social functions became more and more differentiated under the pressure of competition. This differentiation meant that the number of social functions increased so that any individual had to depend upon more and more others to do anything – hundreds of years ago, most people grew their own food whereas we now rely on a chain of suppliers stretching around the world. As this interdependence rose, more and more people had to attune their actions to each other, making it necessary for them to regulate their conduct in increasingly differentiated, more even and more stable ways. This requirement for more complex control had to be instilled into each individual from infancy if society was to function. The more complex forms of control became increasingly automatic, taking the form of unconscious self-compulsion that individuals could not resist even if they consciously desired to do so: 'The web of actions grows so complex and extensive, the effort required to behave "correctly" within it becomes so great, that beside the individual's conscious self-control an automatic, blindly functioning apparatus of self-control is firmly established. This seeks to prevent offences to socially acceptable behavior by a wall of deep-rooted fears, but, just because it operates blindly and by habit, it frequently produces such collisions with social reality. But whether consciously or unconsciously, the direction of this transformation of conduct in the form of increasingly differentiated regulation of impulses is determined by the direction of the process of social differentiation, by the progressive divisions of functions and the growth of the interdependency chains into which, directly or indirectly, every impulse, every move of an individual becomes integrated'.[2] Self-restraint became habitual, or unconscious, through the evolution of societies. Without this, people could not operate in increasingly differentiated societies and without such societies, such self-restraint would not be required. Elias is introducing a notion of unconscious processes, which is simultaneously individual and social.

   Elias also linked the growth of self-control to the growth of centralized institutions of society and the monopolization of force by those institutions. In societies in which force is not monopolized, individuals experience movements between pleasure and pain that are volatile and frequent. People engage more frequently in physical violence against each other, swinging between victory and defeat. Life is uncertain and risks cannot be calculated so that people live more impulsively in the present. As society develops in the direction of the monopolization of physical force, the individual is no longer engaging in feuds but rather in the more permanent and peaceful functions of economic exchange and the pursuit of prestige. The monopolization of force created pacified social spaces that were normally free from acts of violence so that the free use of physical violence by the physically strong was no longer possible. However, nonphysical forms of violence became more frequent, for example, from economic monopolies and from the loss of self-control by individuals when driving cars. Both danger and control, therefore, came less frequently from physical force and more frequently from the very nature of self-control. Individuals are more protected from the violence of others but they in turn have to suppress their own passion and aggression. These forms of compulsion pattern the individual's conduct and the more interdependent people become, the more advantageous they find it to control their emotions and take account of the possible responses of others to what they do. Prediction and foresight become more important than before.

However, the more moderate swings of emotion, the extension of time horizons, less impulse acting, more internal control, all bring pressures for individuals to do with socially correct behavior. These fears, particularly to do with possible social exclusion, become central aspects of an individual's personality and thus of interactions with others. Impulses and fears are banished from public visibility to be revealed only 'behind the scenes', for example, in the bedroom. Self-control encompasses an individual's whole conduct and many impulses and emotions no longer reach the level of consciousness. Although life becomes less dangerous, it also becomes less emotional and this is compensated for in dreams, fantasies, books and pictures. The consequences of growing interdependence in larger groups and the exclusion of physical violence were social constraints that were transformed into unconscious self constraints as 'habitus', that is, the habitual social world in which we live. Perpetual hindsight and foresight is instilled from childhood, becoming conscious self-control and unconscious automatic habit. However, these constraints also produce tensions and disturbances for individuals, taking the form of restlessness and dissatisfaction because impulses can only be partially be gratified. The stresses of self-control can so block people that they are no longer capable of expressing even modified emotions. People may become so surrounded by unconscious automatic fears that they remain deaf or unresponsive to emotion throughout life. Energy may be released in compulsive actions or flow into uncontrollable and eccentric attachments, or predilections for peculiar things, or repulsions, all permitting no real satisfaction. This is all unplanned and there is no end to it, because although the malleable person is shaped to some extent in childhood, with patterns formed and then solidifying afterwards, the process of formation never ceases throughout life. Unresolved conflicts are repeated throughout life in situations reminiscent of childhood and this can lead to contradictions between self-control and unrestrained expression.

Shame, embarrassment and repugnance are particularly important in the formation of 'habitus', that is, individual-social habits. The feeling of shame is a kind of anxiety which arises in an individual when that individual is seen by others to act contrary to the habitual standards of society, and it brings with it feelings of inferiority. People go to great lengths to avoid feelings of shame which therefore acts as powerful forms of social control. The civilizing process has essentially been one of rising levels of shame, repugnance, embarrassment and anxiety which are all forms of simultaneously social and self-control.

Also important in the civilizing process are the dynamics of groupings of people: one group emerges as privileged and others press for emancipation from their underprivileged status. Initially, the poorer 'lower classes' tend to display less self control than the upper classes. The development of foresight and stricter control of behavior by the upper classes are important instruments of their dominance. Offences against manners and etiquette are met with great disapproval so creating classes of superior and inferior people with severe penalties imposed on the inferiors, who lose prestige. Fear of a loss of prestige becomes instilled as a kind of self-compulsion to avoid breaching the code. Although the contrast in conduct between the upper and lower groups diminishes as society evolves, the varieties or nuances of conduct increase. In the evolution of Western society, however, the upper classes eventually had to work in similar ways to the lower classes and the manners of the upper classes spread to the lower so that the differences in conduct between them diminished. Society and individuals are evolving simultaneously in patterns of power relations as patterns of competition and cooperation. The characters and attitudes of people who form power figurations are being formed by these figurations.

The emergence of social order

Elias argued that what we now call Western civilization is not the result of any kind of calculated long-term planning. Individual people did not form an intention to change civilization and then gradually realize this intention through rational, purposive measures. It is not conceivable that the evolution of society could have been planned because that would suppose that 'modern' rational, calculating individuals with a degree of self-mastery already existed centuries ago, whereas Elias' research shows that such individuals did not exist then but were, rather, themselves the products of social evolution. Societal changes produced rational, planning kinds of individuals, not the other way around.

Elias argued that the change in society occurred in an unplanned manner but nevertheless displayed a specific type of order and asked how it is possible that orderly formations, which no human being has intended, arise in the human world. He answers the question in the following way: 'It is simple enough: plans and actions, the emotional and rational impulses of individual people, constantly interweave in a friendly or hostile way. *This basic tissue resulting from many single plans and actions of men can give rise to changes and patterns that no individual person has planned or created. From this interdependence of people arise an order sui generis, an order more compelling and stronger than the will and reason of the individual people composing it*. It is the order of interweaving human impulses and strivings, the social order, which determines the course of historical change'.[3] Although it is highly unlikely that Elias was ever aware of the complexity sciences, what he is describing here is local interaction (self-organization) and emergence. Individuals and groups are interacting with each other, in their local situations, in intentional, planned ways, but the widespread, global consequences of the interplay of these intentions and plans cannot be foreseen by any of them – long-term global consequences emerge. Long-term consequences cannot be foreseen because '. . . each "I" is irrevocably embedded in a "we". . .[and this]. . . finally makes it clear why the intermeshing of the actions, plans and purposes of many "I"s constantly gives rise to something which has not been planned, intended or created by any individual. As is known, this permanent feature of social life was given its first historical interpretation by Hegel. He explains it as a "ruse of reason". But what is involved is neither a ruse nor a product of reason. . . . The interplay of the actions, purposes and plans of many people is not itself something intended or planned, and is ultimately immune to planning. The "ruse of reason" is a tentative attempt, still swathed in day-dreaming, to express the fact that the autonomy of what a person calls "we" is more powerful than the plans and purposes of an individual "I"'.[4]

Individuals can plan their own actions but they are always in relationship with each other in a group or power figuration and none of them can plan the actions of others and so no one can plan the interplay of plans and actions. The fact that each person depends on others means that none can simply realize their plans, but this does not mean that anarchy or disorder results because, Elias says, there is a trend in the evolution of the consequences of the interplay of individual plans and intentions. However, he does not explain why or how there should be such a trend. It is here that the models of the complexity sciences add the insight that nonlinear local interaction between diverse agents has the intrinsic property of producing emergent population-wide patterns which could be creative, or destructive or both. The order, which emerges without individuals planning it, is neither rational, that is, resulting from the purposive deliberation of individuals, nor irrational, that is, arising in an incomprehensible way. It is neither centrally controlled nor lacking in control, because figurations of power, fears of not belonging and of shame are all powerful forms of self and social control.

Social processes and communicative interaction

In reviewing Elias' ideas on social evolution, I have described how the identities of modern self-controlled agents intent on predicting and planning their futures, have emerged in ongoing historical processes of the interplay of the actions and plans of interdependent persons which makes it impossible to plan social patterns despite the felt need to do so. These modern agents are nevertheless forming the patterns of social order that are forming them at the same time, and they are doing so through the interplay of their actions which often produce what none intended. In this way, deliberate plans and emergent social patterns play into each other. I want to claim that the same processes explain how organizations evolve in much shorter periods and suggest that we need to come to understand organizational continuity and change in terms of the interplay between the actions of interdependent people and to understand the simultaneous emergence of human identities. The same features of social control apply in modern organizations as came to apply across modern societies, namely, the constraints provided by processes of shame, embarrassment and anxiety, all expressed as self and social control. This perspective provides a very different and more complex view of the nature of control in organizations, one closer to organizational reality. Instead of equating control in organizations simply with processes of command enforced by monitoring systems, we realize that there are much more powerful forms of organizational control, namely, social pressures and socialized self control that are not designed or enforced by powerful managers and leaders who are actually as subject to self and social control as anyone else. This presents a very different picture of human agents to the autonomous individuals and heroic leaders of the dominant discourse. The same processes of forming privileged and less privileged groups that have been an essential feature of the civilizing process are also still evident in all organizations, meaning that power relations are central to understanding organizational reality. The social order and the nature of institutions and organizations are still evolving, as we saw in Chapter 2, in much the same way as any civilization has been evolving over longer periods. The long-term processes Elias identified as central to the evolution of societies therefore open up a very different view of organizational life to that found in the dominant discourse. I believe it is important to explore in much greater detail the nature of the local interaction in which occurs the interplay between many agents acting in consciously deliberate and unconsciously motivated ways.

As soon as we start asking ourselves what we are doing every day in our ordinary local interactions in which we accomplish our work in organizations, I think we realize how the most fundamental activity is that of communicating with each other. Complaints about lack of communication are very common in almost all organizations and attempts to improve communication are just as common. The problem is that despite all the attempts to communicate more often and more clearly, despite the money spent on consultants, technology and training, the complaints continue. The matter of communication is thus of great practical importance. Perhaps not surprisingly, the way of thinking about communication in the dominant discourse on management is based on work by engineers and was imported along with systems thinking around the 1950s. This most prevalent model of communication is based on the work of radio engineers in which signals are sent from a sender to a receiver.[5] In human terms, this is taken to mean that an idea arises in the mind of one autonomous person, the sender, who formulates it into language signals which are then transmitted to another autonomous person, the receiver. The receiver translates the language back into the idea and in this way, an idea has been transmitted from one mind to another. If the idea was accurately signalled in language, there was no transmission noise usually identified with emotion, and the receiver listened carefully enough to accurately translate the language signalled back into the idea, then communication is optimal. In this way, accurate meaning has been transmitted. However, if the sender lacks formulation and presentation skills, or if emotion distorts the signal, or if the receiver lacks the listening and interpretation skills, then communication will fail and meaning will be distorted. Further attempts at transmission which use the gap between intended meaning and the distortion as feedback can then take place until the gap is closed – here communication is thought of as a cybernetic system. The remedy for failed communication is to train senders in formulation and presentation skills, receivers in listening and interpretation skills and both in avoiding emotional distortions so that there is little gap between what is transmitted and what is received in the first place. This whole approach is based on the assumption that meaning is objectively given in the mind of the sender, an autonomous individual, which can be accurately received provided the receiver refrains from distorting it. There is no notion here that the receiver as well as the sender might be playing a creative role in the making of meaning. However, if we take up the conclusion reached in the last section about the thoroughly interactive social nature of human action we would want to look for a way of understanding communication and meaning making as some kind of interplay between interdependent persons in which they are together constructing meaning. The central concern of the work of the social psychologist and pragmatist philosopher, George Herbert Mead,[6] was just such a social understanding of the nature of human communication as the fundamental social activity. It is of great practical importance, I suggest, to understand this alternative explanation of communication, because it is closer to the reality of organizational life and leads to changes in the communication methods we employ.

Communication as conversation of gestures

Mead held that human societies, that is, forms of cooperative and competitive interaction, are not possible without beings that have human minds, that is, consciousness and self-consciousness, and human minds are not possible without human societies, which means that mind and society must have evolved together. An explanation of the evolution of mind must start with rudimentary forms of social behavior displayed by higher mammals that do not have minds in the human sense and then identify what would be needed for human-like minds to emerge in social behavior, so providing an action-based account of how mind and society have evolved together. Starting with the higher mammals, we can see that they relate to each other in a responsive manner, with a *gesture* by one animal calling forth a *response* from another in the conversation of gestures. Gesture and response together constitute a social act in which meaning arises for both so that knowing is a property of interaction, or relationship. For example, one dog may make the gesture of baring its teeth in a snarl and this may call forth a response of counter snarl, or of flight, or of crouching. The meaning to both animals of the social act of snarl and counter snarl is aggression, while that of snarl and flight is victory and defeat, and the meaning of the social act of snarl and crouching is dominance and submission. This makes it clear that meaning does not lie in the gesture alone but in the social act as a whole; meaning arises in the responsive social interaction between actors. Mead described the gesture as a symbol in the sense that it is an action that points to a meaning but that meaning only becomes apparent in the response to the gesture and therefore lies in the whole social act of gesture-response. The gesture, as symbol, points to how the meaning might emerge in the response. Here meaning is emerging in the action of the living present in which the immediate future (response) acts back on the past (gesture) to change its meaning. Meaning is not simply located in the past (gesture) or the future (response) but in the interaction between the two in the living present. In this way, the present is not simply a point separating the past from the future, because it has a time structure. Meaning does not arise first in each individual and then in the action of transmitting, as in the dominant discourse, but arises in the interaction between the communicating individuals. Meaning is not attached to an object but created in social interaction.

Clearly, there are immediately important implications for communication in organizations. When a CEO, for example, communicates with members of an organization, the meaning does not lie simply in the communication but at the same time in the responses to it. No matter how clearly worded the communication is, it will be interpreted in many different ways and therefore mean different things for different people in a way that the CEO cannot control. Effective communication, therefore, cannot be regarded as a one off event, because it is an ongoing process of negotiation. Effective communication requires staying in the conversation.

Returning to the example of the dogs, we can see gesture-response patterns of competition and cooperation which constitute the kind of society that is widely found in nature. Mostly, such societies rest on functional specialization where, for example, ant societies are structured by specialization into workers and breeders, while mammals may tend to specialize into hunters and breeders and into those that are dominant and those that are submissive. At this stage, meaning is implicit in the social act itself and those acting are unaware of that implicit meaning. Humans must have evolved from mammals with similar rudimentary social structures to those found in present day species of mammals. The mammal ancestors of humans must have evolved central nervous systems that enabled them to gesture to others in a manner that was capable of *calling forth in themselves the same range of responses as in those to whom they were gesturing*. This would happen if, for example, the snarl of one called forth in itself the fleeting feelings associated with counter snarl, flight or submissive posture, just as they did in the one to whom the gesture of snarl was being made. The gesture, as symbol, now has a substantially different role. Mead described such a gesture as a significant symbol, where a significant symbol is one that calls forth the same response in the gesturer as in the one to whom it is directed. Significant symbols, therefore, make it possible for the gesturer to 'know' what he or she is doing. This simple idea is, I think, a profound insight. If, when one makes a gesture to another, one is able to experience in one's own body a similar response to that which the gesture provokes in another body, then one can 'know' what one is doing; one is conscious and can intuit something about the range of likely responses from the other. The body, with its nervous system, becomes central to understanding how animals 'know' anything. Here, there is no split whatsoever between mind and body, or intellect and emotion. From this perspective, it makes no sense whatever to talk about embodiment as some special way of knowing anything, or regard bodily feelings as either superior or inferior to intellect and thinking. All thinking and all feeling are acts of a body. To say that someone 'is too much in their head' and 'ought to be in their body' are mistaken metaphors.

Mead was insistent on talking about interactions between bodies. He argued that any explanation of interaction had to be consistent with the capabilities of an animal's nervous system. The human nervous system had to be such as to make it possible for the gesturer to call forth a response in his or her own body that is similar to that called forth by the gesture in another body. Recent research on the brain provides support for Mead's insight. For example, the neuroscientist, Damasio,[7] argues that the human brain continuously monitors and integrates the rhythmical activity of the heart, lungs, gut, muscles and other organs, as well as the immune, visceral and other systems in the body. At each moment, the brain is registering the internal state of the body and these body states constitute feeling states. This continuous monitoring activity, that is, registration of feeling states, is taking place as a person selectively perceives external objects, such as a face or an aroma, and experience then forms an association between the two. Every perception of an object outside the body is associated, through acting into the world, with particular body states, that is, patterns of feeling. When people encounter situations that are similar to previous ones, they experience similar feeling states, or body rhythms, that orient them to act into the situation. In this way, human worlds become affect laden and the feeling states unconsciously narrow down the options to be considered in a situation. In other words, feelings unconsciously guide choice and when the capacity to feel is damaged so is the capacity to rapidly select sensible action options. Damasio suggests that, from a neurological standpoint, the body's monitoring of its own rhythmic patterns is both the ground for its construction of the world it acts into and its unique sense of subjectivity. Feelings, therefore, are rhythmic patterns in a body and they make it possible for the gesture of one body to call forth in itself a similar response, a similar feeling rhythm, to that called forth in a the body to whom the gesture is made. There seems to be some kind of resonance between the body rhythms of interacting individuals. Possessing this capacity, the maker of a gesture can intuit or predict the consequences of that gesture: he or she can know what he or she is doing, just before the other responds. The whole social act, that is, meaning, can be experienced in advance of carrying out the whole act, opening up the possibility of reflection and choice in making a gesture. Furthermore, the one responding has the same opportunity for reflecting upon, and so choosing, from the range of responses. The first part of a gesture can be taken by the other as an indication of how further parts of the gesture will unfold from the response. In this way, the two can indicate to each other how they might respond to each other in the continuous processes in which a gesture by one calls forth a response from another, which is itself a gesture back to the first. Obviously, this capacity makes more sophisticated forms of cooperation possible. Human social forms and human consciousness thus both emerge at the same time, each forming the other, and there cannot be one without the other.

As individuals interact with each other in this way, the possibility arises of a pause before making a gesture. In a kind of private role-play, emerging in the repeated experience of public interaction, one individual learns to take the attitude, the tendency to act, of the other, enabling a kind of trial run in advance of actually completing or even starting the gesture. Will it call forth aggression, fright, flight or submission? What will be the consequences in each case? In this way, *rudimentary forms of thinking develop*, *taking the form of private role-playing*, that is, gestures made by a body to itself, calling forth responses in itself. Mead said that humans are fundamentally role-playing animals. The simultaneous private and public roles plays so far discussed all take place without verbal language. Mead then argued that the gesture which is particularly useful in calling forth the same attitude in oneself as in the other is the vocal gesture, because we can hear the sounds we make in much the same way as others hear them, while we cannot see the facial gestures we make as others see them, for example. The development of more sophisticated patterns of vocal gesturing, that is, of the language form of significant symbols, is thus of major importance in the development of consciousness and of sophisticated forms of society. Mind and society emerge together in the medium of language. However, since speaking and listening are actions of bodies, and since bodies are never without feelings, the medium of language is also always the medium of feelings.

Both the public conversation of gestures, and the private role-play and silent conversation of each participant, always have biological correlates in the form of body rhythms. Furthermore, these public and private role-plays, or conversations, which constitute the experience of the interacting individuals, actually shape the patterns of connections in the plastic brains of each.[8] Both public and private conversation are shaping, while being shaped by the spatio-temporal patterns of brain and body. This simultaneous public and private conversation of gestures takes place in the medium of significant symbols, particularly those of language, and it is this capacity for symbolic mediation of cooperative activity that is one of the key features distinguishing humans from other animals. Also, human development has depended crucially on the ability to use tools cooperatively and that ability to use tools in ever more sophisticated ways to interact with each other and act in relation to the material and nonhuman contexts is made possible by the ability to speak.

The nature of the social has thus shifted from mindless cooperation through functional specialization of the higher mammals to mindful, role-playing interaction between humans made more and more sophisticated by the use of language in the form of public vocal communication with others (social) and of private, silent conversation with oneself (mind). Mind, or consciousness, is the gesturing and responding action of a body directed towards itself as private role-play and silent conversation, and society is the gesturing and responding actions of bodies directed towards each other. There is no question of separating mind and society as different hierarchical levels and both mind and society are understood as responsive temporal processes of communication which are in no way systems. The spatial metaphor is abandoned and mind is not regarded as being inside anything – instead, it is understood to be the actions of bodies directed to themselves. Society is not regarded as outside individuals, but it is understood as actions of human bodies directed to each other.

The social attitude and the emergence of self

Mead takes his argument further when he suggests how private role-play evolves in increasingly complex ways. As more and more interactions are experienced with others, so increasingly, more roles and wider ranges of possible responses enter into the role-playing activities that precedes the gestures, or to be more accurate, are continuously intertwined with public gesturing and responding. In this way, the capacity to take the attitude of many others evolves, and this becomes generalized. Each engaged in the conversation of gestures can now take the attitude of what Mead calls the *generalized other*. In childhood, most of us are warned by our parents to take account of how 'others' will respond to what we are doing or saying. These 'others' and what 'they' think of you are not actual individuals but generalizations across a particular society. Eventually, individuals develop the capacity to take the attitude of the whole group, or what Mead calls the game. In other words, creatures have now evolved that are capable of taking the social attitude, as they gesture and respond to each other. The result is much more sophisticated processes of cooperative interaction, because there is now mindful, social behavior with increasingly sophisticated meaning and an increasing capacity to use tools more and more effectively to transform the context within which the interacting people live.

The next step in this evolutionary process is the linking of the attitude of specific and generalized others, even of the whole group and the nature of the games they are preoccupied in, with a 'me'. In other words, there evolves a capacity to take the attitude of others not just towards one's gestures but also towards one's self. The 'me' is a person's perception of the configuration of the gestures/responses of the others/society to him or her as a subject, or an 'I'. What has evolved here is the capacity to be an object to oneself, a 'me'. A self, as the relationship between 'me' and 'I', has therefore emerged, as well as an awareness of that self, that is, self-consciousness. In this interaction, the 'I' is the response to the perceived gesture of the group/society to oneself, that is, the 'me'. The 'me' is the attitude of others to the 'I' and they cannot be separated. They do not engage in conversation with each other but together they constitute self-consciousness. Mead argues, very importantly, that this 'I' response to one's perception of the attitude of the group to oneself (the 'me') is not a given but is always potentially unpredictable in that there is no predetermined way in which the 'I' might respond to the 'me'. In other words, each of us may respond in many spontaneously different ways to our perception of the views others have of us. Here, Mead is pointing to the importance of difference, or diversity, in the emergence of the new, that is, in the potential for transformation. Language plays a major role at this stage of evolution and without it, the emergence of human mind, self and society, as we know it would be impossible. These processes, always involving the body and its feelings, both enable and constrain human experience, and they are the basic forms of what I am calling complex responsive processes of relating. In what I have been describing in the foregoing section, it is evident that the conversation of gestures, the complex responsive process of interaction between agents, creates history while that history is forming them. The history referred to here is both the history of the society any person is born into and the life history of the person in that society. It is through ongoing history that people develop some capacity to predict the potential consequences of their gestures to others, and it is through history that people learn to take the attitude of the generalized other.

Back to the complexity sciences as source domain for analogies

As one imagines the process of gesturing and responding between larger and larger numbers of individuals, the complexity of it all becomes quite mind-boggling. How could continuous processes of gesturing and responding between thousands, even millions of people, all in their local interactions produce any kind of coherence? This is not an issue that Mead dealt with, but it is one where the complexity sciences offer important insights, in my view. Models of complex systems demonstrate that nonlinear interactions between large numbers of entities with each responding to limited numbers of others on the basis of their own local principles of interaction will produce coherent population-wide patterns with the potential for novelty, both creative and destructive, when the agents comprising the system are diverse enough. In other words, the very process of local interaction has the inherent capacity to spontaneously produce coherent population-wide patterns without any blueprint or program for those population-wide patterns. Abstract local interaction between abstract symbols produces abstract coherent population-wide patterns which have the paradoxical feature of continuity and novelty, identity and difference, at the same time. By analogy, the continuous local interaction of gesturing and responding in the form of significant symbols between diverse people also has the inherent capacity to produce emergent patterns of interaction across whole populations of humans. This is what I mean by complex responsive process of relating, and it amounts to a particular causal framework, namely, that of transformative cause, where the process is one of perpetual construction of the future as both continuity and potential transformation at the same time. A single causal framework of transformative cause replaces the dual causal framework of rationalist and formative cause upon which the dominant discourse is founded. If one takes this view of the emergence of coherent population-wide patterns of relating in the local processes of relating, then there is no need to look for the causes of coherent human action in concepts such as deep structures, archetypes, the collective unconscious, transcendental wholes, common pools of meaning, group minds, the group-as-a-whole, transpersonal processes, foundation matrix, the personal dynamic unconscious, inner worlds, mental models, and so on. Instead, one understands human relating to be inherently pattern forming.

The key features of communicative interaction and the narrative-like patterning of experience

More detailed accounts of just how communicative interaction works can be found in ethnomethodology,[9] conversational analysis,[10] and social constructionism.[11] The key features of communicative interaction can be classified as: mutual expectations of associative response; turn-taking sequences; sequencing, segmenting and categorizing actions; rhetorical devices.

Mutual expectations of associative response

Whenever people communicate with each other, they quite clearly display, in the very act of that communication, some kind of expectation of each other. People expect those whom they are addressing to reply to what they are saying in some way that is associated with what they are saying. If people do not comply, more or less, with this expectation, there is no communication, and thus no meaning. Associative responding is the very basis of communicative action. Furthermore, people generally expect others to be more or less competent, compliant and reasonable in communicating, just as those others expect them to display those qualities too. People hold each other morally accountable for their communicative and other actions. Alternatively, they may expect others to be incompetent, rebellious, unreasonable and immoral. These expectations have a profound impact on how people proceed together. They undertake very different kinds of communicative action depending upon the expectations they have and if they expect completely uncooperative responses from each other they will try to avoid communication altogether. Even if this is not possible, the meaning arising in the communicative action will be completely different in different contexts of expectation. People do not refer to some set of rules, conscious or unconscious, in order to form those expectations. Instead, they form them in the very action of communication with each other. In that interaction, they may draw on, or point to, local or global sets of rules that have previously been formulated. However, they are not referring to those rules in order to form their expectations, but rather, as resources to be employed in their negotiations with each other. They point to abstract rules to justify their current actions or persuade others to change theirs. They are not simply applying the regularities of rules but referring to them in order to explain, justify or condemn their own, or others', deviations from them. They may refer to rules to guide their joint action together, but since rules can never cover every contingency, what they will often be doing in their communication is negotiating how any rules are to be employed in the current context they find themselves in. Here action, rather than being rule driven, is employing rules as tools, from time to time. This action-based approach emphasizes the social or collaborative nature of the action of talking together in which people make sense of their actions together, taking account of each other's sensibilities, spontaneously sustaining and repairing their unceasing flow of speech entwined activity largely in an unreflective, unforced, unplanned and unintended way. Moreover, in doing all this, they are unconsciously expressing the habitus, the social habits, they live in. The nature of the game they are pre-occupied with is very much formed by their mutual expectations of associative responses from each other.

Turn-taking sequences

The second, strikingly observable feature that imparts coherent pattern to communicative interaction is the turn-taking sequence that creates the rhythms of daily life. The basis of this turn-taking sequence is the expectations people have of each other, as described in the preceding section. People value turns to speak. They compete for them, abandon them and construct them, so making, as well as taking, turns to speak. People make turns for themselves and others by asking questions, soliciting advice, clarifying issues, expressing opinions and so on. They negotiate rights and obligations in this turn-taking process, and it is this negotiating that structures the action of talking and, therefore, most other human actions, because they are accomplished in talking. Everyday turn-taking and turn-making in conversation is simultaneously stable and unstable, predictable and unpredictable. Here, talking, as a recursive and enactive process is structured by interaction.

Sequencing, segmenting and categorizing actions

Third, turn taking/turn making in communicative interaction imparts structure to that communication by actions of sequencing, segmenting and categorizing. One of the most important of these categorization devices is that to do with membership: who may talk and who may not, who is 'in' and who is 'out'. Another important aspect of the turn-taking/turn-making process is referred to as 'adjacent pairs', which urge forward turns and topics.

For example, turn-taking/turn-making exchanges tend to be organized in distinct matching pairs of question and answer, request and response, invitation and acceptance, announcement and acknowledgement, complaint and response and so on.

Rhetorical devices

Fourth, people employ rhetorical devices such as 'directive' and 'instructive' forms of talk in which they are 'arrested' 'moved', 'struck', and 'feel called upon to respond'.[12] In this way, people negotiate with each other, responding to each other's utterances in an attempt to link in their practical activities. They notice and point to the content of each other's speech, including their references to the context; they agree and disagree with each other; they sympathize and fail to sympathize with each other. In doing this, they are constructing living social relationships as they connect, link and orient themselves to each other and to their surroundings in their turn-taking/turn-making communicative interaction. And as with the formation of expectations, the action of turn-taking and turn-making, the actions of categorizing and segmenting, these rhetorical devices express the habitus in which people live; they are all aspects of the games in which we are pre-occupied.

Stability and change in conversational patterns

In responsive processes of communication, people gesture and respond in the form of utterances of one kind or another such as incomplete sentences, stories, propositions and so on, which mutually shape the evolution of their exchanges. The local, situated use of words by one produces responses in others, making momentary, practical differences. People resonate with each other and they may grasp something new, unseen but sensed in the emerging interaction. They are not transmitting information about things but, rather, they are going on with each other in a responsive expression and potential understanding that grows from their very interaction. If they share anything, it is certainly not rules, but sensibilities and responses that are refined and elaborated.[13] It is the very features of the processes of interaction, namely, taking turns, using rhetorical devices, categorizing and so on, in the context of mutual expectations, that impart coherence and pattern to people's ongoing communicative interactions. However, while this patterning produces coherence and stability, it also has within it the possibility of change. That possibility exists, because the beginnings of understanding arise in the moments that strike people and these are often small details that may seem at first to be trivial, but which may amplify into new patterns of relating. It is in the unique variations in each other's expressions, as opposed to the exact regularities of rules, that people have their living understanding of each other. Living moments of the unique variations strike people and so arrest the ongoing routine flow of spontaneously responsive activity. As these variations are articulated, elaborated and refined, people change. Complex mixtures of unique influences shape the actions of people as reciprocally responsive movement between them points beyond the present moment to other possible connections. These movements of conversation are both repetitive and potentially transformative, and it is in the minute variations that the possibility of the novel arises. Given the local unrepeatable nature of context, these moments are inevitably unique, where thought, feeling, perception, memory, impulse and imagination are so tightly interwoven that they cannot be separated. As a result, people's actions are never fully orderly or fully disorderly.

Although a beginning and an end might be ascribed to a particular sequence of communicative interactions, that ascription is purely arbitrary, for even before a particular episode begins, even between total strangers, each has a history of experience. That history has patterned the private role playing of each individual in particular ways that enact, that is selectively enable and constrain, what that individual responds to both privately and publicly. That history establishes what aspects of the gesturing of the other will be striking, will call forth, or evoke, a response and what kind of response it will evoke. These processes of enactment and evocation are made possible, and at the same time limited, by previous history. Moreover, when they are not strangers, the history of their own personal relating to each other, and the histories of the groups they are part of, also become relevant. However, this history is not some kind of 'true' factual account but a reproduction in the living present that always leaves room for potential transformation. Furthermore, those collective and individual histories reproduced in the living present of communicative action are extending those histories into the future. This points to the narrative-like structuring of human experience. Is not simply that people are telling each other stories or that narrative is simply an alternative type of knowledge. The turn-taking, responsive relating of people may be thought of as forming narrative at the same time as that narrative patterns moral responsibility and turn taking. In other words, the experience of the living present, like the past, is structured in narrative-like ways.

I use the term narrative-like, rather than narrative, in order to make an important distinction. A narrative or story is normally thought of in its 'told' sense. A narrative is normally someone's narrative, told from the perspective of a narrator. It normally has a beginning, an end and a plot that moves the listener/reader from the beginning to the end in a more or less linear sequence. This kind of 'narrative told'[14] must be distinguished from the narrative-like process that is narrative in its making. Interaction in the manner described earlier evolves as narrative-like themes that normally have no single narrator's perspective. Beginnings and endings are rather arbitrary, and there are many plots emerging simultaneously. The narrative told is retrospective while narrative-in-its-making is currently emerging in the living present. The former is inevitably linear while the latter is intrinsically nonlinear. Despite these differences, there is a connection, and it is, I think, useful to think of experience as being patterned in a narrative-like way.

The neuroscientist, Damasio,[15] suggests that human bodies construct consciousness and knowledge in interaction with each other in a process in which the biological correlates of this activity take a narrative-like form. Consciousness 'consists of constructing an account of what happens within the organism when the organism interacts with an object, be it actually perceived or recalled, be it within the body boundaries (e.g., pain) or outside of them (e.g., a landscape). This account is a simple narrative without words. It does have characters (the organism, the object). It unfolds in time. Moreover, it has a beginning, a middle, and an end. The beginning corresponds to the initial state of the organism. The middle is the arrival of the object. The end is made up of reactions that result in a modified state of the organism'.[16] Damasio is suggesting that humans become conscious, they develop a feeling of knowing, when their bodies construct and present a 'specific kind of wordless knowledge' to do with being changed by contact with others and he describes in detail how this might happen. 'As far as the brain is concerned, the organism in the hypothesis is . . . the state of the internal milieu, viscera, vestibular system, and musculoskeletal frame. The account describes the relationship between the changing . . . [state] . . . and the sensorimotor maps of the object that causes those changes . . . . As the brain forms images of an object – such as a face, a melody, a toothache, the memory of an event – and as images of the object *affect* the state of the organism, yet another level of brain structure creates a swift nonverbal account of events that are taking place in the varied brain regions activated as a consequence of the object-organism interaction . . . . Looking back, with the license of metaphor, one might say that the swift, second order non-verbal account narrates a story: that of the organism caught in the act of representing its own changing state as it goes about representing something else. But the astonishing fact is that the knowable entity of the catcher has just been created in the narrative of the catching process'.[17] The resonance with Mead's description of the 'I-me' dialectic is striking. Mead talks about interactions between organisms while Damasio focuses on the biological correlates, that is, interactions between neural patterns in different brain regions. In doing so, he in effect provides an explanation of Mead's contention that the mind and self arise in interaction and that the central nervous system is such as to enable this to happen.

The psychologist, Bruner,[18] presents very similar views on the narrative structuring of adult experience. He suggests that humans are born with a predisposition to organize experience in narrative form and that the self is an autobiographical narrative that is continually retold, with variations. The sequential order of narrative provides structure, one that is internal to itself, and it is this internal structure, or plot, that gives the narrative its meaning, one that has nothing to do with a reality, true or false, outside of itself. The meaning of the narrative lies in its overall configuration or plot and each event, happening or mental state takes its meaning from the overall configuration. In order to make sense of the constituent parts of the narrative, one must grasp the overall plot. Narratives are inextricably interwoven truth and possibility and display sensitivity to what is ordinary and what is exceptional in human interaction. The negotiation of meaning between people is made possible by this feature of narrative in which meaning arises in identifying deviations from the ordinary in a comprehensible form. As they interact with each other in a group, each person takes it for granted that others will behave appropriately in a given situation, the norms for such appropriateness having been established by their history of interacting with each other. In other words, the habits, or practices, developed in the past create expectations for current and future action. When people behave in what is taken to be the normal, ordinary way, there is no need for further explanation. It is simply taken for granted, and if pressed for an explanation, people normally reply that such actions are what everybody does or is supposed to do. However, deviations from these expected actions or ways of speaking trigger a search for meaning that is usually provided by a story giving an account of an alternative world in which the unexpected action makes sense, that is, provides reasons for the behavior. Narrative, therefore, mediates between the norms of culture and unique individual beliefs, desires, and hopes. It renders the exceptional comprehensible. It provides a means of constructing a world and identifying its flow as well as regulating the affects of people.

The point I am making is that throughout life, the interactive communication between people forms narrative-like sequences, and it seems that there are biological correlates for this. It is not just that people tell each other stories but that their very experience together is organized in storey-like patterns that emerge in their turn-taking going on together. Experience is narrative-like in its formation and patterning in the living present and afterwards that experience may also be recounted in the form of the narrative 'told', but only ever partially. And such 'narratives told' feature prominently in the ongoing process of communicative negotiation between people in the living present.

The thematic patterning of experience

I am arguing, then, that human relating is human communicating and that human communicating is the action of human bodies in the medium of symbols. Through communicative interaction with each other, and with themselves, humans are able to cooperate in sophisticated ways in joint action using tools to operate within their human and non-human surroundings. It is communicative interaction that enables people to construct significant features of the nonhuman environment they live in: they breed cattle; they build physical structures; they design equipment that extends the range of communication, for example. However, communicative action in the medium of symbols does much more than this in that it constructs both individual mental and social reality. In communicative interaction, people actively respond to each other and in so doing, their experiences are patterned in narrative-like forms. In their relational communication, people are constructing intricate narratives and in reflecting on those narratives, they are also constructing abstract-systematic frameworks of propositions to explain what is going on. When they reflect on what they have been doing, on what they are doing, and on what they hope to do, they select aspects of these dense narratives/abstract frameworks to tell stories or extend their abstract-systematic frameworks of propositions in order to account for what they are doing and make sense of their worlds. In the process, their very identities, individually and collectively, emerge. Life on this view is an ongoing, richly connected multiplicity of stories and propositional frameworks. In this sense, the process is nonlinear, although stories told select a theme in all of this and give it a linear structure. My proposition, then, is that all human relationships, including the communicative action of a body with itself, that is mind, and the communicative actions between bodies, that is the social, are story lines and propositions constructed by those relationships at the same time as those story lines and propositions construct the relationships. They are all complex responsive processes of relating that can be thought of as themes and variations that recursively form themselves in human interaction.

The private role-play, the silent conversation, of each individual and their public interactions can be thought of as themes and variations reproducing history. It is these themes and variations that organize an individual's experience in the living present. However, what those particular themes are at a particular moment will depend just as much on the cues being presented by others as upon the personal history of a particular individual. Each individual is simultaneously evoking and provoking responses from others so that the particular personal organizing themes emerging for any one of them will depend as much on the others as on the individual concerned. Put like this, it becomes clear that no one individual can be organizing his or her experience in isolation, because they are all simultaneously evoking and provoking responses in each other. Together they immediately constitute complex responsive processes of a recursive, reflexive, self-referential kind. In addition, as they do so, themes emerge that organize their experience of being together out of which further themes continuously emerge.

The most obvious themes are, not surprisingly, those that reflect the official ideology of an organization as formal-conscious-legitimate themes. These are the publicly proclaimed visions, values and cultures of an organization, as well as its hierarchically defined roles, policies, procedures, plans and ways of using its tools, that is, its information and control systems and its technologies. They all sustain current power relations, indeed that is usually their purpose, although official ideology may from time to time include policies aimed at shifting power relations, for example, by positive discrimination.

These are the themes of the public transcript or strategic pose that Scott[19] pointed to. It is well known that these formal-conscious-legitimate themes are not sufficient on their own for an organization to function, and it is widely recognized that informal-conscious/ unconscious-shadow themes also pattern communicative interaction. These themes may have qualities of spontaneity and many will reflect unofficial ideologies, conscious and unconscious, that may well undermine official ideology and so shift power relations. These are the hidden transcripts and the arts of resistance that Scott[20] refers to. However, as such shifts in shadow themes emerge, they are reflected in emergent changes in for-mal-conscious-legitimate themes. These themes are continually reproduced and poten-tially transformed in the ongoing relating between people in the living present. It is not that formal-conscious-legitimate themes are of one kind, say intentional and designed, and informal-unconscious-shadow themes are self-organizing/emergent. All are aspects of local processes of continually reproduced and potentially transformed communica-tive interaction, where intentions and designs are themselves themes. They differ in their public visibility and in their fluidity, but they are not different in kind, and they are never separated from each other. They are dynamically interlinked processes of evolution. Why, then, am I making distinctions between them?

I think it is important to make distinctions between different aspects of themes patterning experience, because although they are simultaneous and inextricably inter-linked aspects of the same processes of symbolic interaction, they are often contradic-tory and conflicting. In effect, they often serve completely different purposes. Legitimate themes, as public transcripts and strategic poses, whether they are formal or informal, conscious or unconscious, are largely habitual. They have arisen in previous communi-cative interaction and are being reproduced in communicative interaction in the living present with relatively little variation. It follows that they are stabilizing and largely constructive of continuity. They are constraining in a particular way, namely, one that, in reflecting official ideology, sustains current power relations. In their constraint, legit-imate themes enable repetitive joint action. Whether conscious or unconscious, shadow themes (always informal) as hidden transcripts and the arts of resistance are much more spontaneous and reflect unofficial ideologies, which may either sustain or threaten cur-rent power relations. For example, the official ideology may espouse equal opportunity policies while unofficial ideologies, making it feel natural to continue discriminating against women and minorities, sustain current power relations. On the other hand, shadow themes may express unofficial ideologies that covertly undermine official ideol-ogy and so threaten current power relations. It is in this potential for conflict between shadow and legitimate themes that the potential for transformation arises, because trans-formation always involves some shift in power relations, some shift in current identity.

The currents of communicative interaction, therefore, do not constitute some harmo-nious whole and the living present is as much about conflict and competition as it is about harmony and cooperation. Indeed, without this paradox there could be no trans-formation. Looking backward or forward, no one is able to fully articulate what the themes were or how they linked into each other in reinforcing and contradictory ways. Each articulation is an act of interpretation in the living present as part of communica-tive interaction in the living present. Each act of interpretation in the living present reconstructs the past, potentially changing its meaning. Furthermore, no one can articu-late all the themes in the process of communicative interaction in the living present of a particular local situation, each interpretation being yet another gesture in the ongoing flow of gesture-response. It is even less possible for anyone to articulate all the interacting themes across an organization, an industry or a society. Again, any attempt is simply a localized interpretation in the living present. Nevertheless, coherence emerges in the vast complexity of communicative interactions across enormous numbers of local situations because of the intrinsic capacity of local interaction to pattern itself coherently in the interplay of the intentions of people. However, the pattern of this coherence is not predictable in advance, and it involves both destruction and creation, both stability and instability. Human interaction is imperfect communication between people, misunderstanding and the partial taking into silent conversation by one person of ways of conversing acquired from others in the course of public conversations. Diversity arises in misunderstanding and in the cross fertilization of concepts through interaction between different patterns of conversation. This is where the tension between conformity and deviance becomes important. It is this deviance that imparts the internal capacity to spontaneously evolve new patterns of conversation.

The conversation of gestures, the interplay of local communicative actions and the nature of organizational life

In this chapter, I have been describing how we might understand our ordinary everyday experience of life in organizations as the conversation of gestures in which our local communicative actions play into each other to produce emergent, inseparably merged narrative-like themes and abstract propositions in that experience. I have pointed to how it is we who are producing such themes and propositions and how such themes and propositions are simultaneously organizing our experience of being together. In doing this, I have been in effect drawing attention to the fundamentally interactive, communicative nature of the life games we find ourselves pre-occupied with. It is in our pre-occupation in such games that we express the habitus, the social patterns of habit in which we live, the themes and propositions, all of which we are forming and which are at the same time forming our experience. And this is more than repetition and it is not the creation of fixed structures, but the ongoing iteration of habit in local situations where tiny variations can escalate into altered habits. I am claiming that this approach to human interaction offers a radically different alternative way of thinking about organizations and their management to that of the dominant discourse. Understood in this way, organizations are not systems outside our interaction that the powerful are designing but they are, rather, various games we are all preoccupied with. Alternatively, we can think of organizations as particular evolving patterns of habitus. On the other hand, we can think of organizations as the ongoing conversation of gestures. Moreover, to put the same point in slightly different terms, we can understand organizations as particular narrative and propositional themes emerging across a population of organizational members, and even further across the populations of societies, in local complex responsive processes. To put it as simply as possible, by organization, I mean the ongoing conversation in which people accomplish all their organizational tasks.

I am also claiming that this is an understanding of organizations which gives a more useful account of what we are doing in organizations, because it focuses attention immediately and directly on what organizational members are immersed in doing all day and that is engaging in conversation. It becomes a matter of great importance, therefore, what kinds of conversational pattern are being iterated moment by moment. Some conversations may be characterized by the simplicity of a narrow focus on a few issues and highly repetitive themes – the same few narratives and propositions are endlessly repeated with very little variation indeed. If most ongoing organizational conversations take this form then it is likely that organizational members are 'stuck' in what we might even call neurotic patterns and they cannot change much at all. On the other hand, conversation may be highly complex, drawing attention to wide varieties of issues and questions in which richer narratives and propositions are expressed with considerable variations. Such fluid conversation makes change, creative and destructive, much more possible. In reality, of course, some conversations in an organization will display 'stuckness' while others will be more 'fluid' and yet others will display characteristics of both. The role of effective leader-managers can then be understood as that of participating in the ongoing conversations in ways that encourage fluid conversation in which meaning and possibilities of action are opening up rather than closing down. In other words, we come to understand the primary function of leader-manager as one of widening and deepening communication.[21]

I think the way of thinking about organizations which I am suggesting can illuminate what investment capitalism might mean. After the oil crises of the 1970s, the interplay of communicative actions between corporations, banks, financial regulators, management consultancies, business schools, politicians and policy makers took the form of conversation in many, many local interactions from which emerged narrative themes and propositions across the global economy which could be labelled as 'investment capitalism'. This is a narrative of executives, consultants and investment bankers engaging in activities, conversation, of merger and acquisition. The conversation of organizational life took the form of focusing narrowly on shareholders and the need to satisfy their voracious appetite of share price and earning increases. The propositions emerging in many, many conversations took the form of agency theory and models of capital asset pricing and efficient markets. The narrative of the 'masters of the universe' with their narrow and repetitive themes of 'bottom line', short-term gains, quarterly earnings, share prices, efficient markets, bonuses and increasing earnings expectations, all organized the experience of members of organizations across the globe. Nevertheless, the investment capitalism narrative became increasingly stuck as the twentieth century gave way to the twenty-first. Moreover, the problem with a highly simplified, dominating and repetitive narrative in which conversation is dominated by second-order abstractions, is that it covers over what people are actually doing which is taking increasingly reckless risks in a more and more arrogant belief in their own mastery amounting to fantasies of omnipotence. Of course, what was not being focused on emerged with a vengeance, as it usually does, and created completely surprising and unintended consequences. The alternative way of thinking about organizations, not as systems outside our interaction but as emergent patterns in our conversational interaction, shifts the exclusive focus of attention on second-order abstractions of systems, models and propositions to a focus on how such abstractions are being constructed and used in conversational interaction. This alternative way of thinking about organizations immediately suggests an alternative way of thinking about the roles of leader-managers, not as the designers of systems or masters of anything in particular but as particularly influential participants in the ongoing conversation. They can participate in dominating ways to feed their fantasies of omnipotence and if they succeed in cowing others into submission, they will play an important part in producing highly repetitive stuck conversations which will eventually collapse. On the other hand, they can participate in ongoing conversations in a way that deepens and widens communication, at least some of the time. Just how leader-managers are participating in the ongoing conversation of organizational life, the ongoing ordinary politics of daily life, is therefore a matter of great importance. The importance of local interaction and emergent population-wide patterns means that any claim to mastery by leader-managers must be a fantasy, but this does not reduce leader-managers to ornamental bystanders; it just suggests a more realistic understanding of what they can do and what they actually do, and this is considerable for both good and ill.

Conclusion

The action-based approach I have been describing moves away from the notion of systems of rules operating to cause coherence in human communication and looks for ordering properties in the nature of communicative action itself. It focuses attention on the negotiated nature of turn taking and turn making in conversation and on the intrinsic properties of responsive communicative interaction to produce coherence as both the continuity of habit and the novelty that arises in the variations. It explains that production of coherence and variations in terms of themes that emerge across a population in many, many local interactions consisting, at the same time, of the private experience of mind and the social experience of being together. Organization, coherence and structure are realized as action, which are essentially local processes of turn taking in conversation in the living present. The very constitution of organizations depends on the production of local knowledge through local language practices. Organizations are fundamentally conversational in nature, and they stay more or less unchanged when conversation is stuck in repetition but have the potential for change when conversation is more fluid, more complex. Ordinary, everyday local interaction between people can be most helpfully and most realistically understood, I claim, as the complex responsive processes of ongoing gesture and response. It is in the conversation of gestures that we are creating the games we are so invested in and pre-occupied with. The games we are creating are the habitus, the social habits, we unconsciously enact and which are creating us. It is in this that we are immersed and also in which we are abstracting to construct the second order abstractions of maps, models and plans which we use as rhetorical tools in the ordinary politics of daily life. Only a very small fraction of this activity can be described as decision makers consciously identifying problem situations and selecting the right tools and techniques to use on solving the problem. The dominant discourse tends to focus on this tiny fraction of the reality of organizational life. If we take the conversation of gestures, the local interaction, as central to organizational life the main question then becomes just how population-wide patterns emerge in all this. This is the question to be addressed in the next chapter.

Notes

1   Elias, N. (1939) *The Civilizing Process*, Blackwell, Oxford.
2   Ibid., pp. 367–68.
3   Ibid., p. 366.
4   Elias, N. (1991) *The Society of Individuals*, Oxford: Blackwell, p 62
5   Shannon, C. and Weaver, W. (1949) *The Mathematical Theory of Communication*, Urbana, IL: University of Illinois Press.
6   Mead, G. H. (1932) *The Philosophy of the Present*, Chicago: University of Chicago Press; Mead, G. H. (1934) *Mind, Self and Society*, Chicago: Chicago University Press; Mead, G. H. (1938) *The Philosophy of the Act*, Chicago: Chicago University Press; Mead, G. H. (1923) 'Scientific Method and the Moral Sciences', *International Journal of Ethics*, XXXIII, 229–47.

7 Damasio, A. R. (1994) *Descartes' Error: Emotion, Reason and the Human Brain*, London: Picador; Damasio, A. R. (1999) *The Feeling of What Happens: Body and Emotion in the Making of Consciousness*, London: Heinemann.

8 Siegel, D. J. (1999) *The Developing Mind: Toward a Neurobiology of Interpersonal Experience*, New York: The Guildford Press; Freeman, W. J. (1994) 'Role of Chaotic Dynamics in Neural Plasticity', in van Pelt, J., Corner, M. A., Uylings, H. B. M., and Lopes da Silva, F. H. (eds) *Progress in Brain Research*, Vol 102, Amsterdam: Elsevier Science BV; Freeman, W.J. (1995) 'Societies of Brains: A Study in the Neuroscience of Love and Hate', Hillsdale, NJ: Lawrence Earlsbaum Associates Publishers; Freeman, W. J. and Schneider, W. (1982) 'Changes in the Spatial Patterns of Rabbit Olfactory EEG with Conditioning to Odors, Psychophysiology', 19, 45–56; Freeman, W. J. and Barrie J. M. (1994) 'Chaotic Oscillations and the Genesis of Meaning in Cerebral Cortex', in Buzsaki, G., Llinas, R. Singer, W., Berthoz, A. and Christen, Y. (eds) *Temporal Coding in the Brain*, Berlin: Springer.

9 Goffman, E. (1981) *Forms of Talk*, Philadelphia: University of Pennsylvania Press; Garfinkel, H. (1967) *Studies in Ethnomethodology*, Englewood Cliffs, NJ: Prentice Hall.

10 Sacks, H. (1992) *Lectures on Conversations*, Oxford: Blackwell; Shegloff, E. A. (1991) 'Reflections on Talk and Social Structures', in Boden, D. and Zimmerman, D. H. (eds) (1991) *Talk and Social Structure*, Cambridge: Polity Press; Jefferson, G. (1978) 'Sequential Aspects of Storytelling in Conversation', in Schenkein, J. (ed.) (1978) *Studies in the Organization of Conversational Interaction*, New York: Academic Press; Boden, D. (1994) *The Business of Talk: Organizations in Action*, Cambridge: Polity Press.

11 Shotter, J. (1993) *Conversational Reality: Constructing Life Through Language*, Thousand Oaks, CA: Sage Publications.

12 Shotter, J. (1993) *Conversational Reality: Constructing Life Through Language*, Thousand Oaks, CA: Sage Publications; Shotter, J. and Katz, A. M. (1996) 'Hearing the Patient's "Voice": Towards a Social Poietics in Diagnostic Interviews', *Social Science and Medicine*, 46, 919–31.

13 Ibid.

14 Boje, D. M. (1991) 'The Storytelling Organization: A Study of Performance in an Office Supply Firm', *Administrative Science Quarterly*, 36, 106–26; Boje, D. M. (1994) 'Organizational Storytelling: The Struggle of Pre-Modern, Modern and Postmodern Organizational Learning Discourses', *Management Learning*, 25(3), 433–62; Boje, D. M. (1995) 'Stories of the Storytelling Organization: A Postmodern Analysis of Disney as Tamara-Land', *Academy of Management Journal*, 38(4), 997–1055; Gabriel, Y. (1998) 'Same Old Story or Changing Stories? Folkloric, Modern and Postmodern Mutations', in Grant, D., Keenoy, T. and Oswick, C. (eds) (1998) *Discourse and Organisation*, London: Sage; Grant, D., Keenoy, T. and Oswick, C. (eds.) (1998) *Discourse and Organisation*, London: Sage.

15 Damasio, A. R. (1999) *The Feeling of What Happens: Body and Emotion in the Making of Consciousness*, London: Heinemann.

16 Ibid. p. 168.

17 Ibid. p. 120.

18 Bruner, J. (1990) *Acts of Meaning*, Cambridge MA: Harvard University Press.

19 Scott, J. C. (1990) *Domination and the Arts of Resistance: Hidden Transcripts*, New Haven: Yale University Press.

20 Ibid.

21 Foulkes, S. H. (1964) *Therapeutic Group Analysis*, London: George Allen & Unwin.

8 Turning the dominant discourse on its head

Organizational continuity and transformation emerging in local interaction rather than being chosen by managers

The last chapter looked in some detail at the nature of local interaction as ongoing communicative interaction taking the form of the conversation of gestures. My claim is that it is in many, many ongoing local interactions that there emerges coherent organizational patterns across the population of an organization's members and across the populations of other organizations they interact with. Examples of such patterns are the interconnected activities of producing air transport services at an airline company, patterns of taking turns to speak at meetings which reflect hierarchical position or gender, patterns of designing sophisticated financial derivatives, and patterns of activities that reflect particular beliefs about the nature of education at a university. Examples of coherent patterns across populations of organizations are globalization, recession, credit crunch and rapidly expanding internet services. The intention in this chapter is to explore how such population-wide patterns are linked to local interaction and how local interaction is linked to the population-wide patterns.

People in organizations accomplish whatever it is that they accomplish through continually interacting with a relatively small number of others. We can describe this as local interaction. It does not matter where one is in the hierarchy of an organization; one is still interacting on an hourly, daily basis with a small group of others. Even the CEO of a huge corporation spends his or her day relating to only a small fraction of the organization's membership, just as any clerk much lower down the hierarchy does. The number of colleagues the CEO interacts with may well be larger than those the clerk interacts with, but both are limited and in that sense, both are local. The power ratio is tilted substantially toward the CEO and away from the clerk so that the actions of the CEO may evoke responses from very large numbers of people while the actions of the clerk are attended to by only a few. However, although responses to the CEO's actions may be numerous, their very number means that they cannot be direct responses to him or her. Instead, those responses will be expressed in many, many local situations. In all of these local situations, people are interacting with each other according to patterns, themes, habits or routines, which they may spontaneously adapt at a particular time according to the contingencies of the particular situation they find themselves in. All of this reflects their own personal histories and the histories of the local groupings and wider societies they find themselves in. The point is that, no matter who we are, each of us is always interacting locally to get things done in organizations as well as the other situations of life.

But at the same time, no matter who we are, we are constrained in what we do together locally by what may feel like major *external forces* beyond our control, widespread, overall *structures* we have to take as given, *institutionalized instruments of power* which we have no option but to submit to, pre-existing *technologies* that shape what we do, and *allocations of resources* about which we can do little. We can describe these population-wide patterns as the global. For example, we are constrained by our organization's hierarchical structure, its authorizing and reporting procedures, particularly to do with the allocation of resources, and the accepted ways of talking and doing things that we call the organization's culture. Just as constraining are the 'forces' and 'structures' of the wider society our organization is a part of. For example, the law, government policies for regulating industries and controlling public sector organizations, market allocation of monetary resources, legislation and pressure to provide equal opportunities, collective campaigns to do with animal rights and ecological sustainability, trends such as globalization and so on. To understand how we get things done in organizations, therefore, we need to understand the relationship between local interaction and the global, which may usually be felt as only constraining but which is, of course, at the same time enabling.

Nowadays, the most widespread way of understanding the relationship between the local and the global is in terms of systems. People interact locally in a team, project group or department and this is often thought of as a system produced by the interaction of individual members who are understood as parts of that system. Therefore, each team, group and department has its own purpose, objectives, missions, procedures and local ways of doing things, which together constitute a system and members must conform to this system if it is all to work. In other words, in their interaction, people form the system and that system in turn acts as a causal force on their interactions. However, such a local system cannot operate in isolation but must interact with other teams, groups and departments, also understood as systems. In their interaction, these subsystems form the organizational system and that organizational system is thought to act back on each subsystem as a causal force. Each subsystem must fit in with the purpose, objectives, missions, procedures and organization-wide ways of doing things. It is this higher level, global requirement that is felt as constraining, although it is also enabling. Furthermore, no organizational system can operate in isolation but must interact with other organizational systems, together producing an even higher global level or supra-system such as an industry, market, nation or society. Each organizational system must then fit in with the wider purposes, objectives, procedures and ways of doing things characteristic of the supra-system. Moreover, it is this requirement that is felt to be an external force that constrains members of every organization, although it enables cooperative action as well. The supra-system, therefore, acts back on organizations as causal force shaping organizational systems. Then, there is an even higher-level system of industries, nations and societies interacting with each other to produce global economies and international bodies and these too act back as causal forces on the lower level systems.

In this way of thinking, then, we have the notion of a nested hierarchy of systems in which the higher levels act back as enabling constraints on the lower levels which in turn produce the higher levels. Down at the bottom of this hierarchy is the local interaction of people in their teams, groups and departments and as one moves up this hierarchy, one increasingly encounters the global. At the local level, people are severely constrained in what they can do by the requirements of the various global levels. Furthermore, each level is understood to be subject to its own laws and these become the focus of different academic disciplines. So, at the level of the individual, we need to turn to psychology and at the level of the team or group, ways of understanding group dynamics become relevant. Then, at the level of the organization, explanations are provided by microeconomics and organizational and management theory. At the level of markets and industries, it is macroeconomics that provides the required explanations and at the level of nations and societies, we turn to sociology and political theory.

What happens in this way of thinking is that we increasingly understand what is happening in terms of impersonal forces or systems, which I called second order abstractions in Chapter 4, that become increasingly divorced from ordinary human interaction as we move from the local to higher and higher global levels. For example, neoclassical economics is built on a very simple assumption about humans, summarized in the phrase 'economic man' who is assumed to be a calculating, utility maximizing agent. Thereafter, the modelling and theorizing of economic science broadly continues in terms of impersonal market forces or impersonal routines without much reference to real people. Much the same can be said for the modelling and theorizing to be found in mainstream organizational theory and sociology. Throughout, people, ordinary human bodies, are conspicuous by their absence and their ordinary everyday experiences as they go about their daily work in their local situations are disregarded as rather unimportant. They are thought to be so constrained by the operation of the higher-level systems that the focus of attention is on the design of those impersonal higher-level systems. It is thought that if we are to become more effective, if we are to change, then this requires designed change in some higher-level system. It will not be enough if people try to change anything in their own local interactions. One result of this thinking, so widely taken up now, is that people at local levels feel powerless and alienated from their own experience. In addition, it has important ethical implications in that when things go wrong, we think that the blame must be directed at the higher-level systems and those senior people who are responsible for them. The Hutton Enquiry a few years ago in the UK into allegations that the government had distorted intelligence information to justify the Iraq war provides a very clear example. Hutton concluded that members of the government were not to blame and condemned the BBC for broadcasting inaccurate allegations. In particular, it was concluded that the fault lay in the BBC's editorial system and top executives of the BBC were to blame for this. The Chairman and the CEO were then forced to resign and assurances were given that the system would be improved so that it would never happen again.

What I have been describing so far, is a particular, widely prevalent way of understanding the relationship between local interaction and the global, which I find problematic because of the way it distances us from our own experience. It is based on the assumption that global coherence follows from global design. This chapter will continue an examination of communication as conversation of gestures to provide an alternative way of understanding the connection between the local and the global. I will be arguing in the following sections that, while it may be useful to think in terms of nested systems in the natural sciences, it is not appropriate when it comes to thinking about human action and that what is emerging in the local interaction of human agents is not a system at all but further patterns of interaction both locally and globally at the same time. Mead's further development of the ideas described in the last chapter provides a way of thinking about the relationship between human local interaction and population-wide social patterns.

Generalizing/idealizing and functionalizing: social objects and cult values

Mead's main concern was not simply with a dyadic form of communication which was the main focus of attention in Chapter 7, but with much wider, much more complex patterns of interaction between many people. He was concerned with complex social acts in which many people are engaged in conversation through which they accomplish the tasks of fitting in and conflicting with each other to realize their objectives and purposes. People do not come to an interaction with each other afresh each time, because they are born into an already existing, socially evolved pattern and they continue to play their part in its further evolution. Mead expressed this in the concept of the generalized other discussed in the last chapter. In order to accomplish complex social acts, it is not enough for those involved to be able to take the attitude of the small numbers of people they may be directly engaged with at a particular time; they need to be able to take the attitude, the general tendency to act, of all of those directly or indirectly engaged in the complex social act. It would be impossible to do this in relation to each individual so engaged, but humans have developed the capacity to generalize the attitudes of many. In acting in the present, each individual is then taking up the attitude of a few specific others and at the same time, the attitude of this generalized other, the attitude of the group, the organization or the society. These wider, generalized attitudes are evolving historically and are always implicated in every human action. In play, the child takes the role of another but in the game the child must take on the role of the other and of the game, that is, of all participants in the game and its rules and procedures. In the evolution of society many generalizations emerge which are taken up, or particularized in people's interactions with each other. This is a point of major importance. Mead draws attention to paradoxical processes of generalization and particularization at the same time. Mental and social activities are processes of generalizing and particularizing at the same time. Individuals act in relation to that which is common to all of them (generalizing) but responded to somewhat differently by each of them in each situation in each present period (particularizing).

Mead provided a number of formulations of these generalizing-particularizing processes. One such formulation is his explanation of self-consciousness, referred to in the last chapter, which is a process of a person taking the attitude of the group to himself, where that attitude is the 'me'. The self does not arise in the attitude, the tendency to act, of specific others toward oneself but as a social, generalizing process where the 'me' is a generalization across a whole community or society. For example, what it means to be an individual, a person, a man or a woman, a professional and so on, does not arise in relation to a few specific people but in relation to a particular society in a particular era. We in the West think of ourselves now as individuals in a completely different way to people in the West did four hundred years ago and a different way to people in other cultures. In the 'I-me' dialectic, then, we have a process in which the generalization of the 'me' is made particular in the response of the 'I' for a particular person at a particular time in a particular place. For example, I may take up what it means to be a man in my society in a particular way that differs in some respects to how others see themselves as men in my own society, in other societies and at other times.

Mead's discussion of what he called the social object[1] is yet another formulation of this generalizing and particularizing process. A physical object must be distinguished from a social object, because the former exists in nature and can be understood in terms of itself, while the latter has to be understood in terms of social acts. A physical object is found in nature but a social object is a 'tendency to act' rather than a concept or a thing. In a social setting, then, Mead used the term 'object' in tension with the usual understanding of object as a thing in nature. The pattern or tendency Mead calls an object is in a sense an object in that it is what we perceive in taking it up in our acting but this is a perception of our own acting not a thing. We seem to have a strong tendency to reify patterns of acting and this makes it important to emphasize that the social object is not a thing. Market exchange is an example of a social act: one person offers to buy food and this evokes a complex range of responses from other people to provide the food. However, it involves more than this, because the one making the offer can only know how to make the offer if he is able to take the attitude of the other parties to the bargain. All essential phases of the complex social act of exchange must appear in the actions of all involved and appear as essential features of each individual's actions. Buying and selling are involved in each other. A social act involves the cooperation of many people in which the different parts of the act undertaken by different individuals appear in the act of each individual. The tendencies to act as others act are present in the conduct of each individual involved, and it is this presence that is responsible for the appearance of the social object in the experience of each individual. The social act defines the object of the act, and this is a social object which is only to be found in the conduct of the different individuals engaged in the complex social act. The social object appears in the experience of each individual as a stimulus to a response not only by that individual but also by the others involved – this is how each can know how the others are likely to act and it is the basis of coordination. A social object is thus a kind of gesture together with tendencies to respond in particular ways. Social objects are common plans or patterns of action related to the future of the act. The social object is a generalization which is taken up, or particularized, by all in a group/society in their actions. Social objects have evolved in the history of the society of selves and each individual is born into such a world of social objects. In other words, individuals are forming social objects while being formed by them in an evolutionary process. Social control depends upon the degree to which the individual takes the attitude of the others, that is, takes the attitude which is the social object. All institutions are social objects and serve to control individuals who find them in their experience. The term social object is thus another way of describing what I have been calling population-wide patterns so that we can understand social objects as patterns across a population which are emerging and being sustained in local interactions. Social objects are also what I mean by habitus and game. Examples of social objects are banking, financial regulations and business schools. Social objects also take the form of second order abstractions such as bailouts of banks and increases in money supply to counter recessions.

Mead also linked social objects to values and in another formulation of the interaction between the general and the particular, he draws a distinction between cult values and their functionalization.[2] He pointed to how people have a tendency to individualize and idealize a collective and treat it 'as if' *it* had overriding motives or values, amounting to a process in which the collective constitutes a 'cult'. Members of 'cults' forget the 'as if' nature of their construct and act in a manner driven by the cult's values. Cults are maintained when leaders present to people's imagination a future free from obstacles that could prevent them from being what they all want to be. The visions that leaders of organizations are nowadays supposed to have are examples of this. A cult provides a feeling of enlarged personality in which individuals participate and from which they derive their value as persons. Mead said that they were the most precious part of our heritage and examples of cult values are democracy, treating others with respect, regarding life as sacred, and belief in being American or British. However, it is important to stress that cult values can be good or bad or both. Cult values would include 'ethnic purity' and 'loving your neighbor'. Mead points out that the process of idealization is far from unproblematic and could easily lead to actions that others outside the cult will come to regard as bad, even evil. It is in such cultish behavior that we carry out the most terrible treatment of each other. Mead was pointing to the dangers of focusing on the cult values themselves, on the values of the personalized institution or system, and directly applying them as overriding universal norms, conformity to which constitutes the requirement of continuing membership of the institution. Normally, however, idealization is accompanied by functionalization. Idealizations, or cult values, emerge in the historical evolution of any group or institution to which they are ascribed, and they can become functional values in the everyday interactions between members of the institution rather than being simply applied in a way that enforces the conformity of a cult. For example, the cult value of a hospital might be to 'provide each patient with the best possible care'. However, such a cult value has to be repeatedly functionalized in many unique specific situations throughout the day. As soon as cult values become functional values in real daily interaction, conflict arises, and it is this conflict that must be negotiated by people in their practical interaction with each other.

To summarize, social objects are *generalized tendencies*, common to large numbers of people, *to act in similar ways in similar situations*. These generalized tendencies to act are iterated in each living present as rather repetitive, *habitual patterns of action*. However, in their continual iteration, these general tendencies to act are normally *particularized* in the specific situation and the specific present the actors find themselves in. Such particularization is inevitably a *conflictual process* of interpretation as the meaning of the generalization is established in a specific situation. The possibility of *transformation*, that is, further evolution, of the social object arises in this particularizing because of the potential for *spontaneity* to generate variety in human action and the capacity of nonlinear interaction to *amplify* consequent small differences in their particularization. While physical objects are to be found in nature, social objects can only be experienced in their particularization in complex social acts in the living present. Social objects do not have any existence outside of such particularizing social acts. As well as being generalizations, social objects may also take the form of *idealizations* or cult values. Such cult values present to people a future free of conflicts and constraints, evoking a sense of enlarged personality in which they can accomplish anything. Such values have the effect of *including* those who adhere to them and *excluding* those who do not, so establishing collective or '*we*' *identities* for all of the individuals in both groupings. Social objects/cult values are thus closely linked to *power*. Social objects as generalized tendencies to act in similar ways both enable and constrain the actors at the same time. Social objects are thus forms of *social control* reflected in figurations of power relations between people.

The relationship between local interaction and global patterns

In all his formulations of human communicative interaction, Mead presented the same paradox. Gesture and response are inseparable phases of one social act in which meaningful patterns of interaction arise. Social objects are generalizations found in their particularization. Cult values are idealizations found in their functionalization. I suggest that the meaningful patterns in such particularizing social processes take the form of emerging narrative and propositional themes that organize the experience of being together. Such themes are iterated in each present taking the paradoxical form of habit, or continuity, and potential transformation at the same time. The essentially reflexive nature of human consciousness and self-consciousness means that we have the capacity to reflect imaginatively on population-wide patterns, articulating both the habitual and the just emerging transformations and in doing so, either sustain the habitual or reinforce the transformation of habit.

In our reflection, we generalize the tendencies we observe across many present situations, creating imaginative 'wholes' that have never existed and never will.[3] What we are doing in creating these imaginative 'wholes' is constructing in our interaction perceptions of unity in the patterning of our interactions across a population. That imaginatively perceived unity is then a generalized tendency to act in similar situations in similar ways. What is emerging is the imaginative generalization that is one phase of the social object. The other phase, which is inseparable from the generalization, is the particularizing of the general in the specific contingent situations we find ourselves in. The general can only be found in its particularization in our local interaction and that particularizing inevitably involves conflict. A particularly important form of social object is the norms, the obligatory constraints, that serve as the moral basis for choosing one action rather than another. In reflecting upon our patterns of interaction, in generalizing those patterns and in imaginatively constructing some kind of unity of experience, we employ the tools of writing to codify habits or routines, for example as law, and even design changes in them. However, any intentionally designed change can only ever be a generalization and what that means can only be found in the particularization, that is, in the interplay between the intentions of the designers of the generalization and the intentions of those who are particularizing it.

We not only generalize habitual patterns of interaction to construct some kind of unity of experience, but also inevitably idealize our imaginatively constructed unities or 'wholes'. It is in this process that we experience value, the voluntary compulsions that serve as criteria for selecting what we feel to be good actions.[4] Here again, Mead presented a paradoxical formulation in his distinction between cult and functional values. The idealization must be functionalized in specific contingent situations – the meaning of the idealization is only to be found in the experience of its functionalization. The functionalizing process inevitably involves conflict. Once again, we may employ the tool of writing to articulate and codify the idealizations in the form of ethical propositions, myths and inspiring narratives. They may be presented as intended, crafted vision statements for a corporation, for example. However, although someone can design and intentionally present statements about values, they can only ever be cult values which have no meaning on their own. In other words, the cult value is the first phase of a social act which can never be separated from the other phase, namely, functionalizing. Ideology can also be thought of in paradoxical terms as the simultaneous voluntary compulsion of value and the obligatory restriction of norm. Ideology provides criteria for choosing one action rather than another and it serves as the unconscious basis of power relations, making it feel natural to include some and exclude others from particular groups, thereby sustaining the power difference between those groups.

Given the aforementioned points, we can now understand what we mean by the local and the global and how they are related to each other. The global is the imaginatively created unity we perceive in patterns of interaction across the populations we are members of – it is the generalization and the idealization as one phase of the social object. The local is the particularizing of the general and the functionalizing of the idealization in local interaction. However, these are phases of one social act and can never be separated.

The general is only to be found in the experience of the particular – it has no existence outside of it. The idealization is only to be found in the experience of the particular – it too has no existence outside of it. The process of particularizing is essentially reflective, reflexive and quite possibly imaginative and spontaneous. It is possible for individuals and groups of individuals, particularly powerful ones, to intentionally articulate and even design the general, and the ideal but the particularizing and the functionalizing involves an interplay of many intentions and values and this interplay cannot be intended or designed, except temporarily in fascist power structures and cults. Furthermore, the generalizations and idealizations will further evolve in their particularization and func-tionalization. In short, the global and the local are paradoxical processes of generalizing and particularizing at the same time. In Chapter 2, I described how social objects taking the form of ant-trust legislation were particularized in ways the legislators had not intended. The generalization of ant-trust law was made particular in the interaction of executives in corporations, banks and advisors to managers from which emerged the powerful institution of management consultancies. Similarly the deregulation of finan-cial sectors in the 1980s and 1990s was made particular in the emergence of powerful investment banks and eventually in the patterns of frozen lending known as the credit crunch.

This point about the particularization of generalizations is of great importance and reinforces, for me, the inappropriateness of simply applying the notion of complex adap-tive systems, or any notion of systems for that matter, to human interaction. In complex adaptive systems, the agents follow rules; in effect, they directly and exactly enact gen-eralizations and idealizations. If humans simply applied generalizations and idealiza-tions in their interactions with each other then there would be no possibility of individual imagination and spontaneity and hence no possibility of creativity. We would simply be determined by the generalizations and idealizations. It is in the essentially conflictual particularizing of the generalizations and idealizations, which have emerged over long periods of human interaction, that socially constructed, interdependent individuals dis-play spontaneity, reflection, reflexivity, imagination and creativity as well as conflict. Spontaneity, it seems to me, should be distinguished from impulse. In humans, impulse is an unreflective compulsion to do something, on the spur of the moment, as it were. Impulsive actions, however, are still socially formed and reflexive. Humans are reflex-ive in that their actions are formed by their own histories. Whatever we do, whether impulsive or not, depends upon who we are, upon identity/self, which is socially formed. Humans are also socially reflexive in that what they think and what they do is formed by the group, community and society they are part of and has a history. This social reflexiv-ity is also shaping whatever we do, impulsive or not. Spontaneity is often spoken of as if it were the same as impulse and the opposite of reflection in that spontaneous action also has that spur of the moment quality. However, this is to chop out one event from an ongoing flow of interaction. I would argue that if we pay attention to the interactions preceding the selected moment of spontaneous interaction, we find people exploring the situation they face in ways that are reflective, and it is because of this 'preparation' as it were that someone takes spontaneous action, having the appearance of 'on the spur of the moment'. What distinguishes this kind of spontaneous interaction from mere impulse is that it is a skilful performance, not just a reaction. Spontaneity is what makes it pos-sible for people to deal with the unique contingencies of the situations they always face. Spontaneity generates variety in responses, often as small differences that have the potential for being escalated. In other words, human spontaneity is closely associated with the possibility of transformation and novelty in human interaction. Spontaneity in humans, I would argue, is reflexive, just as impulse is but unlike impulse, the spontaneous act emerges in a history of skilful, reflective performance. Furthermore, spontaneity is never simply located in the individual, or the 'I', because the 'I' can never be separated from 'me', the social.

I have been describing the particularizations of social objects and cult values in local interaction in a way that indicates the habitual, unconscious manner in which people do this. Both Elias and Bourdieu used the term habitus in much the same way as the enactment of the habitual patterns of action of people in a particular society. Both of these writers also likened habitus to the game, as did Mead, and Bourdieu described how in their ordinary local interaction people are pre-occupied in the game in which they are invested and have an interest, for example bankers have an investment in banking which is far more than financial – the investment I am talking about here is the dynamic sustaining of identity. In Chapter 4, I used the term immersing to signify this kind of ordinary local activity in which we are caught up together in our experience of going on together and I contrasted it with the activities of abstracting. I made a distinction between first and second order activities of abstracting. First order abstraction is the categorizing of our perceptions and experiences as when we talk about, say, tables or holidays in general. Such first order abstracting is a necessary part of the activity of thinking and of reflecting on our experience. Furthermore, the development of thought involves second order abstracting which is the manipulation in some way of first order abstractions from direct experience. In second order abstracting, we draw away even further our immersing directly in our ordinary experience and operate in thought with metaphysical concepts, for example, and then in the scientific revolution and the age of reason with the models relating first order abstractions to each other in science, and the use of maps and various techniques in the administration of the modern state. It is the operation in communicative interaction in terms of second order abstracting which provides sufficient simplification of perceptions of the world and our experience to enable us to predict and control to a certain extent from a distance. I think that both first and second order abstracting also constitute both social objects and cult values. Examples of such social objects and cult values are scientific theories of the natural world, for example, neo-Darwinian evolution, and the administrative tools and procedures of organizations such as plans and visions and monitoring procedures. They constitute social objects, because, for example, the theory of evolution is taken up by large numbers of people in similar ways in similar situations and it forms an almost religious belief for some people. Another example is the notion of, say, 'plan' which is also taken up in similar ways by large numbers of people in similar situations. These also can constitute cult values in that rational planning becomes the right thing to do. However, as with other social objects and cult values, the second order abstractions must also be made particular in particular circumstances and that always happens in local interaction, and it is in this local interaction that the social object and cult value of, say, 'plan' evolves.

The making particular of the social objects and cult values taking the form of second order abstractions may be what we could describe as conscious, rational choice, and at the same time, making particular will usually also take the form of unconscious immersing. We become pre-occupied in the game of planning, for example, tending to reify the second order abstract models we build of the world we are acting into and we lose awareness of doing this. In other words, in enacting social objects, cult values, habitus, the game or whatever we want to call it, we are at the same time immersing ourselves in our experience and abstracting from, simplifying, that experience in order to reflect upon it or to achieve some measure of control over others from a distance. I think if we take this attitude, we can see that understanding human organizing in terms of local interaction, the interplay of deliberate plans and unconsciously motivated actions, in which population-wide order emerges as continuity and change, we are not dismissing abstraction, or the plans and tools of governance, or the impact of institutions and laws but understanding all of them as much more complex activities which do not ensure control in any comprehensive or simple way but are nevertheless necessary for some limited form of prediction and control across populations.

An example: the National Health Service (NHS)

Consider government policy relating to the National Health Service in the UK as an example of what I have been describing. The NHS can be thought of as a collective identity, a 'we' identity that is inseparable from the 'I' identities of all who work for it and all concerned with its governance. Such an identity is a social object, that is, generalized tendencies to act in similar ways by large numbers of people in similar situations. On closer inspection, however, there is not one monolithic identity, one social object, but many linked ones. Each hospital, for example, has a distinctive identity, as do the groups of different kinds of medical practitioners and managers. There are, therefore, many social objects, many generalized tendencies by large numbers of people to act in similar ways in similar situations. Furthermore, the medical profession, the NHS and the many different institutions and groupings it is composed are all idealized. Cult values, such as 'providing free health care', 'doing no harm', 'providing all with the highest standard of care' and 'providing the same standard of care in all geographical locations to all classes of person', are essential features of what the NHS means. 'Performance' and 'quality' are recent additions to these cult values. The generalizations and idealizations can all be recorded in written artifacts, sound recordings and films as propositions and/or narratives. These artifacts may take the form of policy documents, legal contracts, procedures, instructions from the Department of Health, and so on. Such artifacts are then used as tools in the communicative interaction and power relating between members within the NHS and between them and those concerned with its governance. However, the artifacts recording the generalizations and idealizations are just artifacts, not the generalizations and idealizations themselves. Whether recorded or not, the generalizations and idealizations only have any meaning in the local interactions of all involved in each specific situation – they are only to be found in the experience of local interaction.

Therefore, for example, when groups of policy makers in the Department of Health and each of the main political parties get together to decide what to do about the NHS, they are clearly interacting locally. What they will be reflecting upon and discussing are the generalizations and idealizations of the NHS or parts of it. They may issue a consultation document, a green paper, to large numbers of people for comment. This is then taken up for discussion in the professional bodies representing different groups in the NHS. Again, the discussion is local interaction, as is the subsequent negotiation of changes in any of the policies. What they are discussing and negotiating in this local interaction is changes to the global, to the generalizations and idealizations as well as second order abstractions. Eventually, a white paper or policy statement, is produced and instructions sent to, say, all of the hospitals in the country setting out what new targets they must meet in order to demonstrate quality and performance and in what way they will be punished if they do not. What I have been describing is processes of local interaction, local negotiation, in which emerges articulations of the general and the ideal as far as the NHS is concerned. The process is one in which people have been trying to design the general and the ideal, and in the way they currently do this in the UK, they reflect a particular way of thinking about the NHS. In setting targets, as second order abstractions, and establishing monitoring process, they display a way of thinking derived from the second order abstraction of cybernetic systems thinking. They are trying to design and install a self-regulating system.

However, the NHS is not a self-regulating system, but many local patterns of interaction in which the general is continually emerging as continuity and change, as it is iterated from one present to the next. What then becomes important is how people are taking up, in their local interactions, the generalizations and idealizations articulated in the artifacts of written instructions and procedures. The meaning cannot be located simply in the gesture which these artifacts represent but at the same time in the myriad responses this gesture calls forth. In a specific situation on a specific day, there may simply not be the physical capacity to achieve the targets set. In each specific situation, there will always be conflicts on what the targets mean and how they are to be adhered to. The target might then become something that has to be avoided, manipulated and even falsified. For example, a specific decision might be to meet, say, a target of reducing waiting lists, by sending people home too early after an operation, leading to a rise in readmissions. The cult value of 'equal treatment' has to be functionalized in a specific situation at a specific time and may mean giving expensive medication to one person and not another. The global generalization/cult value that the policy makers designed is thus being transformed in the local interaction so that it comes to mean something different – instead of uniform high performance, it might come to mean 'cover up' and 'deceit'. As the unexpected emerges in many, many local interactions, the global pattern is transformed and of course, in their local interactions, the policy makers are reflecting upon this. They may then conclude that the now burgeoning number of targets is proving too much of an embarrassment and should be scrapped. However, still thinking in system terms, they feel that they must design some other form of generalization to stay in control and secure adequate performance. They may conclude that 700 targets should be abandoned and be replaced with 22 qualitative standards. Once again, however, the meaning does not lie on the generalization alone but in its particularization in many local situations.

The argument I am presenting here has an immediate implication for processes of policy-making. This is that the almost exclusive focus on the design of a generalization, a second order abstraction, in policy-making will lead to continual cycles of surprise. Greater attention needs to be paid to process of particularizing if policy makers are to avoid some of the endless policy reversals that characterize policy making, at least in the NHS. Norbert Elias is another writer who presents a very similar argument about the relationship between the local and the global.

Long-term social trends

In his explanation of the civilizing process in Europe over the past few hundred years, already referred to in Chapter 7, Elias[5] described in some detail the relationship between local interaction and the slowly evolving global patterns of society. He did not use macromodels and was dismissive of employing concepts such as systems or 'wholes', claiming that using the term 'whole' simply created a mystery in order to solve a mystery. He argued that social evolution could not be understood in terms of social forces, cultural systems, supra-individuals, supra-systems, spirit, élan vital or any other kind of whole outside of experience. Instead, he argued for a way of understanding the global that stayed with the direct experience of interaction between people, the local. So, instead of using macromodels, Elias explored the ordinary patterns of relating between people in their local situations, showing how global patterns emerge in these local interactions and how, at the same time, those global patterns are structuring the very personalities of locally interacting people. 'Though it is unplanned and not immediately controllable, the overall process of development of a society is not in the least incomprehensible. There are no "mysterious" social forces behind it. It is a question of the consequences flowing from the intermeshing of the actions of numerous people . . . . As the moves of interdependent players intertwine, no single player nor any group of players acting alone can determine the course of the game no matter how powerful they may be . . . . It involves a partly self-regulating change in a partly self-organizing and self-reproducing figuration of interdependent people, whole processes tending in a certain direction'.[6]

As Western society evolved, social functions became more and more differentiated under the pressure of competition. He was pointing here to global patterns. However, this differentiation meant that the number of social functions increased so that any individual had to depend upon more and more others to do anything. As this interdependence rose, more and more people had to attune their actions to each other, making it necessary for them to regulate their conduct in increasingly differentiated, more even and more stable ways. He was pointing here to patterns of local interaction and how they could not be separated from the global patterns. The requirement for more complex control had to be instilled into each individual from infancy if society was to function. The more complex forms of control became increasingly automatic, taking the form of unconscious self-compulsion that individuals could not resist even if they consciously desired to do so. Without this local pattern, people could not operate in increasingly differentiated societies, the global, and without such societies, such self-restraint would not be required.

Elias also linked the growth of self-control in local interaction to the global patterns of the growth of centralized organs of society and the monopolization of force by those organs. In societies in which force is not monopolized, the local relationships between individuals are more volatile as people engage more frequently in physical violence against each other. As society develops in the direction of the monopolization of physical force, global patterns, the individual no longer engages in local feuds but rather in the more peaceful local functions of economic exchange and the pursuit of prestige. Therefore, people are taking up different generalizations in their local interactions.

Elias argued that global social evolution results in local fears to do with socially correct behavior. These fears are banished to an individual's own personality and to interactions with others that are shielded from public visibility. The consequence of growing interdependence in larger groups and the exclusion of physical violence was that social constraints were transformed into unconscious self-constraints as 'habitus'.

An example: the development of the internet

In response to the Soviet launch of the first space satellite, President Eisenhower created the Advanced Research Projects Agency (ARPA) to regain the lead in the arms race and this body appointed J. C. R. Licklider to head a new Information Processing Techniques Office (IPTO) organization to develop the Semi Automatic Ground Enthronement (SAGE) program aimed at protecting the US against a space-based nuclear attack. Licklider lobbied for the development of a country-wide communications network and Lawrence Roberts was hired to develop such a network, and which became known as the ARPANET was based on packet switching developed by Paul Baran at RAND Corporation in the USA and by Donald Davies at the National Physics Laboratory in the UK. ARPANET went live in October 1969. In 1990, the ARPANET was retired and replaced by the National Science Foundation Network (NSFNET) which was connected to the academic communication network, Computer Science Network (CSNET) and then with the European research communication network, EUnet, together constituting the Internet. Use of the Internet exploded in the 1990s and the US government trans-ferred management of the Internet to independent organizations in 1995. A mail system was developed for ARPANET soon after its formation and this evolved into the power-ful email technology. This was made possible by the development of timesharing com-puters in the early 1960s when a number of people saw that a natural use of this technology was to extend human communication. In 1971, Ray Tomlinson developed the first ARPANET email application and he chose the 'user @host' form of address. Commercial email appeared in 1988 and in 1993, large network service providers con-nected their proprietary email systems to the Internet after which explosive growth occurred. Alongside these developments, and building on his work at CERN in the 1980s, British scientist Tim Berners-Lee, in collaboration with Robert Cailliau, developed the first web browser in 1990 with the aim of making information more readily available to researchers. He put the CERN (the European particle research facility in Switzerland) telephone directory on the web site and the usefulness of this gained it rapid acceptance. CERN was connected to ARPANET and Berners-Lee used it in 1991 to make his web server and browser available around the world. He persuaded CERN to place the code for the web in the public domain so that anyone could use and improve it. In 1994, Berners-Lee moved to MIT and in 1995 used the term World Wide Web. In just over a decade, the uses to which people have put the web have exploded in an amazing way. This is quite clearly a story of the unplanned interplay of intentions in which one person develops a technology for one purpose and this very rapidly evokes responses from others who use it for purposes no one dreamt of very long before they happened. The Internet, email, World Wide Web and their applications in research, commerce, banking and social networks are all population-wide patterns emerging in many, many local interactions which continue to sustain and change these patterns

A different understanding of social forces/structures

The notions of social forces and social structures are easily reified so that we slip into the habit of regarding them as things with an independent existence outside of our inter-action with each other, even following their own laws. We may even anthropomorphize them and come to think of them as organisms with their own lives quite apart from our own. However, on careful consideration, it becomes clear that what we are referring to when we use these terms is nothing more than widespread, enduring and repetitive pat-terns of interaction with each other that we call routines or habits. When we reify or anthropomorphize these routines and habits, we tend to think of them as external powers causing our interactions. The perspective of complex responsive processes avoids such anthropomorphizing and reifying and does not regard routines and habits as causal powers with regard to our interactions. Instead, we come to see that global routines and habits emerge in our local interactions and continue to be sustained as they are iterated from present to present in those local interactions. Social forces, social structures, routines and habits can all be understood as generalizations that are particularized over and over again in each specific situation we find ourselves in. In other words, they are social objects, generalized tendencies to act. Furthermore, these generalizations are often idealized and come to form the cult values we repeatedly have to functionalize in our interaction.

This way of understanding routines and habits focuses attention on the inevitably conflictual nature of particularizing the general and the idealized. If people simply apply some generalization or idealization in an absolutely rigid way there need be no conflict but particularizing them in specific, unique situations means making choices. Since different individuals and different groupings of them will be making different interpretations of the situation, they will be pressing for different choices to be made. Which of those conflicting choices is actually made will be the result of negotiation and this immediately raises the matter of power. The particular choices made will reflect the figurations of power – the choices of individuals and groups will prevail when the power ratio is tilted in their favor. Power figurations emerge in the interaction between people and like all other organizing themes, there is a strong tendency for them to become habitual, generalized and even idealized. From a complex responsive processes perspective one understands institutionalized instruments, or technologies, of power to be just such generalized/idealized/habitual figurations of power relations. They too are iterated and particularized in each present, and it is in such particularization that they evolve. They are not to be found as things or forces outside of our experience of interaction but only in that experience.

Power ratios are tilted toward those who have something that others need or want. The connection between power figurations and resources then becomes obvious. Since money is the key to controlling resources, power ratios are tilted towards those who can exert more control over money and away from those with little access to it. At this point, it becomes important not to slip into reifying money and regarding it as the external cause of our interactions. Money too is a social object, a generalized tendency to act on the part of large number of people in similar ways in similar situations. This generalization too exists only in its particularization in many, many local interactions. In those local interactions, the power ratio will continue to be tilted towards those individuals and groups whose activities enable them to control more money.

Technology as social object[7]

Technologies can also be thought of not simply as physical objects but also, at the same time, as social objects. The consequence of taking this perspective is that attention is shifted from focusing on technology and competence as things or generalizations designed to achieve given futures, to focusing on the detailed interactions in which they acquire meaning, as they are particularized and potentially transformed. This leads to a very different way of thinking about the role of technology in human action. To identify the difference I want first to give a brief description of how technology is understood in the dominant discourse.

One strand of thinking about technology and organizations derives from neoclassical economics in which technology was understood to be embodied in the physical objects constituting the resource called capital (buildings, plant and equipment). Rational humans design and use technology in an instrumental way to control the environment in the pursuit of human economic interests. No attention was paid to the social aspects of technology use and development or the impact of technology on people. This economic understanding has been taken up and developed in the resource-based view of organizational development,[8] which focuses on how an organization's resources create competitive advantage. However, in an age in which human knowledge has become a more important resource than physical capital, the notion of technology has been developed to encompass the embodiment of knowledge in people. The creation, development and protection of core competences[9] have come to be seen as key sources of competitive advantage, and it is the organization's managers who are responsible for sustaining and developing these core competences,[10] as well as managing the creation of new knowledge[11] upon which they depend. In the resource-based view, technology is understood as a system amenable to intentional cultivation and management. The instrumental approach of neoclassical economics to technology, mainly thought of as physical objects, has thus continued but a social dimension has been added in the emphasis placed on the role of teams in knowledge creation and technology development, although human knowledge is still ultimately located in the individual. However, the resource-based view greatly simplifies the connection between technology and the social, paying very little attention to how technology acquires meaning and so impacts on the manner in which people interact and experience themselves in organizations.

Other strands of thinking about technology and organizations originate in sociology and psychology. They pay much greater attention to the social implications of technology development. Some writers have pointed to the alienating effects of technology which often destroys the dignity of people's work and the pride they take in it. The result is widespread feelings of alienation where people feel themselves to be powerless objects controlled and manipulated by technology.[12] These feelings are exacerbated by hierarchical, bureaucratic organizational structures which create a mode of social domination.

The sociotechnical tradition[13] paid particular attention to the wider social dimensions of technology. A study[14] of the coal mining industry compared the pattern of social relations of successful and unsuccessful teams and found that the cause of the success lay not in the technology, since both used the same technology, but in patterns of work relations. In successful teams, the members were very involved in detailed decision-making about how the technology was to be used in specific situations – they were self-managing teams. In the unsuccessful teams, on the other hand, members operated in a very hierarchical manner and displayed great dependency on the team leader. The self-managing teams were able to deal more flexibly with the complex details of specific situations and consequently felt safe in the dangerous conditions of underground mining. In the hierarchical teams, leaders were not able to provide all of the control necessary to guarantee safety and failed to see that complex technology and role fragmentation made hierarchical control impossible. These authors concluded that technology, no matter how sophisticated, would fail if not mated with a social system designed to operate it. The requirement was for joint optimization of the interrelated technical and social systems, where the optimization of the whole might require less than optimization of the subsystems taken separately. They argued that work relationship systems needed to be designed to bring the two subsystems together. By reconciling human needs and technical efficiency, many of the problems created by the introduction of new technology could be overcome. In this view, humans and technology are a whole.[15] They function together and are dependent on each other and must be seen as a whole system evolving together. The result is a way of thinking about technology that incorporates the social in a much richer way than the resource-based view described earlier. However, the development of both the technical and the social systems is as much caused by human design, as is the case in the resource based view. There are still rational designers, now designing both social and technical systems (rationalist causality), and there are still systems unfolding the enfolded design (formative causality).

Actor-network theory[16] is concerned with how actors construct networks, where the network is composed not only of humans but also nonhumans such as technological artefacts. The theory claims that it is the actors, the network and the social relations between them that shape and constitute an organization. The interplay of technology, the objects it handles and changes in knowledge and action (learning) are the outcome of a process of local struggle. The core of actor-network theory is 'a concern with how actors and organizations mobilize, juxtapose, and hold together the bits and pieces out of which they are composed; how they are sometimes able to prevent those bits and pieces from following their own inclinations and making off; and . . . so turn a network from a heterogeneous set of bits and pieces each with its own inclinations, into something that passes as . . . [an] . . . actor'.[17] This theory treats human and nonhuman elements of any network symmetrically, giving equal status to both.[18] Actor-network theory, therefore, loses the distinction between humans and things and in the process turns the social into mere appearance. There is still the implication of humans as rational designers (actors construct networks). Furthermore, artefacts are now also actors or agents. Once again, there are confusing implications of people having choices as to overall technology design, on the one hand, and none, on the other.

To summarize, the key distinctions between the different views of technology described in the foregoing section relate to whether they see the evolution of technology as:

- Predictably determined by rational choice as in the resource-based and sociotechnical systems (rationalist causality), or whether they see technology evolution as driven by chance and competitive selection and so moving to an unknown future (adaptionist causality) as in actor-network theory;
- Involving the social/psychological in rather limited forms of teamwork as in the resource-based view, or involving the social/psychological as a separate system interacting with a technical system to form a whole as in sociotechnical systems, or involving the social/psychological as elements having very little difference to artefacts as in actor-network theory.

I now want to suggest another perspective, one that understands technology development as an essentially social process in which the causality is transformative. This makes the social/psychological central, as in sociotechnical systems theory, but avoids any separation between the two and avoids thinking in systems terms at all. It also avoids any equation of human beings with artefacts in the evolution of technology and explores just how one might think about the implications of technology for social evolution.

An alternative way of taking account of the social: complex responsive processes and technology

Taking a transformative perspective on causality, with its implication of fundamental unpredictability, leads to a substantial shift in thinking about organizations. In a world where patterns are emerging unpredictably, it becomes highly problematic to think of technology development simply as a human choice or design. Instead, one thinks of technology and knowledge as being perpetually created in the communicative interaction and power relating between people in local interaction in the living present. These social-technological patterns can be understood as social objects. The tools involved in a technology can be understood as physical objects designed and constructed by people to purposefully accomplish their activities. As such, technology is to be found in nature as other physical objects are. However, techniques for using tools, that is, people's knowledge, skills, practices and methods of tool use, always involve complex social acts. As such, technology is a social object to be found only in experience. Technology in the form of physical objects is also, in use, immediately a social object, that is, generalized tendencies for large numbers of people to act in fairly similar ways in using the physical objects of technology. In their particularization, these generalized tendencies evolve further as small differences are amplified – the causality is transformative. Technology is then understood, not simply as physical objects to be found in nature, but at the same time, as social objects to be found in our experience of complex social acts. This gives us an understanding of technology as being perpetually iterated in the particularizing of the generalized tendencies to act in the present.

An example is provided by Internet and email technologies. The tools are computers, servers and software programmes. Their mere existence creates tendencies for large numbers of people to communicate with each other through email and accessing databases. This is the generalized tendency to act in similar ways. These generalized tendencies are iterated in each present as rather repetitive, habitual techniques. In their continual iteration, technologies are particularized in specific situations in the present. We send emails to each other and conduct transactions over the Internet, for example, with banks. Such particularization is inevitably a conflictual process in that techniques are adapted to the demands of particular situations with their specific understanding of the past and expectations of the future. For example, as the use of email spreads in organizations, conflicts arise as to the purposes it can be used for. People start using emails for personal use and this conflicts with business requirements leading to policies specifying what uses are to be allowed or prohibited. The possibility of technological transformation arises in this particularizing as techniques are spontaneously adapted to variations in specific situations and then potentially amplified. For example, the Internet has become a means of transacting payments. Then there is the development of fraud and viruses and ways of dealing with them. Technology as social object only exists insofar as it is taken up, or particularized, in the ordinary everyday social interactions between people.

Thinking about technology in this way focuses attention not only on the physical objects of tools but also on the complex responsive processes of relating in which the generalized social object called technology is particularized. This brings to the fore questions of power, control and identity. Consider some examples.

Reading and writing is a technology that is essential to scientific progress and the development of tools and techniques. However, reading and writing are also social objects. Abram points out how reading and writing have led to the replacement of the sensuous, embodied style of consciousness found in oral cultures with a more detached, abstract mode of thinking.[19] When concepts such as 'virtue' and 'justice' are recorded in writing, they acquire an autonomy and permanence independent of ordinary experience. Abstraction becomes a way of thinking and speaking as well as writing. Reading and writing not only eclipse nature but also tend to eclipse local, bodily human interaction in the present.[20] New technology (including writing and printing) can be understood as emerging in an unplanned process which transforms the society which has produced it.[21] Literacy and printing have influenced human patterns of relating. The technology of writing fosters logic and abstraction.[22] Writing also sets up the conditions for objectivity. It fosters precision and distanced forms of communication between people. Writing led to a shift from 'hearing dominance' to 'sight dominance' and print continued the trend.

Modern technologies of information and communication are other examples of social objects that profoundly affect the pattern of our interactions and even the conceptions we have of ourselves. The development of computers has been accompanied by the development of cognitivist psychology in which mind has come to be thought of as an information-processing device rather like a computer. The mind has come to be thought of as models and maps, again reflecting technology. The development of the camera obscura some 250 years ago was accompanied by a view of mind as an internal world that made representations of objects in outside reality. As social object, technology shapes our thinking in many areas apparently unconnected with that technology itself. Technology provides metaphors for our thinking about everything around us. So we think of organizations as machines or as ships to be steered by their leaders. The social objects of technology, therefore, affect how we experience ourselves, our identities, and they of course impact on patterns of social relations. One only has to think of the technology of fast foods and that of contraception to see what enormous shifts in social relations accompany the evolution of technology.

The relationship between people and technology: social objects and meaning

Most approaches see the relationship between people and technology in an instrumental way. Technology is that which people design and manipulate in order to control their environment. The notable exception is actor-network theory which treats both people and technology as agents in social evolution. The interaction between people and between people and technology is regarded as so much the same that there is no need for a distinction. In the complex responsive processes, perspective on technology outlined in the preceding section, both of these positions are avoided. First of all, it is argued that humans do not have a relationship with things in anything like the same way as they have with each other, even though they may feel as if they do and metaphorically talk as if they do. People and things do not engage each other in the social act of gesture and response. The gesture-response is an understanding of the detailed way in which humans interact with each other. It is not just one person doing something and the other reacting to it. In gesturing, one is taking a similar attitude to one's action as the other is taking to it. Furthermore, in human relating, one person is not simply taking the attitude of the specific other but always at the same time the attitude of the generalized other/me (which is the same as the social object). Both the gesturer and the responder are self-conscious and selves are social objects. Clearly, nothing like this goes on when using a tool.

The key point is that we are not interacting with or relating to a tool in anything like the sense we use these words with respect to human relating or interaction. What we are doing is using, even playing with, the tool.

However, tools and other physical objects in nature are not just objects we operate with and upon, because they have meaning for us, including highly emotional significance. The key point here has to do with *meaning*. We respond emotionally and intellectually to the *meaning* physical objects such as cars, clothes, jewelry, our own bodies, mountains, lakes and so on, have for us. However, Mead makes the profoundly important point that meaning cannot be located in a physical object. Physical objects have no meaning because meaning cannot be 'had'. For Mead, meaning is the social act and the social act is meaning. In this way of thinking, meaning is the activity of inter-acting, and it does not exist anywhere, even as the vocal act of the word, let alone in a physical object. Therefore, it follows that a physical object can only be meaningful insofar as it is somehow taken up in our interactions with each other. Meaning arises as the particularizing of the social object in specific situations. Take a car as an example. The car in itself, as a physical object, has no meaning and can therefore arouse no emotion in those using it. However, a car is not simply a physical object but also, at the same time, a social object, that is, a generalized tendency to act which is common to a number of people. This generalized tendency could take the form of respecting those who own big cars, for example. What is evoking the response of respect here is not the physical object of the big car but the social object of 'big car'.

Conclusion

The way of thinking about social structures, institutionalized instruments of power and resources, suggested in this chapter focuses our attention on local interaction as the way of understanding the global. It is an invitation to take seriously our experience of immersing and abstracting at the same time in our ongoing local interactions. I think that this whole way of thinking in terms of social objects and cult values, of pre-occupation in the game and the manner in which we use the second order abstractions of models, plans and administrative procedures which grant us only limited predictive ability and the limited control across a population, are much more consistent with the organizational reality described in Chapter 1. Thinking in this way enables us to understand how it could happen that the world could experience credit crunches and recessions, companies could collapse while others continued to thrive, while not simply dismissing articulations of abstractions from population-wide policies and plans. The latter do have an impact, often a major impact, but this is only expressed in many, many local interactions and policies and plans will always also produce surprises. The nature of local interaction and the links with population-wide patterns will be further explored in the next chapter in terms of power relations.

Notes

1 Mead, G. H. (1938) *The Philosophy of the Act*, Chicago: University of Chicago.
2 Mead, G. H. (1914) 'The Psychological Bases of Internationalism', *Survey*, XXIII, 604–7; Mead, G. H. (1923) 'Scientific Method and the Moral Sciences', *International Journal of Ethics*, XXXIII, 229–47.
3 Dewey, J. (1934) *A Common Faith*, New Haven, Conn: Yale University Press.
4 Ibid.

5 Elias, N. (1939/2000) *The Civilizing Process*, Oxford: Blackwell.

6 Elias, N. (1970/1978) *What is Sociology?*, Oxford: Blackwell, pp. 146–47.

7 The section on technology is taken from: Johannessen, S. and Stacey, R., 'Technology as Social Object', in R. Stacey (ed.) (2005) *Experiencing Emergence in Organizations: Local Interaction and the Emergence of Global Pattern*, London: Routledge.

8 Penrose, E. T. (1959) *The Theory of the Growth of the Firm*, New York, Wiley; Wernerfeldt, B. (1984) 'A Resource-based View of the Firm', *Strategic Management Journal*, 5, 171–80.

9 Prahalad, C. K. and Hamel, G. (1990) 'The Core Competence of the Corporation', *Harvard Business Review*, 68, 78–91.

10 Hamel, G. (2000) *Leading the Revolution*, Boston: Harvard Business School Press.

11 Nonaka, I. and Takeuchi, H. (1995) *The Knowledge Creating Company: How Japanese Companies Create the Dynamics of Innovation*, New York: Oxford University Press.

12 Blauner, R. (1964) *Alienation and Freedom*, Chicago: University of Chicago Press.

13 Trist, E. and Bamforth, K. (1951) 'Some Consequences of the Longwall Method of Coal Getting', *Human Relations*, 4(1), 3–33; Trist, E. (1981) 'The Evolution of Socio-Technical Systems', *Occasional Papers No.2*, Ontario; Emery, F. E. and Thorsrud, E. (1969) *Form and Content in Industrial Democracy*, London: Tavistock.

14 Trist, E. and Bamforth, K. (1951) 'Some Consequences of the Longwall Method of Coal Getting', *Human Relations*, 4(1), 3–33.

15 Emery, F. E. and Trist, E. L. (1973) *Toward a Social Ecology*, London: Tavistock.

16 Fox, S. (2000) 'Communities of Practice, Foucault and Actor-Network Theory', *Journal of Management Studies*, 37(6), 853–67.

17 Law, J. (1992) 'Notes on the Theory of the Actor-Network: Ordering, Strategy, and Heterogeneity', *Systems Practice*, 5(4), 12.

18 Callon, M. and Latour, B. (1981) 'Unscrewing the Big Leviathan: How Actors Macro-structure Reality and How Sociologists Help them to Do so', in Knorr-Cetina, K. and V. Cicourel (eds) *Advances in Social Theory and Methodology: Toward an Integration of Micro- and Macro-Sociologies*, Boston, Mass, USA: Routledge & Kegan Paul Ltd. Callon, M. (2002) 'Writing and (Re)writing Devices as Tools for Managing Complexity', in Law, J. and Mol, A. (eds) *Complexities: Social Studies of Knowledge Practices*, Durham, NC, USA: Duke University Press.

19 Abram, David (1996) *The Spell of the Sensuous*, New York: Vintage Books.

20 Donaldson, A. (2005) 'The Technology of Writing in Organisational Life', in Stacey, R. (ed.) (2005) *Experiencing Emergence in Organizations: Local Interaction and the Emergence of Global Pattern*, London: Routledge.

21 Ibid.

22 Ong, W. J. (2002) *Orality and Literacy*, London and New York: Routledge.

9 Local and population-wide patterns of power relations and ideology

The dynamics of inclusion and exclusion in organizations

In discussing the emergence, in vast numbers, of local communicative interactions, of relational patterns across whole populations, I have from time to time mentioned the power aspects of human relating and their ideological underpinnings. In this chapter, I will be exploring in more detail the questions of power relations and the ideological basis of human choice, linking them to the dynamics of inclusion and exclusion in human interaction and how those dynamics create our identities, which are also expressed in institutional forms. In talking about power I will be departing from the view of power which tends to prevail in the dominant discourse on organizations and their management in which power is thought to be possessed by some who can use 'it' to get others, sometimes force others, to do what they would not otherwise have done. Here power tends to be reified and regarded as the possession of the few with the many possessing very little power and sometimes none at all. Understood in this way, the use of power is often judged to be unethical, especially because it is often equated with manipulation. This view leads to a call for the empowering of the many by the few (meaning that the few should give some of their power to the many), and even those who do not share the view that power is unethical at least argue that empowerment is a form of motivation that improves performance and so is desirable in a rational kind of way. The ideology of equality and improvement, of avoiding the manipulation of others, makes the use of power rather shameful and how it is being used becomes undiscussable, covered over and denied. Indeed, many equate power with what they call 'politicking' and then regard power as something that disrupts the effective functioning of organizations. Leaders and managers are exhorted to remove power from 'the equation' and cease the 'politicking' involved in serving their own personal agendas and concentrate instead on serving the community. In the academic disciplines of management, power features as a special factor to be discussed in specific books and papers on the subject or presented as a chapter in textbooks on strategy and organizational behaviour. If I am to depart from this dominant discourse on power and the downgrading and covering over of power, where do I turn? What I find very helpful in understanding the ordinary politics of everyday life in which we are always negotiating our interactions with each other, is the view of power and ideology presented by Elias.

Elias held that power is not a thing that a person carries around and gives to others or takes away from them.[1] Such a view of power is very much tied up with the notion that we are independent autonomous individuals, 'closed' off from each other. However, for Elias there are no autonomous human beings simply because individuals are quite obviously dependent on each other in an essential and fundamental way – society is the society of interdependent individuals. We can accomplish nothing without each other, without cooperating and competing with each other. In other words, we need each other for many different reasons – we need others to love and to hate; we need others to depend upon or rebel against; we need others to victimize or be victimized by; we need enemies for wars and friends and opponents for peace. It follows that to claim that humans are essentially interdependent is to claim a fundamental 'fact' about life, not simply an ideological position that interdependence and relating are good, because our interdependence accounts for the horrific destructiveness of human action as well as its creative beauty. The ideology arises in our judgment of what is beautifully creative and what is horrifically destructive about relating to each other. Interdependence explains how both the good and the bad arise, indeed how particular judgments or ideologies arise. If human individuals are interdependent in this way, it follows that we need each other, and it is this need which explains why *power* is an aspect of *every act of human relating*. Since I need others, I cannot do whatever I please; and since they need me, neither can they. We constrain each other at the same time as enabling each other, and it is this paradoxical activity that constitutes power. Furthermore, since need is rarely equal, the pattern of power relations will always be skewed more to one than to another. Therefore, if I need you more than you need me, then the power distribution is tilted toward you. However, if as we relate to each other, we discover that now you need me more than I need you, then the pattern of power relations moves and is tilted toward me. Power then refers to usually fluid patterns of perceived need and is expressed as figurations of relationships. These figurations are social patterns of grouping in which some are included and others excluded, and it is in being included in this group and excluded from that group that we acquire identity. I am included in a group called academics and excluded from a group called footballers, so when asked *who I am*, I say that *I am* a teacher: collective 'we' identity is inseparable from individual 'I' identity so that individual identity is fundamentally social, a matter of power relations. I am claiming as a fact of our experience that humans need each other and that relative need will rarely be equal, meaning that power is always an aspect of every act of human relating and that it is always expressed in patterns of inclusion and exclusion that give identity. I am also claiming that it is in these very acts of power relating as the ordinary politics of everyday life that ideology arises as our judgment of what is good and what is right about our acts of power relating. At the same time, these ideological judgments are shaping our acts of power relating. Figurations of power can come to have a kind of semipermanence in which they are expressed in intuitional arrangements. It is the examination of these phenomena that this chapter proposes to take further.

Understanding social processes through the metaphor of games

Elias maintained[2] that sociology could not be reduced to the psychology of individuals, because the figurations of human interdependence cannot be reduced to the actions of individual people. On the contrary, the actions of individuals can only be understood in terms of their patterns of interdependence, that is, in terms of the figurations they form with each other. 'Some people tend to shrink from this insight. They confuse it with a metaphysical assumption of long standing which is often summed up in the saying "the whole is more than the sum of its parts". Using the term "whole" or "wholeness" creates a mystery in order to solve a mystery. This aberration must be mentioned because many people appear to believe that one can only be one or the other – either an atomist or a holist'.[3]

Elias contests this either/or position and explores how people, because of their interdependence and the way their actions intermesh, form figurations while those figurations form them. To illustrate this, he uses a number of game models to demonstrate the relational character of power in a simplified form. These are game contests in which the relative power of the contestants is explored to bring out the features of various power figurations. He starts with a game in which two groups of antagonists face each other in an all-out struggle in which there are no rules. For example, two groups might struggle with each other for limited food resources. When one group does something, say, raids the territory of the other group to steal their cattle, then that other group will have to respond to this, perhaps by mounting a counter-raid or building better fortifications, or entering into an alliance with a third group. It is because of this continuing need on the part of all groups to respond to what the others are doing that they obviously depend on each other – there can be no cattle raiders if there are no farmers who possess cattle, and farmers who possess cattle would not have to build fortifications if there were no cattle raiders. Groups perform a function for each other, even if such a functional relationship is not desired, and the way each group is internally organized reflects their expectation of what they will need to do next. One group, the raiders, will probably organize themselves into a pattern of a fierce leader-commanding warriors, while the other, intent on improving fortifications, will probably show greater functional differentiation with soldiers distinguished from builders and both distinguished from ruling groups. Each group then is serving a function for the other even in patterns of hostility – they need each other as enemies if they are to conduct skirmishes. 'It is not possible to explain the actions, plans and aims of either of the two groups if they are conceptualized as the freely chosen decisions, plans and aims of each group considered on its own, independently of the other group'.[4]

The central question relates to how people have come to be able to regulate their interdependence so that they need not resort to all-out struggle as a regular pattern of interaction. This can be explored by comparing a number of games in which the strength differential between two playing groups diminishes. As the power ratio declines, the possibility of either of the groups controlling both the other group and the course of the game diminishes. This game becomes more like social processes and as this happens, it resembles less and less the implementation of individual plans: 'to the extent that the inequality in the strengths of the two players diminishes, there will result from the interweaving of moves of two individual people a game process *which neither of them has planned*.'[5] The social cannot be reduced to the individual and it is because of this that no one in the game can control its evolution. The explanation has to do with the constraints they place on each other and the unpredictability of their responses to each other.

As the number of players in each playing group increases, some groups of players might disintegrate, splintering into a number of smaller groups, which move further and further apart from each other, playing the game without trying to cooperate or compete with each other. For example, the weaker groups might migrate to new territories where they can live independently of other groups, at least for a time. On the other hand, the splinter groups could carry on playing with each other but in doing so, they will develop a new power figuration of interdependent groups, in which each may have some autonomy but will also have to develop forms of cooperation, as they compete with each other for certain resources. If this happens, it becomes even less helpful to try to understand the evolution of the game in terms of individual plans – it will be even less possible for any grouping to control the course of the game. It is also possible, of course, that as the number of players in a group increases, they could choose to remain together but this will require a much more complex figuration in which a two-tier group might develop with one sub-group being rulers, say, while the other becomes, say, the common people, so that a specialization develops. Special functionaries now coordinate the game: representatives, delegates, leaders and governments which together form a smaller group, playing directly with and against each other. However, they are also bound together in some way with the mass of players, the second tier. Both levels depend on each other but the distribution of power between them can vary. Elias then explores what happens when the power differentials decline. 'Even in a game with no more than two tiers, the figuration of game and players already possesses a degree of complexity which prevents any one individual from using his superiority to guide the game in the direction of his own goals and wishes. He makes his moves both *out* of the network and *into* the network of interdependent players, where there are alliances and enmities, cooperation and rivalry at different levels.'[6]

This game analogy demonstrates the evolving effects of interdependence on power figurations and the ability to control the game and in so doing, points to explanations of the kinds of processes in which the functions of upper and lower classes in, say, Western Europe changed as the power differential diminished. The game analogy also points to explanations of the processes in which the financial sectors of most countries have become increasingly differentiated and interdependent over the last few decades, making it impossible for any group of players – financial institutions, borrowers and lenders, regulators and governments – to control the evolution of the global financial game. Despite this, however, we continue to blame one or other of the groups of players for what happened so that they can be punished, and we also continue to ascribe the problem to the system, calling for it to be redesigned so that it all 'never happens again'. In their explanations of what is happening, people use metaphors 'which oscillate constantly between the idea that the course of the game can be reduced to the actions of the individual players and the other idea that it is of a supra-personal nature. Because the game cannot be controlled by the players, it is easily perceived as a kind of superhuman entity. For a long time, it is especially difficult for the players to comprehend that their inability to control the game derives from their mutual dependence and positioning as players, and from the tension and conflicts inherent in this interweaving network'.[7] The game analogy shows clearly how social evolution is an emergent change in patterns of relationships across a population, arising in many local interactions. However, this insight is clouded by the persistent tendency of the dominant discourse to either locate the cause of change in an individual or in some 'whole' outside of the direct experience of interaction. Increasingly, elaborate chains of connections between people produce shifting power figurations leading to processes and outcomes which are more and more difficult to understand and intend.

I want to turn now to just how, in our local communicative interaction with each other, we produce local figurations of power relations between us, and how these relate to the wider figurations of power across populations.

Turn-taking, power and ideology

In Chapter 7, I described how communication can be understood as the conversation of gestures involving local processes of interaction between people who take conversational turns for themselves and make such turns for others in associative ways. It is in such associative communicative interaction between human bodies that patterns of meaning and relating emerge in the form of narrative and propositional themes and variations of them; and at the same time, these emerging themes and variations pattern the associative turn-taking/turn-making. For example, as a group of people work together in an organization, one of their number takes more turns while others make more turns for him in their conversation in which a leadership narrative emerges of a visionary and somewhat temperamental founder-leader. However, this narrative leadership theme is not only emerging in the pattern of turn-taking and turn-making; it is at the same time forming the pattern of turn-taking and turn-making. Conversational themes do not emerge out of nowhere but are iterated and potentially transformed in the very actions of communication; and what is being reproduced, each time with unique variations, is themes that have emerged in the previous history of each individual, in the previous history of the grouping they currently find themselves in, and in the wider communities and societies they are part of.

Of particular importance in these conversational processes is the emergent reproduction of themes and variations that organize communicative actions into membership categories. These tend to be themes of an ideological kind that establish who may take a turn, as well as when and how they may do so. It is the thematic ideological patterning of turn-taking/turn-making that enables some to take a turn while constraining others from doing so. So, particular ideologies of deference and the role of women may be reflected in a particular grouping of senior men who take more turns than others do while those others make more turns for them: the result is categories of conversational participants in which some are included as senior men, from which category junior men and all women are excluded. There is also another aspect: to go on together, people have to account to each other for what they do, which means that they not only enable each other to do what they could not do alone, but they also constrain each other, with the effect of excluding some communicative actions and including others. Since turn-taking/turn-making is both enabling and constraining at the same time, it immediately establishes power differences in which some people are 'in' and others are 'out', and some ways of talking are 'in' while others are 'out'. This process of power relating, with its dynamic of inclusion and exclusion, is ubiquitous in all human communicative inter-action, that is, in all human relating. The very process of turn-taking/turn-making renders the dynamic of inclusion and exclusion an inevitable and irremovable property of human communicative interaction quite simply because when one person takes a turn, others are at that moment excluded from doing so. Moreover, this inevitable dynamic has very important consequences. If communicative interaction is essential, not only for the survival of every individual, but also for the continued reproduction and transformation of their very selves or identities, then any exclusion must be felt as very threatening. For a being for whom the social is essential to life itself, the deepest existential anxiety must be aroused by any threat of separation or exclusion since it means the potential loss or fragmentation of identity, even death. Also, categorizing people into this or that kind, with this or that kind of view, may be experienced as threatening. This is because it creates potential misrepresentation of identity and potential exclusion from communication.

I am suggesting, then, that the process of conversational turn-taking/turn-making that reproduces and transforms themes of collaboration, at the same time reproduces and transforms themes to do with inclusion and exclusion, or power, and these arouse feelings of existential anxiety, which trigger themes to deal with that anxiety in some way. The themes triggered by anxiety may well have to do with repatterning the dynamic of inclusion and exclusion, with shifting the relations of power. These and other themes triggered by anxiety may well disrupt collaboration and they may also be highly destructive. However, without such disruptions to current patterns of collaboration and power relations, there could be no emergent novelty in communicative interaction and hence no novelty in any form of human action. The reason for saying this is that disruptions generate diversity. One of the central insights of the complexity sciences is how the spontaneous emergence of novelty depends upon diversity. Furthermore, there is a link between anxiety and the use of fantasy to cope with it. By this, I mean that an individual who experiences, not necessarily consciously, the anxiety aroused by exclusion, may well elaborate on his or her own actions and those of others in the private role-play/ silent conversation of mind, in a way that has little to do with what they are actually doing. The result can be fantasy and misunderstanding to varying degrees, even serious breakdown in the whole process of communicative interaction. Again, however, there is a close relationship between fantasy and misunderstanding, on the one hand, and the emergence of novelty, on the other. Fantasy is close to imaginative elaboration and misunderstanding triggers a search for understanding thereby provoking continued imaginative elaboration and communication. It is in such continued struggles for meaning, and the imaginative elaboration going with it, that the novel emerges. Processes of communicative action, that is, processes of power relating, are such that they both preserve continuity, or identity, and promote transformative change at the same time.

The anxieties of organizational life are also defended against by what some have called social defences against anxiety.[8] For example, nurses may develop patterns of working that make it difficult to get to know patients too well and may resist changing such work patterns, because they need some defence against getting close to people who keep dying. Many social and organizational routines serve mainly as defences against anxiety. Although managers experience the surprising outcomes of their long-term plans they continue to fiercely defend elaborate planning procedures. This may well be a response to the anxiety of not knowing what outcomes will be and not being in control.

Power relations are both stabilized and changed by particular ways of talking that have to do with the membership categorization that is part of the pattern forming processes of communication. It is in this categorization that the dynamics of inclusion and exclusion emerge, and those dynamics have the characteristics of stability and change at the same time. Consider how this happens.

The dynamics of inclusion-exclusion, gossip and identity

The typical dynamics of inclusion and exclusion are vividly illustrated in a study of a small town in Leicestershire, England, by Elias and Scotson.[9] The town, called Winston Parva to conceal its identity, was founded in the late nineteenth century by an entrepreneurial industrialist who built a factory and also a village, mainly to house the ordinary workers who were to be employed in the factory but also for a small number of supervisory staff whose houses were clustered at one end of the village. Life continued in the village until World War II broke out in Europe in 1939, and soon after this event, the government took the factory over to make products for the war effort. The government expanded the factory and built a number of new, somewhat larger houses, in what came to be called the 'estate' located right next to the village. The new houses enabled the government to rehouse working-class people whose homes had been bombed in East London, some 80 miles away. Elias and his student Scotson studied conditions in

Winston Parva nearly a quarter of a century later and noticed how those dwelling in the village and those dwelling in the estate constituted two quite separate communities. Although the men from both communities worked every day together in the factory without any problems and although their children went to the same local schools, there was no social intercourse outside factory and school. There was a pub in the village in which only people from the village met for a drink and a gossip in the evening and there was a pub in the estate which was used only by people from the estate. Women from the village never visited women from the estate and their children did not play with estate children outside school hours. The same applied to women and children in the estate. It was also noticeable that the elected local government consisted entirely of village dwellers.

This situation struck Elias and Scotson as very odd, because there was no immediately obvious difference between the two groups of people: both groups were white English people; both used the same language and after a quarter of a century, there was not much difference in their accents; and both were working-class people. The only difference was that one group, the newcomers, had been there for only a quarter of a century, whereas the other group, the established, had been there for over a century. On inquiring into the separation, Elias and Scotson were struck by the nature of the gossip prevailing in both communities. Villagers described estate dwellers as rather dirty people who did not maintain their houses and gardens. They were not well educated and their children behaved badly. The villagers described themselves as clean people who maintained their homes and gardens in good condition, were educated and had well-behaved children. The villagers were thus articulating an ideology which polarized the two groups in terms of binary opposites, with all bad ascribed to the estate dwellers and all good to the villagers. This enabled them to denigrate the estate dwellers without any difficulty and made it feel natural that they should occupy the power positions. What is being demonstrated here is how a simplistic ideology which splits good from bad, locating them in different groups, sustains the pattern of power relations between the groups. People are being included in one group and excluded from another in a dynamic which expresses a pattern of power relations reflecting an underlying ideology. Furthermore, the prime mechanism sustaining this ideology is gossip: praise gossip is directed by villagers to their own group and blame gossip or stigma is directed to the other. What was rather shocking, however, was not simply the prejudice of the villagers. On enquiry, it became evident how the estate dwellers had taken into their own self-perception the assertions about them made by the villagers. Estate dwellers reluctantly agreed that their neighbors did tend to be rather dirty people who did not maintain their properties and had rather badly behaved children. The stigma articulated by the one group had been driven into the self-perception of the other group. Although there was no real difference between the communities, with some in both communities maintaining their properties and disciplining their children and some in both communities failing to do this, the villagers were uniformly identifying themselves with the best in their midst, namely, the upper working-class factory supervisors, while the estate dwellers identified themselves with their worst members. The two groups were unconsciously caught in processes in which they served a function for each other, the function being to do with the maintenance of superiority and inferiority. Ideology can thus take the form of communication that preserves the current order by making that current order seem natural. In this way, ideological themes organize the communicative interactions of individuals and groups. Ideology here is mutually reproduced in ongoing communicative action rather than being some fundamental hidden cause located somewhere. Ideology is a patterning process, that is, narrative themes of inclusion and exclusion which are iterated. Ideology exists only in the speaking and acting of it.

This inclusion-exclusion dynamic was also intimately linked to the identities of members of both groups. Those living in the village had the identity of village dwellers with all its positive attributes – when asked 'who are you?' they could reply 'I am a villager'. If a villager questioned the simple binary distinction being drawn about village and estate, he or she would take the risk of antagonizing neighbors, and this could well lead to exclusion. The sustaining of identity, therefore, required compliance with the ideology. Similarly, estate dwellers derived their identities from membership of the despised estate group and would also risk exclusion if they challenged this. Elias and Scotson explained this dynamic of identity formation and processes of inclusion and exclusion in terms of the cohesion that had emerged over time in the already-established group of inhabitants. They had come to think of themselves as a 'we', a group with common attachments, likes, dislikes and attributes that had emerged simply because of their being together over a period. They had developed an identity. The new arrivals lacked this cohesive identity, because they had no history of being together and this made them more vulnerable. The more cohesive group therefore found it easy to 'name' the newcomers and ascribe to them hateful attributes such as being dirty or liable to commit crimes. Therefore, although there was no obvious difference between the two groups, one group used the fact that the other was newly arrived to generate hate and so maintain a power difference. This was, in a sense, 'accepted' by the newcomers who took up the role of the disadvantaged. I would describe what happened here as follows. Organizing themes of an ideological nature had emerged in the communicative interaction within and between both the established and the newcomer groups. That ideology established, and continued to reinforce, membership categories and differences between those categories.

However, eventually what usually happens is that some 'deviants' in one or other or both of the groups takes issue with the ideology and opposes it, usually in a way that can be described as 'shrill cries from the margin'. The official, legitimate ideology expressed in public transcripts and strategic poses conflicts with the unofficial shadow ideologies of the deviants, at first as hidden transcripts expressed in subtle acts of resistance but then as often extreme acts of rebellion.

What I have been describing is a very illuminating insight into how gossip sustains ideology, which generates processes of inclusion and exclusion, which sustain identities, all of which sustain patterns of power relations. These are clearly the processes that produce racism, sexism, ageism, homophobia and any other 'ism' we care to mention. In all these cases, we have seen how some at the margins in both groups mount oppositions which the more powerful regard as shrill and hysterical, or downright terrorism. The liberators of black people everywhere have usually been cast as terrorists or at least perpetrators of hysterical over response – 'if only they would be reasonable, is the cry, then we could sort something out'. The same response was made to those pursuing women's liberation in the early twentieth century and in the gay liberation movement of the late twentieth century. It seems, however, that reasonable arguments do not bring major change all on their own to deep-seated patterns of inclusion and exclusion. However, the processes I have been describing also apply no less importantly if much less obviously in everyday organizational life. Finance houses may have groups of front-office staff and groups of back-office staff, while hospitals have groups of managers, physicians and nurses, each of which is further divided into subgroupings.

Although senior executives may be designing task flows for these groups, they cannot organize or police the way they actually interact with each other – their patterns of inclusion and exclusion, their identities, are being unconsciously sustained in much the same way as the groups at Winston Parva, with much the same consequences. Other examples of inclusion-exclusion dynamics are when we debate differences in our theories using terms and concepts that exclude from the conversation those not already in the know, or when we talk in particular ways in ordinary everyday life, we are often using differences to sustain power relations and exclude some from the conversation. If we want to have a deeper insight into the dynamics of organizational life and why it produces surprises, then we must be sensitive to the ordinary organizational reality of inclusion, exclusion, gossip and ideology.

One of the principal ways that power differentials are preserved, then, is the use of even trivial differences to establish different membership categories. This suggests that it is not that a racial or religious difference generates hatred of itself, but rather that such differences are given an ideological form and then used to stir up hatred in the interests of sustaining power positions in a dynamic of inclusion and exclusion.[10] This as an unconscious social process in that the hatred between the groups emerges in an essentially unintended organizing process that no one is really aware of or actually intends. The very differences that are essential to the emergence of the new are, at the same time, generators of destructive processes of hatred.

The inclusion-exclusion dynamic I have been describing is not some aspect of power relations and communicative interaction that humans could somehow decide to do without. The very process of categorizing itself makes the dynamic inevitable. The act of naming or categorizing an experience is an act of breaking that experience up into different parts and relating those parts to each other. To categorize is to place experience in one category rather than another, thereby identifying a difference from other experiences not placed in that category. The effect is to locate similarity within the category, so obliterating differences between experiences in that category, and locate difference between categories while obliterating any similarity between them.[11] In this way, experience is unconsciously polarized into similarity and difference and the paradox of simultaneous similarity and difference within and between categories is lost sight of. So, when some in a group are named 'British', the others all become 'not-British' and the differences between members within each group are obliterated and the fact that this is being done is unconscious. At the same time, there is a difference being drawn between the two groups and the similarity between them, the fact that both are human, say, tends to be obliterated. Talk about differences between one group and other groups can be used to stir up hatred against others in order to preserve unconsciously sensed power differences and this is sustained by the categorization of experience into binary opposites that become entrenched as ideologies, which make behavior seem right and natural.[12]

How do the processes of inclusion and exclusion appear in ordinary everyday life in organizations?

The dynamics of inclusion and exclusion in organizational life

A few years ago I was asked to take part in an exercise to be undertaken by a healthcare trust that faced drastic reorganization. The intention was to split the large trust into four smaller ones in line with changes in government policy. No one yet knew who was to fill what management position in the new organization, or even where they would be located, and the changes were only some months away. There was no doubt that everyone was carrying on with their day-to-day tasks in an atmosphere of great confusion and increasing levels of frustration, stress and anxiety. The need to do something to prepare for the change was indeed pressing. One course of action proposed by senior management was that an exercise be undertaken to identify the existing qualities of good leadership that should be taken into these new organizations, whatever they turned out to be. A number of focus groups of management and staff were to be set up to identify what these qualities were and they would then be used as criteria for selecting people to fill the management positions in the new organizations and then also used as criteria against which management performance was to be judged. I was asked to attend a planning meeting to decide just what these focus groups should do and then facilitate the work of one of those groups. Some of the themes emerging in that planning meeting, themes organizing the experience of being together at that meeting, seemed to be as follows: designed criteria must be established in advance of any change; measures for performance should be set so that people knew what they had to do; performance should be judged and rewards given according to the criteria; action plans should be articulated and the meeting of targets was to be ensured; the discussion of the groups should be focused so that they talked only about leadership and did not 'open the can of worms' that constituted the current situation; and so on. Another theme that ran through the meeting had to do with an exercise mounted two years previously called a 'Better Future'. It was very difficult to raise critical questions about the benefits of this program over the past two years.

There were two people at this meeting who expressed some skepticism and wondered what the proposed focus groups could hope to achieve. However, the intervention was dismissed by others, particularly the Head of Organization Development. There was clearly a particular pattern of talking structured by and structuring the particular themes I have just mentioned. Those who talked in this way were the 'in' group and those who did not were clearly being excluded. I joined the 'out' group in their skepticism and began to suggest other ways we might proceed, perhaps by focusing attention on what was going on now and what the next step might be, as an alternative to some abstract exercise about leaders and a future which none of us knew much about. This caused great irritation for some and a debate ensued. Why the irritation? The person most irritated was a member representing senior management and in charge of Organization Development (OD). The themes structuring the talk and making it 'in' were themes from the language of OD professionals. Any attempt to shift the language and talk about self-organizing processes and emergence would clearly shift the figuration of power and in so doing, create a new figuration of who was 'in' and who was 'out'. The ideology of OD, therefore, had to be defended, because it was the basis of the current power structure, certainly at that meeting and, I am sure, more widely. In the end, the dominant pattern of talking held out and the focus group proposal went ahead. However, the meetings themselves never took place and when I asked why, I was told that it was a long story.

I am suggesting, then, that it is only when the themes organizing and organized by communicative interaction shift that there will be any change in this organization and I am pointing to just how difficult this is, because any such shift immediately alters power relations and insider/outsider dynamics. If the ensuing anxiety cannot be borne, then great efforts will be undertaken to reproduce existing patterns of communicative interaction with as little variation as possible. Living with this anxiety is very difficult, perhaps impossible, in a situation in which people's complete work situation is undergoing massive and uncertain change. Faced with the death of their existing organization, people may be trying to save something to do with good leaders. Perhaps the whole idea of focus groups and the criteria they must design, which all sounds so rational, is part of a fantasy of salvation, the pursuit of which makes it unnecessary to confront the truly distressing situation people find themselves in. Such fantasy has an advantage of a defensive kind, but it disrupts communicative action directed at the current source of difficulties and as such may block change.

In exploring central issues about power so far in this chapter, I have made repeated references to ideology. The rest of this chapter will focus on values, norms and ideology in order to gain some insight into what they are and how they arise.

Desires, values and norms

A distinction can be drawn between desires and preferences, on the one hand, and values or ideals and norms, on the other hand,[13] and a further distinction can be made between first and second order desires.[14] First order desires or preferences are fluid and particular bodily impulses expressed as unreflective action and experienced as compulsive motivations for actions, which lack evaluative criteria and so are not intrinsically linked to ethics or morals. However, humans also have desires directed to their desires, second order desires, in that they can desire to have desires, or not, and they can desire that their desire be strong enough to make it possible for them to desire to be different to what they are. Desires directed to our desires arise in reflective self-evaluation so that human desiring is essentially reflective and self-evaluative and so fundamentally social. For human action, it is not possible to take desire (bodily impulse or first order desire) on its own because of the human capacity, essentially social, to formulate the desirable and the judgment or evaluation that this always involves. Only in the rarest of circumstances, I would argue, do humans simply act on bodily impulse – there is almost always some kind of discrimination arising in a history of social interaction, although that discrimination could quite easily have become unconscious. This discrimination inevitably implicates norms and values. Therefore, what are they and how do they arise?

Norms are evaluative in that they provide criteria for judging desires and actions to realize them. They are experienced as obligatory and constraining and so that they inevitably restrict opportunities for action, being intimately connected with morals in that they provide criteria for what *ought* to be done, what is *right*. Norms, then, provide a basis for evaluating and choosing between desires and actions, and they emerge and evolve as people in a society become more and more interdependent and as the use of violence is monopolized by the state.[15] Desires are taken more and more behind the scenes of daily life as more detailed norms emerge about what can and cannot be done in public and these norms become part of individual personality structures, adherence to which is sustained by the social process of shame. Norms, therefore, are constraints arising in social evolution that act to restrain the actions and even desires of interdependent individuals, so much so that the constraints become thematic patterns of individual identities. In complex responsive process terms, norms are themes organizing experience in a constraining way. However, norms are inseparable although different from values.

Values and ideals are evaluative in that they provide general and durable criteria for judging desires, norms and actions. However, unlike norms, they are attractive and compelling in a voluntary, committed sense which motivates and opens up opportunities for action. Values attract us, giving life meaning and purpose, and so are experienced not as restrictive but as the highest expression of our free will, presenting a paradox of compulsion and voluntary commitment at the same time. Values are intimately connected with ethics in that they provide criteria for judging what *is* the *good* in action, differentiating between good and bad desires, as well as good and bad norms. Values are essentially concerned with what it is good to desire. When we reject a perfectly realizable desire because we believe it is unacceptable then we are distinguishing between higher and lower virtues or vices, profound and superficial feelings, noble and base desires. Such evaluations refer to feelings such as outrage, guilt and admiration and they indicate a life we hold to be of higher value, a view of the kind of person we want to be. Values, as inspiring, attractively compelling motivations to act toward the good, are continually arising in social interaction, that is, in our ongoing negotiation with each other and ourselves as we go on together, as inescapable aspects of self-formation. It follows that values are contingent upon the particular action situations in which we find ourselves and although they have general and durable qualities, their motivational impact on action must be negotiated afresh, must be particularized, in each action situation. Dewey[16] combines such an intersubjective understanding of self and value formation with experiences of self-transcendence. The communicative interaction, in which self is formed, is more than a means to coordinating action; it opens human beings up to each other, making possible the experience in which values and commitments to them arise. Shared experiences overcome self-centeredness, producing altruism, which is a radical readiness to be shaken by the other in order to realize oneself in and through others. This opening, or transcending, of the self toward others is the process in which values arise. Dewey also brings in the role of imagination and creativity in the genesis of values and value commitments. Imagination idealizes contingent possibilities and creates an imaginary relation to a holistic self. While imaginary, this relation is not an illusion or a fantasy. Idealization allows us to imagine a wholeness, a unity of experience, which does not exist and never will, but it seems real because we have experienced it so intensely. This is not a solitary but a social process. The will does not bring about the imagined wholeness; rather, the will is possessed by it. The description of values and value commitments so far may easily be taken as meaning that values are unequivocally good. However, this is not so. The notions of cult values, the power dynamics of inclusion and exclusion, and the way in which groups of people may get caught up in destructive unconscious processes of self-loss, focus our attention on the darker aspects of values/ideals and value commitments. These processes point to the particular problems that arise from the tendencies to idealize imagined wholes and immerse in imagined participation in them.

   What I have been describing is a perspective in which values are a paradox in that they arise in: processes of self-formation and self-transcendence at the same time; interaction between people but at the same time experienced by them as beyond their own positing; critical reflection and in experience beyond conscious deliberation at the same time; intense actual experience of interaction and idealizing acts of imagination at the same time. Values may be good or bad or both, depending upon who is doing the judging. Values do not arise either from conscious intentions or through justification and discussion, although such intention, justification and discussion may be applied later. Values cannot be produced rationally and they cannot be disseminated through indoctrination. A purpose in life cannot be prescribed. Instead, the subjective experience of values arises in specific action contexts and types of intense experience. Values and value commitments arise in the process of self-formation through processes of idealizing key intense experiences and through the imaginative construction of a whole self to yield general and durable motivations for action directed toward what is judged as the good. These generalized idealizations must always be particularized in specific action situations as people negotiate their going on together. Values cannot be prescribed or deliberately chosen by anyone, because they emerge, and continue to be iterated, in intense interactive experiences involving self-formation and self-transcendence. To claim that someone could choose values for others would be to claim that this someone could form the identity, or self, of others and form the self-transcendence of others.

Therefore, value formation is very much a central aspect of what pre-occupation in the game is all about. When we articulate these values, we are engaging in first order abstracting, and when we see these values as a system that the leaders can change, then we are engaging in second order abstraction and splitting off the immersing in local experience.

Norms, values and ideology

In complex responsive processes terms, values are themes organizing the experience of being together in a voluntarily compelling, ethical manner, while, paradoxically, at the same time norms are themes of being together in an obligatory, restrictive way. In their ongoing negotiation of the enabling-constraining actions they choose, all are taking the attitude of others, specifically and in a generalized/idealized ways. In other words, they are continually negotiating the evaluations of their actions and the criteria for evaluation are at the same time both obligatory restrictions taking the form of what they ought and ought not to do (norms) and voluntary compulsions, taking the form of what they are judging it good to do (values). The evaluative themes forming and being formed by human interaction are norms and values at the same time, together constituting ideology. How is this so?

The generalization/idealization (the imagined whole or unity of experience) has the qualities of obligatory restriction (norm) and, at the same time, the qualities of voluntary compulsion (values) and so is evaluative. In dialectical terms, the opposition (negation) of norm and value, of restricting and opening up, is transformed (Aufhebung or negation of negation) as ideology. Ideology, a whole that is simultaneously the obligatory restriction of the norm and the voluntary compulsion of value, constitutes the evaluative criteria for the choice of communicative interactions and the sustaining of power relations. As such, it is largely habitual and so unconscious processes of self and social at the same time. If people in a group rigidly apply the ideological whole to their interactions in all specific, contingent situations, they cocreate fascist power relations and cults which can easily be taken over by collective ecstasies. The result is to alienate people from their ordinary everyday experience and so create a false consciousness. Alternatively, if the ideological whole is so fragmented that there is little generalized tendency to act, then people will be interacting in ways that are almost entirely contingent on the situation, resulting in anarchy. Usually, however, people particularize/functionalize some ideological wholes in contingent situations, and this is essentially a conflictual process of negating the whole, which always involves critical reflection.

The discussion of norms and values can, I think, further illuminate the nature of the 'I-me' dialectic. The 'I' can be thought of as the voluntary compulsion that arise in intense iterative experience, grasped by the imagination and idealized in a manner that opens up possibilities for action. Spontaneity, imagination and idealization, voluntary compulsion impervious to argument, are all characteristics of the 'I'. On the other hand, one can think of the 'me' in terms of the obligatory restriction of the ought/right (norm). However, 'I' as value and 'me' as norm can never be separated in the process of self-formation. In dialectical terms, the opposition (negation) of voluntary compulsion ('I') and obligatory restriction ('me') is transformed (Aufhebung or negation of negation) as self. Self-formation is thus a fundamentally social process, and this is a fundamentally evaluative process of norm and value. Nevertheless, there is a further negation, because in altruistic social interaction, the self is opened up to others, and it is in this experience of self-transcendence that values arise. I would argue that, for humans, the spontaneity of the 'I' has little to do with bodily impulses as such, because bodily impulses are already socially formed. Furthermore, I would argue that human spontaneity is not the opposite of reflection. Dewey, James and Joas all link the experience of value with the critical examination of action, with reflection. One might think of the 'I' as the impulsion to enact values and this inevitably involves reflection. For me, the spontaneity of the 'I' refers to the feeling that I must respond, even in ways that surprise and frighten me, if I am to be able to live with myself.

From a complex responsive processes perspective, there are no universals outside of human interaction, but this does not mean that norms and values are purely relative in an 'anything goes' kind of way, because generalizations and idealizations, can only be found in their particularization in specific interactive situations. This always involves negotiation of conflict and power relating, in which 'anything goes' is impossible. From a complex responsive processes perspective, desires, values and norms are all understood to be particular narrative and propositional themes emerging in interaction and at the same time patterning that interaction. Norms are constraining aspects of themes, providing criteria for judging desires and actions. Emotions, such as shame and fear of punishment or exclusion, provide the main constraining force. Values, on the other hand, are highly motivating aspects of themes that arise in particularly intense collective and individual experiences, involving imagination and idealization, and serve as the basis for evaluating and justifying desires and actions, as well as the norms constraining them. Emotions such as gratitude, humility, altruism, guilt and feelings of self-worth provide the attractive, compelling force of value experiences. For each person, these intense value experiences are particularly linked to interactions over a life history with important others, such as parents, who are perceived to enact values ascribed to them. These important others cannot unilaterally prescribe such values, because they emerge in the relationship. However, while the separation of values and norms is an aid to understanding, it is an abstraction from lived experience in which norms and values are inseparable aspects of the evaluative themes, the ideologies, which are choices of actions.

What is the part a leader plays in all of this? Leadership arises in social processes of recognition[17] in which, in imagination, the leader can be recognized as embodying the idealized whole. Here the leader is not designing the values and persuading others to commit to them. The leader is participating in the intense experience in which the values are arising and in which he or she comes to be imagined as embodying them. He/she and the others may be so caught up in the process that they all lose sight of the imaginative nature of their construct. The leader is then idealized as a person and denigration is never far away. Leadership is a social object and cult value.

I want to turn now to the connections between the foregoing theory of value/norm genesis and the spiritual.

Complex responsive processes and spirituality

Joas, Dewey and James all regard religious experience as an aspect of 'values in general' and hold that the exploration of the nature of religious experience brings deeper insight into the genesis of values and value commitments. For example, having broken away from his own religious background and belief in any supernatural being, Dewey[18] was not concerned with institutionalized religion but with the experience of religious feeling, which many refer to as the spiritual. For him, religious experience was real but was culturally mediated without supernatural origin so that both religious and aesthetic experiences are imaginary orientations to a whole self, which is an ideal or imaginative projection that permeates and transforms life, bringing a sense of security and peace. Participation in conversation, as a social experience of value involving self-formation and self-transcendence, could lead to the experience of wholeness and so constitute an ideal inspiring reverence, thereby sacralizing community and democracy. Unlike Dewey, James[19] did not take a social perspective on self-formation but sought to understand the religious by taking the religious experience of the solitary individual. However, like Dewey, he sees self-transcendence, self-opening, as the process in which 'values in general' arise and faith, like love, is a special case of this. He too broke away from his own religious background and was not concerned with theology or religious institutions but with personal religious experience, which he defined as the feelings and acts of people in their solitude as they understand themselves in relation to the divine. To study such experience is to study human experience in one of its most intense and universal manifestations. Accounts of conversion experiences, prayer, mystical experiences and personal rebirth conclude that the religious is always experienced anew by living individuals as natural emotions directed towards religious objects. James said that the divine is a primal reality which one feels impelled to respond to gravely and solemnly. He distinguished religious experience from moral experience in that the moral person concentrates the will in order to lead a moral life, and this morality restricts possibilities for action. However, the religious person lives life with passion, excitement and fervor and this experience is liberating, empowering and morality transcending, so increasing possibilities for action. This experience of religiosity arises in the impulse to yield the self to the Self. Religiosity is a state of assurance and certainty in which there is a loss of worry and a feeling of peace, harmony and willingness to be. It is a passion of acquiescence and admiration involving the perception of truths impossible to articulate in language. The appearance of the world is altered and a feeling of bliss or ecstasy flows through one, involving the conviction of the presence of a stronger power than oneself. Conversion is a unification of the self and prayer opens one up to supra-individual forms of power. Such experience cannot be instilled by proofs and is impervious to argument. Religious and closely related aesthetic experiences are, therefore, particularly intense examples of the experience of values in general. Religious experience, as an experience of value, has particular qualities and emotions to do with awe, reverence and love, accompanied by feelings of peace and assurance that give meaning to life. This may have nothing to do with anything supernatural but arises as idealization of an imagined whole.

From a complex responsive processes perspective, religious or spiritual experiences are easily understood as particularly intense and powerfully attractive experiences of value. The key aspect, perhaps, of religious and spiritual experience is a particularly powerful experience of that self-transcendence, the emptying, losing and opening the self to otherness and so finding the self, which is common to all experiences of value. Without this, we get the cult and collective ecstasy with its loss of self. For some, the experience of self-transcendence is not accompanied by the need to postulate some transcendent divine and is presumably, therefore, not accompanied by any experience of the transcendent divine. For others, however, the spiritual experience of self-transcendence and the experience of the transcendent divine are inseparable. The theory of complex responsive processes has, of course, absolutely nothing whatsoever to say about the question of whether there is, or is not, a transcendent divine or what the nature of that transcendent divine might be. The theory is concerned with how either or both of these beliefs are taken up in action in organizations.

However, the theory of complex responsive processes rests upon a theory of causality in which there is no causal power outside human interaction accounting for the patterning of that interaction, because interaction is being patterned by interacting people. The theory is, then, saying that any transcendent divine is not the cause of human interactions. It is we who cause our interactions through individual evaluations and choices of action but not simply as individuals for although each of us may evaluate and choose our next action, the pattern that emerges is the result of the interplay of all those evaluations and choices and none of us can choose that interplay. To say that God is the cause of an individual's actions or the cause of the interplay of individual actions would be to escape our own ethical responsibility for what we do in particular situations and run into the unsolved problem of how a loving God could choose the terrible things we do to each other. Furthermore, just as with any value, the spiritual value experience has its dark side. Those who have powerful spiritual experiences may well come to believe that this entitles them to occupy the moral high ground, leading to the particularly destructive dynamics of inclusion and exclusion, with their often terrible consequences. The result is a loss of negotiated value orientations in highly normative institutional structures with the direct application of cult values.

It might be objected that denying a causal role for the divine in the patterning of human interactions amounts to claiming either that God is irrelevant or that religious experience is being split off from all other experience. I argue that this objection is unfounded. Persons who believe in God and experience the religious are experiencing what is, for them, the most powerful and motivating of all values. This experience, therefore, infuses all their actions and evaluations. The religious experience is thus taken up in the actions of those who are religious and this must play its part in what emerges in the interaction between them and others who will have different or no religious experience, but will all, nevertheless, experience value in some way. It is in negotiations of these differences, and the conflict they bring, that human futures emerge. The religious experience is not split off from the other actions of the religious person and the belief in God is not irrelevant to them. They play their part through the actions of religious persons in ways that cannot be understood in terms of simple causality.

When I talk to groups of managers about understanding organizations as complex responsive processes, I am frequently asked about the connection with the spiritual. When I ask people what they mean by the spiritual, they reply that it has to do with personal peak or ecstatic experiences, often related to nature; the connectedness of everything to everything forming a whole; the infinite; and a higher purpose, the ultimate meaning of life. What is it about the theory of complex responsive processes that triggers this question of spirituality for managers in organizations that ostensibly have nothing to do with spirituality? I think it is because this theory emphasizes the unpredict-ability of human futures. When I talk about the unknowable, the perpetual construction of the future in the never-ending iterative processes of the present, this is easily linked in the hearer's perception to some notion of the infinite. I also talk about the emergence of individual and collective identity in social interaction, thereby challenging ways of thinking and talking about identity as an essence or a pre-given self existing inside an individual person. This challenge touches on questions about the meaning of life and its purpose. Furthermore, a key aspect of the theory of complex responsive processes is its notion of transformative causality where human interaction is patterned as repetition and potential transformation at the same time, from within that interaction. In other words, interaction is its own cause without any 'whole' having causal power above or below that interaction. It is then taken that I am denying anything mysterious, mystical, or spiritual in human experience. It is taken that the notion of a transcendent divine, or any higher purpose in life, is incompatible with the perspective of complex responsive processes. It is understandable, therefore, that the theory of complex responsive proc-esses should trigger questions to do with spirituality.

However, it is striking how often this question is raised when we are talking about organizations that have nothing to do with religion. Why does this happen? Perhaps it has something to do with the fact that most people in Western Europe and a sizeable minority in the USA now have no religious practice and for more than a century soci-ologists, philosophers and politicians have raised concerns about the basis of ethics and values in such a secular society. There was a time when religion gave most people a sense of the ultimate meaning of life but now in a secular society where is one to look for such meaning? Perhaps people have come to look for some kind of ultimate purpose in life in the organizations for which they work, and this is why the question of spiritual-ity quickly comes to mind when taken-for-granted notions of the nature of organizations are questioned.

For me, there are a number of reasons for not appealing to the mythological and the mystical in our explanatory frameworks relating to organizations. First, when we move to the mystical, to an ineffable and unknowable God, for example, we move away from the possibility of reasoned explanation because, by definition, we cannot articulate explanations of the ineffable and unknowable. In relation to the mystical, we have to move away from explanation to intuitive experience which we might try to talk about in terms of mythology or theology and experience in ritual. However, when talking about human organizations, I feel it is incumbent upon us to explain what we think we are doing together, even when we point to mythology or engage in ritual. Second, some of those importing notions of the spiritual into their discussions about organizations seem to me to use the spiritual in a prescriptive, instrumental or utopian way, thereby positing a cause of human interaction which lies outside that interaction. For me, this is a debas-ing of the most precious aspect of human experience and an easy way out of taking ethical responsibility for what we are doing in the ordinary daily conduct of our lives. Third, it seems to me that most organizations exist in order to provide goods and serv-ices of many different kinds. Most organizations do not exist to meet people's spiritual needs – for these, we have religious organizations.

I now turn to how norms, values and the spiritual are dealt with in the organizational literature and in the section after that to how people take these matters up in organiza-tional practice.

Values and spirituality in organizational discourse

One prominent approach to values in organizations regards them as key aspects of organizational culture, which is then closely connected to the role of leaders. Values are thought to arise as the response of some individual to a problem in contrast to the factual and the real aspects of the problem.[20] If the values are successfully involved in solving the problem, they are then reflected in the observable behavior of other members of the group and then as they become habits, they fall below the level of awareness to become the cause of ongoing patterns of group behavior. If these deep underlying values become inappropriate then they need to be deliberately changed by leaders. Deep values are unconsciously shared, and it is possible to make them conscious and engineer changes in them.[21] The origin of culture/norm/value is usually located in the founder of a group and the possibility of changing culture in leaders. If a mature organization is to avoid blindly perpetuating itself and the leadership it has created, then the leader must break the tyranny of the old culture. Such a leader must acquire objectivity and insight into the elements of culture, and it is his essential function to manipulate the culture.[22] This is completely different to the theory of values set out in the previous section. First, the term value is used to mean what *ought* to be, rather than what *is*. In the views expressed earlier in this chapter, a norm is what ought to be and a value is about what is judged to be good. The formulation common in the dominant discourse loses the attractive, motivating nature of values in the obligatory and restrictive nature of norms. Second, the dominant discourse locates the genesis of values-norms quite clearly in the individual arising as a rational solution to a problem. From a complex responsive processes perspective, values arise in social processes of self/identity formation and self-transcendence. Third, the dominant discourse holds that deeply seated norms can be changed by deliberate choice, which is explicitly rejected as a possibility in this chapter, because values and norms both arise in social interaction which no one can control. They have to do with self and identity, both individual and collective, and these cannot be deliberately chosen or engineered. There is no notion of functionalization; so in the end, the dominant discourse is talking about cult values. It is rational individual choice that generates values rather than conflictual interaction between people with its potential for amplification as in the theory of complex responsive processes.

The theory of the learning organization[23] is also concerned with the matter of values, as an aspect of personal mastery involving the experience of increased connectedness between people and between people and their environment. This experience of connectedness leads to the values of compassion and a genuine commitment to something larger than us, namely the whole. This is a commitment of the heart and a sincere desire to serve the world, naturally leading beyond self-interest to a broader vision. Great leaders are those who see spiritual welfare, the self-actualization of their people, as part of their task, because this will lead to a person being committed to a higher purpose. The discipline of personal mastery requires spiritual growth but goes beyond it to approach life from a creative viewpoint. Those who display personal mastery have a special sense of purpose and for them, vision is a calling. They are called to work creatively with the tension between vision, what we want for the future, and current reality. This discipline of personal mastery is not a soft option but one that leads to better organizational performance and higher profit.

In the end, the dominant discourse, no matter what the angle taken, presents a view of organizational life and the role of values in it, in which the leader is the one who designs the values and manages their widespread sharing on the part of organizational members. Writers and managers may talk somewhat ambivalently about values emerging, but at the same time, they claim that in successful organizations leaders design them and persuade or train others to follow them. They see nothing contradictory about this – all it means is that it is difficult to achieve. The genesis of values is located in individuals with any social process coming into the sharing phase. For some, the process of value genesis and commitment is largely a rational one which may involve emotion but has little to do with spirituality. For others, however, there is a strong spiritual aspect to the learning organization where all are called upon to serve a higher purpose, because they are interconnected and part of the whole – dialogue is a special form of communication that causes a common pool of meaning to flow through people. Some even go so far as to recommend meditation for managers as a way of discovering what they should do.[24] Spiritual aspects are not to be dismissed as soft, because they lead to superior performance and so greater profit. Therefore, while some writers do introduce the strongly attractive, motivating nature of values in the form of spirituality, they see it as the kind of climactic experience of an individual act of self-mastery. From a complex responsive processes perspective, such moments are not simply individual choices but, rather, they have to do with values arising in social processes of self-formation and self-transcendence. Values cannot be deliberately designed or rationally chosen, because they arise in interaction and spiritual experience has the quality of a gift rather than a choice. Implicitly, the suggestion is that organizations should use the spiritual to improve their performance. The spiritual is then being dealt with in a prescriptive and instrumental manner to secure improved organizational performance. In the approach taken in this chapter, there is no prescription or instrumentalization, because I argue that all values, including the spiritual, cannot be designed and built in the first place.

Some other writers take the emphasis on spiritual matters in relation to organizations even further.[25] They point to the clash between work and family life, to the despair of young people, the impact of economic growth on the planet, the pervasive feeling of not being valued at work leading to reduced job satisfaction and morale, frustration and anger that is detrimental to business. To reverse this, they call for organizations to nurture people's souls at work and allow their souls to emerge, linking this to improved business results. They claim that current economic and organizational systems are not working and call for a metanoia, a change of mindsets, hearts and ways of acting, so the sacredness of work is regained and a more relational world is created. Some turn to the new sciences which are said to make us more aware of our yearning for simplicity and how this is a yearning we share with natural systems. Organizations are called upon to trust in the power of values, because they can shape every employee into a desired representative of the organization. Effective leadership communicates simple rules, guiding visions, inspiring values, and then allows individuals in the system to meander in seemingly random, chaotic ways. The movement to participative management is rooted in the changing perception of the organizing principles of the universe. They conclude that when relationships in an organization are care-full then a community of care develops, creating space for the soul at work to emerge. When the individual soul is engaged, people naturally want to add value. The collective soul is where people become connected to a larger purpose, transforming the 'protean' spirit of the organization to infinite possibilities through a culture of care, support and fulfillment. The collective soul benefits the whole.

What we see here is the bringing together of a number of themes that constitute what many are now talking about when they link spirituality with organizations. There is the call for organizations to meet the spiritual needs of individuals, the development of the individual's soul. This is linked to a relational world, the community and the sacralization of community and work. Relationships are taken to be entirely good. Soul and community are then closely linked to deep ecology and sustainability, often understood in mythological, even mystical, terms, and this in turn calls for a return to ancient wisdom. Nature too is to be re-sacralized. These are all elements of a whole that is unquestionably good, so establishing a particular ethics of a universalist kind in that those who participate in this whole are good and those who do not are bad. All of this points to the need for a sense of higher purpose and creates a utopian prescription for organizational success thereby instrumentalizing the spiritual. What is so created is what Mead called cult values and those putting them forward pay no attention to just how these cult values are functionalized as good and bad in ordinary daily life. The natural complexity sciences are used to justify particular cult values without any interpretation of what the insights of those sciences might mean in human terms or any attempt to explain how such cult values are functionalized in daily life. There are the same ethical implications as before, namely, that those ascribing to the cult of care are good and those not ascribing to it are bad.[26] Here we see the mythological elevation of nature to the status of some whole that we must all participate in, for it provides our higher purpose. The effect is to hold out the hope of a utopia, a hopelessly idealized future, if only we would all conform. This is, of course, Mead's definition of a cult value. Rather than the self-transcendence that Dewey talks about in his view of the genesis of values, we have in the perspective of Wheatley and others what can only be described as the loss of self in participation in a whole. This is in sharp contrast to the perspective of complex responsive processes theory, which seeks to understand just how such cult values are functionalized in ordinary, everyday conflictual social life as both good and bad. Compared to Dewey, the writers reviewed in this section lose sight of the imaginary nature of the whole and of the role of self-transcendence or altruism, the opening of the self, in the genesis of values. For Dewey, care means opening the self to others rather than participation in some actual whole in which the self is lost rather than transcended. A view of care as the opening of the self to others does not exclude conflict. The writers reviewed in this section miss the contingent, conflictual and negotiated nature of values but see them rather as universals. They confuse ethics and norms and do not see the link between idealization and denigration.

Values and organizational practice

The literature on spirituality and organizations, examples of which were discussed in the last section, may not have had a major impact on how practitioners in organizations think and act but the views of those writing about values in general, particularly Schein and Senge, certainly have. Most large organizations now pay attention to their values, taken as synonymous with norms, and seek to specify those that should govern the behavior of their members. The questions of values/norms and leadership feature prominently in a great many of the management and leadership development programs that organizations put their most promising managers through.

For example, GE has specified in great detail what it calls 'The GE Values' so taking seriously the views of Schein and Senge that it is the role of leaders to design the values/

norms that members of an organization are to live by. GE requires all employees to sign a form undertaking to abide by the 'GE Values' which are specified in a large volume given to each employee. Employees are also given 'Blue Forms' which they are encouraged to use to report on those who are infringing these values in some way. Such reports initiate disciplinary procedures against those infringing the values. These are, of course, not values in the terms of this chapter but norms constraining what people can do and the use of procedures to inform on people breaking the norms is the practical illustration of the point made earlier on the conformist ethics that this promotes.

Many companies mount initiatives to develop new values, so carrying out the prescriptions of Schein, Senge and others that it is the role of leaders to redesign the values when the old ones are no longer appropriate. For example, the chief executive of one major company I worked with appointed a task force of 'high flyer' managers to identify a new set of values for their organization so that people would act in more entrepreneurial ways. Despite intense effort, this task force could not come up with a new value set that they felt to be meaningful and they floundered in trying to identify how they could get everyone to behave according to such a values set, even if they could come up with one. What I found intriguing about this attempt to carry out the prescriptions of Schein, Senge and others, was that the members of the task force showed no signs of reflecting on what the concept of 'values' might mean or how values might arise and be sustained or change. They simply took the prescription for granted.

Given the presumably unwanted consequences of a conformist ethics and the enormous difficulty, I would say impossibility, of carrying out the mainstream prescriptions to do with values in organizations, the question arises as to why managers still try. Furthermore, why is there a considerable interest expressed by many in organizations in that form of value called the spiritual, most commonly meaning higher purpose and the 'whole', linked to nature? The reason probably has to do with the experience of many of a loss of value in their lives. The response to this loss may well be reflected as a call for the organizations in which they work to fill this loss. However, the resulting mythological and utopian thinking amounts, for me, to an escape from explanation and in practice leads to an ethics of conformity. From the perspective of complex responsive processes, the value statements produced by organizations amount to gestures and although such gestures can be designed the response to them cannot. What kind of response might one expect? One response would be cynical disregard. However, if the publication of a value statement, a list of desired behaviors, is accompanied by strong pressures to conform, then the value statement amounts to an articulation of norms and fear, and shame may lead people to be seen to conform even though they do not really agree. The inspirational qualities of values simply do not arise. Finally, if accompanied by sufficient rhetorical skill on the part of leaders, the response might be some kind of collective ecstasy, some kind of cult. What one would not get from designed values is the compelling and attractive force of authentic values which arise in intense interactions between people in processes of self-formation and self-transcendence.

Institutions and legitimate structures of authority

This chapter has been exploring the local interactions which form and are formed by population-wide patterns of power relations, as expressed in the identity-creating dynamics of inclusion and exclusion which are always reflections of ideologies. Ideology is constituted in the paradoxical interplay of desires, norms and values as restrictions, compulsions and voluntary commitments to choices of action. It is these complex responsive processes of relating that constitute the game in which we are all daily immersed. However, this activity of immersing in the game is by no means mindless. The activity of immersing is in fact a highly skilled performance and some of the skills take the form of thinking and reflecting in terms of both the first order abstracting of categories of experience and each other and the second order form of abstracting in which we construct maps, models, system designs and plans to increase our ability to control from a distance. In this way, we take up and continue to evolve in our local interactions the generalized and idealized narratives and propositions of our history, and a feature of great significance in this activity is the formation of institutions and legitimate patterns of authority. From a complex responsive processes perspective, such institutions and legitimate 'structures' of authority are not primarily the realizations of rational designs and plans to achieve clearly defined objectives but, rather, the articulations of actual or desired population-wide power figurations and ideologies, very much to do with identity, that are emerging in many local interactions. It is in these highly complex, responsive processes of interaction that we jointly carry out our tasks in organizations.

For example, Chapter 2 described the evolution of university-based business schools. This did not happen as the result of a central decision to set up a population-wide network of business schools to provide an education that would produce more efficient managers upon whom profitability and continuing economic growth depended. Instead, business schools began to appear as an expression of the ideologies of wealthy industrialists who believed that managers should be ethically responsible stewards of society's resources. As institutions, they were expressions of the search for legitimacy and acceptable identity on the part of a new class of functionaries called managers. The continuing evolution of business schools expressed changing ideologies, power figurations and identities, recently reflecting and shaping investment capitalism, for example. In the UK, there are now central government policies with the rational aim of refocusing universities and business schools on training people to meet the needs of the economy, and such policies are affecting how universities are governed, but it is by no means clear that this is having the intended effect of producing more efficient managers; many are concerned at the decline in educational standards which economic instrumentalist approaches are producing while others cynically claim that the response of the universities to such policies is simply a public relations façade behind which business as usual continues. Chapter 2 also mentioned the emergence of powerful independent management consultancies in the USA which later spread across Europe and then the rest of the world. Here again, there was no central intention to create an industry of independent management consultants. The opportunity for independent management consultancies was opened up by the Glass-Steagall Act passed by Congress in 1933 and the potential for rapid growth in consulting activities was also create by government policies requiring due diligence and other reports.

The point I am making is this. It is easy, from the emphasis I have been placing on how population-wide patterns emerge in local interaction, to conclude that any attempt to design institutions or intentionally formulate and promulgate policies is futile or at least flawed. Such a conclusion, however, simply shifts the focus of attention from one pole, autonomous design, to the other pole, emerging pattern, and the effect of doing this is to be left still with an inadequate explanation of what we are doing in our experience of organizational life. Quite clearly, central authorities do develop and enforce central policies and institutions are designed. Nevertheless, to understand the effect of such activities we need to see how they only ever have any impact insofar as they are taken up in many, many local interactions and the impact depends on just how they are taken up. So, policies and institutions emerge in the local interactions of policy makers who articulate the patterns that are emerging in the form of policies, laws and intuitional arrangements the effects of which emerge in the local interactions of the many, many people affected by the policies laws and intuitions. The policies laws and intuitions all take the form of generalizations, frequently second order abstractions, and also idealizations and what effect they have depends upon the particularizing in local interaction in which the policies, laws and institutions will evolve further.

Conclusion

This chapter has presented a view of the reality of organizational life as complex responsive processes of local interaction between people taking the form of communicative interaction in which they construct patterns of power relations, expressed as categories of inclusion and exclusion, reflecting their ideologies and constructing their identities. In this everyday activity of the ordinary politics of organizational life, people are making choices selected by their ideologies even when those choices look like rational calculations. Together they are engaged and pre-occupied in the games, the habitus, of everyday organizational life. The game, or habitus, is the general and the ideal which is continually particularized by people in their local interactions. The local interactions are therefore being formed by the generalizations and the idealizations of the game, often expressed in central government policies and laws, as well as in institutional forms. But at the same time as being formed by the generalizations and idealizations across the population, people in their local interactions are forming them and in so doing contributing to their further evolution. The possibility of evolution lies in the differences between people, their power positions and ideologies, and this means that the evolution of patterns of human conduct is inevitably conflictual. Such an account accords, for me, far more with the kind of organizational reality I was describing in Chapters 1 and 2 than the perspective provided by the currently dominant discourse.

Notes

1 Elias, N. and Scotson, J. (1994) *The Established and the Outsiders*, London: Sage.
2 Elias, N. (1970) *What is Sociology?* New York: Columbia University Press.
3 Ibid. p. 72.
4 Ibid. p. 77.
5 Ibid. p. 82.
6 Ibid. p. 86.
7 Ibid. p. 92.
8 Menzies Lyth, I. (1975) 'A Case Study in the Functioning of Social Systems as a Defence Against Anxiety', in Coleman, A. and Bexton, W. H. (eds) *Group Relations Reader*, Sausalito, CA: GREX.
9 Elias, N. and Scotson, J. (1994) *The Established and the Outsiders*, London: Sage.
10 Dalal, F. (1998) *Taking the Group Seriously*, London: Jessica Kingsley.
11 Matte-Blanco, I. (1975) *The Unconscious as Infinite Sets: An Essay in Bi-logic*, London: Duckworth; Matte-Blanco, I. (1988) *Thinking, Feeling and Being*, London: Routledge.
12 Dalal, F. (1998) *Taking the Group Seriously*, London: Jessica Kingsley.
13 Joas, H. (2000) *The Genesis of Values*, Cambridge: Polity Press; Dewey, J. (1934) *A Common Faith*, New Haven, Conn: Yale University Press; James, W. (1902) *The Varieties of Religious Life*, Cambridge, Mass.; Mead, G. H. (1934) *Mind, Self and Society*, Chicago: Chicago University Press.

14 Frankfurt, H. (1971) Freedom of the Will and the Concept of a Person, *Journal of Philosophy*, 67(1), 5–20.

15 Elias, N. (1939/2000) *The Civilizing Process*, Oxford: Blackwell.

16 Dewey, J. (1934) *A Common Faith*, New Haven, Conn: Yale University Press.

17 Griffin, D. (2001) *The Emergence of Leadership*: *Linking Self-organization and Ethics*, London: Routledge.

18 Ibid.

19 James, W. (1902) *The Varieties of Religious Life*, Cambridge, Mass.

20 Schein, E. H. (1985) *Organizational Culture and Leadership*, San Francisco: Jossey-Bass.

21 Ibid.

22 Ibid.

23 Senge, P. M. (1990) *The Fifth Discipline*: *The Art and Practice of the Learning Organization*, New York: Doubleday.

24 Scharmer, C. O. (2000) 'Presencing: Using the Self as Gate for the Coming-into-presence of the Future', Paper for conference on *Knowledge and Innovation*, May 25–26, 2000, Helsinki, Finland.

25 Fox, M. (1995) *The Reinvention of Work*, San Francisco: Harper Collins; Lewin, R. and Regine, B. (2000) *The Soul at Work*, London: Orion Business Books; Wheatley, M. J. (1992) *Leadership and the New Science*: *Learning about Organization from an Orderly Universe*, San Francisco: Berrett-Koehler.

26 Griffin, D. (2001) *The Emergence of Leadership*: *Linking Self-organization and Ethics*, London: Routledge.

10 Implications of a theory of complex responsive processes for policy making, consultancy, leadership, management, organizational research and management education

This book is drawing attention to the inadequacy of the current dominant discourse on organizations and their management and the lack of congruence between the underlying thinking in this discourse and the reality of organizational life. The dominant discourse explicitly and implicitly claims that management is scientific, more or less, and that there is an organization science focused on the objective study of organizations in order to identify the causal laws governing them. This thinking makes a usually implicit assumption about efficient causality and predictability. If management and organization are sciences, then they are the sciences of certainty. Closely allied with the assumptions of science are the ideologies of control and improvement which are reflected in taken-for-granted views of the roles of managers and leaders as the controllers of organizational evolution. It can be argued that the linking of organization and management to science, particularly engineering, had essentially to do with the quite explicit search for the legitimacy of management roles. The link to science was a powerful move in the professionalization of management, which was expressed in the institutions of research-based business schools, professional management education, professional associations of managers and the rise of a profession of expert advisors to managers in the form of management consultants.

However, these developments have covered more than a century now and it has become clearer and clearer that the claim for management legitimacy through science has a rather shaky basis. Despite the massive increase in numbers of professionally educated managers and the millions of pieces of research, there is no adequate scientific evidence base for the dominant prescriptions for managing and leading organizations. Furthermore, the economic events of the first decade of the twenty-first century provide a dramatic experience of the lack of congruence between the dominant discourse and the quite evident reality of organizational life. The collapse of investment capitalism calls for more than a new regulatory regime; it calls for a major rethink of the roles of managers and leaders and a serious examination of the ideologies of control and improvement. If we are to turn to science then we should move from thinking in engineering terms of the sciences of certainty to ways of thinking indicated by the sciences of uncertainty, the sciences of complexity. However, this should be done in a way that avoids the error of the dominant discourse in directly applying the natural sciences to organizations. In turning to the natural sciences of uncertainty, they should be used only as sources of analogies for organizations, to be interpreted in terms of sociology and psychology. Perhaps we need to accept that management and leadership are not sciences but fundamentally social phenomena which cannot be understood simply in terms of the application of science, both the sciences of certainty and those of uncertainty.

However, reaching this conclusion does not have to mean that leadership and management are simply 'arts' to be practiced without much attention to theory. This book argues for a rigorous development of theory that is more congruent with our experiences of organizational reality. This book advocates a more paradoxical way of thinking about organizations in terms of the simultaneous activities of abstracting from and immersing in the experience of local interaction in organizations, which is understood to produce emergent patterns across populations in organizations and societies. From this perspective, we are perpetually constructing 'the organization' as patterns that emerge in our ordinary local interaction while at the same time the pattern of organization is perpetually expressed in our local interactions as we together perpetually create the future. Local interaction thus becomes central to our understanding of organizations, leadership and management. That local interaction takes the form of ongoing, ordinary conversation between members of an organization and between them and members of other organizations. It is in these ordinary conversations that patterns of power relations emerge, not just in the local interactions themselves but across populations, and these patterns of power relations take the form of figurations of inclusion and exclusion which confer identity on people. Furthermore, the power relations of local interaction are reflections of ideologies, and these ideologies are the basis, largely unconscious, of our choices. Together we are perpetually iterating and potentially transforming patterns of interaction across populations in our ordinary, everyday conversations, power figurations and ideologically based choices, all of which can be summarized as the complex responsive processes of the ordinary politics of everyday life. Central to understating what we are actually doing in organizations, the reality of organizational life as opposed to the abstract idealized prescriptions of the dominant discourse, is the recognition of the interplay of our intentions in our pre-occupation in the game, our expressing of habitus, of social objects and of cult values, all quite different to the single dimensionality of autonomous 'rational' decision-making.

The principal implication of a shift in ways of thinking is the refocusing of attention. The dominant perspective quite naturally leads to a focus on decision makers and the problem situations they are required to deal with, where the problem could be to do with correcting what has gone wrong or responding to new opportunities in innovative ways. The question immediately posed is that of how to make the *right* decisions, and this is frequently taken to mean identifying and following *rational*, analytical techniques using the right decision-making tools to make decisions which *optimize* outcomes. This approach is sometimes recognized to be an idealization and more sophisticated decision-making techniques such as those found in soft and critical systems thinking take account of the emotional, ideological and political basis of decision-making in an uncertain world, characterized by webs of interconnection which makeit unwise to try to deal with any problem situation in one best way in isolation from other problem situations. This leads to prescriptions for multiple definitions of problem situation boundaries and the application of many mental models or paradigms to the identification of helpful decisions and solutions. The problem situations generally relate to macro issues with long term consequences, such as how to develop more innovative products, or how to design a reporting structure, or how to improve quality, or what procedures should be put in place to reduce risks of accidents at work, or how to improve systems of health care and education, or how to cut crime, or how to reduce poverty, or how to design financial products to reduce risk and maximize profit and so on.

In other words, the problem situations generally relate directly to what I have been calling population-wide patterns of interaction, usually without paying much, if any, attention to what I have been calling local interaction. However, the decision-makers are basically concerned with taking some action, exerting some control, in relation to many local interactions in which they themselves are not directly involved. They may be trying, for example, to decide on procedures for avoiding accidents in a particular type of work which they themselves do not undertake. They are then making decisions affecting and seeking to control local interactions taking place some distance away. They therefore face the kind of problem situation, referred to in Chapter 2, which the modern state encountered in improving the system of taxation. Central decision-makers could only deal with this situation by simplifying and generalizing across many local interactions by, for example, preparing cadastral maps. The need to 'see like a state' leads naturally to the building of models and the drawing of maps and 'rich pictures' to simplify and delineate distant, widespread problem situations. In Chapter 5, I pointed to how this approach to problem situations necessarily amounts to both first and second order abstracting from the experience of ordinary local interaction, and we seem to have a strong tendency to forget the abstract nature of our maps and models and deal with them as the things of reality, while people and their local interactions disappear from view. Consequently, the decisions made about the problem situations identified produce unexpected results that are difficult to make sense of because local responses have disappeared from view. I suggested in Chapter 1, that this way of thinking becomes increasingly incongruent with the reality that we are experiencing in ordinary organizational life.

Chapters 7, 8 and 9 have presented an alternative way of thinking which focuses attention on the experience of local interaction in organizations, including the local interaction of 'seeing the big picture like a state' and the local interaction of responding to those who make and enforce decisions to do with population-wide patterns. Attention is thus refocused so that we 'see like state' but at the same time notice the local nature of our seeing and the local responses to macro decisions, including the practice of the arts of resistance. In other words, I am calling for a paradoxical way of thinking which holds together both the activity of immersing in the game and the activity of abstracting from it all at the same time. If we think in this way then we see that formulating what we are doing in terms of decision-makers and problem situations immediately moves to one pole of the paradox of local interaction, namely, the simplifying macro, objective, abstracting activity with the danger of covering over the far from simple, micro, subjective immersing activity. In the local interaction of participating in organizational processes of communication, power relating and ideologically based choices, people hardly ever go through step-by-step procedures of distinguishing decision-making techniques and defining problem situations. They may do this from time to time in special events such as strategy away days or 'open space' events, but mostly managers and leaders are as pre-occupied in the various games of organizational life as anyone else, and it is in this pre-occupation that there emerges what are later called 'decisions'. A shift in ways of thinking along the lines I am suggesting, of course, has major implications for how we think about the roles of policy makers, management consultants, management educators, organizational researchers, managers and leaders. This final chapter will briefly sketch out what some of the implications for thinking about these roles might be.

Policy making and public sector governance

In Chapter 1, I mentioned the growing orthodoxy on the form that public sector governance is taking. This section explores the ideology and the way of thinking which this orthodoxy reflects, taking as a particular example the health service in the United Kingdom, although the same points apply to other public sector activities and other countries too and they also raise more general questions to do with impact of government policies generally, for example, to do with regulatory frameworks.

As I said in Chapter 1, over the past few decades there has been a movement in the United Kingdom away from a model of governance for public sector health and education, which was highly decentralized in national terms with services delivered by institutions which were internally governed in a collegial manner. However, during the 1980s, politicians presented the whole public sector as inefficient, irresponsible, nonaccountable for quality delivery and far from innovative, and made unfavourable comparisons with the private sector. Policy makers responded by making attempts to mimic markets in the public sector, and managerialism, the private sector theory of management, was imported and increasingly imposed by central government on the whole of the public sector. This required the setting of targets, the formulation and implementation of plans, the monitoring of achievement of targets, or lack of it, and the punishment of those who failed to achieve targets. The public sector was supposed to work as a market but this proved to be impossible and behind the rhetoric of the market there has emerged its opposite; namely, heavy regulation directly from the central government in the form of setting targets and monitoring performance against them. The result is a highly centralized form of national governance and a major change in the power figuration within delivering organizations in which power relations are now tilted firmly towards the top of the hierarchy of managers and away from the professionals who actually deliver the service. The collegial form of public sector governance has all but vanished, or perhaps more accurately, is still practiced to some extent in the shadow of the legitimate surveillance procedures. However, the particular form of power figuration which has emerged is sustained by a very different ideology to that which prevailed before. This is an ideology of efficiency, measurable quality and improvement, managerial control to produce uniformity of service; in short, an ideology of the market which takes precedence over the older ideology of vocation.

In this section, I explore the consequences of this change in corporate governance and ask whether the new model of governance actually works, reaching the conclusion that, while there may have been pockets of improvement, there is very little evidence indeed of overall improvement. In the face of this conclusion, it becomes important to ask why it is so hard to argue against this mode of governance. The first reason is that doing so amounts to challenging the dominant ideology and power figuration. The second reason is that the underlying way of thinking which supports the new governance model is so taken for granted, that an alternative way of thinking is not immediately apparent, and there seems to be no way out. After all, who can be against improvement and efficiency? This is why I think it is of central importance to reflect upon current taken for granted ways of thinking about the public sector and explore the implications of alternatives.

The way of thinking underlying today's public sector governance is a rather crude form of first order cybernetic systems thinking and the ideology underlying it creates a cult of performance, which replaces purpose. It has the hallmarks of the cult, namely, the presentation of a hopelessly idealized future and heavy demands for conformity. The approach is characterized by the instrumental use of naming and shaming people and institutions to enforce compliance, aided by a form of emotional blackmail as people are exhorted not to let their colleagues down. This cult of performance is actually operationalized in ways that involve the manipulation of figures and the distortion of clinical decisions to ensure the appearance of meeting targets. The result is a culture of deceit and spin in which appearance and presentation replace substance so that people become alienated from their experience. Instead of leading to authentic quality, I argue that the whole approach amounts to a system of counterfeit quality on the surface, while hard-pressed clinical staff continue to provide a 'good enough' service. This section concludes with an argument for moving away from systems thinking to the perspective of complex responsive processes where organizations are thought of, not as things, but as patterns of relationships between people. If an organization is patterns of relations between people but policy makers think they are systems, then what will happen as they enforce their policies? From the complex responsive processes perspective, such policies are simply second order abstractions, gestures which articulate social objects and cult values which have to be particularized in local interaction. So how are people in the health service particularizing central government policies on the governance of the public sector, while nevertheless fulfilling their purpose of being there together? And what are the consequences?

The consequences of performance management in the health service

The first consequence of the current mode of public sector governance relates to the pattern of employment.[1] Managers and central staff in hospitals have been growing so rapidly that they now significantly outnumber qualified doctors, no doubt reflecting the growing apparatus for the surveillance and control of the NHS (National Health Service), indicating just how substantial the cost of this form of public sector governance is. However, supporters of the new mode of governance argue that it has led to big increases in the number of patients treated, real progress in improving quality, significantly reduced waiting times for treatment and improved performance generally so that it is worth the enormous cost.[2] However, other sources repeatedly tell a different story[3] of no discernable connection between the amount of money going into the NHS and the number of patients treated. We repeatedly read newspaper reports telling us how targets are claimed to have been met when they are consistently missed, how apparent progress towards the key target for accident and emergency patients is unreliable, how hospitals distort their activities during periods when waiting times are being checked,[4] how second waiting wards are set up to remove patients from Accident and Emergency Ward counts. Doctors sometimes meet targets for waiting times for new patients by cancelling follow up appointments[5] and arbitrary targets simply push patients from one waiting list to another.[6] There have been many other reports on rising readmission rates, the falsification of data and the use of fine definitional differences to operate from two waiting lists, only one of which is officially published. These newspaper reports indicate how it is only possible for medical professionals and their managers to survive in the new cult of performance by practicing some form of deceit, or to put it more mildly, 'gaming the system'.[7] Although the clinical staff does continue to deliver a 'good enough' service, they do so despite the managerialist form of governance, not because of it.

Furthermore, one does not have to rely on newspaper reports in the United Kingdom to reach this conclusion. Researchers in Canada have found that managers and other professionals in public sector organizations develop techniques to corrupt the implementation of centralized control techniques, expertly practicing the arts of resistance.[8] These researchers argue that applying techniques of control drawn from a theoretical framework which is not compatible with the actual work environment inevitably leads to the corruption of those techniques in order to resist organizational change, with consequent unexpected consequences. The original intention of the techniques is lost in the political gaming between institutional professionals and government administrators: 'plans are serving as a tool in negotiations with the institutional environment represented mainly by the government . . . rather than serving as an instrument of change the technique is co-opted (corrupted)'.[9] The researchers argue that this 'failure' is not due to management but to the techniques themselves. Because of the incompatibility between the theory and the actual setting it seeks to understand, norms represented by the techniques contradict the practice of the organizations and the result is hypocrisy, which in turn breeds the destructive force of cynicism. This cynicism is exacerbated by the frequency with which the control techniques are changed: 'Lower-level managers avoid overt opposition, going through the motions of conformity rather than risk sanctions. In the process the very idea of quality management has been perverted. However, considerable energy has been expended.'[10] There are parallel research findings in the United Kingdom which argue that formal attempts at bureaucratic reform in the NHS have had little impact.[11] 'One impact of externally driven change is to feel disempowered or 'driven' in a particular direction . . . in the case of the quasi-market, for example, the drivers are central Government and both managers and professionals alike experience the impact. Within this context, some professionals perceive that their position and freedoms have been eroded and frequently blame 'management' for these changes.'[12] In the USA, despite its very different way of structuring healthcare, similar conclusions are reached by researchers. In 1999, The Institute of Medicine published a report titled *To Err is Human*. This revealed that tens of thousands of Americans were dying each year because of medical mistakes and poor performance. There is virtually no indication that American healthcare has become safer despite large-scale programs for improvement.[13] The responses to this failure typically continue to be a call to analyze and publish 'best practice': 'Although newly organized medical error reduction initiatives now abound, a close inspection of what is actually being accomplished through these initiatives may unfortunately lead one to believe that many of these "quality" efforts are geared more toward a socially and legally defensible public relations stance rather than an actual attempt to produce lasting improvement in medical outcomes . . ... The application of human factors research . . . would suggest that socio-cultural factors and task specific "change management principles" may provide hints on the reason that global "best practice" mandates and top-down reengineering are rarely successful'.[14] 'Best practice' in one local situation may not be 'best practice' in another indicating that health care initiatives should be local rather than global: 'if one understands how and why techniques are socially constructed in the course of ongoing interactions, herein lies a way to rethink management intervention that reaches beyond the impasse.'[15] It is the shift in thinking, which these and other authors are calling for, that I wish now to explore.

Taking it for granted that organizations are systems

In previous chapters, I have pointed a number of times to how we have come to think that rational individuals, governed by a rationalist causality, can objectively study higher level systems called groups, organizations and societies and redesign or re-engineer such systems to produce improved outcomes. In effect, these rational designers are enfolding visions, targets and so on, the human systems which will then, it is assumed, be unfolded by the formative operation of the systems, that is, by the interaction of the individuals (parts) constituting them. The most frequent conception of such systems is derived from the cybernetic notion of s a self-regulating system, a theory of control imported from engineering. Quality assurance systems were particularly well developed by engineers for manufacturing processes and later taken up in most repetitive administrative procedures as well. The engineer's notion of control became the most visible form of control in private sector organizations in practice and occupied most of the space in the literature on management and organizations. This emphasis on control focused attention on procedures, bureaucracies and paper trails to such an extent that the fundamental importance of human interaction, trial and error, and the highly political ways in which private sector organizations in fact function tended to be obscured. We could say that the ordinary day-to-day, rather messy nature of managing in commercial organizations became invisible, cloaked by a myth of calculating rationality. Human beings became resources used by an 'it' called an organization. Human beings became a 'dimension' of this 'it'.

It was this myth of instrumental, calculating rationality, I would argue, that was taken up and propagated by politicians in the 1980s and ever since as *the* way to govern the public sector. A whole taken-for-granted way of thinking is represented in target setting and procedures for monitoring performance. What seems beyond question in the rhetoric of improvement and modernization is its underlying way of thinking. And this is to implicitly assume that public sector organizations, even those as large as the National Health Service, are actually cybernetic systems and can be operated as such. It seems that we have come to think of public sector organizations as actually being like large central heating appliances with all those persons operating in them actually being like little central heating appliances. I argue that a particularly naïve form of systems thinking has become the fundamental notion underlying public sector governance today. The hypothetical nature of a system in which reality is thought of 'as if' it were a system seems to have been completely obliterated in the idea that a health system actually exists, and there seems to be little awareness of the problems inherent in applying a way of thinking about human action which is at odds with the potential for human choice, novelty and spontaneity and the need to continually respond to local contingencies. The much more sophisticated second order systems thinking seems to have had little impact on formulating national policy on the governance of the health sector, although some have occasionally used the tools and techniques of second order system thinking to design and run events for health care managers who are trying to work out how they might respond to governance policies. It is little wonder, therefore, that the consequences take the form described earlier.

The implications for public sector governance of the theory of complex responsive processes

From the perspective of complex responsive processes, the National Health Service is thought of as a social object, that is, as generalized tendencies of large numbers of people to act in similar ways in similar situations. On closer inspection, however, there is not one monolithic social object but many linked ones. Each hospital, for example, is to some extent a distinctive social object, as are groups of different kinds of medical practitioners and managers in that hospital. There are, therefore, many social objects, many generalized tendencies for large numbers of people to act in similar ways in similar situations, many games in which people are pre-occupied. Furthermore, the medical profession, the National Health Service and the many different institutions and groupings it is composed of are all idealized. Cult values, such as 'providing free health care', 'doing no harm', 'providing all with the highest standard of care' and 'providing the same standard of care in all geographical locations to all classes of person', are amongst the essential features of what the National Health Service means. 'Performance' and 'quality' are recent additions to these cult values. The generalizations of social objects and idealizations of cult values can all be recorded in written artifacts such as policy announcements and monitoring reports and sound recordings and films, all in the form of propositions and narratives. Such artifacts are then used as tools in the communicative interaction and power relating between members within the National Health Service and between them and those concerned with its governance, and between all of them and the users of health services. However, whether articulated in the form of artifact or not, the generalizations and idealization only have any meaning in the local interactions of all involved in each specific situation – they are only to be found in the experience of local interaction.

So, for example, when groups of policy makers meet to decide what to do about the NHS, they are clearly interacting locally. What they will be reflecting upon and discussing are the generalizations and idealizations of the NHS or parts of it. They may issue a consultation document, a green paper, to large numbers of people for comment. This is then taken up for discussion in the professional bodies representing different groups in the NHS. Again, the discussion is local interaction, as is the subsequent negotiation of changes in any of the policies. What they are discussing and negotiating in this local interaction is changes to the global, to the generalizations and idealizations or second order abstractions. Eventually a white paper, or policy statement, is produced and instructions sent to, say, all of the hospitals in the country setting out what new targets they must meet in order to demonstrate quality and performance and in what way they will be punished if they do not. What I have been describing is processes of local interaction, local negotiation, in which emerges articulations of the general and the ideal as far as the NHS is concerned. The process is one in which people have been trying to design the general and the ideal and in the way they currently do this in the UK they reflect a particular way of thinking about the NHS. In setting targets and establishing monitoring processes they display a way of thinking derived from cybernetic systems thinking. They are trying to design and install a self-regulating system.

However, the NHS is not a self-regulating system, but many local patterns of interaction in which the general is continually emerging as continuity and change as it is iterated from one present time to the next. What then becomes important is how people are taking up, in their local interactions, the generalizations and idealizations articulated in the artifacts of written instructions and procedures. The meaning cannot be located simply in the gesture of second order abstraction which these artifacts represent, because it is also located at the same time in the myriad local responses this gesture calls forth from those immersed in many organizational games. In a specific situation on a specific day, there may simply not be the physical capacity to achieve the targets set. In each specific situation, there will always be conflicts on what the targets mean and how they are to be adhered to. The target might then become something that has to be avoided, manipulated, and even falsified. For example, a specific decision might be to meet, say, a target of reducing waiting lists, by sending people home too early after an operation, leading to a rise in readmissions. The cult value of 'equal treatment' has to be function-alized in a specific situation at a specific time and may mean giving expensive medica-tion to one person and not another. The global generalization/cult value that the policy makers designed is thus being transformed in the local interaction so that it comes to mean something different – instead of uniform high performance, it might come to mean 'cover up' and 'deceit', involving the skilful practice of the arts of resistance so that they can continue to deliver the service while apparently complying with the targets.

As the unexpected emerges in many, many local interactions, the global pattern is transformed and of course, in their local interactions, the policy makers are reflecting upon this. They may then conclude that the now burgeoning number of targets is prov-ing too much of an embarrassment and should be scrapped. However, still thinking in system terms, they feel that they must design some other form of generalization to stay in control and secure adequate performance so that 700 targets should be abandoned, only to be replaced with 22 qualitative standards. Once again, however, the meaning does not lie on the generalization alone but in its particularization in many local situa-tions. This way of understanding focuses attention on the inevitably conflictual nature of particularizing the general and the idealized. If people simply apply some generaliza-tion or idealization in an absolutely rigid way there need be no conflict but particular-izing them in specific, unique situations means making choices. Since different individuals and different groupings of them will be making different interpretations of the situation, they will be pressing for different choices to be made. Which of those conflicting choices is actually made will be the result of negotiation and this immedi-ately raises the matter of power. The particular choices made will reflect the figurations of power – the choices of individuals and groups will prevail when the power ratio is tilted in their favor. While this is going on, public attention is focused on a strategic pose as an attempt to 'see like a state'.

If one takes this perspective, then the cooption and corruption of the tools and tech-niques, the game playing and deceit all become perfectly understandable aspects of hidden transcripts and the arts of resistance. They are the manner in which people find it possible to give at least the appearance of compliance and yet go on together to do the work of health care. All of this happens because the policies, tools and techniques reflect a way of thinking about organizations that is inappropriate in that it completely covers over the ordinary, everyday contingencies which people must negotiate in order to carry on doing what they need to do. An enormously expensive mode of public sector governance may produce some improvements but at the cost of distorting judgments in local situations and the requirement to expend huge amounts of emotional energy to get the work done while appearing to comply. The question then becomes that of how we are to develop forms of public sector governance that do take account of the essentially local nature of human interaction; the essentially contingent and conflictual manner in which people are able to go on together to do their work. Instead of importing mecha-nistic notions of quality from manufacturing, we need to be asking ourselves what quality actually means in the local situations in which health care and education are actually delivered. The aim of doing this is for policy makers to develop more appropri-ate generalizations, more appropriate ways of 'seeing like a state' which recognize the inevitability of the practice of the arts of resistance. Ongoing exploration of ways of 'seeing like a state' are essential, because some kind of control from a distance is still necessary for widespread improvement and accounting for resource use. There can be no one best way of doing this. The implication is that the centralized target setting form of governance should be scrapped altogether as other more appropriate ways are negotiated.

I am claiming that the kind of thinking I have been trying to develop in this book is more congruent with organizational reality than the dominant discourse is. I am suggesting that we might develop a better understanding of policy making, with regard to health, for example, if we move away from thinking that we are dealing with a system and realize that we are dealing with social objects. To put this in another way, any health policy will necessarily engage the habitus, the social habits, of health service providers, users, regulators and policy makers. In other words, policy makers are players in the health game in which they and health service providers, users and regulators are pre-occupied. The policy makers are producing policies in the form of second-order abstractions whose meaning arises in the immersion of all players in the health game. The moves in the game alter patterns of power relations, creating new categories of inclusion and exclusion, and the moves also reflect and affect competing ideologies. The implication for policy makers must surely be significant. If, as a policy maker, I think I am to design a system of performance incentives and monitoring regulation which will be implemented, more or less, by people of goodwill, it would make perfect sense for me to focus attention on designing the right system, formulating the right plans, putting the right procedures and policing mechanisms in place. I will be focusing on designing the right tools and techniques. However, if as a policy maker I think of myself as a player in the health game who needs to reflect carefully on the nature of the game and the likely local moves all the other players may or may not make, it would make sense to pay far less attention to the tools and techniques of control and far more attention to the far more important dynamics of the game, to the potential for coopting and corrupting the tools and techniques as other players practice the arts of resistance. I will be reflecting upon how my proposed techniques for motivation and control may affect patterns of power relations, who is being included and excluded with all the consequent powerful effects on identities, remembering that threats to identity will always arouse anxiety and the defenses necessary to live with it. I am not talking here about greater consultation with health providers and users – after all, consultation is simply another aspect of the game. I am talking about a different kind of sensitivity reflected in a different kind of conversation between policy makers themselves and between them and those for who they are making policies. I am convinced that the conversations of policy makers would be patterned in terms of very different narrative and propositional themes if they thought in complex responsive processes terms. Furthermore, these points apply to all other policy making, not just in relation to health. For example, it seems highly likely that the next few years will see major changes in the regulatory frameworks for the finance sector. What policies might be put forward if they are formulated not simply as techniques of risk reduction and control but as moves in the game of finance?

The roles of leaders and managers after the collapse of investment capitalism

Implicit in the dominant discourse on leadership is a view of the leader as one who stands outside the organizational system, formulates the values and visions it should unfold and then charismatically persuades others to implement the vision and values. From the complex responsive processes perspective developed in previous chapters, it is impossible for anyone to step outside of their interaction with others. A leader, like everyone else, can only interact with a limited number of others and cannot control the vast number of local interactions in which population-wide patterns of power and economic relations emerge that cannot have been have planned or directed by the leaders. Such patterns constitute social objects which people will always be particularizing in their local interaction. No one can step outside of interaction to design that interaction and from this perspective, it does not make sense to think of leaders setting directions or designing population-wide patterns of interaction which they can then realize. Leaders are particularly visible, particularly powerful players in games they are not in control of but are probably more pre-occupied with than any of the other players. When leaders 'set directions' or formulate organizational 'designs', they are in effect articulating social objects and cult values as second order abstractions, making statements about generalizations and idealizations as gestures, but what happens as a result of doing this depends upon how people take up such social objects and cult values in their local interaction with each other. While there is no overall program, design, blueprint or plan causing population-wide patterns, there are many individual designs, programs, blueprints and plans developed by players in the game in their local interactions which may express desires for some imaginative 'whole'. The population-wide patterns will emerge in the interplay of all of these designs and plans and no leader can control this interplay. Any statements that the most powerful make about organizational designs, visions and values are understood as gestures of second-order abstractions calling forth responses from many, many people immersed in their local interactions. The most powerful can choose their own gestures but will be unable to choose the responses of others, which may well reflect the arts of resistance, so that the outcome of their gestures will frequently produce surprises. The complex responsive processes perspective, therefore, casts considerable doubt on the mainstream understanding of leadership. If one thinks of organizations as widespread narrative patterns emerging in local interaction, then it is impossible for leaders to determine values, change cultures or move whole organizations along their own envisioned direction. Nevertheless, how, then, is one to think about the role of leader and the nature of leadership?

From the complex responsive processes perspective, the role of leader *emerges*, and is continually iterated, in *social processes of recognition*.[16] In organizations, people work together in groups and working together means engaging in communicative interaction and power relating in which people are continually choosing what to say and do next on the basis of ideology, so evoking and provoking responses from each other in their ongoing game in which that very game, or habitus, evolves. These social processes most commonly take the form of ordinary, everyday conversations.[17] It is this social interaction which forms and is formed by individual selves and what emerges, and is continually iterated, is a diversity of selves, where each recognizes and is recognized in their identity and differences. One such identity and difference is that of the role of leader. The role of leader is cocreated by all in these processes of recognition. The leader is as much formed by the recognition of the group as he or she forms the group in his or her recognition of the others.

As far as organizational reality is concerned, what is being mutually recognized is extremely complex. People may recognize and unconsciously collude in creating abusive forms of leadership. Typically, relational complexity is reduced to two stereotypical positions, one being the leader and the other being the followers. As they interact on the basis of these stereotypes, people may be unconsciously creating fantasized leadership in which all can act out their interlocking patterns of neurosis. As we know only too well, leaders are sometimes psychotic or become so through the pressures of filling the role. Leaders are embodied symbols of all sorts of things for people, and they play extensive roles in the fantasy lives of those they 'lead'. On the other hand, and at the same time, what is being recognized in leaders are important features in the ability to go on productively together. I will start by setting out what I think we recognize in the leaders we find helpful and effective and will then turn to what we need to think about in relation to the shadow side of leadership.

What is being recognized in an effective leader is the ability of the leader to *articulate emerging themes* in the ongoing organizational conversation, or to deconstruct and so present anew a theme that has become highly repetitive, so as to help the group to take the next conversational step. Complexity means that as they interact, people are producing further patterns of interaction that are known and unknown at the same time. It is particularly as they deal with the creative, the novel and the uncertain that people find that they must act into the unknown. It is in the process of exploring what to do next in such situations that members of a group turn to those who are able to articulate some meaning in what is emerging between them. This is not the same as drawing boundaries around problem situations, identifying the requisite tools and techniques, finding a solution or providing the answer – after all, the leader is acting into the unknown just as much as anyone else is. It is, rather, the tentative expression of what might be going on that triggers further exploration by others. In fact, from this perspective, the primary activity of an effective leader is to constantly evoke and provoke further exploration by members of a group, as they together act into the unknown and then respond to what they produce. Moreover, leaders in such groups are not simply, not even primarily, seeking to articulate what is emerging between them in their own local interaction in isolation. What they are trying to do is articulate what is emerging across populations of organizational members and across the populations of wider societies. They are seeking to formulate some view of what is emerging at a distance; in other words, they are attempting to 'see like a state'. They may well be using systemic techniques in these activities aimed at impacting on patterns much wider than immediate local interaction.

The aim of the effective leader here would be to widen and deepen communication between members of a group through exercising skills of conversation that keep opening up the possibility of new meaning rather than closing down on further exploration. Stuck conversation of a repetitive kind is what stuck unchanging organizations are, while more complex, fluid conversations are changeful organizations. The leader is recognized as the one who can deal with *not knowing* a little longer than others can, thereby providing some confidence for others to continue in their exploratory activities. Leaders encourage wider and deeper communication when they are recognized as persons with an *enhanced capacity for taking the attitude of others*, including the generalized other. It is this capacity that enables one recognized as leader to articulate emerging themes, especially those reflecting the particularization of social objects across wider populations. What I mean here relates to the capacity for empathy and attunement, as well as emotional awareness and skill. Also involved in this is the capacity to take the attitude of others is a particular ability to recognize and articulate the generalizations, the wider social patterns or social objects, which are being particularized in the interaction. Another important aspect recognized in effective leaders will be that of *displaying greater spontaneity* than others display. Here, spontaneity does not mean impulsiveness but rather acting imaginatively, and this involves reflection. Reflection can be understood as a paradox of immersing in and abstracting from experience. Spontaneity then means the capacity to act in a wider range of ways, taking risks and often surprising oneself and others. Such a capacity must be particularly valuable when it comes to acting into the unknown. One recognized as leader has a *greater capacity than others to live with the anxiety* of not knowing and of not being in control. The leader is recognized as one with the courage to carry on interacting creatively despite not knowing. It follows from the previous points that one recognized as an effective leader displays an *enhanced capacity to think, feel, reflect and imagine*.

What is being recognized in the leading-following relationship is a particular *figuration of power* in which the power balance is tilted toward the leader. Power figurations always create collective identities as patterns of inclusion and exclusion, with all the emotions and responses to those emotions that inclusion-exclusion always brings. Leading effectively requires considerable sensitivity to the dynamics of inclusion and exclusion. Furthermore, one recognized as leader will often be identified with what is ideal. There is a *powerful tendency to idealize* leaders where others come to perceive leaders as embodying idealized values. Norms and values are particular emergent themes organizing the experience of being together – they arise in process of self-formation.[18] The leader does not design them but rather participates in particularly influential ways in the processes of interaction with others in which *values and norms are continually iterated and potentially transformed*. It is the idealization that makes the leader particularly influential in this process. However, such idealization brings with it considerable danger in which the leader can easily become a cult leader. In addition, the price paid for the experience of being idealized is the experience of being denigrated and being made a scapegoat. Leadership is then essentially about ethics.[19]

In listing the capacities being recognized in the emergence of the role of leader, I am not talking about the attributes of an autonomous individual which that individual has been given, learned or can choose to have. Particular individuals have particular tendencies to act, formed in a life history of acting. However, in any specific situation such tendencies, the capacities referred to earlier, are all cocreated, they all re-emerge in social interaction, in ongoing social processes of self-formation and the recognition by others of that self, while recognizing the selves of others. One cannot identify the attributes of some individual and then conclude that one with the requisite attributes will perform effectively as a leader, because how the leader performs will depend just as much on the kinds of recognition, the kinds of responses of others. These kinds of recognition are not necessarily all good. I referred earlier to the tendency to idealize leaders, and this becomes a particularly powerful tendency when people experience high levels of uncertainty and anxiety. The expectations of the idealized leader can very easily become completely unrealistic and when they are not met, denigration soon replaces idealization. The good and the bad will emerge at the same time. It follows that it is extremely important for leaders to be aware of these, usually unconscious, group processes, enabling them to resist the idealization and prepare to deal with the denigration. The processes I am referring to easily create neurotic and pathological forms of leadership. In states of great anxiety, groups easily become submerged in group ecstasy or enact unconscious defenses, taking the form, for example, of excessive unrealistic dependency, aggression and scapegoating of others.[20] This may destroy the capacity for rational work and lead to forms of cult leadership and fascist power structures.

So, what is the practice of effective leadership from the perspective of complex responsive processes? It is a very different way of understanding the role of leader to that of the dominant discourse in which the leader stands outside the system, designing and manipulating variables and pulling levers in order to stay in control. From a complex responsive processes perspective, the practice of effective leadership is that of participating skillfully in interaction with others in reflective and imaginative ways, aware of the potentially destructive processes one may be caught up in. It is in this practice of immersing while abstracting from the games of organization that one is recognized as leader, as one who has the capacity to assist the group to continue acting ethically, creatively and courageously into the unknown. In this way, a leader may be exerting a powerful influence on what others think and do, and so on what happens, but all of this can only be done through the quality of the leader's participation in the conversation. I am not presenting this as prescription for a new form of leadership but as a pointer to what I think effective leaders already do.

However, not all leaders are effective in this sense, and there is not and never has been any leader who participates all the time in the manner I have been suggesting is recognized in effective leaders. Leaders are sometimes, some perhaps most of the time, destructive, greedy, neurotic, psychotic, criminal and despotic, or at best ineffective. We could say that what is being recognized by others in these forms of leadership is some kind of fantasy or myth of, say, savior or fight leader, or some kind of masochistic fantasy of being dominated by bullying leaders, all involving some kind of collusion and manipulation. I am talking here about the symbolic function of leadership. Moreover, all of this is coconstructed in often ordinary, mundane daily politics in which we cocreate leaders who may be abusive or patronizing, as well as inspiring and helpful. Leaders often fail to listen, while followers collude with this in not standing up to them, often for obvious reasons to do with economic security. In the dominant discourse, leaders are assumed to be perfectly healthy, balanced people, who set the direction of the organization for others to follow. However, as soon as it is recognized that anxiety can have strange effects on groups, the possibility arises that leaders can also be the neurotic creations of the group. It is quite possible that leaders are vainly trying to act out the fantasies that those in the management team are projecting on them. Leaders affect what groups do, but groups also affect what leaders do through processes of unconscious projection. As soon as we recognize the shadow side of leadership, it becomes clear that those taking up leadership roles have an ethical duty to reflect upon their own neurotic disposition and develop capacities for recognizing and coping with the neurotic dispositions of those around them.

Neurotic forms of leadership

Kets de Vries[21] explains the nature of neurotic leadership in the following way, drawn from psychoanalysis. Everyone behaves in a manner that is affected by what one might think of metaphorically as an inner theatre. That theatre consists of a number of representations of people and situations, often formed early in childhood, and those that have come to play the most important roles are core conflictual relationships. It is as if people spend much of their lives re-enacting conflicts that they could not understand in childhood, partly because these conflicts are familiar to them, and partly, perhaps, because they are always seeking to understand them. What they do, then, is project this 'inner' play with conflictual situations out onto the real world they have to deal with.

Leaders do this just as others do, the difference being that they project their 'inner' conflicts onto a much larger real-world stage that includes their followers. A leader projects 'internal' private dialogues into 'external' public ones and these dialogues are about core conflictual themes from childhood. The particular neurotic style a leader practises will be determined by the nature of these core conflicts. Followers also project their inner plays onto the leader and these leader/follower projections keep leaders and followers engaged with each other in a particular manner. Followers project their dependency needs onto leaders and displace their own ideals, wishes and desires onto them too. The 'inner' theatre in which leaders and followers join each other contains scenarios which are the basis of imagined, desired and feared relationships between them. There are typical scenarios that are found over and over again and they constitute typical dispositions, typical ways of defending against, repressing, denying and idealizing particular leader/follower relationships. Everyone uses such devices and everyone has a number of prominent dispositions that constitute that person's neurotic style. This is quite normal, and it becomes a problem only when people massively, compulsively and habitually use a rather small number of defences. This blocks their ability to relate to reality effectively, and it is then that they might be labelled 'neurotic'.

A number of such dispositions, or neurotic styles, can be distinguished. Every leader will display a combination of some of these styles, and it becomes a problem only when a rather small number of them come to dominate the behavior of the leader and the followers. For example, there is the *aggressive* disposition which tends to characterize many who become leaders and rather fewer who are followers – aggression is often acceptable in leaders but creates problems for followers. Tough chief executives who are socially forceful and intimidating, energetic, competitive and power oriented fall into this category. People are not important to them and they want to dominate. They tend to be impulsive and to believe that the world is a jungle. They expect people to be hostile to them and they become aggressive in advance to counteract such expected hostility. Of course, their behavior may well provoke the hostility they expect. Such leaders probably experienced parental rejection or hostility. Then there is the *paranoid* disposition, found frequently amongst leaders and less amongst followers. Such people are always looking for hidden motives and are suspicious of others. They are hyper-vigilant, keep scanning the environment and take unnecessary precautions. They deny personal weakness and do not readily accept blame. They tend to be restricted and cold in relationships, with little humor. They are fond of mechanistic devices to measure performance and keep track of people. Such people may have had intrusive parents and may feel uncertain of themselves. Others display the *histrionic* disposition which is characterized by a need to attract the attention of others at all costs. Such people are alert to the desires of others; they are sociable and seductive with their sense of self-worth heavily dependent on the opinion of others. They love activity and excitement and tend to overreact to minor incidents, often throwing tantrums. Such people may have had difficulty attracting the attention of parents. Yet, others display the *detached* disposition when they find it difficult to form close relationships. They tend to be cold and aloof, and this may be a response to parental devaluation. The *controlling* disposition is high in leaders and low in followers, and it is displayed by people who want to control everything in their lives. They have an excessive desire for order and control. This is a way of managing hostile feelings that may have arisen from the behavior of controlling parents. The resultant hostility may emerge as tyrannical ways of behaving or its opposite of submission. The *passive–aggressive* disposition tends to be found more in followers than in leaders. Such people are highly dependent but tend to attack those they depend upon. They resist demands for performance, they are defiant, provocative and negative, complaining all the time and demanding much from their leaders. They tend to blame others all the time, they are ambivalent and pessimistic. This difficulty might arise because such people find it difficult to assess what is expected of them. They are likely to have had parents who presented them with conflicting messages. Other dispositions are the *narcissistic* one when people see themselves as exceptional and special; the *dependent* disposition in which people are excessively dependent upon others; and the *masochistic* disposition.

It is not just the style of the leader or the style of the followers on their own that determines how their joint behavior unfolds. It is how the styles engage each other that will create the environment within which they have to work. So, an aggressive, controlling leader interacting with dependent, masochistic followers will produce a rather different context and pattern of behavior compared with such a leader interacting with, say, passive–aggressive followers. These patterns of interaction will have a powerful impact on how effectively people interact in an organization.

Leadership and ethics

In the dominant discourse, the conception of ethics is one which requires individuals to submit themselves to the visions and values revealed to them by their leaders, or democratically chosen by them as empowered individuals. Participation then becomes submission to a harmonious whole variously described as shared values, common purpose, common pool of meaning, transpersonal processes, group mind, collective intelligence, simple rules and so on. The ethical choice is that of voluntary submission to a larger harmonious whole. This way of thinking about ethics and leadership has many consequences. The freedom to choose actions and explore their ethical implications is located primarily in the leader, while the other members of an organization are required to conform to the emerging leadership of the whole, as indeed must the leader in the role of steward and teacher. Positing a harmonious whole removes diversity and conflict. Since diverse persons, by definition, are not submitting to the whole and so not losing their individuality, there is bound to be conflict, but this is either ignored or condemned. Theories of learning organizations and living organizations, as well as most applications of complexity theory to organizations, ignore diversity and conflict and their role in generating novelty. By setting up a whole outside of the experience of interaction between people, a whole to which they are required to voluntarily submit if their behavior is to be judged ethical, this way of thinking distances us from our actual experience and makes it feel natural to blame something outside of our actual interaction for what happens to us. It encourages the belief that we are victims of a system, on the one hand, and allows us to escape feeling responsible for our own actions, on the other. We come to feel that our actions are insignificant parts of some greater whole and that there is nothing much we can do about it, especially when management becomes a matter of changing *whole* organizations. An ethics based on the autonomy of the individual or of a systemic whole, is an ethics based on universal moral principles, which do not depend upon social or natural contingencies. They do not reflect the present context in which people are interacting with their particular life circumstances, aspirations and motivations. This is an idealized view of ethics as cult values in which autonomous leaders exercise their freedom independently of the contingencies of nature and society.[22]

Leaders act and leadership is action. This immediately means that a theory of leadership is also a theory of ethics. Ethical values emerge in interaction as a reflection of the emergence of leaders. Leadership, as a theory of ethics, is thus concerned with action in the present constructing the future, and this means that it has to do with 'who' is acting into the future, the matter of identity. The underlying concern has to do with persons and the notion of person combines two opposite aspects, namely changeability and stability. This combination of transformation and continuity is at the core of what identity is about and therefore at the core of what ethics and leadership are about. One can avoid thinking in terms of ethical universals as 'fixed reality' against which human conduct is to be judged, apart from and before action with meaning known in advance. Instead, one can think of ethics as the interpretation of action to be found in the action itself, in the ongoing recognition of the meanings of actions that could not have been known in advance. Motives then do not arise from antecedently given ends but in the recognition of the end as it arises in action. The moral interpretation of our experience is then found within the experience itself as new points of view that emerge in the conflictual interaction in which the future is perpetually being created. This view of ethics avoids simply idealizing in a cult manner and focuses on how idealizations are functionalized in the everyday conflicts in which we are always negotiating the future on the basis of the past. It avoids detaching from the everyday present of social interaction and instrumentalizing ideologies that go unnoticed and unchallenged.

Management

In Chapter 2, I referred to how definitions of the roles of leader and manager reflected a Platonic distinction between a concern with what to do and a concern with how to do it. It is then easy to allocate each to different roles with the leader in the elevated position of deciding what to do and the manager in the more instrumental role of determining how to do it. However, from the late nineteenth century up to the last quarter of the twentieth century, the roles of leaders and managers were not sharply distinguished from each other. Leaders also had to manage and managers of people inevitably had to lead as well. Khurana[23] points to the articulation in the early 1980s of a split between leaders with the more glamorous roles and managers with the more mundane roles. He suggests that this had to do with the relegation of management to the role of acting as agents for shareholders with the sole function of maximizing shareholder value. This role was conceived in narrow, instrumental and calculating terms. A more elevated role was then presented for leaders as charismatic figures who presented visions and converted people to the right values. This split off view of leadership thus seems to be very much part of investment capitalism, and after its collapse, the further evolution of capitalism may yield a more integrated view of leadership and management.

From the perspective of complex responsive processes, leadership roles and all other roles in an organization, including those of managers, are cocreated by all members of an organization in their ongoing local interaction. However, if leaders and managers are both cocreated in social processes then sharp distinctions between them, indeed between them and other roles, are unlikely to be sustained. For me, leadership and management are inseparable and neither can exist in some pure form. The points I have been making on leaders therefore apply just as much to managers. Furthermore, no leader-manager is always and everywhere *the* leader. Leadership as mutual recognition is much more fluid and shifts around the group even though legitimate authority continues to be identified with those 'higher' in the hierarchy. Also, leadership-management is interacting locally with others and so is concerned with patterns of local interaction, but at the same time, it is concerned with wider population-wide patterns as second-order abstractions, increasingly so with movement up the hierarchy, so as to be able to make legible distant local interactions as some form of 'seeing like a state' which enables some limited and imperfect influence across populations.

Organizational and management research

The complex responsive processes way of understanding life in organizations has implications for appropriate methods of research in management and leadership. The emphasis on participation in local interactions raises fundamental questions about objectivity in social research and focuses our attention much more clearly on the subjective nature of experience in organizations. The method of research then becomes that of making sense of one's own experience. The method is that of taking one's experience seriously with the aim of reflexively exploring the complex responsive processes of human relating. Experience is the experience of local interaction, and this immediately suggests that organizations need to be understood in terms of the experience of their members and others with whom those members interact. From the perspective of complex responsive processes, the appropriate method for understanding, for researching into, organizations is itself complex responsive processes. Research itself is also complex responsive processes, and the research method becomes reflection on ordinary everyday experience. Experience is felt, meaningful engagement in relating to others and to oneself as we do whatever we come together to do. Experience refers to interdependence, to the social, as the fundamental human reality. Since such interaction between living bodies is patterned primarily as narrative themes, taking one's experience seriously is the activity of articulating and reflecting upon these themes. In other words, the method is that of giving an account, telling the story, of what I think and feel that I and others are doing in our interaction with each other in particular contexts over particular periods of time and what sense we are together making of the much wider emergent patterns across populations. Since what I and we are doing is inseparable from who I am and who we are, a meaningful narrative is also always expressing, that is, iterating or cocreating, individual and collective identities. Taking one's experience seriously, through articulating the narrative themes organizing the experience of being together, is an essentially reflexive activity and in its fullest sense, this is a simultaneously individual and social process, including the social patterns that are much wider than our own immediate interaction.

It is the explicitly reflexive nature of the narrative that distinguishes it as a research method from the literary story. The research narrative is explicit and ordinary, as opposed to the poetic license of the literary story which has the potential for drawing attention to the epic nature of human experience or simply describing imaginative fantasy. The narrative as research method is reflexive in an individual sense insofar as the narrator is making explicit the way of thinking that he or she is reflecting in the construction of the story. In other words, the reflexive personal narrative is explaining why it has the particular focus it has and how the narrator's past experience is shaping the selection of events and their interpretation. The narrator is making explicit, as far as possible, the assumptions being made and the ideology being reflected, in explicating the particular meaning being put forward in the narrative. At the same time, the narrative as research method is no less importantly reflexive in a social sense. Social reflexivity requires the narrator to explicitly locate his or her way of thinking about the story being told in the traditions of thought of his or her society, differentiating between these traditions in a critically aware manner. In other words, the narrator as researcher engages intensively with literature relevant to his or her particular narrative accounts and makes explicit the ideological underpinnings and power relation implications. The literary story leaves interpretation of meaning largely to the reader while the narrative method of research rigorously sets out the writer's interpretations an assumptions.

An example of this approach to research is provided by the Doctor of Management Programme, at the Business School of the University of Hertfordshire. All participants are part time and must be working in some capacity in an organizational setting. Their research is their current experience of their organizational practice. The final thesis is built up through writing a number of projects, each of which is a reflexive narrative in the sense described in the foregoing section – the research method is for each participant to take his or her own experience seriously. In the first project, each participant provides a narrative account of the events, influences, literature and traditions of thought that are now shaping his or her practice and how he or she makes sense of it. Each of the following projects takes a particular situation the author is involved in and presents a narrative account of what the author and others are doing in that situation. They may, for example, be involved in quality improvement initiatives or they may be trying to choose how to respond next to some action that people in another organization have taken. The reflective narrative of some person's organizational experience is, however, only the 'raw material' of complex responsive processes of research into organizational life. It serves as the basis for discussion with others in a deepening reflection on the meaning of the narrative. The discussion may be one involving others in the narrator's organization and/or one involving members of some community of researchers. Therefore, on the Doctor of Management Programme, participants work in small learning groups of three to six members and a supervisor. They discuss each others' narratives, commenting, questioning and probing the accounts given, the literature drawn on or omitted, and the meaning being made of the experience. Each person then rewrites the narrative account and presents it once more to the group for discussion. Typically, there are at least three such iterations. The purpose of this iterative approach is to make richer sense of experience and as the researcher goes through this process, he or she experiences movements in his or her thought. The purpose is not to solve a problem or make an improvement to the organization but to develop the practitioner's skill in paying attention to the complexity of the local, micro interactions he or she is engaged in, because it is in these that wider organizational patterns emerge. However, the movement of thought is not an abstract matter, because the practitioner-researchers are making sense of their own current experience of what they and others are doing in their organization and as they do so, their practice inevitably evolves, hopefully for the better, although there can be no guarantee of this.

In this way, participants on the program build up a portfolio of projects, over a two- to three-year period, in which there emerge, usually more and more clearly, overall themes of importance to the participants in their organizational practice. The projects also chronicle movements of thought and shifts in organizational practice of the participants as they iterate through the projects to develop a thesis on organizational life. A further iteration involves discussing this movement through the projects and writing a synopsis and critical appraisal of the major themes, the movement in thought and

practice, and the contribution the researcher is making to his or her community of practitioners. Instead, then, of requiring the formulation of an hypothesis which is then
explored, the complex responsive processes research method offers a process in which
meaningful themes about organizational life emerge. Instead of resulting in a retrospec-
tively tidy write up, the complex responsive processes method leads to a research
account that tracks its own actual development as further reflexivity.

There is yet further reflexivity involved in the complex responsive processes research
method, and this involves making sense of the local, contingent process of the research
itself. Therefore, a key aspect of the program is the time made available, and the importance attached to, reflection by supervisors and researchers on the processes of learning
and researching together. This is done in regular community meetings of staff and
research students of the program. The way of working together in this meeting is very
much influenced by the group analytic tradition.[24] As with group analytic large groups,
all sit in a large circle and talk about whatever they want to talk about and this
will inevitably include the sense that they are making of the program and its research
method.

The community meeting on the program differs in some respects from the usual
group analytic one in that no one takes the role of group conductor. Although there is an
acknowledged power difference between supervisory staff and participants working
toward a degree, the staff members do not adopt behaviors likely to enhance that power
difference. For this reason, no staff member takes on the role of conductor, leader or
consultant. Instead, staff members participate fully as members of the group and do not
keep themselves separate from others on social occasions, except for staff meetings. The
experience of the large group is an important one for a number of reasons. First, it provides group support for what is an anxiety provoking process – the degree of critical
reflection required by the complex responsive processes approach inevitably leads to
some undermining of taken-for-granted aspects of ways of thinking and thus personal
and collective identities. Second, the group meetings provide a live experience of the
emergence of themes organizing the experience of being together and the power relations they reflect. Early on in the program, members may be invited to form themselves
into small learning groups and negotiate for a supervisor. This inevitably creates the
inclusion-exclusion dynamics of power relations and the often-stressful emotions that
go with it. This and other experiences have close similarities to the kinds of patterns
people experience in their own organizations and the group meetings provide opportunities for noticing and discussing these.

There are three important questions which must be addressed by any research method,
and these relate to ideology, ethics and validity or legitimacy. The ideology of the complex responsive processes research method will be addressed in the next section. The
use of narratives of personal experience of interaction with others raises important ethical questions. The first matter has to do with writing about people one is interacting with
and the related issue of disclosing confidential material. In a more conventional approach,
involving say interviews, the ethical approach is usually to inform those one is writing
about of what one is doing and then show them what one has written, concealing identities as appropriate. However, a researcher writing about his or her own personal experience of his everyday work activities can hardly keep informing people that he might
possibly write about what they are doing together. The best that can be done is to inform
colleagues in general about what one is doing and then write about the experience in a
way that does not reveal their identities but still presents a 'reliable' account of what is

going on. Other than this, there is no general ethical rule to guide the researcher in the traditional sense of thought before action. Consistent with the complex responsive processes approach, the ethics of what one does as a researcher, as with what one does in all other situations, is contingent upon the situation and the emerging and ongoing negotiation with those with whom one is interacting. The second ethical matter has to do with inviting people to undertake a form of research that can carry with it considerable risks. The risks are potentially hostile responses from others one is writing about, and the threats what is written might present to existing power relations and one's own job security. Here again, there can be no general ethical rule, only the contingent negotiation of how to proceed in particular situations so that the research work does not create undue risks for the researcher. Finally, there is the matter of validity or legitimacy. Clearly, there can be no objective validity for the obvious reason that the research is an interpretation, a subjective reflection on personal experience. However, it is not any arbitrary account in that it must make sense to others, resonate with the experience of others and be persuasive to them. Furthermore, it must be justifiable in terms of a wider tradition of thought that the community being addressed finds persuasive, or at least plausible. The value of this kind of research, I would claim, is that it presents accounts of what people actually experience in their organizational practice with all its uncertainty, emotion and messiness, rather than highly rational, decontextualized accounts and their hindsight view.

The reflexive, reflective approach I have been describing as a research method is much more than 'simply research'. It is also an indication of how leader-managers might conceive of themselves as 'researchers' using this method to explore who they are and what they are doing together as well as who they wish to become, and what they would like to do together. The approach is not simply research, because at the same time, it is the exploration of the fundamental questions of strategy – the strategic exploration of identity.

Further clarification of the complex responsive process research method can be obtained by comparing it with another form of qualitative research, that of action research, particularly the collaborative inquiry strand in that tradition.[25] The action research and the complex responsive processes approaches have many interests in common in that both: argue that positivist scientific methods and the simple position of the objective observer are not appropriate for researching social phenomena; are theories of social action; seek to avoid splitting theory and practice; are concerned with emergent phenomena; focus on participation and relationship; focus on the everyday and narrative aspects of experience; and engage with but do not move to postmodernism. However, there are fundamental differences between the two approaches and these may not be all that immediately obvious, because although both may use the same words, they have different meanings. In particular, the words action, participation, relationship, experience and emergence have substantially different meanings in the two approaches. The differences become evident in comparing how the two perspectives deal with metaphysics; the individual and the social; and ideology, power and ethics.

Metaphysics or a worldview

Metaphysics, that is, 'beyond physics' or appearances, refers to all encompassing claims about an ultimate reality. For many of those pursuing action research, it constitutes more than a methodology; it is an all encompassing worldview or paradigm of the social as systemic, holistic, relational, experiential and participatory.[26] From this perspective, action research is, therefore, built upon a metaphysical foundation in which the cosmos is seen as a systemic whole that is integrated, interacting, self-consistent and self-creative. Humans are parts of this whole, and participation means participation in this whole in a way that produces the whole. Those arguing in this tradition talk about a given cosmos, a primordial reality in which the mind actively participates and can experience a pristine acquaintance with, unadulterated by preconceptions.[27] Some action researchers then link this participative worldview to some notion of spiritual, ecstatic experiences in which people become aware of their own interconnectedness, and in doing so experience their true selves in the ecstatic I-Thou encounter with another.

Complex responsive processes, however, is a responsive temporal process theory which, when it comes to understanding human action, argues against systems thinking. Human interaction is patterned in the interaction between bodies and there is no need to look for any causal agency outside human interaction itself. This way of thinking is not holistic. Wholes emerge as our own imaginative constructs taking the form of ideologies. As described in the foregoing section, the methodology is that of exploring our own experience of interaction with each other and the ways in which this patterns our experience. What we are doing is exploring interaction as complex responsive processes of relating. The theory/method is therefore not based on any 'pre-given', and it has no metaphysical or spiritual foundations. Experience is the experience of interacting with other people in the context of the physical world, in which metaphysical themes and spiritual understanding emerge in human interaction and are available for exploration if that is what interests the researcher. Therefore, in participating, in interaction with, in relating to, each other, people are not producing a whole, other than as an imaginative construct, but only further patterns of interaction. These patterns are narrative themes that organize the experience of being together. Some of these themes can be described as metaphysical or spiritual. Instead of a starting point consisting of pre-given, universal wholes, the foundation of the argument consists of a number of generalized propositions about the nature of human interaction – a claim to a general human reality which is social interaction between bodies living in a physical world. Accounts and understandings emerging in such interactions are constrained by the physical world and by social relations of power. Nevertheless, the patterns are always contingent and evolving.

The individual and the social

The action research approach is therefore one that understands the social as a system at one level constructed by individuals at another level. For some writers on action research, individuals are thought to possess a true or real self that can be actualized in what is essentially a spiritual, often pantheistic, experience. Complex responsive processes theory, however, does not distinguish the individual and the social as separate levels but regards them as the same phenomenon. Human minds and human societies arise together, with the individual as the singular and the social as the plural of interdependent embodied persons. Individuals are paradoxically forming and being formed by the social *at the same time*. This is a very different theory of psychology to the humanistic and existential psychology of action research. Instead of thinking in terms of individuals actualizing themselves through what is ultimately a spiritual experience, the complex responsive process approach is concerned with understanding how individual and collective identities arise at the same time in the social interaction of interdependent individuals.

The methodology is one in which individuals take their own experience of these social processes seriously and try to understand the nature of that experience in which their identities are under perpetual construction.

Ideology, power and ethics

Action research starts with a clear ideology and takes, as given, values to do with cooperation, collaboration, democracy, emancipation, liberation, challenge to existing power structures, human flourishing and sustainable development.[28] Within this holistic and systemic framework, ethics then takes the form of thought before action. Action research has a clear political agenda which is inherent in the method. It is about empowering people. Some action researchers talk about restoring meaning and mystery to life so that the world is experienced as a sacred place. The theory/method of complex responsive processes reflects a different ideology. What it idealizes is human interaction itself with its paradoxical cooperation and competition/conflict, difference and sameness. However, central to the approach is the claim that the idealization cannot be taken on its own as a given or universal, because it only arises in its particularization in contingent, local situations. The exploration concerns how ideologies, and the power relations they sustain or change, emerge. Ethics is ongoing negotiation as participative interaction. Truth is 'truth for us'. Value orientations are unavoidable in the explanatory frameworks of the social sciences and such value orientations guide scientific inquiry, while the inquiry acts back on the value orientations. So, what are the value orientations of the method of complex responsive processes? What is particularly valued is the activity of exploring and explaining the differences between alternative ways of making sense of experience. The value may be summarized as 'taking one's own experience seriously' thereby attaching particular value to the subjective. This method does not presuppose a worldview or systematic ideology but rather seeks to explore how values, including its own, emerge in experience. It is an essentially reflexive method.

The implications for methodology

If global pattern emerges in local interaction in the absence of any plan or blueprint for that global pattern, then it follows that one can only really understand an organization from within the *local interaction* in which global tendencies to act are taken up. This means that the insights/findings of the research must arise in the researcher's *reflection* on the microdetail of his or her own *experience* of interaction with others. It follows that the research method is subjective, or rather, a paradox of immersing in and abstracting from experience. The term immersing refers to the pre-occupation in the game with the inevitable emotion that is aroused in the experience of interacting with others in order to accomplish some joint task. It is quite possible that heightened anxiety, in conditions of not knowing, will submerge us in highly emotional, or 'involved', thinking which could take 'magico-mythical' forms. Clearly, such thinking cannot qualify as research. However, if we can never avoid immersing then it follows that it is impossible for any of us to achieve fully detached, objective, abstract, rational thinking about the action of engaging with others. In relation to human action, then, the approach to research that is called for is paradoxically immersed and abstract at the same time.

If one takes the view that knowledge emerges and evolves in a *history* of social interaction, rather than being developed by an autonomous individual, then one attaches central importance to research as a participative, social process. Research on organizations is then done by participating in a community of researchers who are together exploring the meaning they are making of their experience. This inevitably involves conflict as people explore their differences and, indeed, this conflict is essential for the movement of thought. Research proceeds by researchers engaging in argument around difference, feeling themselves compelled to justify the perspective they take in its difference from other perspectives. Research, from this perspective, is not an activity which is separate from practice, because the reflective practitioner is, on the view so far presented, inevitably also a researcher in that both are engaged in reflecting upon their own experience. It follows that research is closely linked to the iteration and possible transformation of identity. This is because identity is the answer to the questions: Who am I? Who are we? What am I doing? What are we doing? What is going on? How do we now go on together? Effective research is potentially transformative of identity and is therefore bound to expose vulnerability and raise existential anxiety with all the emotion this brings with it.

What I have been saying has focused attention on research as an activity of the researcher making sense of his or her own experience of local interactions. However, researchers can and do focus on interactions of others at a distance, often concerned with population-wide patterns and second order abstractions from them. I am not trying to suggest that this is an invalid or inferior form of research. Clearly, it is not, just as macropolicy is not rendered invalid or inferior to local interaction. What is being suggested, though, is that even when concerned with the second-order abstractions of population-wide patterns, the activities of the researcher are, nevertheless, reflexive engagement in the local interactions of some research community.

Management education

Chapter 2 described how the establishment of business schools played an important role in the development of the professional identity of the manager and in so doing developed a professional identity for business school teachers and researchers. The early years were a struggle by both managers and business school academics for recognition, where the former were engaged in a struggle with trades unions and the latter with already established academic disciplines who regarded with disdain the claims for management as an academic discipline. At first, managers strove to be perceived as the stewards of society's resources and business school staff as educators of general managers drawing for their thinking on sociology as well as scientific management imported from engineering. Over the years, the roles changed so that in the most recent era, managers became agents for shareholders supposed to operate as decision-making technicians, and the role of business school staff became that of training managers in the right tools and techniques. The technical role of managers was split off by some from the more glamorous role of leader and the role of business school academics, especially at elite schools, became one of preparing high performers for leadership roles. Then investment capitalism rested very much on powerful investment banks and powerful management consultancies with the business schools, especially the elite ones, training people for roles in the banks and consultancies. All of this was occurring against a backdrop in which policy makers were increasingly regarding universities as instruments of economic progress through education aimed at providing trained business resources and research producing direct applications of techniques and products to economic activity.

As a result of all of these developments, the situation of business schools is now very different to what it was when they were struggling for academic recognition. The situation is now one in which business schools are the parts of universities most clearly identifiable with the current ethos of economic instrumentalism; they attract the largest inflow of students and produce financial surpluses which subsidize other academic activities. However, the freedom that such a position might be thought to bring is highly constrained by the form of public sector governance they are subjected to which is much the same as that I described in relation to the health services. The question now is what role business schools will play as investment capitalism evolves into some other form of capitalism.

If one thinks of organizations in complex responsive processes terms, then the role of business schools will be to provide opportunities for managers and leaders to understand what they are doing in reflexive ways that take account of the conversational life of organizations, the figurations of power they create and the ideologies which underlie the choices they make. The educational contribution would be that of providing greater insight into the games we are all preoccupied in and such insight would also be the aim of business school research activities. Perhaps we will become acutely aware of the absurdity of training future managers in terms of abstract decision-making techniques only, largely ignoring the complex dynamics of real life in organization. Perhaps the focus will shift to greater attempts to prepare future managers to deal with difficult people, surely one of their main roles.

Management consultancy

Chapter 2 briefly indicated how the roles of management consultants emerged first from the need for financial advice on investment projects and from cost accounting requirements in efficiently carrying out projects. Legislation created the need and opportunity for independent management consultancies to conduct due diligence procedures and prepare other legally required reports, while attempts to prevent monopoly agreements between corporations created an opportunity for management consultants to become disseminators of knowledge on best practice. Much later, management consultants found themselves in heavy demand from government bodies as well as universities, hospitals and, late on, charities. Management consultancy has therefore grown very rapidly over the past century or so, and it continued to grown into the era of investment capitalism as they provided a source of training in the techniques and tools of strategic management and the maximizing of shareholder value. They have come to be regarded as experts in management and leadership, well equipped to help identify problem situations and provide the right management tools for optimal decision making. Any significant change in corporate regulatory frameworks and any evolution of capitalism will undoubtedly affect the opportunities for and the roles performed by management consultants.

Corporate managers in almost all kinds of organizations take it for granted that what consultants do is very practical in that they provide the tools and techniques managers widely talk about and expect to be provided with. However, taking a complex responsive process perspective on organizations changes the meaning of what is practical. The tools and techniques come to be understood as second order abstractions of a highly generalized even idealized kind. This does not make them useless, because they are very much a requirement for 'seeing like a state' and exercising at least limited control from a distance. However, they can also easily be used as a rational cover for the far less orderly interaction of ordinary politics in everyday life in organizations. The focus on supposedly practical tools reflects figurations of power relations; the dynamic is of inclusion and exclusion, with their impact on identity and corporate performance. Managers can easily become rationally blind to highly relevant matters to do with ideology. It is attending to matters such as this through provoking and evoking richer more complex forms of conversation that become eminently practical from the perspective of complex responsive processes. The role of the consultant then becomes primarily one of participating in the local interactions of organizational life with the purpose of aiding the development of more fluid conversation in which the potential for both continuity and change emerge.

Conclusion

When I talk to managers about the matters I have been raising in this chapter I am sometimes told that what I am saying is very depressing. On enquiry, it transpires that what is found depressing is the inability to predict and so to stay in control of what is happening over a whole population. For me, there is nothing depressing about thinking in terms of the interplay of the intentions that all of us are forming and being formed by. In many ways, it is exciting and inspiring to notice how we and others around us have developed skills in carrying on interacting creatively, and also destructively, in our not knowing. I think this way of thinking connects more closely with the experience of organizational reality, making it both more intelligible, less anxiety provoking and more amusing.

Notes

1 For example, figures published by the Department of Health in their document *NHS Staff Overview 1998–2008* show how various categories of staff in the Health Service in England have been changing. Total employment in the NHS in England has increased by about 28 percent between 1998 and 2008 to reach nearly 1.4 million. Within this total, the number of qualified doctors (including general practitioners) has increased by around 44 percent to reach around 134,000, while doctors in hospitals only have increased by 55 percent to reach about 96,000. Over the same period, the number of qualified nurses has increased by just over 27 percent to reach a total of about 408,000. However, the total of managers and senior managers has increased by 76 percent over the ten-year period to reach nearly 40,000, while staff in central functions has increased by just over 48 percent to reach 105,000. Taking managers and central staff together, they now amount to 145,000, an increase of 55 percent since 1998. Managers and central staff at 145,000 now significantly outnumber qualified doctors in hospitals at 96,000. This continuing growth in numbers of managerial and administrative staff no doubt reflects the growing apparatus for the surveillance and control of the NHS, indicating just how substantial the cost of this form of public sector governance is.
2 For example, on 21 June 2003, *The Sunday Times* (pp. 12–13) referred to a report by the NHS chief executive.
3 For example, on 21 June 2003, *The Sunday Times*, p. 12, referred to research by the King's Fund showing that the number of scheduled operations and consultant appointments had fallen. On 11 January 2008, *The Telegraph* reported that almost 400,000 patients were still waiting for treatment for more than a year.
4 Ibid. p. 12.
5 On 29 July 2003, *Evening Standard* referred to a report by an all party Public Administration Select Committee of Parliament.
6 On 30 July 2003, *The Times* described research published in the *British Journal of Cancer* which showed that after targets for breast screening were introduced in 1999, the proportion of women who saw a consultant within two weeks rose from 66 percent to 75 percent. However, the proportion who received treatment within five weeks of this first appointment fell from 84 percent to 80 percent.

7 Williams, R. (2005) Leadership, Power and Problems of Relating in Processes of Organizational Change, in Griffin, D. and Stacey, R. (eds) (2005) *Complexity and the Experience of Leading Organizations*, London: Routledge.

8 Lozeau, D., Langley, A. and Denis, J. (2002) 'The Corruption of Managerial Techniques by Organisations', *Human Relations*, 55(5), 537–64.

9 Ibid. p. 547.

10 Ibid. p. 553.

11 Ferlie, E., Fitzgerald, L. and Wood, M. (2000) 'Getting Evidence into Clinical Practice an Organizational Perspective', in *Journal of Health Services and Policy*, 5(2), 96–102, 726; Fitzgerald, L., Ferlie, E. and Hawkins, C. (2003) 'Innovation in Healthcare: How Does Credible Evidence Influence Professionals?', *Health and Social Care in the Community*, 11(3), 219–28.

12 Ferlie, E., Fitzgerald, L. and Wood, M. (2000) 'Getting Evidence into Clinical Practice an Organizational Perspective', in *Journal of Health Services and Policy* 5(2), 96–102, 726.

13 Macklis, R. D. ((2001) 'Successful Patient Safety Initiatives: Driven from Within', *Group Practice Journal*, November/December: 65–91.

14 Ibid. p. 1.

15 Lozeau, D., Langley, A. and Denis, J. (2002) 'The Corruption of Managerial Techniques by Organisations', *Human Relations*, 55(5), 560.

16 Griffin, D. (2001) *The Emergence of Leadership*: *Linking Self-organization and Ethics*, London: Routledge.

17 Shaw, P. (2002) *Changing Conversation in Organizations*, London: Routledge.

18 Joas, H. (2000) *The Genesis of Values*, Cambridge: Polity Press.

19 Griffin, D. (2001) *The Emergence of Leadership*: *Linking Self-organization and Ethics*, London: Routledge.

20 Bion, W. (1961) *Experiences in Groups and Other Papers*, London: Tavistock.

21 Kets de Vries, M. F. (1989) *Prisoners of Leadership*, New York: Wiley. Kets de Vries adopts a psychoanalytic perspective in understanding neurotic forms of leadership. In its focus on the individual and the system, I argue that psychoanalysis falls with a neo-Kantian way of thinking that I have been critiquing in this book (see also Stacey, R. [2003] *Complexity and Group Processes*: *A Radically Social Understanding of the Individual*, London: Routledge). However, while recognizing major theoretical differences, the psychoanalytical approach is particularly informative when it comes to neurotic patterns.

22 Griffin, D. (2001) *The Emergence of Leadership*: *Linking Self-organization and Ethics*, London: Routledge.

23 Khurana, R. (2007) *From Higher Aims to Hired Hands*: *The Social Transformation of Business Schools and the Unfulfilled Promise of Management as a Profession*, Princeton, NJ: Princeton University Press.

24 Foulkes, S. H. (1964) *Therapeutic Group Analysis*, London: George Allen & Unwin; Kreeger, L. C. (ed.) (1975) *The Large Group – Dynamics and Therapy*, London: Maresfield Reprints.

25 Reason, P. and Bradbury, H. (2002) *Handbook of Action Research*: *Participative Inquiry and Practice*, London: Sage.

26 Ibid. p. 7.

27 Heron, J. and Reason, P. (1997) 'A Participative Inquiry Paradigm', *Qualitative Inquiry*, 3(3), 274–94.

28 Reason, P. and Bradbury, H. (2002) *Handbook of Action Research*: *Participative Inquiry and Practice*, London: Sage.

References

Abernathy, W. J. & Hayes, R. (1980) Managing our Way to Economic Decline, *Harvard Business Review*, July–August, 67–77.

Abram, D. (1996) *The Spell of the Sensuous*, New York: Vintage Books.

Ackoff, R. L. (1981) *Creating the Corporate Future*, New York: Wiley.

— (1994) *The Democratic Organization*, New York: Oxford University Press.

Akhavein, J. D., Berger, A. N. & Humphrey, D. B. (1997) The Effects of Megamergers on Efficiency and Prices: Evidence from a Bank Profit Function, *Review of Industrial Organization*, 12(1), 95–139.

Aldrich, H. (1979) *Organizations and Environments*, Englewood Cliffs, NJ: Prentice-Hall.

Allen, P. M. (1998a) Evolving Complexity in Social Science, in Altman, G. & Koch, W. A. (eds) *Systems: New Paradigms for the Human Sciences*, New York: Walter de Gruyter.

— (1998b) Modeling Complex Economic Evolution, in Schweitzer, F. & Silverberg, G. (eds) *Selbstorganization*, Berlin: Dunker and Humbolt.

— (2000) Knowledge, Ignorance and Learning, *Emergence, Complexity & Organization*, 2(4), 78–103.

— (2001) What is Complexity Science? Knowledge of the Limits of Knowledge, *Emergence, Complexity & Organization*, 3(1), 24–42.

Allen, P. M., Strathern, M. & Baldwin, J. S. (2006) Evolutionary Drive: New Understandings of Change in Socio-Economic Systems, *Emergence, Complexity & Organization*, 8, 2.

Ameriks, K. (ed.) (2002) *The Cambridge Companion to German Idealism*, Cambridge: Cambridge University Press.

Amihud, Y. & Miller, G. (1998) *Bank Mergers & Acquisitions*, Amsterdam: Kluwer Academic Publishers.

Anderson, C. & McMillan, E. (2003) Of Ants and Men: Self Organized Teams in Human and Insect Organizations, *Emergence*, 5(2), 29–41.

Anderson, P. (1999) Application of Complexity Theory to Organization Science, *Organization Science*, 10(3), 216–32.

Andrade, G., Mitchell, M. L. & Stafford, E. (2001) New Evidence and Perspectives on Mergers, *Harvard Business School Working Paper* No. 01–070.

Andre, P., Kooli, M. & L'Her, J. (2004) The Long-Run Performance of Mergers and Acquisitions: Evidence from the Canadian Stock Market, *Financial Management*, 33(4), 15–25.

Arendt, H. (1958) *The Human Condition*, Chicago: University of Chicago Press.

Ashby, W. R. (1945) The Effects of Control on Stability, *Natura*, 155, 242–43.

— (1952) *Design for a Brain*, New York: Wiley.

— (1956) *Introduction to Cybernetics*, New York: Wiley.

Ashmos, D. P., Duchon, D., McDaniel, R. R. & Huonker, J. W. (2002) What a Mess! Participation as a Simple Managerial Rule to 'Complexify' Organizations, *Journal of Management Studies*, 39(2), 189–206.

Barnes, P. A. (2003) The Origins of Limited Liability in Britain, The First 'Panic', and their Implications for Limited Liability and Corporate Governance Today, Available at SSRN: http://ssm.com/abstract+488703.

Bateson, G. (1973) *Steps to an Ecology of Mind*, St Albans: Paladin.

Bateson, W. (1851) *Materials for the Study of Variation, Treated with Special Regard to Discontinuity in the Origin of Species*, New York: Robert Schalkenbach Foundation (1970).

Beer, S. (1966) *Decision and Control: The Meanings of Operational Research and Management Cybernetics*, London: Wiley.

— (1979) *The Heart of the Enterprise*, Chichester: Wiley.

— (1981) *The Brain of the Firm*, Chichester: Wiley.

— (1994) *Beyond Dispute: The Invention of Team Syntegrity*, New York: Wiley.

Beinhocker, E. D. (1999) Robust Adaptive Strategies, *Sloan Management Review*, Spring, 95–106.

Beiser, F. C. (ed.) (1993) *The Cambridge Companion to Hegel*, Cambridge: Cambridge University Press.

Bertalanffy, L. von (1968) *General Systems Theory: Foundations, Development, Applications*, New York: George Braziller.

Bion, W. (1961) *Experiences in Groups and Other Papers*, London: Tavistock.

Blauner, R. (1964) *Alienation and Freedom*, Chicago: University of Chicago Press.

Boden, D. (1994) *The Business of Talk: Organizations in Action*, Cambridge: Polity Press.

Boisot, M. (2000) Is There a Complexity Beyond the Reach of Strategy?, *Emergence, Complexity & Organization*, 2(1), 114–34.

Boje, D. M. (1991) The Storytelling Organization: A Study of Performance in an Office Supply Firm, *Administrative Science Quarterly*, 36, 106–26

— (1994) Organizational Storytelling: The Struggle of Pre-modern, Modern and Postmodern Organizational Learning Discourses, *Management Learning*, 25(3), 433–62.

— (1995) Stories of the Storytelling Organization: A Postmodern Analysis of Disney as Tamara-Land, *Academy of Management Journal*, 38(4), 997–1055.

Boulding, K. E. (1956) General Systems Theory: The Skeleton of Science, *Management Science*, 2, 197–108.

Bourdieu, P. (1998) *Practical Reason: On the Theory of Action*, Cambridge: Polity Press.

Boyne, A. G. & Walker, R. M. (2002) Total Quality Management and Performance: An Evaluation of the Evidence and Lessons for Research on Public Organizations, *Public Performance and Management Review*, 26(2), 111–30.

Broekstra, G. (1999) An Organization is a Conversation, in Grant, D., Keenoy, T. & Oswick, C. (eds) (1998) *Discourse and Organisation*, London: Sage.

Brown, S. L. & Eisenhardt, K. (1998) *Competing on the Edge: Strategy as Structured Chaos*, Boston, MA: Harvard Business School Press.

Bruner, J. (1990) *Acts of Meaning*, Cambridge, MA: Harvard University Press.

Burgelman, R. A. & Grove, A. S. (2007) Let Chaos Reign, then Rein in Chaos – Repeatedly: Managing Strategic Dynamics for Corporate Longevity, *Strategic Management Journal*, 28, 965–79.

Burke, W. W. (2008/1982) *Organization Change: The Theory and Practice*, Thousand Islands CA: Sage Publications Inc.

Callon, M. (2002) Writing and (Re)writing Devices as Tools for Managing Complexity, in Law, J. & Mol, A. (eds) *Complexities: Social Studies of Knowledge Practices,* Durham, NC, USA: Duke University Press.

Callon, M. & Latour, B. (1981) Unscrewing The big Leviathan: How Actors Macro-structure Reality and How Sociologists Help them to do so, in Knorr-Cetina, K. & Cicourel, V. (eds) *Advances in Social Theory and Methodology: Toward an Integration of Micro- and Macro-Sociologies*, Boston, Mass, USA: Routledge & Kegan Paul Ltd.

Campbell-Hunt, C. (2007) Complexity in Practice, *Human Relations*, 60(5), 793–823.

Carlisle, Y. & McMillan, E. (2006) Innovation in Organizations from a Complex Adaptive Systems Perspective, *Emergence, Complexity & Organization*, 8(1), 2–9.

Cartwright, S. & Cooper C. L. (1996) *Managing Mergers, Acquisitions and Strategic Alliances*: *Integrating People and Cultures*, London: Butterworth-Heinemann.

Checkland, P. B. (1981) *Systems Thinking, Systems Practice*, Chichester: Wiley.

Checkland, P. B. & Schles, J. (1990) *Soft Systems Methodology in Action*, Chichester: Wiley.

Chia, R. (1998) From Complexity Science to Complex Thinking: Organization as Simple Location, *Organization*, 5(3), 341–69.

Chiles, T. D. & Meyer, A. D. (2001) Managing the Emergence of Clusters: An Increasing Returns Approach to Strategic Change, *Emergence*, 3(3), 58–89.

Churchman, C. West (1968) *The Systems Approach*, New York: Delacorte Press.

— (1970) *The Systems Approach and its Enemies*, New York: Basic Books.

Cilliers, P. (1998) *Complexity and Postmodernism*: *Understanding Complex Systems*, London: Routledge.

Cohen, M. D., March, J. G. & Olsen, J. P. (1972) A Garbage Can Model of Organizational Choice, *Administrative Science Quarterly*, 17, 1–25.

Coleman, H. J. (1999) What Enables Self-Organizing Behavior in Business, *Emergence*, 1(1), 33–48.

Collins, J. (2001) *Good to Great*, New York: Harper Business.

Connor, D. R. (1998) *Leading at the Edge of Chaos*: *How to Create the Nimble Organization*, New York: John Wiley & Sons.

Dalal, F. (1998) *Taking the Group Seriously*, London: Jessica Kingsley.

Damasio, A. R. (1994) *Descartes' Error*: *Emotion, Reason and the Human Brain*, London: Picador.

— (1999) *The Feeling of What Happens*: *Body and Emotion in the Making of Consciousness*, London: Heinemann.

Darwin, C. (1859) *The Origin of Species by Means of Natural Selection or, The Preservation of Favoured Races in the Struggle for Life*, London: John Murray.

— (1871) *The Descent of Man*, London: John Murray.

Dawkins, R. (1976) *The Selfish Gene*, New York: Oxford University Press.

de Certeau, M. (1988) *The Practice of Everyday Life*, Berkeley, CA: University of California Press.

de Geuss, A. (1988) Planning as Learning, *Harvard Business Review*, March-April, 70–74.

Dickerson, A., Gibson, H. D. & Tsakalotos, E. (1997) The Impact of Acquisitions on Company Performance: Evidence from a large Panel of UK Firms, *Oxford Economic Papers*, 49(3), 344–61.

Dewey, J. (1934) *A Common Faith*, New Haven, Conn: Yale University Press.

DiMaggio, P. J. & Powell, W. W. (1991) Introduction, in Powell, W. W. & DiMaggio P. J. (eds) *New Institutionalism in Organizational Analysis*, Chicago: Chicago University Press, pp. 1–38.

Donaldson, A. (2005) The Technology of Writing in Organisational Life, in Stacey, R. (ed.) (2005) *Experiencing Emergence in Organizations*: *Local Interaction and the Emergence of Global Pattern*, London: Routledge.

Downs, A., Durant, R. & Carr, A. N. (2003) Emergent Strategy Development for Organizations, *Emergence*, 5(2), 5–28.

Edelenbos, J, Gerrits, L. & Gils, M. (2008) The Co-evolutionary Relation Between Dutch Mainport Policies and the Development of the Seaport Rotterdam, *Emergence, Complexity & Organization*, 10(2), 49–61.

Effron, D., Niedenthal, P. M., Gil, S., & Droit-Violet, S. (2006) Embodied temporal perception of emotion, *American Psychological Association*, 6, 1.

Eldridge, N. & Gould, J. (1972) Punctuated Equilibria: An Alternative to Phyletic Gradualism, in Schopf, T. J. M. (ed.) *Models in Paleobiology*, San Francisco: Freeman, Cooper and Co.

Elias, N. (1939/2000) *The Civilizing Process*, Oxford: Blackwell.
— (1953/1987) *Involvement and Detachment*, London: Blackwell.
— (1970) *What is Sociology?* New York: Columbia University Press.
— (1989) *The Symbol Theory*, London: Sage Publications.
— (1991) *The Society of Individuals*, Oxford: Blackwell.
Elias, N. & Scotson, J. (1994) *The Established and the Outsiders*, London: Sage.
Emery, F. E. & Trist, E. L. (1973) *Toward a Social Ecology*, London: Tavistock.
Eskildson, L. (2006) TQM's Role in Corporate Success: Analyzing the Evidence, *National Productivity Review*, 14(4), 25–38.
Ezzamel, M., Willmott, H. & Worthington, F. (2001) Power, Control and resistance in 'The Factory that Time Forgot', *Journal of Management Studies*, 38(8), 1054–79.
Fayol, H. (1916) *Industrial and General Administration*, London: Pitman (1948).
Ferlie, E., Fitzgerald, L. & Wood, M. (2000) Getting Evidence into Clinical Practice: An Organizational Perspective, in *Journal of Health Services and Policy*, 5(2), 96–102.
Fisher, R. A. (1930) *The Genetic Theory of Natural Selection*, Oxford: Oxford University Press.
Fitzgerald, L., Ferlie, E. & Hawkins, C. (2003) Innovation in Healthcare: How Does Credible Evidence Influence Professionals?, *Health and Social Care in the Community*, 11(3), 219–28.
Flood, R. L. (1990) Liberating Systems Theory: Towards Critical Systems Thinking, *Human Relations*, 43, 49–75.
Forrester, J. (1958) Industrial Dynamics: A Major Breakthrough for Decision-Making, *Harvard Business Review*, 36(4), 37–66.
— (1961) *Industrial Dynamics*, Cambridge, MA: MIT Press.
— (1969) *The Principles of Systems*, Cambridge, MA: Wright-Allen Press.
Foulkes, S. H. (1964) *Therapeutic Group Analysis*, London: George Allen & Unwin.
Fox, M. (1995) *The Reinvention of Work*, San Francisco: Harper Collins.
Frankfurt, H. (1971) Freedom of the Will and the Concept of a Person, *Journal of Philosophy*, 67(1), 5–20.
Freeman, W. J. (1994) Role of Chaotic Dynamics in Neural Plasticity, in van Pelt, J., Corner, M. A., Uylings, H. B. M., & Lopes da Silva, F. H. (eds) *Progress in Brain Research*, Vol 102, Amsterdam: Elsevier Science BV.
— (1995) *Societies of Brains: A Study in the Neuroscience of Love and Hate*, Hillsdale NJ: Lawrence Earlsbaum Associates Publishers.
Freeman, W. J. & Barrie J. M. (1994) Chaotic Oscillations and the Genesis of Meaning in Cerebral Cortex, in Buzsaki, G., Llinas, R., Singer, W., Berthoz, A. & Christen, Y. (eds) *Temporal Coding in the Brain*, Berlin: Springer.
Freeman, W. J. & Schneider, W. (1982) Changes in the Spatial Patterns of Rabbit Olfactory EEG with Conditioning to Odors, *Psychophysiology*, 19, 45–56.
Gabriel, Y. (1998) Same Old Story or Changing Stories? Folkloric, Modern and Postmodern Mutations, in Grant, D., Keenoy, T. & Oswick, C. (eds) (1998) *Discourse and Organisation*, London: Sage.
Gardner, H. (1985) *The Mind's New Science: A History of the Cognitive Revolution*, New York: Basic Books.
Garfinkel, H. (1967) *Studies in Ethnomethodology*, Englewood Cliffs, NJ: Prentice Hall.
Gell-Mann, M. (1994) *The Quark and the Jaguar*, New York: Freeman & Co.
Gershenson, C. & Heylighen, F (2003) When Can We Call a System Self-organizing?, in Banzhaf, W., Christaller, T., Dittrich, P., Kim, J. T. & Ziegler, J. (eds) *Advances in Artificial Life*, pp. 606–14.
Gleick, J. (1988) *Chaos: The Making of a New Science*, London: William Heinemann Limited.
Goffman, E. (1981) *Forms of Talk*, Philadelphia: University of Pennsylvania Press.
Goldberger, A. L. (1997) Fractal Variability Versus Pathological Periodicity: Complexity Loss and Stereotypy in Disease, *Perspectives in Biology and Medicine*, 40(4), 553–61.

Goldsmith, W. & Clutterbuck, D. (1984) *The Winning Streak*, London: Weidenfeld & Nicholson.

Goldstein, J. A., Hazy, J. K. & Silberstang, J. (2008) Complexity and Social Entrepreneurship: A Fortuitous Meeting, *Emergence, Complexity & Organization*, 10(3), 3, vi-x.

Goodwin, B. (1994) *How the Leopard Changed its Spots*, London: Weidenfeld and Nicholson.

Goodwin, R. M. (1951) Econometrics in Business-style Analysis, in Hansen, A. H. (ed.) *Business Cycles and National Income*, New York: W. W. Norton.

Goold, M. & Quinn, J. J. (1990) *Strategic Control: Milestones for Long Term Performance*, London: Hutchinson.

Grace, M. (2003) Origins of Leadership: The Etymology of Leadership, *Selected Proceedings from 2003 Conference of the International Leadership Association*, 1–15.

Grant, D., Keenoy, T. & Oswick, C. (eds) (1998) *Discourse and Organisation*, London: Sage.

Greenley, G. E. (1986) Does Strategic Planning Improve Performance? *Long Range Planning*, 19(2), 101–9.

Griffin, D. (2001) *The Emergence of Leadership: Linking Self-organization and Ethics*, London: Routledge.

Grimshaw J. M. & Eccles, M. (2004) Is Evidence-based Implementation of Evidence-based Care Possible? *Medical Journal of Australia*, 180, 50–51.

Grol, R. & Wensing, M (2004) What Drives Change? Barriers to and Incentives for Achieving Evidence-based Practice, *Medical Journal of Australia*, 180, 57–60.

Haldane, J. B. S. (1932) *The Causes of Evolution*, New York: Harper Brothers.

Hamel, G. (2000) *Leading the Revolution*, Boston: Harvard Business School Press.

Hannan, M. T. & Freeman, J. (1989) *Organizational Ecology*, Cambridge, MA: Harvard University Press.

Haynes, P. (2003) *Managing Complexity in the Public Services*, Maidenhead, Berkshire: Open University Press (McGraw-Hill Education).

Hegel, G. W. F. (1807) *The Phenomenology of the Spirit*, Bamberg: Joseph Anton Goebhardt. Translated by A. V. Miller, Oxford: Oxford University Press.

Hendricks, K. B. & Singhal, V. (1997) Does Implementing an Effective TQM Program Actually Improve Operating Performance? Empirical Evidence from Firms That Have won Quality Awards, *Management Science*, 43(9), 1258–74.

Hendricks, K. B. & Singhal, V. (2000) Firm Characteristics, Total Quality Management and Financial Performance, *Journal of Operations Management*, 238, 1–17.

Hendricks, K. B. & Singhal, V. (2001) The Long Run Stock Price Performance of Firms with Effective TQM Programs, *Management Science*, 47(3), 359–68.

Heron, J. & Reason, P. (1997) A Participative Inquiry Paradigm, *Qualitative Inquiry*, 3(3), 274–94.

Hertzberg, F. (1966) *Work and the Nature of Man*, Cleveland, OH: World.

Hickson, C. R. & Turner, J. D. (2005) Corporation or Limited Liability Company, in McCusker, J. J., Engerman, S., Fischer, L. R., Hancock, D. J. & Pomeranz, K. L. (eds) (2005) *Encyclopaedia of World Trade Since 1450*, New York: Macmillan.

Hodge, B. & Coronado, G. (2007) Understanding Change in Organizations in a Far-from-Equilibrium World, *Emergence, Complexity & Organization*, 9(3), 3–15.

Hodgson, G. M. (1999a) *Evolution and Institutions: On Evolutionary Economics and the Evolution of Economics*, Cheltenham: Edward Elgar.

Hodgson, G. M. (1999b) Structures and Institutions: Reflections on Institutionalism, Structuration Theory and Critical Realism, Paper for the 'Realism and Economics' workshop, King's College, January.

Holland, J. (1998) *Emergence from Chaos to Order*, New York: Oxford University Press.

Holmes, J. & Stube, M. (2003) *Power and Politeness in the Workplace: A Sociolinguistic Analysis of Talk at Work*, London: Pearson Education.

Houchin, K. & MacLean D. (2005) Complexity Theory and Strategic Change: An Empirically Informed Critique, *British Journal of Management*, 16(2), 149–66.

Huselid, M. A., Jackson, S. E. & Schuler, R. S. (1997) Technical and Strategic Human Resource Management Effectiveness as Determinants of Firm Performance, *Academy of Management Journal*, 40(1), 171–88.

Huxley, T. (1863) *Man's place in Nature*, New York: D. Appleton.

Ingham, H., Kran, I. & Povestam, A (2007) Mergers and Profitability: A Managerial Success Story? *Journal of Management Studies*, 29(2) 195–208.

Jackson, M. C. (2000) *Systems Approaches to Management*, New York: Kluwer.

James, W. (1902) *The Varieties of Religious Life*, Cambridge, Mass.

Jensen, M. C. & Meckling, W. H. (1976) Theory of the Firm: Managerial Behavior, Agency Costs, and Ownership Structure, *Journal of Financial Economics*, 3, 303–60.

Jensen, M. C. & Smith, C. W. (eds) (1984) *The Modern Theory of Corporate Finance*, New York: McGraw-Hill.

Joas, H. (2000) *The Genesis of Values*, Cambridge: Polity Press.

Kant, I. (1790) *Critique of Judgement*, trans. W. S. Pluhar, Indianapolis: Hackett (1987).

Kast, P. & Rosenzweig, F. (1970) *Management and Organization*, New York: McGraw-Hill.

Kauffman, S. A. (1993) *Origins of Order*: *Self Organization and Selection in Evolution*, Oxford: Oxford University Press.

Kauffman, S. (1995) *At Home in the Universe*: *The Search for the Laws of Complexity*, London: Viking.

Kelly S. & Allison, M. A. (1999) *The Complexity Advantage*: *How the Science of Complexity Can Help Your Business Achieve Peak Performance*, New York: McGraw-Hill.

Kets de Vries, M. F. (1989) *Prisoners of Leadership*, New York: Wiley.

Khurana, R. (2007) *From Higher Aims to Hired Hands*: *The Social Transformation of Business Schools and the Unfulfilled Promise of Management as a Profession*, Princeton, NJ: Princeton University Press.

King, D. R., Dalton, D. R., Daily, C. M. & Covin, J. G. (2003) Meta-analyses of Post-acquisition Performance: Indications of Unidentified Moderators, *Strategic Management Journal*, 25(2), 187–200.

Kreeger, L. C. (ed.) (1975) *The Large Group – Dynamics and Therapy*, London: Maresfield Reprints.

Lamarck, J. B. (1984) *Zoological Philosophy*: *An Exposition with Regard to the Natural History of Animals*, Chicago: University of Chicago Press.

Law, J. (1992) Notes on the Theory of the Actor-Network: Ordering, Strategy, and Heterogeneity, *Systems Practice*, 5(4), 12.

Lewin, R. (1993) *Complexity*: *Life at the Edge of Chaos*, London: J. M. Dent.

Lewin, R. & Birute, R. (2000) *The Soul at Work*, London: Orion Business Books.

Lewin, R. & Regine, B. (2000) *The Soul at Work*, London: Orion Business Books.

Lewontin, R. C. (1974) *The Genetic Basis of Evolutionary Change*, New York: Columbia University Press.

Lichtenstein, B. B., Uhl-Bien, Marion, R., Seers, A., Orton, J. D. & Schreiber, C. (2006) Complexity Leadership Theory: An Interactive Perspective on Leading in Complex Adaptive Systems, *Emergence, Complexity & Organization*, 8(4), 22–12.

Lickert, R. (1961) *New Patterns of Management*, New York: McGraw-Hill.

Lozeau, D., Langley, A., & Denis, J. (2002) The Corruption of Managerial Techniques by Organisations, *Human Relations*, 55(5), 537–64.

Luhman, J. T. & Boje, D. M. (2001) What is Complexity Science? A Possible Answer from Narrative Research, *Emergence*, 3(1), 158–68.

Luhman, J. T. (2005) Narrative Processes in Organizational Discourse, *Emergence, Complexity & Organization*, 7(3–4), 15–22.

MacIntosh, R. & MacLean, D. (1999) Conditioned Emergence: A Dissipative Structures Approach to Transformation, *Strategic Management Journal*, 20(4), 297–316.

Macklis, R. D. ((2001) Successful Patient Safety Initiatives: Driven from Within, *Group Practice Journal*, November/December, 65–91.

Maguire, S. & McKelvey, B. (1999) Complexity and Management: Moving from Fad to Firm Foundations, *Emergence*, 1(2), 19–61.

Marion, R. (1999) *The Edge of Organization*: *Chaos and Complexity Theories of Formal Social Systems*, Thousand Oaks, CA: Sage Publications.

Maslow, A. (1954) *Motivation and Personality*, New York: Harper Brothers.

Matte-Blanco, I. (1975) *The Unconscious as Infinite Sets*: *An Essay in Bi-logic*, London: Duckworth.

Matte-Blanco, I. (1988) *Thinking, Feeling and Being*, London: Routledge.

Mayo, E. (1949) *The Social Problems of Industrial Civilization*, London: Routledge and Kegan Paul.

McCulloch W. S. & Pitts, W. (1943) A Logical Calculus of Ideas Imminent in Nervous Activity, *Bulletin of Mathematical Biophysics*, 5, 21–35.

McKelvey, B. (1999) Complexity Theory in Organization Science: Seizing the Promise or Becoming a Fad, *Emergence*, 1(1), 5–31.

McKelvey, B. (2002) *Postmodernism vs. Truth in Management Theory,* in Locke, E. *Post*: *Modernism & Management*: *Pros, Cons and Alternatives*, Amsterdam: Elsevier.

McKelvey, B. (2003) From Fields to Science: Can Organization Studies Make the Transition?, in Westwood, R. & Clegg, S., *Point/Counterpoint*: *Central Debates in Organization Theory*, Oxford: Blackwell.

McKenna, C. D. (2006) *The World's Newest Profession*: *Management Consulting in the Twentieth Century*, Cambridge: Cambridge University Press.

Mead, G. H. (1914) The Psychological Bases of Internationalism, *Survey*, XXIII, 604–7.

Mead, G. H. (1923) Scientific Method and the Moral Sciences, *International Journal of Ethics*, XXXIII, 229–47.

Mead, G. H. (1932) *The Philosophy of the Present*, Chicago: University of Chicago Press.

Mead, G. H. (1934) *Mind, Self and Society*, Chicago: Chicago University Press.

Mead, G. H. (1938) *The Philosophy of the Act*, Chicago: Chicago University Press.

Mead, George H. (Petras, J.W., Editor) (1968) *Essays on Social Philosophy*, New York: Teachers College Press.

Meek, J. W., De Ladurantey, J. & Newell, W. (2007) Complex Systems, Governance and Policy Administration Consequences, *Emergence, Complexity & Organization*, 9(1–2), 24–36.

Menzies Lyth, I. (1975) A Case Study in the Functioning of Social Systems as a Defence Against Anxiety, in Coleman, A. & Bexton, W. H. (eds) *Group Relations Reader*, Sausalito, CA: GREX.

Midgley, G. (2000) *Systemic Intervention*: *Philosophy, Methodology, and Practice*, New York: Kluwer.

Miller, E. J. & Rice, A. K. (1967) *Systems of Organization*: *The Control of Task and Sentient Boundaries*, London: Tavistock.

Mintzberg, H. (1973) *The Nature of Managerial Work*, New York: Harper & Row.

Mintzberg, H. (1994) *The Rise and Fall of Strategic Planning*, Hemel Hempstead: Prentice Hall.

Mintzberg, H. & Waters, J. A. (1985) Of Strategies Deliberate and Emergent, *Strategic Management Journal*, 6, 257–72.

Mitleton-Kelly, E. (2006) Co-evolutionary Integration: The Co-Creation of a New Organizational Form Following a Merger and Acquisition, *Emergence, Complexity & Organization*, 8(2), 56–81.

Mowles, C. (2009) 'Emerging Evidence' (to be published in *Development in Practice*).

Nelson, R. R. & Winter, S. G. (1982) *An Evolutionary Theory of Economic Change*, Cambridge, MA: Harvard University Press.

Nicolis, G. & Prigogine, I. (1989) *Exploring Complexity*: *An Introduction*, New York: W. H. Freeman.

Nonaka, I. & Takeuchi, H. (1995) *The Knowledge Creating Company*: *How Japanese Companies Create the Dynamics of Innovation*, New York: Oxford University Press.

O'Loughlin, M. (1995) Intelligent Bodies and Ecological Subjectivism: Merleau-Ponty's Corrective to Postmodernism's 'Subjects' of Education, *Philosophy of Education,* 12(2), 15–23.

Ong, W. J. (2002) *Orality and Literacy*, London and New York: Routledge.

Pascale, R. T. (1999) Surfing the Edge of Chaos, *Sloan Management Review*, 40(3), 83–95.

Pascale, R. T., Millemann, M. & Gioja, L. (2000) *Surfing the Edge of Chaos*: *The Laws of Nature and the New Laws of Business*, New York: Crown Business.

Penrose, E. T. (1959) *The Theory of the Growth of the Firm*, New York, Wiley.

Peters, T. J. & Waterman, R. H. (1982) *In Search of Excellence*, New York: Harper & Row.

Pfeffer, J. & Sutton, R. (2006) *Hard Facts, Dangerous Half-Truths and Total Nonsense*: *Profiting from Evidence-Based Management*, Boston: Harvard Business School Press.

Philips, A. W. (1950) Mechanical Models in Economic Dynamics, *Econometrica*, 17, 283–305.

Pinkard, T. (2000a) *Hegel*: *A Biography*, Cambridge: University of Cambridge Press.

Pinkard, T. (2000b) Hegel's Phenomenology and Logic: An Overview, in Ameriks, K. (ed.) (2002) *The Cambridge Companion to German Idealism*, Cambridge: Cambridge University Press.

Pinker, S. (1994) *The Language Instinct*: *The New Science of Language and Mind*, New York: William Morrow.

Prahalad, C. K. & Hamel, G. (1990) The Core Competence of the Corporation, *Harvard Business Review*, 68, 78–91.

Prigogine, I. (1997) *The End of Certainty*: *Time, Chaos and the New Laws of Nature*, New York: The Free Press.

Prigogine, I. & Allen, P. M. (1982) The Challenge of Complexity, in Schieve, W. C. & Allen, P. M. (eds) (1982) *Self-Organization and Dissipative Structures*: *Applications in the Physical and Social Sciences*, Austin Texas: University of Texas Press.

Prigogine, I. & Stengers, I. (1984) *Order Out of Chaos*: *Man's New Dialogue with Nature*, New York: Bantam Books.

Purser, R. E. & Cabana, S. (1998) *The Self Managing Organization*: *How Leading Companies Are Transforming the Work of Teams for Real Impact*, New York: The Free Press.

Rappaport, A. (1986) *Creating Shareholder Value*: *The New Standard for Business Performance*, Simon & Schuster.

Ray, T. S. (1992) An Approach to the Synthesis of Life, in Langton, G. C., Taylor, C., Doyne-Farmer, J. & Rasmussen, S. (eds) *Artificial Life II*, *Santa Fe Institute, Studies in the Sciences of Complexity*, *Volume 10*, Reading, MA: Addison-Wesley.

Reason, P. & Bradbury, H. (2002) *Handbook of Action Research*: *Participative Inquiry and Practice*, London: Sage.

Reynolds, C. W. (1987) Flocks, Herds and Schools: A Distributed Behaviour Model, Proceedings of Siggraph '87, *Computer Graphics*, 21(4), 25–34.

Richardson, K. A. (2008) Managing Complex Organizations: Complexity Thinking and the Science and Art of Management, *Emergence, Complexity & Organization*, 10(2), 13–27.

Robertson, D. A. (2003) Agent-Base Models of a Banking Network as an Example of a Turbulent Environment: The Deliberate vs. Emergent Strategy Debate Revisited, *Emergence, Complexity & Organization*, 5(2), 56–71.

Robertson, D. A. & Caldart, A. A. (2008) Natural Science Models in Management: Opportunities and Challenges, *Emergence, Complexity & Organization*, 10(2), 49–61.

Rost, J. C. (1991) *Leadership for the Twenty First Century*, New York: Praeger.

Rousseau, D. M. (2006) Is There Such a Thing as Evidence-based Management?, *Academy of Management Review*, 31(2), 256–69.

Rousseau, D. M., Manning, J. & Denyer, D. (2008) Evidence in Management and Organizational Science: Assembling the Field's Full Weight of Scientific Knowledge through Synthesis, *Annals of the Academy of Management*, 2, 475–515.

Sacks, H. (1992) *Lectures on Conversations*, Oxford: Blackwell.

Sanders, T. I. (1998) *Strategic Thinking and the New Science: Planning in the Midst of Chaos, Complexity and Change*, New York: The Free Press.

Saussure, F. de (1974) *Course in General Linguistics*, London: Collins.

Scharmer, C. O. (2000) Presencing: Using the Self as Gate for the Coming-into-presence of the Future, Paper for conference on *Knowledge and Innovation*, May 25–26, 2000, Helsinki, Finland.

Schein, E. H. (1985) *Organizational Culture and Leadership*, San Francisco: Jossey-Bass.

Schore, A. N. (1994) *Affect Regulation and the Origin of the Self: The Neurobiology of Emotional Development*, Hillsdale, NJ: Lawrence Earlbaum Associates Inc.

Schreiber, C. & Carley, K. M. (2006) Leadership Style as an Enabler of Organizational Complex Functioning, *Emergence, Complexity & Organization*, 8(4), 61–76.

Scott, J. C. (1990) *Domination and the Arts of Resistance: Hidden Transcripts*, New Haven: Yale University Press.

Scott, J. C. (1998) *Seeing Like a State: How Certain Schemes to Improve the Human Condition Have Failed*, New Haven: Yale University Press.

Seddon, J. (2008) *Systems Thinking in the Public Sector: The Failure of the Reform Regime and a Manifesto for a Better Way*, Axminster: Triachy Press.

Senge, P. M. (1990) *The Fifth Discipline: The Art and Practice of the Learning Organization*, New York: Doubleday.

Shannon, C. & Weaver, W. (1949) *The Mathematical Theory of Communication*, Urbana, IL: University of Illinois Press.

Shaw, P. (2002) *Changing Conversation in Organizations*, London: Routledge.

Shegloff, E. A. (1991) Reflections on Talk and Social Structures, in Boden, D. & Zimmerman, D. H. (eds) (1991) *Talk and Social Structure*, Cambridge: Polity Press.

Shilling, S. (1999) Towards an Embodied Understanding of the Structure/Agency Relationship, *British Journal of Sociology*, 50, 4.

Shotter, J. (1993) *Conversational Realities: Constructing Life through Language*, Thousand Oaks, CA: Sage Publications.

Shotter, J. & Katz, A. M. (1996) Hearing the Patient's 'Voice': Towards a Social Poietics in Diagnostic Interviews, *Social Science and Medicine*, 46, 919–31.

Siegel, D. J. (1999) *The Developing Mind: Toward a Neurobiology of Interpersonal Experience*, New York: The Guildford Press.

Soltani, E. & Pei-Chun Lai (2007) Approaches to Quality Management in the UK: Survey Evidence and Implications, *Benchmarking: An International Journal*, 14(4), 429–54.

Sommer, S. C., Loch, C. H. & Dong, J. (2009) Managing Complexity and Unforeseeable Uncertainty in Startup Companies: An Empirical Study, *Organization Science*, 20(1), 188–133.

Stacey, R. (2001) *Complex Responsive Processes in Organizations: Learning and Knowledge Creation*, London: Routledge.

Stacey, R. (2003) *Complex and Group Processes: A Radically Social Understanding of Individuals*, London: Brunner-Routledge.

Stacey, R. (2005) *Experiencing Emergence in Organizations: Local Interaction and the Emergence of Global Pattern*, London: Routledge.

Stacey, R. (2007) *Strategic Management and Organisational Dynamics: The Challenge of Complexity*, London: Pearson Education (5th Edition).

Stacey, R. & Griffin, D. (2005) *Taking Experience Seriously: A Complexity Perspective on Researching Organizations*, London: Routledge.

Stacey, R., Griffin, D., & Shaw, P., (2000) *Complexity and Management: Fad or Radical Challenge to Systems Thinking?*, London: Routledge.

Stewart, I. (1989) *Does God Play Dice*, Oxford: Blackwell.

Surie, G. & Hazy, J. K. (2006) Generative Leadership: Nurturing Innovation in Complex Systems, *Emergence, Complexity & Organization*, 8(4), 13–26.

Sword, L. D. (2007) Complexity Science Conflict Analysis of Power and Protest, *Emergence, Complexity & Organization*, 9(3), 47–61.

Tait, A. & Richardson, K. A. (2008) Confronting Complexity, *Emergence, Complexity & Organization*, 10(2), 27–41.

Taylor, C. (1975) *Hegel*, Cambridge: Cambridge University Press.

Taylor, C. (2007) *A Secular Age*, Cambridge, MA: The Belknap Press of Harvard University Press.

Taylor, F. ([1911] 1967) *Scientific Management*, New York: Harper Brothers.

Taylor, W. A. & Wright, G. H. (2002) A Longitudinal Study of TQM Implementation: Factors Influencing Success and Failure, *Omega*, 3(2), 97–111.

Tichy, G. (2001) What Do We Know about Success and Failure of Mergers? *Journal of Industry, Competition and Trade*, 1(4), 347–94.

Tolbert, P. S. & Zuckner, L. G. (1996) The Institutionalization of Institutional Theory, in Clegg, S. R., Hardy, C. & Nord, W. R. (eds) *A Handbook of Organization Studies*, London: Sage.

Trist, E. (1981) The Evolution of Socio-Technical Systems, *Occasional Papers No. 2*, Ontario.

Trist, E. & Bamforth, K. (1951) Some Consequences of the Longwall Method of Coal Getting, *Human Relations*, 4(1), 3–33.

Truss, C. (2001) Complexities and Controversies in Linking HRM with Organizational Outcomes, *Journal of Management Studies*, 38(8), 1121–49.

Tsai, S. D., Hong-quei, C. & Valentine, S. (2003) An Integrated Model for Strategic Management in Dynamic Industries: Qualitative Research from Taiwan's Passive-component Industry, *Emergence, Complexity & Organization*, 5(4), 34–56.

Tsoukas, H. (1993) Analogical Reasoning and Knowledge Generation in Organization Theory, *Organization Studies*, 14(3), 323–46.

Tsoukas, H. & Hatch, M. J. (2001) Complex Thinking, Complex Practice: The Case for a Narrative Approach to Organizational Complexity, *Human Relations,* 54(8), 879–1013.

Tustin, A. (1953) *The Mechanism of Economic Systems*, Cambridge, MA: Harvard University Press.

Twomey, D. F. (2006) Designed Emergence as a Path to Enterprise Sustainability, *Emergence, Complexity & Organization*, 8(3), 12–23.

van Dyck, W. & Allen, P. M. (2006) Pharmaceutical Discovery as a Complex System of Decisions: The Case of Front-loaded Experimentation, *Emergence, Complexity & Organization*, 8(3), 40–56.

Varga, L. & Allen, P. M. (2006) A Case-study of the Three Largest Aerospace Manufacturing Organizations: An Exploration of Organizational Strategy, Innovation and Evolution, *Emergence, Complexity & Organization*, 8(2), 48–64.

Veblen, T. B. (1899) *The Theory of the Leisure Class*: *An Economic Study in the Evolution of Institutions*, New York: Charles Scribeners.

Veblen, T. B. (1934) *Essays on our Changing Order*, Ardzrooni (ed.), New York: The Viking Press.

von Foerster, H. (1984) On Constructing Reality, in von Foerster, H. (ed.) *Observing Systems*, Seaside, CA: Intersystems.

von Glasersfeld, E. (1991) Knowing Without Metaphysics: Aspects of the Radical Constructivist Position, in Steier, F. (ed.) *Research and Reflexivity*, London: Sage.

Waldrop, M. M. (1992) *Complexity*: *The Emerging Science at the Edge of Order and Chaos,* London: Penguin.

Wernerfeldt, B. (1984) A Resource-based View of the Firm, *Strategic Management Journal*, 5, 171–80.

Westphal, K. (1993) The Basic Context and Structure of Hegel's Philosophy of Right, in Beiser, F. C. (ed.) (1993) *The Cambridge Companion to Hegel*, Cambridge: Cambridge University Press.

Wheatley, M. J. (1992) *Leadership and the New Science*: *Learning about Organization from an Orderly Universe*, San Francisco: Berrett-Koehler.

Wiener, N. (1948) *Cybernetics*: *or Control and Communication in the Animal and the Machine*, Cambridge, MA: MIT Press.

Williams, R. (2005) Leadership, Power and Problems of Relating in Processes of Organizational Change, in Griffin, D. & Stacey, R. (eds.) (2005) *Complexity and the Experience of Leading Organizations*, London: Routledge.

Wright, S. (1931) Evolution in Mendelian populations, *Genetics*, 16, 97–159.

Wright, S. (1940) Breeding Structures of Populations in Relation to Speciation, *American Naturalist*, 74, 232–48.

Zaleznik, A. (1977) Managers and Leaders: Are They Different?, *Harvard Business Review*, 70(2), 126–35.

Zhu, Zhichang (2007) Complexity Science, Systems Thinking and Pragmatic Sensibility, *Systems Research and Behavioral Science*, July.

Author index

Subject index